The Structure and Operation of
THE JAPANESE ECONOMY

the structure and operation of the

JAPANESE ECONOMY

K. Bieda

Reader in Economics

The University of Queensland

John Wiley and Sons Australasia Pty Ltd

SYDNEY

New York   London   Toronto

ISBN and National Library of Australia
Card Number: Cloth   0 471 07220 6
            Paper   0 471 07225 7
Library of Congress Catalog Card Number: 76 – 127033

Registered at the General Post Office, Sydney, for transmission through the post as a book

Printed at The Griffin Press, Adelaide, South Australia

日本文化の研究を志望する
わが娘 ヴァンダに捧げる
K・ビェダ

Foreword

Why has Japan achieved a high economic growth rate? How did the government's economic plans and fiscal and monetary policies affect this growth? What impact did the post-war farmland reform and the peculiar characteristics of Japan's monetary and industrial structures have on economic growth? This book presents interesting analyses on these and related topics.

The views of eminent foreign economists on Japan's economy can be enlightening to us Japanese in many respects. This book is especially interesting because the author, having lived in Japan for extended periods between 1967 and 1969, not only knows the statistics but has first-hand knowledge of the working of Japan's economy in addition to his extensive knowledge of the Western economic systems. As the author himself points out, Japan's economic system, while apparently similar to that of Western Europe, has in reality many features that have been modified to suit Japan's culture. Judging merely from the documents and statistics on Japanese economy, foreign economists may draw false conclusions. On the other hand, the Japanese themselves may not be fully aware of the peculiar features of their economy and may also believe that they have adopted the economic system of Western Europe unmodified. Mr Bieda's book serves to fill this gap in understanding Japan's economy. Among the many interesting features of this book, I would like to cite as an example the author's appraisal of the role of economic plans in Japan's economic growth. Since the end of World War II, the Japanese government has been drawing up economic plans approximately every three years. A foreigner looking only at these documents may get the impression that Japan's economy has been growing exactly according to these plans. In fact, however, equipment investment by Japanese enterprises has always far exceeded the amount envisaged in the plans and the economic growth rate has been much higher than was announced. Some Japanese economists therefore consider that the government plans have been merely ornamental. Both these views are probably too extreme. Mr Bieda states that "in Japan the execution or implementation of the plan rests solely on the announcement effect of the plan", but he holds that "the impact of the plan is increased by several facts typical for Japan". By analysing these typical facts, he brings forth a third view, different from either of the two mentioned above. The role of the government plans in Japan's economy cannot be fully understood unless one takes into account the facts that in Japanese society the government's advice is apt to command respect and attention, that the private planners use the government plans as the basis for their own plans, and that for the implementation of the plans Japan has peculiar fiscal and monetary policies as well as independent controls by various government institutions. This book discusses these points in detail and succeeds in clarifying the peculiar role of the government plans in Japanese economy.

In addition, this book presents a fairly detailed study of the Japanese tax system, agricultural situation, the capital market and the *keiretsu*. These aspects of Japanese economy are relatively little known abroad, and are interesting from an academic point of view as well as being of practical use to those engaged in business with Japan. The book is up-to-date throughout.

SABURO OKITA
President, The Japan Economic Research Centre

Tokyo, May 1970

Table of Contents

List of Tables

List of Illustrations

Preface

Japan's remarkable economic and cultural achievements over the last 100 years, and in economic matters especially in the last twenty years, have captured the attention of the world. For some people the centre of interest lies in the "miraculous" economic growth rate. For others, particularly in the developed countries, the interest is in Japan's economic planning, in the effectiveness of the Japanese monetary control, or in the flexibility of the economy.

For the readers in under-developed countries which now aspire to follow Japan's footprints, this book (especially Chapters 1, 7 and 8) may perhaps have some useful positive and negative pointers, but they will have to be on the look-out to choose only that which is applicable to their conditions, and then that which is desirable.

Although this book is aimed at people in various walks of life, the author has primarily had in mind the needs of university students in economics and in Asian Studies. Some sections of the book will be of use to geography students. Chapter 2 will be of interest to students of government. The content of several chapters was influenced by the needs of men in the business world or in government who have to deal with, or in, Japan. It is hoped that the book will save them some frustration and some misunderstandings in their work. Japanese economic institutions often appear imitations of the West, but in fact they have invariably been adapted to the local culture, and the apparent similarity can be misleading.

The general literate reader will not find the book indigestible, especially if he is prepared to skip over technicalities and if he just looks for the "message" of the tables and not their detailed content.

Western books on the Japanese economy, considering its size and its sophistication, are only moderately plentiful. Some of them are extremely good, but most of them describe Japan as it once was, not as it is. Japan has been undergoing such rapid and fundamental changes that any book, no matter how good it was in the 1950s or 1960s, would now be utterly misleading other than as a piece of economic history. These books have lengthy discussions of the *zaibatsu* and how they were dissolved. This book just mentions what the *zaibatsu* were and that they were dissolved and proceeds to discuss in detail the structure, characteristics and the effects of their modern counterpart: the *keiretsu*. The present problems of Japanese agriculture, that now utterly un-Asian industry, cannot be gleaned from the existing books, because developments in the Japanese economy in general and in agriculture in particular have turned the circumstances of 1950s or early 1960s upside down. Economic planning and its role are not discussed in some books, and in some Western literature they are misunderstood. In some rare cases where it is apparently well analysed, readers are still misled, in particular with respect to implementation, perhaps because they wilfully though unconsciously misread them. This book tries to explore and show up the "implementation" of the plans.

This book is as up-to-date as the availability of Japanese statistics and the publication lag of the statistics allow. In coverage it attempts to deal with the essential features only, keeping in mind the various categories of potential readers. In one sentence, it shows how the Japanese economy now "ticks".

No doubt, there are some errors of commission and omission. The readers' comments on them would be welcomed by the author for his own private benefit in the first instance, and for improvement of the book for later editions.

In the case of a book like this the author drew heavily on the aid of many institutions and writers so that it would be impracticable to acknowledge them all individually. The author gratefully acknowledges the hospitality of the Japan Economic Research Centre for periods in 1967, 1968 and 1969. He is indebted to Mr Nobuo Miyamoto of the Japanese Ministry of Foreign Affairs for introductions to numerous government departments and business institutions, all of whom without exception went to much trouble to provide assistance.

In writing this book the author was especially assisted by comments of two Japanese economists, Mr Hisao Kanamori, senior economist of the Japan Economic Research Centre, now about to take a senior staff position in the Japan Economic Planning Agency, and Professor Sumihiro Korenaga of Hosei University, now a post-doctoral Research Fellow at the University of Queensland. Both of those authorities on the Japanese economy generously read and commented on the whole of the earlier draft of this book.

Professor Kenzo Hemmi of the Department of Agricultural Economics, Tokyo University, has read Chapter 8 on Agriculture and has made a number of most valuable suggestions. While without the comments of these authorities the book would have been much poorer, they are in no way responsible for any of its imperfections.

Thanks are also due to Mr T. Kawabata, the Consul of Japan in Queensland, who very kindly did the artistic paint-brush work on the Japanese inscriptions in the book.

Brisbane, August 1970   K. BIEDA

CHAPTER ONE

The Growth of the Japanese Economy

Japan is the most exciting and *ex ante* the most improbable case of rapid rate of economic growth in history. At the time of the Meiji Restoration in 1868, Japan was faced with stark poverty, one of the meanest natural resource endowments, a backward technology after two and a half centuries of almost complete self-imposed isolation from the rest of the world under the Tokugawa Shogunate (a military dictatorship in a feudal setting, 1603-1867), and a culturally "traditional society" with a feudal structure. Within a mere hundred years Japan has overtaken a number of European countries in respect to income *per caput* and technology, and has become one of the world's three economic super-powers. It is now becoming evident that Japan will become the Country of the Century. Even in the earlier part of the century the growth rate of Japan's income of about 4 per cent p.a.* was remarkable by an international yardstick (1-2 per cent p.a. long-run), and it continued to be high even during the Great Depression of the 1930s, which severely reduced incomes in virtually all countries.

Then Japan joined World War II, which destroyed the Empire, and income was cut in half by the end of the War. This was followed, however, by a rapid economic recovery and now an extraordinary reach for economic ascendancy. The unique rate of growth achieved since the early 1950s, and the pent-up energy for a great Japanese Leap Forward in the rest of this century have never been in the vision of European observers of Japan, or even in the hopes of the Japanese, except perhaps those remarkable leaders of the Meiji Period. Even as late as 1949, E. A. Ackerman, an economic geographer on the staff of the American occupation authorities wrote:

> In the light of an analysis of its resources, the Japan of the next three decades appears to have one of two aspects if its population continues to grow to 100 million or more:

* Kazushi Ohkawa, in association with M. Shinohara, M. Umemura, M. Ito and T. Noda, *The Growth Rate of the Japanese Economy Since 1878*, Kinokuniya Book Store, Tokyo, 1957, p. 21.

1. It may have a standard of living equivalent to that of 1930-34 if foreign financial assistance is continued indefinitely.
2. It may be "self-supporting", but with internal political, economic and social distress, and a standard of living gradually approaching the bare subsistence level.†

Twenty years later Japan's G.N.P. became the second largest in the non-Communist world, after the U.S.A., and she is an important donor of economic aid. Although in income *per caput* Japan ranks at the time of writing only twentieth in the world (U.S. $1141 in the Japanese Fiscal Year ending 31 March 1969) she is in some ways extremely modern. Indeed she is almost completely up-to-date in the ownership of all new industrial gadgets.

Table 1.1. Diffusion Rate of Consumer Durables in Japan, per 100 Households, as at February, 1969.

	%		%
Sewing Machines	84·6	Refrigerators	84·6
Knitting Machines	37·2	Electric Fans	80·1
B & W Television	94·7	Air-conditioners	4·9
Colour Television	13·9	Organs	18·0
Stereo Record Players	27·3	Pianos	6·1
Tape Recorders	28·6	Passenger Cars	17·3
Cameras	62·7	Vans	9·8
Washing Machines	88·3	Small Trucks	6·9
Vacuum Cleaners	62·6		

Source: *Japan Economic Yearbook*, Toyo Keizai Shimposha, Tokyo, 1969, p. 244.

On the other hand, the Japanese family ownership of cars and the availability of square metres of housing space are very low. It is in these two fields that the main thrust of increased Japanese consumer expenditure is now going. *Consumer* spending of an average *wage-earner's* household in Japan in 1968 was 65,400 yen *per month* (U.S. $182). It grows very rapidly: in 1968 it grew 11·3 per cent over the preceding year. How were these increases in consumption distributed?

Foodstuffs expenditure increased 7·8% (domestic rice declined, meat and dairy products increased *very slightly*, beverages and similar "luxury" products increased significantly, and so did eating-out). *Housing expenditure* increased 22·8% over the preceding year. *Motor car purchases* increased 50% over the preceding year.* Total private housing investment in Japan trebled between 1960-1968.

In fact the ownership of electric hair-dryers, cameras and possibly tape

† E. A. Ackerman, *Japanese Natural Resources*, Tokyo: G.H.Q., S.C.A.P., N.R.S., 1949. Quoted by Shigeto Tsuru in *Essays on Japanese Economy*, Kinokuniya Book Store, Tokyo, 1958, pp. 36-37.
* *Japan Economic Yearbook*, p. 110.

recorders, is more common in Japan than in any other country in the world. It is, however, in housing, public amenities and the level and the quality of nutrition that Japan still lags substantially behind the most advanced countries. As for housing, individual families have consciously given it lower priority compared to savings and education of children. The public authorities' restraint in providing developed land together with extreme shortage of reasonably flat land have contributed to this state of affairs too. Above all housing credit by Western, say American or Australian, standards is almost not available. Even a university professor would not get a loan if he did not have collateral security. It has to be remembered that the housing stock of any community at any moment of time is the result of the conditions of some thirty years past, and in that period Japan could not have afforded better housing, and although she now can, it will take some time before she catches up to her present and future income status in the world. The present housing shortage is mirrored by the flat rentals in Tokyo and other world cities:

Table 1.2. *Monthly Rent of a Furnished 3-bedroom Western Style Flat in US$*

Tokyo	1000	New York	650	Vienna	200
Delhi	200	Zurich	280	Washington	260
Athens	300	Montreal	275	Dublin	48
Rome	360	Dusseldorf	137	Wellington	84
Paris	260	London	288	Singapore	158
		Sydney	139	Hong Kong	200

Source: *The Australian Financial Review*, 11 December 1968. Quoted by permission of *The Financial Times*, London.

Of course the average Japanese does not pay those rents. Very often his employer provides housing which is, however, of extremely modest quality, at a nominal rent. Social amenities again are a product of past periods (the length depending on the amenity), and again the community and the authorities were until recently giving priority in investment works to income generation rather than to amenities. As is indicated by the very names of the last economic plan of Japan, the Social and Economic Development Plan 1967-1971, and the present New Social and Economic Development Plan 1971-1976, the authorities intend to make up this deficiency in the future.

As for nutrition, a Westerner would have to say that the average Japanese is still poorly fed. In 1965 the average daily calorie intake of the Japanese was only 2,300 compared to 3,270 in the U.K., 3,251 in Australia, 3,150 in U.S.A., 3,150 in Canada and 1,880 in India. In protein intake Japan's position is even worse. Medical authorities consider protein consumption the hall-mark of nutritional welfare. The

Japanese daily protein intake was 77·6 grams of which less than one-third was of animal origin. The Australian figures were 91·3 grams of which about two-thirds was of animal origin.*

Indeed in the hundred years of the extraordinary growth of the Japanese economy and income *per caput* the standard of nutrition of that statistical abstract "the average Japanese" improved only very little, though the "consumption" of the modern industrial gadgets has grown, and in the post-war period has grown at a very rapid rate. According to Ohkawa, writing in 1957, at the outset of the Meiji period in 1868 the average daily calorie intake was 2,042† and rose to only 2,300 between 1934-1938 and has not surpassed that figure even today. Since Ohkawa wrote his book, J. I. Nakamura‡ came to the conclusion that food production in the early Meiji period had been grossly underestimated because farmers under-reported both the acreage and the yields. To the extent this is valid it strengthens the argument that in the 100 years of a remarkable economic growth the *average* nutrition levels changed very little.

There is, of course, a view that the Asians, being smaller in height and living in warmer climates than the Europeans, may require less food. But firstly the Japanese are not that small, and in any case, the relationship here might be the reverse of this. Now with better nutrition the average height of the Japanese is going up. In any case when we consume for example sugar or meat, we do not do it because we need the calories, so that the physical stature cannot explain the differences satisfactorily. As for the climatic factor, Japan is not very much warmer than West European countries and certainly not warmer than Australia.

Table 1.3.   Consumption of Sugar in a Few Selected Countries in the period 1957-1959, annual, per caput, kilograms.

Australia	51
United Kingdom	50
Denmark	47
Canada	44
New Zealand	42
U.S.A.	41
Finland	40
Ceylon	18
Pakistan	15
Japan	13

Source: U.N., *The Compendium of Social Statistics,* 1963, pp. 167-168.

* Japanese figures are taken from: Ministry of Foreign Affairs, Government of Japan, *Japan's Agriculture Today*, Tokyo, 1967, p. 15. Australian figures: Commonwealth Bureau of Census and Statistics, *The Official Yearbook of the Commonwealth of Australia 1967*, Canberra, p. 1217. All other figures: *The Times of India Directory and Yearbook 1967*, Bombay, p. 309.
† Ohkawa, *et al*, p. 76.
‡ J. I. Nakamura, *Agricultural Production and Economic Development in Japan 1873-1922*, Princeton University Press, 1966, Chs. 2-5.

Table 1.4. Consumption of Proteins grams per caput *per day (1957/8-1959/60)*

	Total	Animal Origin
New Zealand	106	72
Argentina	98	57
France	97	50
Ireland	97	57
Yugoslavia	95	26
Canada	94	63
Finland	94	53
Denmark	93	57
Greece	93	26
U.S.A.	92	65
Turkey	90	14
United Kingdom	86	51
Syria	78	17
United Arab Republic	73	13
Mexico	68	20
Japan	67	17
Taiwan	57	14
Libya	53	10
India	52	6
Ceylon	42	6

Source: U.N., *The Compendium of Social Statistics,* 1963, pp. 165-166.

It is clear from Tables 1.3 and 1.4 that in Japan the consumption of sugar, proteins in general and animal proteins in particular, is at the level of under-developed countries. However, it is in the consumption of meat and eggs, and milk proteins that Japan lags even more behind the developed countries, as well as behind the under-developed ones, and for beef the contrast would be even greater.

In *per caput* consumption of meat Japan is exceeded by such countries as the United Arab Republic, Mexico, Turkey, Syria, the Philippines, Libya and many others. In the consumption of eggs and milk proteins Japan is also among the few lowest ranking countries in the world. It is only in fish consumption that Japan ranks very high, possibly the highest in the world, but the figure is not high enough to bring the total protein consumption to anywhere near the level of the advanced countries.

In vegetables the Japanese consumption ranks roughly at the level of advanced countries, though her place in that ranking is the thirteenth in the world, close after Libya, United Arab Republic, Chile, Peru and Turkey. It is only in the starchy foodstuffs, cereals and potatoes, that Japan beats the advanced countries, but that is in fact a sign of a poor nutrition standard.

It is difficult to know to what extent this low Japanese food consumption is due to traditional frugality, that is, psychological pressures to save, or is due to the exorbitantly high (by world standards) food prices imposed

Table 1.5. Annual per caput *Consumption of Meat, Eggs, Fish and Milk Proteins, kilograms (1957/8-1959/60).*

Country	Meat	Eggs	Fish	Milk Proteins
Australia	116	11	5	7
Argentina	109	7	2	4
Uruguay	109	7	1	6
New Zealand	106	15	7	10
U.S.A.	92	20	5	9
Canada	78	17	7	9
Denmark	72	9	15	8
United Kingdom	71	15	10	7
France	71	11	5	7
Belgium and Luxemburg	58	15	6	7
Ireland	58	15	4	11
West Germany	54	12	7	7
Switzerland	54	10	3	10
Austria	52	10	3	8
Sweden	50	12	18	9
Paraguay	48	1	—	2
Netherlands	44	12	4	9
South Africa	44	3	7	3
Colombia	41	3	1	2
Japan	6	4	22	1

Source: U.N., *The Compendium of Social Statistics,* 1963, pp. 167-8.

upon the population by all Japanese governments over the period in order to protect domestic agriculture. In other words, it is difficult to know whether the modest food consumption is a virtue or vice in this case. The fact, however, that the mass-produced and cheap electronic gadgets are so widely diffused in Japan suggests that the main part of the reason for such frugal food consumption lies in price. There is no doubt at any rate that an informed Westerner would say that in Japan today the greatest and easiest increase in "income" in the true sense, that is in economic welfare, would be produced by a reduction of import barriers on foodstuffs. It seems, however, in view of the revealed Japanese set of values and the strongly entrenched policy of protecting agriculture, that the improvement in the food sector of consumption in Japan will be the last to come. But it will come very soon because of the rapid economic growth. At present, however, protectionism together with extreme short-age of cultivable land has pushed food prices, even of basic foods, very high indeed; rice is three times as dear as in the world markets, and beef between four and nine times dearer than in Australia, for example.

Growth in the Meiji Period

The fact that Japan has had a remarkable growth record in the last 100 years is now well known. What is not well known, however, is the growth rate and its nature in the period up to World War I, and that this period has been crucial to Japan. If the process of that growth were better understood it could throw some light on the problems of the present under-developed countries. The other not unconnected problem is: what were the changes, if any, in the economic position of the peasants and the wage earners in that early period?

On both these issues there are some conflicting opinions and in a way too many statistical estimates. It is probably fair to say that none of those statistics for the period up to World War I should be taken very seriously. Quite apart from the inadequacy of data and all sorts of somewhat dubious, makeshift devices to fill the gaps, there are numerous conceptual problems like the index number problem in the conversion of the current money values into the constant money values, or the problem of making sure that classes and categories have the same coverage throughout. All the same various discordant estimates do exist, and, what is worse, lead to quite different interpretations of the process of the economic growth.

Until 1965 it was widely accepted among students of Japanese economic growth that the early growth up to World War I was in fact financed by an historically unique high rate of growth of output in agriculture, with more or less constant input of labour and capital. According to Ohkawa and his collaborators who calculated "moving average" rates of growth of income and output (in order to smooth out short-term variation) between overlapping ten-year averages, the annual growth rate was 2·4 per cent for the period 1878-87 to 1883-92, 4·3 per cent for the period 1883-92 to 1888-97, and also 4·3 per cent for 1888-97 to 1893-1902.* That model was often put up for possible imitation by the present under-developed countries. It seemed to offer a short-cut to economic growth *and* an early increase in consumption.

J. I. Nakamura's studies undermined to some extent that intellectual structure.† He started from a basic claim that the early Meiji government assessment of the output of agriculture, used hitherto by scholars, was grossly understated because it was made on the basis of returns for land tax, made substantially by the villagers themselves when the new land tax legislation of 1873 was applied. He claims that the undervaluation took the form of understating the area under cultivation and the yield of land, as a result of which the total yield of agriculture was understated. He recalculated the output of agriculture from 1878-1882 to 1913-1917 and found as a result that the annual rate of increase was about 1 per

* Ohkawa, *et al*, p. 21.
† (a) J. I. Nakamura, "Growth of Japanese Agriculture 1875-1920", in *The State and Economic Enterprise in Japan*, edited by W. W. Lockwood, Princeton University Press, 1965.
  (b) Nakamura, *Agricultural Production and Economic Development*.

cent p.a., instead of 2·4 per cent as estimated by Kazushi Ohkawa and others. Nakamura also claimed that the growth of output of the secondary and tertiary industries was also *overstated*, as development proceeded, and *understated* in the period before commercialisation accelerated. In this latter claim he is not at all original and is substantially wrong as far as some of his conclusions go. His claim is based on the well-known elementary fact of social accounting that usually the national income estimates cover only the market-bound activities, that is, exclude goods produced and services performed inside the family for use by the family. In the pre-industrial society many goods and services were supplied—clothing was produced and food was prepared by the family members for love, not for payment—and therefore often they are not counted as national income, but when commercial production of those products develops their value comes to be counted as part of the national income. Consequently, the accepted system of social accounting understates the early income and overstates the subsequent growth of income as industrialisation advances. But this really leads Nakamura nowhere. This criticism applies equally well to all the other developed countries and consequently it cannot bring the Japanese figures of growth to a lower level, like that experienced by the present developed countries in their early days of growth.

While he was at it, Nakamura could have just as well added that much of the civilised man's consumption expenditure is purely defensive—it represents a cost of living in an industrial society and not an addition to his welfare. Here are a few examples. The vast majority of car owners use that expensive machine almost exclusively to travel to and from work, their residence of necessity being very far from the vast modern business centres. This method does not nowadays save time, and certainly does not make commuting to work any safer or pleasanter than it was in an earlier age. Yet the cost of modern roads, cars, petrol stations, car repairs and panel beating is treated as an *addition* to the nation's income. Further, the price of food that we consume contains now a large element of transport cost because the food has to be brought from large distances. That cost of food transport is treated as an *increase* in income, and it is obvious that this "increase in income" was foregone in the older days when most families were self-sufficient in virtually all consumption. One could go on listing such situations for a long time. Nakamura did not discuss any of them although they are on a par with his argument about the weakness of the social accounting practice. He raised another argument in favour of his general thesis. He argued that the overstatement of the growth rate in the industrial sector had also come from the inclusion of new classes of products as they "became available" and new firms, which were "previously uncounted". It is not clear exactly what he means here.

His argument can mean either that he is again referring to his previous statement about the formerly non-market-bound activities being taken over by the market-bound producers, and in such case he is merely repetitious, or it can mean that the coverage of the firms was grossly inadequate at first, but greatly improved later. He may be right on those imperfections of social accounting, but if he is, should we attach any weight to income estimates?

What is then left of Nakamura's thesis?

The early Meiji period agricultural output was probably understated in the official statistics and this has inflated the subsequent rate of growth as the statistical series gradually eliminated the understatement. As a result the early economic growth of Japan becomes much less spectacular and much more like the old, relatively unexciting Western pattern of growth. Since population was growing at about 1 per cent p.a. and the agricultural output grew at about a similar rate (Nakamura), (admittedly with a more or less constant labour force in agriculture) there was no special surplus created there for industrialisation, and the resource flow, apart from labour, would have to come out of an increased propensity to save. Further, this adjustment of the agricultural output time series would pull down the overall rate of growth of the G.N.P. in the period from the estimate of 4 per cent p.a. (Ohkawa and others) to a much more normal though still respectable $2 \cdot 8$ per cent p.a. But if agriculture had not produced substantial increases of output with an unchanged input of factors of production, where had the resources for industrialisation come from, asked Nakamura. His answer is interesting and much of it may be valid even if the underestimation thesis is rejected in the future. The resource flow, he said, had come from the "previously untapped resources" under the all-embracing Tokugawa system of feudal regulations and restrictions.

One resource flow out of agriculture to the modern sectors is, of course, the supply of manpower and womanpower leaving the countryside for the towns. While the population of Japan grew in the period at about 1 per cent p.a., the agricultural labour force hardly changed. Although there are several published estimates of the labour force in agriculture, the most widely accepted one is that of Hemmi, according to whom the agricultural labour force declined very slightly until World War I. In any case all of the estimates lead to the conclusion that all or virtually all of the increase in the rural population went to the manufacturing and services sectors.

As for capital, Nakamura holds that agriculture did provide the required savings, but not at the rate previously believed, and not because there was any spectacular growth of incomes in agriculture. The Meiji Restoration produced very substantial socio-economic changes in the country, which increased the marginal propensity to save, in other words, the rate of saving due to a 100 yen increase in income. The destruction of the feudal system meant that farmers obtained ownership of the land that they cultivated, while the *samurai* and the *daimyō* lost the lands but were *partly* compensated for the loss of the feudal revenues. Although the new land owners now had to pay a new and heavy land tax, on a balance they gained; income was redistributed to them from the *samurai* and the *daimyō*. In the end the main losers were the *samurai*, because the *daimyō*'s incomplete cash and government bond compensation was improved by the abolition of the old rule of the *shoguns* that the *daimyō* had to spend a part of each year at the *shogun*'s court, and when he went to inspect his country properties he had to leave his wife and children at the court as permanent hostages. This meant that the *daimyō* had to maintain two households, one in the capital and one in the country, which was very expensive in itself, and also involved the additional costs of long travel with "proper staff" each year.

In addition the *shogun*, who himself spent lavishly, induced the *daimyō* to overspend to keep them poor and therefore more pliable and obedient. When those feudal burdens were removed from the *daimyō* their finances were improved *to that extent*, through the fact that their consumption (wanted and unwanted) was reduced, so that on a balance the deterioration in their position was not so bad as it would appear on first look. The incomes of the *samurai* were substantially reduced. The incomes of the landowners, however, were increased. The landowners had a lower marginal propensity to consume than the *samurai* and the *daimyō* of the old system, and as a result this redistribution of incomes increased savings of the country. In addition the *samurai* and the *daimyō*, well educated and disciplined as a group, were now pressed by the economic circumstances to look for jobs in the new capitalist system. Ultimately they provided much of the business leadership, though in the short-run, while not absorbed into the economic system, they presented a grave political danger.

Briefly, savings for development of the country were provided by agriculture, but not out of any dramatic increase of productivity (though there was some increase). Further, the Government in that period took about 10 per cent of the value of the output of agriculture in the form of the land tax. The monies thus collected were used in part for universal education (investment in the human capital) and for the economic infrastructure: railway, telegraph, land improvement and pilot manufacturing industries.

From a study of capital formation in Japan by H. Rosovsky it appears that between 1887 and 1916 net domestic capital formation was at a modest level from 4·5 to 6·8 per cent of the net national product. Nakamura considers those figures a low level of capital formation and tries hard to explain the actual high rate of growth of income. Indeed, the net investment rate of 4·5 to 6·8 per cent (out of which more than 40 per cent was public investment) goes ill with the reported growth rate of income of 4 per cent p.a. (Ohkawa). In this situation either one can say, like Simon Kuznets did, that Japan had by far the lowest ratio of marginal net domestic capital formation to marginal net domestic product among all the developing countries, and a really exceptionally low one, or one can say, as Nakamura did, that there was nothing very exceptional there and that the ratio was not really so low. Nakamura said that in the first instance the growth rate in the period 1878-1882 to 1913-1917 was not 4 per cent p.a., but only 2·8 per cent, and secondly, the capital investment in the early period was also under-rated. These two propositions together would tend to make the capital/output ratios more plausible.

It should be noted here that Ohkawa does not accept the main lines and conclusions of Nakamura's work, although he admits that the early Meiji agricultural output may perhaps have been under-rated slightly.*
Even a study of Nakamura's book itself would tend to suggest that he is pushing the growth-understatement thesis somewhat hard. All the same on *à priori* grounds and on historical grounds some of his conclusions seem to be plausible. Intellectually it is much more acceptable to believe that the Japanese economic growth from the Restoration until World War I was not a sudden explosion but a continuation of some developments in the late Tokugawa period at least. Although the shogunate was feudal and applied many economically irrational regulations and restrictions, it gave Japan two centuries of peace and stability, during which education gradually developed (not only for the *samurai*), and some progress in various arts was made. Crawcour stresses the pre-Restoration levels of achievement in Japan.† He says that already in the late Tokugawa period some merchants applied quite modern accounting techniques and a rational calculation of alternative courses of economic action, so it was not all a traditional society.

Crawcour also stresses the extent to which production was commercialised, or market-bound, and this is also a sign of advancement to a modern economic system. The population, he says, was comparatively well educated and more responsive to economic opportunities than traditional societies usually are. Nakamura stated that in most provinces in the Tokugawa period there was a policy of retaining as much labour as possible in order to achieve economic self-sufficiency of the province. Similarly the peasants had instructions to produce rice—to assure the

---

* Kazushi Ohkawa and Henry Rosovsky, "A Century of Japanese Economic Growth" in *The State and Economic Enterprise in Japan*, ed. Lockwood, pp. 68-69.
† Sydney E. Crawcour, "The Tokugawa Heritage" in *The State and Economic Enterprise in Japan*, ed. Lockwood, pp. 17-44.

supply of the basic food even in lean years—and there were prohibitions of producing other crops such as silk on the land suitable for rice growing. Briefly, there was both overallocation of labour on land, and also misallocation of labour. There were also the numerous *samurai*, who, while educated, were prevented by the social system from playing any positive role in the economy. The destruction of the old system with its regulations and social constraints released much labour for the growth of a modern society.

The Rate of Economic Growth Since World War II

Although the war left Japan in ruins, economically completely exhausted (a quarter of her material wealth was destroyed, the G.N.P. at the end of the war was only a half of the pre-war peak) and with the necessity to resettle over six million Japanese repatriated from the former colonial possessions, by the early 1950s Japan regained her pre-war income *per caput*. Then it was felt by most observers that after the rapid process of recovery the Japanese economic growth would slow down. Events proved otherwise. The Japanese economy accelerated its growth, doubling the national income in real terms every seven years. Again when this growth was a demonstrated fact observers claimed that it would slow down once the pool of unemployed labour was exhausted.

Table 1.6.   Average Annual Rates of Growth of Total G.N.P. in Real Terms.

Country	1950–55	1955–60	1960–65
Japan	12·1	9·7	9·6
West Germany	9·3	6·3	4·8
Italy	6·0	5·5	5·1
Austria	6·1	5·2	4·3
Netherlands	5·5	4·2	4·8
France	4·3	4·6	5·1
Switzerland	4·8	4·0	5·3
Canada	4·7	3·3	5·5
Australia	4·0	4·0	5·0
U.S.A.	4·3	2·2	4·5
Norway	3·5	3·2	5·2
Belgium	3·1	2·5	4·5
Sweden	3·2	3·6	5·1
U.K.	2·7	2·8	3·3

Source: Saburo Okita, *Causes and Problems of Rapid Growth in Japan*, Japan Economic Research Center, Paper No. 6, 1967.
The Australian figures were added by the author.

The figures in the preceding table are *total* G.N.P. figures (not *per caput*) but since Japan's population grows very slowly the *per caput* figures would be even more striking. The rapid economic growth in Japan shown in Table 1.6 has not yet slowed down, again despite predictions, this time on the grounds of decline of the total labour force growth rate. In the Japanese Fiscal Year ended 31 March 1968, the real rate of growth of the G.N.P. was 13·3 per cent and in the Fiscal Year ended 31 March 1969, it was 12 per cent. However in the next decade there will be so great a decline in the growth rate of the labour force, from 1·3 per cent in the decade ended 1967 to well below 1 per cent in the first half of 1970s,* that the income growth may slow down.

Saburo Okita and Fumiro Murobuse of the Japan Economic Research Center estimate that by 1985 and since 1965 Japan will have overtaken twenty countries in income *per caput* to become the fourth richest country in the world, after the U.S.A., West Germany and the Soviet Union. Some non-Japanese economists estimate that in thirty-one years' time from now Japan will be the second richest country in the world, after the U.S.A. Perhaps this appears scarcely plausible to some, but it has to be remembered that at each stage of her economic growth during the last century the next rise was improbable. Of course, life always brings surprises, but a surprise we should also consider is that Japan may cut that time-table.

Anyone can make estimates when Japan will overtake the advanced Western countries in income *per caput*. The result depends on whether we expect the recent trends to continue, and if not what changes in trends we assume. This also depends on how much we wish to under-state the probable trends, in order to be conservative (and credible). The Japanese Ministry of Finance has also made some estimates. (*The Japan Economic Journal*, 25 March 1969). The Ministry of Finance made two alternative assumptions:

(a) that the growth rates between 1956-1966 will continue;
(b) that the growth rates of the other countries will continue but that of Japan will slow down.

Assumption (a), that the growth rates of the period 1956-1966 will continue, that is, that Japan will grow at 12·9%, gives the following result: Japan will overtake in income *per caput all the countries* of the world by 1988 when she will overtake the *then* richest country, Sweden. The U.S.A. will be overtaken in 1984 and Germany will also be over-taken in that year. France will be overtaken in 1980 and Britain in 1974.

The more cautious assumption (b) that Japan's growth will slow down in future to 11·9 per cent p.a. up to 1986 and to 9·9 per cent after-wards, postpones the time-table slightly. Japan would overtake Sweden (the then richest country in the world) in 1992, U.S.A. in 1985, West Germany in 1986, France in 1980 and Britain in 1974.

* Economic Planning Agency, *The Economic and Social Development Plan 1967-1971*, Government of Japan, 1967, pp. 30-31.

Japan's fast economic growth, not to speak of her present reach for economic ascendancy has *ex ante* always seemed improbable, simply because of the extreme paucity of her natural endowment *per caput* of population. Japan's total land area is only 370,000 square kilometres— less than one-twentieth of the United States, and one-and-a-half times as big as the United Kingdom. On that land live now just over 100 million people, and the Economic Planning Agency of Japan estimates that by 1985 the population will rise to 113 million.* (This growth will not be because of the birth rate, which is very low, but because of reduction of mortality.) The country's mineral resources are negligible. The density of population in 1967 was 271 persons per square kilometre, which is exceeded only by the Netherlands with 346 persons and Belgium with 301 persons. These figures are, however, misleading. Population should be related to land that is usable and to other resources. In Japan, because of the extremely mountainous nature of the country, only 16 per cent of the total land area is arable. This fact makes her the most densely populated country in the world. Japan is also very poor in other natural resources except for the hydro-electric power supply which is high owing to the prevalence of mountains and the high rainfall. Under these circumstances and given the fact that foreign capital has never played a large role in Japan's development, how has that country lifted itself by its own bootstraps to a modern, prosperous and rapidly advancing country?

The Main Factors in Japan's Economic Growth

It is not necessary to argue that an analysis of the economic background of a country that has produced growth as fast as Japan must be interesting to the developing and developed countries. Yet the lessons from the Japanese growth cannot be applied easily, certainly not as a parcel of policies to be adopted wholesale. The factors that produce or speed up economic growth are numerous, very complicated in their operation, and not yet fully agreed upon by economists. In life there is a diversity of situations, no two countries are alike, no single country faces exactly the same situation in one period as in another. In addition, often the favourable factors of growth have to be operating in appropriate combinations before they can produce favourable results. All the same a study of the remarkable Japanese economic success story must contribute to understanding of some key factors in economic growth.

THE IMPORTANCE OF STRUCTURAL CHANGE IN THE ECONOMY

It seems to be part of the "conventional wisdom" to hold that the road to higher national productivity lies in working harder at one's job, and

* E.P.A., *Shin-zenkoku Sogo Kaihatsu Keikaku*, 1968, p. 15.

indeed, whenever a nation is in economic difficulties there are always appeals to do just that. But quite apart from the fact that no one likes to work harder, there are close limits to working harder. Of course, one can always do the job more intelligently but this requires great originality, and this spark of creativity is rare. Quite often the easier road to high national productivity is in adaptability as to what job one would do. At any time in the domestic and the world markets there are always new products and new needs appearing. The key to success both in private business and for a nation as a whole is to switch as rapidly as possible into those new products, or the products for which the demand increased. It is, of course, best to be an initiator of the products or processes, but imitation of others is almost as good. For a while the new products have high income elasticity of demand and low price elasticity of demand; the first of these assures rapid growth of sales without the need for cutting the price, and the second allows a price to be charged which includes a sort of "quasi-rent" (monopoly) element. As soon as this quasi-rent is squeezed out by the hordes of other (slower) imitators the wisdom is to switch quickly into something else. Of course, that very ability to switch quickly postulates in fact the existence of some qualities, at least, of a developed, non-traditional society.

As for the all-important structural change of the economy it should be further noted that in Japan the pattern of development has in the main been in the direction pointed out by the principle of "comparative advantage". Although this comparative advantage has usually been seen in "dynamic" terms, in terms of what the comparative advantage would be in the future, it has almost always been a realistic interpretation of potentialities in the *near* future. Such is not always the case in some other countries, which often pick up quite unlikely "infant industries" and push them indefinitely at a very high cost to the rest of the country. In Japan the structural change was aimed first at labour-intensive indus-tries—which was sound there because the country had plenty of labour—and later has been aimed at skilled-labour and know-how-intensive products. It was a steady, step by step movement, with a massive effort to introduce universal education as a pre-condition of structural change and growth, while at the same time rapid improvements were taking place in agriculture, for a long time the very basis of growth and the source of resources for growth in other sectors. Then came the develop-ment of light consumer-goods industries, especially textiles, to be followed by a stress on simpler heavy industries, and in the present stage an entry into the most sophisticated modern gadget industries and the chemical industry.

The remarkable fact is that in Japan, unlike in most other countries, all "infant industries" have already become or are on the verge of becoming "adult industries". Many other countries seem to carry indefinitely the heavy burden of a large number of "infants" which are not growing, but often are even slipping back. Not so in Japan! This matter would surely deserve a deep detailed study, but in the absence of it, one could make two generalisations. The first is that Japan has almost invariably picked the right "infants" (those requiring plenty of skilled labour force) for her circumstances and the government and families put a high priority on the education of that labour force. The second probably lies in the unique Japanese combination (elsewhere an unlikely one) of large scale oligopolistic organisation of industry *together* with a high degree of competition. The large size of industrial units gives the economies of scale, and the so-called "excessive" competition protects the country from the evils of oligopoly.

SOME GEOGRAPHIC ADVANTAGES

It should be stressed that although natural endowment of Japan has been meagre by comparison with most countries, she has had some advantages denied to most of the present under-developed countries. To begin with, Japan is situated in a temperate climate and this seems to have been favourable to development of civilisation in the past (though in future, technology may remove some of the handicaps of tropical climates). Then she is an island country and in the past the sea allowed the easiest communications. This was obviously of importance to Japan for both domestic and international communications before and after the period of her self-imposed isolation of two and a half centuries. Japan has also been a very homogenous country with a high degree of patriotism, an awareness of being different from the rest of the world and an ambition to excel over the foreigners. Above all, nurtured on a partly assimilated ancient Chinese culture, Japan of the nineteenth century was not a primitive country like some African countries are today. At the beginning of the Meiji era the Japanese had a civilised society with considerable skills, even though that civilisation could not stand up to the technological skills of Europe.

CULTURAL CHANGE AND "THE TRADITIONAL SOCIETY"

Although in 1868 Japan emerged from the Tokugawa Shogunate as an apparently "traditional society", it was not "traditional" in the sense that India or the Indonesian countryside is today. The famous English economist F. Y. Edgeworth* wrote late in the nineteenth century of "stationary Japan", but Japan was not stationary in all respects. Although she had some of the features of the "traditional society" at the grass-roots level among the peasantry, there was a considerable degree

---

* F. Y. Edgeworth, "The Stationary State in Japan", *Economic Journal*, September 1895.

of intellectual restlessness and experimentation with farming methods. Kenzo Hemmi reports:

> On these pilgrimages (to the holy shrines) in the second half of the Tokugawa period the peasants studied the farming conditions and methods of other clans, and whenever they came across any interesting rice-seed, they would fill their bamboo walking sticks with it and take it home secretly. . . . This trend became all the more apparent with the Meiji Restoration (1868) and it became possible to hold open rice-seed exchanges and peasants' get-togethers for the exchange of information.†

Hemmi mentions the names of several nineteenth century Japanese peasants who experimented for years to produce a better variety of rice. It is obvious that this empirical and innovative spirit does not exist at all in the villages of most of the present under-developed societies. They still live and work in the traditional way and often are content with following the work methods inherited from immemorial time, so that the main problem is at first to make them dissatisfied with the old ways. (An adviser helping an under-developed country was once asked what were the results after five years of work in a group of villages. His answer was: "Very good! We have succeeded in making them unhappy about their lot.")

DRAWING LABOUR FROM THE BACKWARD SECTOR

At this stage it can only be stated (pending elaboration and documentation in later pages) that although the Japanese "economic miracle" has been produced *partly* by the mass of the Japanese workers learning to do their job better (not working harder), ultimately the biggest source of growth has been in a continuing, conscious and deliberate structural change of the economy. In other words, factors of production were induced, and assisted in various ways, to move out of unprofitable and unpromising industries into industries that promised greater returns. This last factor is so important that it cannot be over-stressed. Indeed, in part, the extraordinarily high rate of Japanese economic growth is explainable by the simple fact that Japan has had a very large *inefficient* sector of the economy (agriculture, small-firm manufacturing and distribution) to start with, from which it has been rapidly shifting the factors of production into the advanced modern sector. It is obvious that each of the millions of workers removed, for instance, in the post-war period from low-wage (and in Japan unprofitable) agriculture, or from small retailer and small manufacturer sectors into the high-wage modern profitable industrial sector, produces large increases of G.N.P. without the necessity for working harder, or without the people necessarily

† Kenzo Hemmi, *Japanese Agriculture*, Department of Agricultural Economics, University of Tokyo, 1968, p. 8.

working with any greater originality or intelligence. This point, however, could easily be misconstrued to minimise Japan's extraordinary achievement. Having a large inefficient sector in the economy is not a sufficient condition for economic growth. Many countries, indeed in a sense all countries, have a relatively inefficient sector, but none grows at the Japanese rate, and some do not grow at all. The crux of the problem lies in the fact that the larger the inefficient sector in the economy, the greater the inertia of that economy, and the harder the task of performing the structural shift. This is so because:

(a) an economy with a large inefficient sector usually is a result of a "traditional society", and such society is very difficult to change at the top and/or at its grass-root levels;
(b) such an economy has extreme difficulty (based on cultural and on physical factors) in accumulating enough capital which is necessary to make the structural shift.

THE WILL TO CHANGE

Japan, however, was culturally equipped to solve those two problems. Although the shogunate system imposed a "traditional-society" veneer and rigid feudal ways of social behaviour, individually the peasantry (the most conservative element in any society) was open to new ideas and to new ways. When the Meiji Restoration brought a remarkable and progressive ruling class, the rulers did not have to fight a mass inertia. The peasants were ready for most innovations (though not for the heavy land taxes), wanted more education for their children and more freedom in their economic activity.

The rulers were motivated largely by the external danger. At the time of the Meiji Restoration, European imperialism at its peak threatened any remaining independent Asian country, and Japan was shocked into an essentially single-minded effort. The Western imperialism of the nineteenth century encroached directly upon Japanese sovereignty in several ways:

(a) Commodore Perry's visit in 1854 with the naval ships and his demands that Japan open up her boundaries for trade.
(b) The "unequal trade treaties" of 1858 with the Western Powers which forbade Japan to impose tariffs higher than 5% *ad valorem*, and which were repealed only in 1899.
(c) The bombardment of Shimonoseki and Kagoshima by American and British warships in 1862/3.

The Government slogans: "Wealth and Military Strength", "Promotion of Industry", and "Development of Culture and Civilisation", caught the imagination of the people. Similarly after World War II, Japan has single-mindedly adopted the principle: "Economic Growth First".

The mobilisation of the national effort for development was aided by early and rapid introduction of universal education. The mobilisation of capital (for the structural shift) almost exclusively from domestic sources was made possible by several features of the Japanese social and economic system, which are uninformatively called "frugality" of the Japanese, together with a relatively rapid improvement in the traditional industry—agriculture, and later textiles. Initially, however, the increased incomes, or productivity, came not from the improvement of productive processes, but from opening up of domestic trade (foreign trade liberalisation also brought large and important gains but they were slower to come).

REMOVING REGIONAL AND NATIONAL TRADE BARRIERS

Under the Tokugawa Shogunate the various clans collected their own customs tariffs on movement of goods, while foreign trade was reduced to a tiny trickle confined to medicines. The removal of the trade prohibition after Commodore Perry's visit, and of the clan-imposed tariffs after the Meiji Restoration, produced an increase in income and in the value of production as soon as transport problems were resolved. It should be noted that prior to 1868 there was no freedom of transportation of goods or movement of persons in Japan. In economic theory it can be proved that if an area removes trade barriers and opens up trade with another area, the income effect is the same as if a very important technological invention were applied in the country removing trade barriers. Also, the abolition of numerous other feudal restrictions at once allowed more economic use of resources, especially as the "unequal treaties" prevented Japan from imposing protective tariffs until the end of the century, when the treaties were repealed. In that period the country went through a process of sifting the industries, which by eliminating the inefficient industries (such as cotton-growing which disappeared), assisted the efficient ones (for example, silk).

The Role of Education

The remarkable speed with which Japan introduced universal elementary education and generally produced structural changes in the economic and social fabric of society was aided by the fact that Japan has been the most homogenous country in the world. It has had practically no religious, ethnic, linguistic, or other social and cultural divisions that would hinder modernisation of the country. (The Ainu Aborigines have not been a problem.)

Even before the Meiji reforms Japan had for the times a remarkable spread of education, though from today's standpoint the most important things were not always taught in the schools. Under the Tokugawa Shogunate the Japanese noblemen were taught Chinese classics, and

the warriors military virtues. But there were private schools for com-
moners too, called *terakoya*, where reading, writing and arithmetic were
taught. Just before the Meiji Restoration, in the middle of the nineteenth century, there were about 16,000 of those *terakoya* schools. The
bureaucrats even in the Tokugawa period were educated—they could
read and write. They kept better and earlier records than did their
counterparts in the European countries; for example, Japan already
had registrations of births and deaths in the seventeenth century, earlier
than the United Kingdom did.

Before the twentieth century began, literacy in Japan was almost 100
per cent.* Almost immediately after the Meiji Restoration Japan introduced a modern educational system with universal free and compulsory
primary education of at first four and later six years, and secondary
schools, by setting up Government primary and secondary schools
throughout the country in 1872.†

This progressive educational measure introduced so early in Japan com-
pares more than favourably with countries such as England and
Australia.‡ By 1874 Japan had over 20,000 elementary schools and by
1875 over 24,000, when it must be concluded that the elementary
school provision all over the country was ample because since then the
number of elementary schools has increased very little, to over 26,000
in 1962§ in spite of more than doubled total population.

The number of elementary school pupils in Japan was 1,326,190 in
1873, almost two million in 1875, three million by 1882, over four
million by 1898, over five million by 1902, over six million by 1910,
and over seven million by 1917. The numbers of students in secondary
and tertiary schools rose at a similarly fast rate. The preceding figures
show that Japan was among the pioneers of universal compulsory

---

* When one bears it in mind that to read or write Japanese one must know three
systems of writing: *Hiragana* and *Katakana* (which are syllabaries resembling
the Latin alphabet as they stand for sounds) and *Kanji*, which consists of
thousands of Chinese characters (which stand for meaning), 100 per cent literacy
was no mean achievement.

† Ministry of Foreign Affairs, *The Japan of Today*, Government of Japan, Tokyo,
1967, p. 71.

‡ In England ". . . the Elementary Education Act of 1870 accepted the *principle*
of compulsory education. By the end of the nineteenth century elementary
education had become *virtually* both compulsory and free of charge. Public
provision of secondary education (already begun in Wales) started in England
under the Act of 1902". Italics provided by this author. Source: *Britain: An
Official Yearbook*, H.M.S.O., London, 1964, p. 162.
In Australia compulsory education began in 1872 in Victoria, 1875 Queensland,
1875 South Australia, 1880 New South Wales, 1893 Tasmania, 1893 Western
Australia. Source: *Official Yearbook of Australia 1966*, p. 582.

§ Ministry of Education, *Japan's Growth and Education*, Government of Japan,
1963, pp. 150-153.

education and that it made an all out effort to reach the whole population of school age almost in one big step—in one generation's time.

In the post-war period Japan continued to place great emphasis on education, at both the levels of public and family expenditure.

Table 1.7. Public Expenditure on Education in Selected Countries as Percentage of National Income.

Country	Year	Percent of N.I.
U.S.S.R.	1960	7·1
Finland	1959	6·3
Uganda	1958–59	5·9
Japan	1958–59	5·7
Belgium	1959	5·6
Norway	1959	5·5
Netherlands	1958	5·2
Congo (Leopoldville)	1960	5·1
East Germany	1959–60	5·0
Poland	1959	4·8
U.S.A.	1957–58	4·6
U.K.	1959–60	4·2
South Korea	1960	4·1
Austria	1959	3·9
Bulgaria	1960	3·9
New Zealand	1959–60	3·7
West Germany	1959–60	3·6
Sweden	1959–60	3·2
Italy	1960–61	3·2
Switzerland	1958	3·1
Israel	1960–61	3·0
France	1960	3·0
Yugoslavia	1958	2·8
Australia	1959–60	2·2
Portugal	1960	2·0

Source: UNESCO, *Basic Facts and Figures 1961*, pp. 72-79. Reproduced with the permission of Unesco.

Not only did the government in Japan spend the fourth highest percentage of national income among all the countries of the world, but the family expenditures on education are also known to be very high in Japan. Japanese parents are prepared to make very great financial sacrifices to obtain admission to university for their children. The number of places in the publicly-owned universities is inadequate relative to the number of applicants (760,000 candidates for 450,000 places in 1968). The pressure is so great that more than 70 per cent of students were educated in private universities in 1968. The admission to a university is highly coveted and consequently the parents are often prepared to pay very high admission fees, apart from the subsequent tuition fees. Those "admission fees" are often unofficial, or semi-voluntary. The private universities have some difficulty in increasing tuition fees because students would fight, so they sometimes openly invite "donations" before the admission examinations. One private university in 1968 sent out a circular letter to the candidates for admission examinations advising that those who would donate 300,000 yen (US$833) would obtain admission "outside the normal admission quota". The *Japan Times* (25 February 1968) reported that one professor of a private university earned something like fifty million yen

Table 1.8.   Percentage of Male and Female Population 25 Years of Age and Over with Tertiary Education.

Country	Year of Census	Males	Females
Japan	1950	2·7	0·1
Japan	1960	11·0	2·3
Israel (Jewish pop.)	1954	6·1	2·8
Israel (non-Jewish)	1954	0·6	0·2
Taiwan	1956	5·8	0·8
Hong Kong	1961	5·0	2·0
Hungary	1949	3·5	0·6
Hungary	1960	4·1	1·1
Bulgaria	1946	2·4	0·6
Bulgaria	1956	3·8	1·2
Poland	1960	3·7	1·4
Finland	1950	3·6	2·5
Rumania	1956	3·6	1·4
Philippines	1948	3·4	2·0
Greece	1951	3·4	0·7
Chile	1952	3·4	1·4
France	1954	3·3	0·7
Canada	1951	3·1	1·2
Italy	1951	2·5	0·5
Norway	1950	2·4	0·2
Yugoslavia	1953	1·0	0·7
Yugoslavia	1961	2·3	0·3
Scotland	1951	2·0	2·4
Turkey	1950	1·9	0·3
Mexico	1950	1·8	0·5
England and Wales	1950	1·7	1·3
Portugal	1950	1·6	0·3
Spain	1950	1·1	0·1
Spain	1960	1·5	0·2
Pakistan	1951	1·5	0·2
Argentina	1947	1·4	0·2
Brazil	1950	1·4	0·1
Cuba	1953	1·2	0·3
India	1951	0·5	0·1
Iran	1956	0·1	0·0

Source: U.N., *The Compendium of Social Statistics*, 1963, pp. 312-322.

(US$138,888) over three years from student bribes for aiding their admission.

The average Japanese teenager is under tremendous social and family pressure to do well in the admission examinations. The family pressure is reflected by the common nickname "education mama". A university degree is now essential for most white collar jobs, and it is not uncommon for factory foremen to have university degrees. As a result of such social and economic pressures, Japan produces a large number of university graduates. In 1960 there were eleven graduates in every 100 males, 25 years old or over, which is certainly the second highest rate in the world. As the following table shows, this tremendous increase in the number of graduates occurred almost exclusively during the 1950s.

Table 1.9. Number of Graduands in One Year (about 1958) per 100,000 Total Population and Economic Growth Rate.

Country	All graduands per 100,000 total pop.	Science, Technology, Agriculture graduands per 100,000 total pop.	The rest, non-science graduands per 100,000 total pop.	G.N.P. *per caput* growth rate 1951–1959 %
Japan	175	30	145	7·2
Canada	130	33	97	1·0
Czechoslovakia	100	43	57	6·6
Bulgaria	98	43	55	7·1
Hungary	72	28	44	4·9
South Korea	72	20	52	2·6
Finland	69·5	15·5	54	3·0
India	65	17	48	1·6
Poland	64	35	29	6·0
Sweden	64	17	47	2·8
West Germany	59	30	29	6·1
Taiwan	59	22	37	3·7
Yugoslavia	57	15	42	8·0
United Kingdom	55	21	34	2·1
Australia	47	14	33	1·2
Austria	44	12	32	5·6
Switzerland	44	15	29	2·7
Italy	42	11	31	5·2
Spain	33	6	27	3·9
Brazil	24	3	21	3·2
Thailand	21	3	18	1·8
Chile	19	4	15	1·0
Turkey	15	4	11	3·2

Sources: Data on graduates: UNESCO, *Basic Facts and Figures 1961*, pp. 69-71. Reproduced with the permission of Unesco.
Economic Growth Rate data: U.N., *Compendium of Social Statistics*, 1963, pp. 562-568.
Data on total population: U.N., *Statistical Yearbook 1963*, pp. 23-41.

In the year 1958 Japan produced 160,000 tertiary institution graduates,*
an absolute number which was exceeded in the whole world only by
the U.S.A., India, and the U.S.S.R. (except for the U.S.A., this is only
because of the larger size of the total populations of those countries).
Not only is the overall Japanese educational effort impressive, but also
the pattern of education there is interesting. Japan has by far the highest
proportion of students (and the absolute number per 100,000 total
population) in social sciences in the whole world and, on the other
hand, a very low proportion indeed of students in pure natural sciences,
while in the applied natural sciences and in the agricultural sciences she
ranks high (seventh in the world in both).

This author has carried out a number of correlation tests between the
educational effort of various countries and their economic growth rate
with a time lead, and with two different time lags.† The study shows
that there is a statistically significant correlation between public expenditure on education and economic growth rate, especially if a time
lag of several years is applied to economic growth rate. Similarly, there
is a statistically significant correlation between the number of tertiary
institution graduands in all fields in one year per 100,000 total population and economic growth rate a few years later. The importance
of the time lag is in the fact that much of total expenditure on
education goes for intermediate stages of education and it is only
when a suitably long time lag is applied to economic growth rate that
expenditure on scholars affects economic growth.

More disaggregated tests of correlation could have been carried out only
for tertiary students (not graduands) in various subjects. It has then
turned out that there is no correlation at all between the number of tertiary
students in humanities, education and fine arts in a year per 100,000
of total population and economic growth rate. What is more surprising,
no correlation at all was found between the numbers of students (per
100,000 of total population) in pure sciences and economic growth.
This would require some explanation. There is a well-known, and no
doubt well-founded, belief that pure science lies at the bottom of every
applied scientific achievement. We do not deny this at all. But two
qualifications must be made here. Firstly, such a dependence of man's
material achievements on pure theory is a very long-term one, for example
when the great Greek philosopher Pythagoras produced his now well-
known geometrical theorem, for a long time it was purely a speculative
geometrical exercise, and it probably took many centuries before that
theorem came to be used by builders to mark out square angles on the

---

* The figures for education are taken from UNESCO, *Basic Facts and Figures*,
    1961.
† K. Bieda, "The Pattern of Education and Economic Growth Rate", to be pub-
    lished in *The Economic Record*, September 1970.

ground. While in modern times this time lag of practical application after the appearance of theory is not so extraordinarily long, it is still usually fairly long. Secondly, pure sciences and their findings are fully and easily importable, especially nowadays. Thus for any single country it is not necessary to make a very big effort in pure natural sciences, though, needless to say, some effort is needed to give meaning to the findings of the applied sciences.

The study has found, however, a statistically significant correlation between students in the applied sciences, especially agriculture, and economic growth. And surprisingly again, it found even a stronger

Table 1.10. Numbers of Tertiary Students in One Year (about 1958) per 100,000 of Total Population and Growth of G.N.P. per caput 1951–1959.

Country	*All Students	Humanities Education Fine Arts	Social Sciences	Pure Natural Sciences	Engineering	Agriculture	Growth Rate of G.N.P. per caput
							%
Australia	877	321	68	83	134	25	1·2
Japan	723	194	325	29	100	31	7·2
Bulgaria	635	85	107	47	199	109	7·1
Canada	619	336	53	54	89	18	1·0
Czechoslovakia	588	169	63	26	192	52	6·6
Yugoslavia	541	157	101	24	85	39	8·0
Finland	487	209	89	55	49	17	3·0
Austria	476	101	69	35	124	15	5·6
Denmark	457	194	69	26	45	22	2·8
Poland	419	70	30	25	155	39	6·0
West Germany	400	152	42	50	61	7	6·1
Switzerland	384	105	50	67	51	7	2·7
Sweden	383	161	19	48	60	9	2·8
Rumania	377	66	32	49	106	41	7·5
Spain	373	153	17	33	23	7	3·9
Italy	359	73	85	40	44	6	5·2
Hungary	347	64	20	20	93	47	4·9
South Korea	341	60	103	44	33	26	2·6
Taiwan	304	78	69	29	64	28	3·7
Chile	261	97	30	3	26	16	1·0
India	228	132	16	51	8	3	1·6
U.K.	215	71	13	47	21	5	2·1
Turkey	188	22	47	13	20	9	3·2
Thailand	143	13	66	8	6	4	1·8
Brazil	136	27	20	5	16	4	3·2

* This figure will not agree with the sum of the five branches listed because it includes also students of law, medicine and miscellaneous unspecified.

Source: See Table 1.9.

correlation between students in "social sciences" (including economics) and economic growth. The correlation in the case of social sciences was so strong that the statistical chances of such a result coming by a chance were less than 1 per cent. As a demonstration of how pragmatic and how sound Japanese decisions in economic matters are, it should be mentioned that Japan has by far the highest number of students in "social sciences" in the world per 100,000 of total population, and that although her total student population is extremely large by any yardstick, she has a very small number of students in pure natural sciences. In the applied sciences, however, which has a close connection with economic growth, Japan again has a large number of students.

The preceding figures reveal how single-mindedly Japan pursues the goal of economic growth. Of course, a wholesale dedication to economic growth, while producing income increases—with a time lag—has a price attached to it. Current consumption of goods and services has to be kept down in order to devote resources to capital formation. Similarly, in the educational structure the humanities have to be kept at a lower level if educational resources are to be increased in the vocational, the applied studies. Many subjects in humanities can be compared to durable consumer goods which make life more interesting or comfortable, but do not increase income. A poor country can best serve even its humanist tastes by sacrificing them a little for a while to produce a fast economic growth. This is so because in the twentieth century there are precious few humanist values out of the expanding vast range potentially available that can be enjoyed by a poor peasant. Theatre, museums, art galleries, lectures and so forth require money and leisure, and these last two goods come only with advanced economic development.

The Importance of Exports and the Flow of Foreign Exchange

The development of a backward country requires a substantial flow of foreign exchange for the purchase of foreign capital equipment and expertise which cannot be obtained at home. This means that unless there is a possibility of substantial foreign borrowing and aid, the developing country must develop a healthy and lively export industry. In addition to this very important need, there is another reason why the development of export trade is vital. A rapid development of a backward country contains an inherent contradiction which must be resolved: the under-developed country must keep on saving and investing a large proportion of its income, at the same time, however, that it is producing goods which are only in part suitable for domestic investment. If the increased output of the rapidly developing country is not sold abroad, and it is not available mostly in the form of investment goods (because many of those are too sophisticated for an under-developed country to produce), they must be sold as consumer goods in the domestic market. If the bulk, or all of the increased output is sold at home as consumer goods, this implies that all, or almost all, of the income is consumed at home, that is, saving and investment are low. This, of course, would be serious as it would undermine the whole basis of development. (Indeed this problem is the main reason why the Soviet Union laid so much stress on the heavy industries in her development which was autarchic, that is based on the home economy.) If, on the other hand, saving is maintained at a high level, if there is no attempt to consume the bulk of the increase in output, and the increased output is not sold readily abroad, then it would be unsaleable, and as such would constitute a most serious drag on the level of activity and on growth. The importance of "effective demand" for *employment* has been dramatically demonstrated by J. M. Keynes, but its importance for *development* has never been stressed, yet if the demand is not there, the entrepreneurial spirit will be severely discouraged.

There is an additional reason why a healthy and growing export market is vital for development. A small domestic market in an under-developed country does not allow the development of large scale production with its important economies of scale. But if the developing country can find a substantial market abroad either because of sheer luck (for instance the deposits of oil in the present age) or through its own efforts to create an export industry, it cannot help growing. For any single country the world market is so large that it will take increasing quantities of output without the necessity of lowering the price.

Export- or Domestic-Oriented Economic Growth

The relative importance of the export market and the domestic market in the growth of any economy is not easy to determine. Indeed there is some controversy about the matter. In the economic development theory there has been a strong presumption that foreign trade is important as a factor initiating and stimulating growth in a backward economy. That view has been most strongly put by Hla Myint. Miyohei Shinohara tried to find some empirical evidence for that theory in Japanese economic growth, and in that of other countries. He posed the question: "To what extent [relative to other factors] has the expansion of foreign trade been responsible for Japan's economic development . . . [has] domestic demand or foreign demand played the major role?"*

Shinohara made a study of the correlation of the export growth rate

* Miyohei Shinohara, *Growth and Cycles in the Japanese Economy*, Kinokuniya Book Store, Tokyo, 1962, p. 43.

and the industrial growth rate of various countries for a period prior
to the Great Depression, 1911-1913 to 1926-1929, and for a post-war
period 1953-1959. He found that in both periods there was a very
close correlation between the high rates of growth of exports and high
rates of growth of industrial production, or national output.

*Table 1.11.   International Comparison of Export and Industrial Growth Rates for
1953–1959 (average annual rates)*

Country	Export Growth Rate %	Industrial Growth Rate %
Japan	19·5	12·7
West Germany	14·5	8·7
Italy	11·8	7·4
France	5·5	9·1
Sweden	7·2	3·7
United Kingdom	3·7	2·5
U.S.A.	3·4	1·3

Source: Shinohara, *Growth and Cycles*, p. 46.

It is quite obvious that fast economic growth goes together with a lively
export performance. However, as with all correlations, statistics will
never answer the question of which way the causal relationship goes.
Do high exports promote high economic growth rates or the other way
around, or do they promote each other, or are they both independent of
each other, but promoted by a third factor? Shinohara concludes that
the high growth of exports "seems to have a leading, causative role
in industrial development". He adds a general qualification that even if
the export growth *rate* is very high, its impact on the growth of the
economy may not be great if the economy is not highly dependent on
exports, that is if exports represent a very low proportion of G.N.P.
However, he points out that Japan was very dependent on export markets
before World War II, especially in some important manufacturing
industries like textiles. Shinohara may have been right but unfortunately
he relies almost exclusively on correlations and that is not a sufficient
proof.

The opposing school of thought is represented by W. W. Lockwood,
who says: "Sometimes, indeed, the growth of Japanese industry from
Meiji times is attributed mainly to the expansion of overseas demand.
This is a misconception . . . and fails to offer any intelligible explanation
of the substance and breadth of Japanese economic development."† It

† William W. Lockwood, *The Economic Development of Japan: Growth and
Structural Change 1868-1938*, Princeton University Press, 1954, p. 364.

should be mentioned, however, that in several other places he seems to espouse the opposite thesis too.

Lockwood also based his view on statistics. He considered the export/production ratios for various products, and found that during the years 1928-1937 between 25-35 per cent of the entire product of Japanese manufacturing was exported abroad (including the outer parts of the Japanese Empire). He admitted that this was a high percentage by world standards, but he proceeded to argue that this percentage included raw silk and cotton piece goods, where the bulk of the output (75% and 55% respectively) was exported, and these pushed the overall percentage up. He argued that if these two goods were excluded, the overall percentage of output of manufactures that was exported in 1930 was between 15-20 per cent, and this when broken down into single goods revealed great variation, with 50 per cent of pottery and 30-50 per cent of output of wheat flour, rubber goods, bicycles, enamelled ironware and canned foodstuffs being exported, but only 10 per cent of engineering products such as machinery, industrial equipment, vehicles, clocks and scientific instruments, and even less of the products of the chemical industry as a whole. From this he concluded that although ". . . the fortunes of the export trade made the difference between prosperity and depression in Japan . . . it was in the domestic market that was 'the chief stimulus to growth'."

Before we assess the two opposing views we should mention the views of Chikashi Moriguchi of Kyoto University. He is of the opinion that in the period preceding World War II (which was analysed by Lockwood) the Japanese economic growth *was* "export-oriented or export-led", but that in the post-war period it was not export-oriented or export-led, but "heavily dependent upon the expansion of the domestic market".*

Moriguchi seems to base his split attitude on the fact that Japan was much more dependent on foreign trade before World War II than she is now. He said further: "Historically, the process of Japan's industrial growth has been a constant repetition of import—import substitution—expansion of domestic demand—exports process applied to newly emerging modern industries." This last statement is, of course, of necessity true for any country that is about to catch up on the advanced countries. As a truism it does not explain the forces making this process possible, that is, it does not explain from what source come the means of payment for the new-fangled foreign product imports, the money for the imports of foreign capital and know-how, and whence comes the effective demand in an economy that is poor *and at the same time* tries

* Chikashi Moriguchi, *Japanese Trade Policies*, cyclostyled paper read to the 1968 Winter School of the Economic Society of Australia and New Zealand, Sydney, pp. 3-4.

to save much! In other words that truism does not explain the dynamism of the process.

As for Lockwood, although undoubtedly his book is an outstanding piece of scholarship, he allowed himself to be misled by his mass of statistics. To test Lockwood's view let us *suppose* that in fact the fast economic growth *was* export-led or export-oriented. Does it not follow that the very fast economic growth of the Japanese economy produced by that export explosion having produced large domestic income and therefore purchasing power, would ultimately *have to* make the newly rich domestic market the main source of effective demand? To put this argument in another way: *ex post* any case of successful economic growth *must* of necessity look as if it had been oriented to the domestic market, consequently any figures of the proportion of output sold in the domestic market, which Lockwood so elaborately provides, only mean that the Japanese economic growth, however led, was successful, and there is nothing exciting about such a statement. What we need here is the *ex ante* relationships, and these cannot be gleaned from statistics which always provide an *ex post* picture. The meaningful relationships have to be found in logic and an historical study. These two suggest that Japan's lively export performance provided both the fuel and the spark to ignite the fuel in the engine of economic growth. In other words, in the end we incline to the view taken by Shinohara, except that Shinohara tried to prove it solely by correlations and these *never* prove anything and their implied message has to be found and checked outside statistics.

The Role of Foreign Capital

Japan, in spite of her meagre natural endowment, has been quite fortunate in respect to foreign trade and foreign exchange availability although she has borrowed very little and permitted very little foreign investment at home. To this day she retains a very strong disinclination to let in foreign investment, in spite of the *equally strong* present diplomatic pressure by the U.S.A. to allow more foreign capital investment in Japan. It is interesting to mention that in the matter of foreign investment, Japan's attitude has been exactly opposite that of Australia, which has been doing its best to attract foreign capital.

In fact, one can say that the Japanese economic growth "miracle" has been performed virtually without foreign capital. The main reasons for this are very strong Japanese nationalism and fear of foreign economic and political domination. One of the political motivations of Meiji Restoration was fear of European and American imperialism. Japan saw what was happening in Asia and Africa and was afraid of becoming another colony. Although Japan saw the need for imports of goods and of technology from the West she was afraid that "the flag might follow the trade". The fear was so strong that a single German farmer, invited in the last years of the shogunate to set up a model cold-climate farm in Hokkaido, was immediately bought out by the Meiji Government.†

However, the government was prepared to borrow money from foreigners in political or military emergencies. The Tokugawa Shogunate, preferring isolation, did not, indeed could not, borrow abroad at all. The early Meiji Government obtained in London two small loans amounting together to about £3 million in 1870 and 1873 (which were used to compensate the former *samurai* for their old feudal rights) though the loans were at the rather high rates of interest of 9 and 7 per cent respectively. The next time, twenty-five years later, the borrowing was in different circumstances and at the rates of interest almost half as much. Japan had then won a victory in the 1894-5 War with China, which in itself improved the credit standing of the Japanese govern-ment. In addition she obtained a large (for those days) war "indemnity" of £stg.38 million, which created a substantial monetary reserve for Japan, since sterling was then on the gold standard, and which allowed Japan to put the yen on to the gold standard in 1897. Putting the yen on the gold standard at any time, but especially in those days, put a cloak of full respectability on the yen and the financial management of the Japanese government and thereby facilitated borrowing abroad.

In preparation for the next war, with Russia in 1905, during and after that war, Japan floated many loans in England and France. That was the only period of heavy Japanese borrowing abroad. From figures supplied by Lockwood,‡ if one subtracts the 1894-5 War and the Boxer War indemnities, one obtains the approximate figures of about 1500 million yen (about £stg.159 million) for all net foreign capital inflow in the period up to 1913-1922. This includes local authority, the Industrial Bank of Japan, and the Oriental Development Company borrowing plus a quite small amount of private direct foreign capital investment in Japan. Against this capital inflow should be offset an outflow of capital from Japan to Asia and the rest of the world. All the same, the total of capital inflow to Japan in the period was undoubtedly a large sum for those days. However, its direct effects on economic development of Japan were negligible because the loans were for military purposes, though it is possible that the indirect effects of the increased military expenditures were favourable, especially as the wars were short and victorious.

During World War I, Japan was able to take full advantage of excellent trade conditions. Her commodity exports and her shipping services earned such large foreign currency surpluses that Japan became a creditor

† Lockwood, *Economic Development*, p. 322.
‡ Lockwood, *Economic Development*, pp. 254-255.

country for a brief period, having accumulated large holdings of foreign currencies and having granted loans to the French, British, and Russian governments. However, the Russian loan was repudiated by the Soviet Government, and the other loans when repaid, together with the foreign currency holdings, were substantially used up in the twenties.

All the same, in the thirties and up to World War II, Japan continued to be a net creditor country, that is if one set off in the reckoning the total of the foreign assets owned by Japan against foreign-owned assets in Japan. That creditor position was, in fact, quite substantial, especially if the assets in the Japanese colonial territories were included.

Foreign investment in Japan since World War I until the last War was exclusively private direct investment in some modern industries— quantitatively unimportant, but very important qualitatively, because it was the vehicle of spreading know-how and modern technology.

Since the last War Japan has raised some fixed interest loans abroad, especially from the World Bank, and has received some direct private investment, mainly during the period of American Occupation, because after obtaining independence the Japanese government has virtually prohibited foreign ownership of and control of business. Since the 1950s when the Foreign Investment Law was passed to enable foreign borrowing, Japan has again become a borrower in the world financial markets. But it has been mainly fixed-interest borrowing from the World Bank, the U.S. Export-Import Bank and some oil companies. At the same time, however, Japan started to export capital, mostly in equity form, to countries in all parts of the world, mainly to assure herself of steady supplies of raw materials.

In her growth Japan has admitted very little foreign equity capital, but she has used quite consciously and deliberately the advantage that equity capital usually brings, namely imported know-how. The Japanese Government encourages Japanese firms to import know-how, and indeed keeps detailed statistics of its inflow. From 1950 to 1960 the Government records reveal Japan received foreign technology in 3,500 cases.

Japan A Creditor Country Again

It is a complicated matter to estimate the outstanding (cumulative) total of the assets held by a country abroad and its domestic assets owned by foreign countries. Published official estimates for Japan do not exist. However, there are some private estimates made anonymously by a few "city banks". Below is one such estimate.

As can be seen from Table 1.12, in recent years Japan emerged from the status of a net debtor country into again being a clear net creditor. From now on Japan's creditor status will grow steadily, barring any really extraordinary developments in the world. This will be so for

Table 1.12. Outstanding (Cumulative level) External Assets and Liabilities of Japan, million US $.

Assets:	End of Dec. 1962	End of Dec. 1963	End of Dec. 1964	End of Dec. 1965	End of Dec. 1966	End of Dec. 1967	End of Dec. 1968
Long-term assets:	1,476	1,760	2,041	2,503	3,209	4,085	5,168
Direct investment	393	515	562	639	746	866	1,087
Trade credit	633	737	1,072	1,315	1,716	2,200	2,775
Yen credit	64	124	175	287	436	655	893
Subscriptions to Int. Organisations							
Open A/c credit	386	384	234	262	311	361	413
Other assets							
Short-term assets:	3,058	3,513	4,221	4,697	4,801	5,196	6,827
Liquid assets of "foreign exchange banks"	1,155	1,501	2,173	2,549	2,661	3,105	3,828
Of this:							
(Export usance)	(749)	(7)	(1,345)	(1,652)	(1,896)	(1,982)	(2,734)
Other assets	62	54	45	41	66	86	108
Foreign exchange and gold	1,841	1,878	1,999	2,107	2,074	2,005	2,891
Total assets	4,534	5,273	6,262	7,200	8,010	9,281	11,995
Liabilities:							
Long-term liabilities	2,428	3,243	3,898	3,927	3,825	3,880	4,717
Direct investment	274	376	477	522	522	598	651
External bonds	327	481	635	708	683	669	789
Loans	1,144	1,557	1,894	1,915	1,896	1,925	2,403
Bonds	156	276	291	231	206	275	504
Trade credit	37	95	176	167	135	94	81
Aid debt to U.S.A.	490	458	425	389	355	319	289
Short-term liabilities:	2,770	3,490	4,402	4,404	4,114	5,600	6,267
Liquid liabilities of the Government and Bank of Japan	580	356	360	338	359	362	354
Liquid liabilities of "foreign exchange banks"	1,854	2,699	3,362	3,452	3,179	4,133	4,617
Of this:							
(Import usance)	(1,037)	(1,698)	(1,904)	(2,035)	(1,806)	(2,211)	(2,302)
Other short liabilities	336	435	680	614	576	1,105	1,296
Total liabilities	5,198	6,733	8,300	8,331	7,939	9,480	10,984
Net balance	−664	−1,460	−2,038	−1,131	71	−199	1,011

Source: *Nihon Keizai Shimbun,* 15 March 1969.

three separate reasons. Firstly, owing to the remarkable competitiveness of Japanese products in the world markets (evidence of undervaluation of the yen?) the Japanese share of world trade is growing very fast, and her balance of payments is very healthy. As a result the Japanese Government will very likely easily give approvals for investment abroad and may even encourage it in order to disarm international pressures on Japan for liberalisation of import barriers and/or for upward revaluation of the yen because large overseas investment will tend to prevent foreign currency reserves from growing excessively. Investment abroad by Japanese residents is controlled by the Foreign Investment Council which consists of representatives from the Economic Planning Agency, the Ministries of Finance, Foreign Affairs, Agriculture and Forestry, Transportation and Construction.

The second reason why Japan is likely to increase her foreign investment abroad is rapid growth from now on of the motive—domestic know-how. Export of capital usually has as a vehicle and as an engine some form of superior know-how.

Another reason lies in the fact that such foreign investment confers several indirect benefits on Japan or Japanese firms, apart from the obvious direct benefit in the form of dividend. Japanese foreign investment, like any investment abroad, can have the following indirect effects:

(a) Investment made for the purpose of utilising local (foreign) resources may increase exports of Japanese capital equipment and parts for the finished product, especially where under-developed countries are involved.

(b) Industrial investment made abroad under the protective trade barriers of the country in question may be an effective means of beating competition of other countries in that market.

(c) Some investments abroad are made to facilitate marketing, such as distribution agencies and servicing or repair agencies.

(d) Because Japanese industry and government are very conscious of their dependence on foreign supplies of essential raw materials, they have developed a remarkable policy of investing in foreign extractive industries. In this case extraordinary care is taken not to put all their eggs into one basket. The supply sources under long-term contracts, and the Japanese investment in the foreign source of supply are carefully and deliberately dispersed in various parts of the world, so that no single supplier country has a dominant position. The dispersal of the source of supply protects Japanese industry from disruption of supply by industrial unrest abroad, or by politically determined withdrawal of supplies. To understand this near obsession with security of supplies it is necessary to know that Japan has been an object of trade discrimination and even trade embargoes in the past. In this case again the Japanese have shown their ability to turn a disadvantageous situation into one which has favourable effects. By offering different supplier countries long-term contracts and by putting some capital into the extraction venture (usually minority shareholding) the Japanese stimulate price undercutting and competition among the supplying countries and stimulate an increase in the world capacity of the particular mining industries. This must bring down the prices of the raw materials—which is to the advantage of Japan— it improves her terms of trade. Even if this development of a high, or excess capacity might produce a fall in the return on the Japanese capital invested in the supply of the material, this loss is small relative to the gain in the cheaper supplies because the

Japanese capital shareholding is a minority one and it will be mainly the foreign capital that will bear the squeeze, and the other entirely foreign owned factors of production will bear a good deal of the burden of the squeeze. The government of that foreign country might even give some assistance to that industry then.

The Japanese Government assists the development of foreign mineral resources through the Metallic Minerals Exploration Agency of Japan and the Japan Petroleum Development Corporation.

Table 1.13. Japan's Foreign Investments by Region and Industry (authorised cumulative amounts from April 1951—March 1967)

		Amount millions of US$	%
	North America	348·5	29·6
	Europe	27·2	2·3
	Oceania	11·4	1·0
Region	Latin America	329·3	27·9
	Asia	226·6	19·2
	Middle and Near East	220·5	18·7
	Africa	15·0	1·3
	Total	1,178·4	100
	Natural Resource Development	504·4	42·8
	Trade	187·9	15·9
Industry	Finance and Transportation	41·8	3·5
	Manufacturing and others	444·3	37·7

Note: (i) The Source of regional break-down is Ministry of Finance.
  (ii) Analysis by industry was made by the Economic Planning Agency.
     Investments in natural resource development are those made with the purpose of importing the commodity exploited thereby.
     Investments in trade are those made in relation to overseas activities of trading firms of their sales agencies.
Source: *The Economic White Paper,* Government of Japan, Tokyo, 1968.

Windfall Foreign Exchange Gains

The Meiji Government inherited a good deal of gold and silver (of domestic origin mainly) from the Tokugawa Shogunate which prohibited foreign trade mainly to avoid "cultural contamination" from foreigners, but partly also because of a "bullionist" sentiment to protect the gold stock. That gold was later used to cover the balance of payments deficits. Next the 1894-5 Sino-Japanese War "indemnity", payable in sterling or gold and amounting to a quarter of the annual national income of Japan at the time was received by Japan.* Japan escaped all the

* Miyohei Shinohara, "Factors in Japan's Economic Growth", *Hitotsubashi Journal of Economics,* Vol. 4, No. 1-2, February, 1964.

destruction of World War I that Europe suffered, and in fact made large gains from trade and shipping during that war.

Finally the U.S.A., after some hesitation, decided to give Japan economic aid after World War II, which in the end amounted to around US$2 billion for the whole period of economic recovery of Japan. This aid came, of course, in the form of essential goods, but since the authorities in Japan sold them to the public for the yen, the money so accumulated (called the "Aid-Counterpart Funds") was used for lending to private businessmen to assist industrial recovery.

The issue of foreign, mainly U.S., economic aid to Japan as a factor assisting growth is very complicated. Japan received the following amounts of aid:

1946	US$193 million
1947	US$404 million
1948	US$461 million
1949	US$519 million
1950	US$357 million
1951	US$151 million
Total	US$2,085 million†

This aid took the form of straight grants by the U.S.A. to enable Japan to obtain the most essential foodstuffs and other imports. Considering the fact that it was the victor who was making those gifts to the then hated enemy this was undoubtedly generous (even if political objectives also played a role). In the first three post-war years this aid paid for 68 per cent of all imports by Japan. This shows how important the aid must have been.

However, if we view the aid as one of the factors assisting economic growth of Japan, then we should consider also the aid's counterpart —the "occupation costs" paid by Japan to the U.S.A. During the occupation period 1946-1952 Japan paid 550 billion yen as "occupation costs". According to Takahashi this sum converted into the U.S. dollars at the various rates of exchange of the period would be 4·8 billion dollars. Thus, although the U.S. aid was undoubtedly generous, if one views the aid *in its wider context* and as a factor of growth, it is clear that the aid cannot be considered the cause of fast economic growth.

On the other hand when the Korean War and the Vietnam War came, the fact that U.S. troops were stationed in Japan gave some stimulus to the Japanese earning of dollars by sales of goods and services directly or indirectly connected with the two wars. Of course much of the goods, if not services, would have been bought by the U.S.A. even if Japan had not been used as a base.

†Masao Takahashi, *Modern Japanese Economy Since 1868*, Kokusai Bunka Shinkokai, Tokyo, 1968, pp. 153-154.

In the post-war period Japan received windfall foreign currency earnings as a result of the Korean and Vietnam Wars. Although Japan did not desire those wars, and would have done much to prevent them, she may have turned out to be the chief, perhaps the only, beneficiary of them. The Korean War was especially important as Japan was only recovering from World War II and would have suffered extreme constraints in the external sector because of shortage of foreign exchange, and in the domestic economy because of lack of "effective" demand. Shigeto Tsuru* estimated that the U.S. "special procurements" in Japan directly due to the Korean War were ". . . 44, 65 and 63 per cent respectively of commercial exports in 1951, 1952 and 1953. . . ."

In the late sixties the U.S. purchases, directly or indirectly attributable to the Vietnam War, ran at a billion U.S. dollars a year out of the total export receipts of US$9·7 billion in 1966 and US$11·6 billion in 1967.

Japanese sales to the U.S.A. under "special procurement" have been so large because of Japan's geographical proximity and ability to make quick deliveries (often direct deliveries to the theatre of war) to the U.S. armed forces in East Asia.

Against those windfall gains, however, one should set off the windfall losses that Japan had on account of the war reparations to countries that she occupied during World War II. Those reparations started in the fifties and in the late fifties reached the level of about US$70 million a year and continued into the sixties.†

The Importance of Silk

In view of the facts that for almost all of the 100 years since the Meiji Restoration Japan did not obtain much foreign capital, and that in the present century she has invested more than she received from abroad, it has to be concluded that as far as capital goes Japan raised herself up by her own shoe strings. But more than any other country so far, she drew heavily on foreign know-how and technology. In the early Meiji years this took a double form: employment of *numerous* foreigners as technical experts and as teachers in government offices, schools and industry; and sending government officials and young students abroad to foreign schools and business firms. Therefore the question arises, how did Japan raise the foreign exchange to pay for the imports of capital equipment and foreign know-how? In this regard Japan has been rather lucky, given the fact that she did her best to make use of any trade opportunity open to her.

* E. E. Hagen, editor, *Planning Economic Development*, Richard D. Irwin, Home-wood, Illinois, 1963, p. 126.
† For detailed figures see: I.M.F., *Balance of Payments Yearbooks*.

In the first half of the century since the Meiji Restoration Japan pulled herself up on the thin silken thread in somewhat the same way as Australia and New Zealand have ridden on the sheep's back. Silk dominated Japan's trade for more than half of the hundred years, indeed right until World War II, when nylon was developed. Production of raw silk in Japan was 2·3 million pounds in 1868 but quadrupled in the next fifteen years in the first display of Japanese export perform- ance. It grew to twenty-eight million pounds average annual output in the period 1909-1913.‡ In the early part of the last hundred years the other exports were: Japanese tea, rice, copper, coal, marine products and handicrafts such as pottery, paper, lacquer and bronze, which were replaced in the thirties by exports of textiles made of imported raw materials, though silk was then still the most important export item. Japan's luck here consisted in the fact that European silk production was greatly reduced by silkworm disease in Europe in the nineteenth century, while with the growth of standards of living in Europe and America the demand for silk grew very rapidly, especially for "fully fashioned" ladies' stockings before nylon. If nylon had appeared fifty or sixty years earlier, Japan's success story would have been much slower and much less dramatic. By the time nylon had come in quantity during the last war, Japan was already geared for production of other manufac- tured exportables. But while silk reigned supreme as a textile material, Japan did her best to make use of the opportunity. She produced many improvements in sericulture: the output of silk was increased through double-cropping, but the quality of silk was also improved. One great virtue of silk for Japan was that the production of the silk cocoons required leaves of mulberry trees that grow on land not suitable for food produc- tion, so that silk production did not compete with food production.

In this availability of a good foreign exchange earner Japan was more fortunate than her later would-be imitators, the other under-developed countries, except those that have discovered oil. Silk also had another advantage for domestic growth: it lent itself easily to domestic processes of manufacture gradually growing in intensity and sophistication, which led Japan on the path of development of textile manufacturing. Here again Japan found herself better placed than the present under- developed countries. At the time she entered textile and other manufac- turing, there were few countries with low-wage labour which were technologically geared to create effective competition. Today the under- developed countries all want and are ready to develop textile industry— which means that growth of exports is frustrated, and the expansion of production held in check for each developing country.

It is interesting to note Lockwood's objections to this "early bird" thesis.

‡ Lockwood, *Economic Development*, p. 27.

He argued that Japan could not have "benefited from the continuing poverty of Asia" and that a more prosperous Asia would have in fact assisted Japan's development.* But it would appear that in this respect Lockwood misunderstood the situation which is an ambivalent one. If one thinks of the rest of Asia (and the under-developed world in general) *in terms of a market to sell goods in,* then his statement is undoubtedly true, indeed, so true that it would be unnecessary to make it. However, one also has to consider those countries as Japan's competitors for a market that it was both difficult and important to get. If those under-developed countries in Asia (and elsewhere) had not been poor and in "industrial stagnation" they would have been either at the same or a higher level of technological development as Japan. They would have been pushing their own exports, similar to those of Japan, and in such a situation Japan would have been unlikely to expand her exports faster than the rest of the world, as she has in fact done. The optimal situation for Japan would have been one where Asia and the under-developed world in general had *some* growth, but not as much as Japan, so that they would not become serious competitors of Japan in their domestic markets and in the third markets. If the under-developed countries had been growing, but were a step or two behind Japan, this would have given Japan the best of both worlds. Actually, Japan found her situation almost of that kind, but the under-developed countries of today face the Lockwood situation and do not do well in it.

Further, Lockwood argued that Japan's trade with the United States, the British Empire and the continental Europe had equalled that with Asia. This was meant to show that Japan's access to the markets of the under-developed countries had not in fact been so important, but one could easily draw the opposite conclusion here. In any case, if the rest of Asia had an equal or higher growth rate than Japan, Japan would not have been able to dominate the U.S. silk market, for example, as she did, because China and others would have gained a lion's share of it. On the other hand, for Japan to obtain a large share of the presumably larger Chinese market (if China had been advancing fast) would not have been probable, because of the other under-developed countries, especially those who tend to have the same manufactured exports. Surely a rapidly developing China would not have bought more Japanese silk, tea, or cotton manufactures!

Undervaluation of the Yen and the Cost-of-Living Paradox

In part of the pre-war period and in the post-war period, Japan had the advantage of undervaluation of the yen which gave a stimulus to exports

* Lockwood, *Economic Development*, pp. 398-399.

and thereby to domestic expansion, directly and indirectly. Of course, any *single* country could attempt to undervalue its currency by an administrative fiat of fixing the exchange rate at a level that would be likely to produce rapidly growing exports, faster than the growth of the total world exports. (Although in fact for various, mostly wrong, reasons, most countries attempt to do the opposite—to *overvalue* the currency, and defend the overvalued rate by various import trade barriers and payments restrictions.) But even if some developing countries tried to undervalue their currency, it is one thing to undervalue it in fixing the exchange rate, and another matter to make that undervaluation "stick". A surplus in the balance of payments created by an undervaluation of the currency creates domestic inflationary pressures. As long as there is some unemployed manpower to absorb, and wage rates are held down by some means or other, *and consumption is held down* by social forces or fiscal policies as the total of incomes goes up, the undervaluation of the currency can be maintained. In such a case the increases in export receipts can be used for importing producer goods for increased investment (instead of having them accrue as liquid foreign exchange holdings of the banking system, which would produce powerful inflationary pressures of all sorts, as has been happening in West Germany during the sixties). In most countries, though not in Japan, when a currency has been deliberately, or more likely, unwittingly undervalued when the exchange parity was chosen, the increased exports, together with the "multiplier effect" which creates a great increase in demand for labour, resulted in increased wage rates, the whole cost-price structure of the country has risen in relation to that of the rest of the world, and the initial undervaluation has been eaten up. Japan, however, has been able to maintain an undervaluation of her currency in the post-war period, because of the restraint discussed before and also because much of the present exports are not labour intensive but capital intensive and come from industries with large economies of scale and fast technological progress. Consequently, the inflationary pressures that have appeared in the sixties have not affected the export prices. A short-term visitor to Japan cannot fail to be puzzled by the very low value of the yen in Japan—the high cost of living—and the low cost of Japanese exports abroad. This apparent paradox becomes less puzzling when one looks at the wholesale price index (which covers the bulk of exports). This has either actually declined or stayed constant during the sixties, while the cost of living index has gone up at very high rates every year to make Japan one of the dearest, if not the dearest, country to live in. The main reason for this is that the cost of living index covers goods and services where technological improvements of productivity have been slow, and where there has not yet been much use made of the economies of large scale production (and distribution). The additional, minor reasons include drastic import restrictions on foodstuffs and the high cost of the excessive multiplication and over-extension of distribution channels in Japan; and the fact that the large "trading companies" which do most of Japan's export and import business are prepared to take low mark-ups on exports in order to foster exports, and cover most of their operating costs through high mark-ups on imports.

Capital Formation

Although it is widely accepted that economic progress is closely con-nected with a wider and deeper use of capital, there is some doubt whether a high degree of availability of (say, foreign aid) capital is decisive for economic growth of an under-developed country. Although fast growing countries do use up a great deal of capital, it is not certain that a sudden and lavish provision of capital for an under-developed country would necessarily trigger off rapid and self-sustained growth. On the other hand there *is* evidence for the view that many countries have lifted themselves up initially with relatively little capital, and that others have not, although they have had as much capital, but have used up the potential for capital accumulation in consumption, or in accumulation of idle hoards of precious metals or bank accounts in the safe countries of the West.

Availability of capital, or rather the potential availability of capital alone, is not decisive. Capital has to become available but it has to be in the right setting.

The role of capital in a wide sense is to provide the existing workers, and the workers newly arriving on the market, with tools. This implies that with a faster population growth the country needs more capital. Thus the population growth rate becomes one of the critical factors. Those people who for various reasons (sometimes a religious dogma, sometimes lack of understanding of basic economic principles), argue that Malthus was wrong, are barking up the wrong tree. Technological progress in agriculture (not so significant in Malthus's time) does indeed bring closer the possibility of the advanced countries producing enough carbo-hydrates for the population of the world—if that population does not explode. But no one has yet shown that there is a mechanism which would *guarantee* that a faster population growth would be accompanied by a faster technological growth to keep everybody fed on the present standard, not to mention that the technological progress should allow a steady raising of that standard.

Technological growth in agriculture and other industries occurs mainly in the developed countries and this is poor consolation for the under-developed nations. The modern variety of the Malthusian theory must be largely based on the shortage of capital *per caput* and not so much on the shortage of land *per caput*. While it is true that technological know-how could theoretically solve the mankind's calorie problem (if necessary even by chemical synthesis), all of that technological know-how and its application are directly or indirectly based on increasing availability of capital *per caput*. Moreover, the prospects of merely filling hungry people is not that exciting, as it barely lifts us to the level of welfare of animals in a zoo. The modern expression of the Malthusian theory must be that excessive population growth spreads the available capital (or savings) so thinly that a decent human life is not possible on its basis.

The experience of Japan in economic growth does not have very many simple doctrines that could be applied directly to under-developed countries, but population control is certainly one of them. From the Meiji Restoration to the end of the century the population growth in Japan did not exceed 1 per cent p.a.,* and in the twentieth century it has never exceeded 1·5 per cent p.a. Many under-developed countries at present have a population growth of about 3 per cent p.a. These figures imply that if the present under-developed countries wanted to imitate the Japanese performance but maintained their present birth-rates, they would have to make about three times as large a savings effort as the Japanese did. This is difficult to conceive as being feasible. In addition, it should be mentioned that 100 or even fifty years ago catching up required much less capital than it does today.

More capital is also needed to improve the economic infrastructure of the society, which includes transport, communications, etc. ("social capital") and to improve the manpower and the womanpower of the country ("human capital") through training and education.

It is obvious then that a certain minimum supply of capital is indispensable in any country. Yet in an under-developed society the supply of that minimum is often difficult to achieve. Since we have argued earlier that in Japan this development capital has not come from abroad, how was the domestic supply engineered? For a successful capital formation three basic ingredients are necessary: the existence of entrepreneurial spirit in the community; the willingness to provide savings out of a meagre income; and the prospects that the product of the invested capital can be sold at home or abroad.

Lockwood says that the rate of capital formation has been high in Japan ". . . because the incentives to invest in newly-produced capital assets were raised and sustained at a high level . . . by both market forces and political drives."†

This is undoubtedly a substantial part of any explanation of the Japanese

---

* For details of the Japanese population growth see: Ohkawa, *et al*, p. 19.
† Lockwood, *Economic Development*, p. 268.

economic achievement. In fact, from 1868 till the second World War, the Japanese deliberately concentrated their efforts to realise their their slogan: "Wealth and Military Strength", to the almost total exclusion of all other objectives (such as consumption). Since the last war they have concentrated exclusively on catching up with the West in technology and production. In the first period they were motivated directly by their strong nationalism, based on a sense of being unique in the world, and by a fear of foreign imperialism. Since the last World War that strong nationalism has had to be sublimated into economic drives, and until recently Japan has behaved like a *"homo oeconomicus"* of the textbooks—everything has been subordinated to economic growth. The national slogan in this period has been "Production First". In that single-mindedness Japan has been similar to the communist countries, only even more so. In Japan the economic drive of the national leadership has been met by fullest co-operation of the whole population. Consumers showed great restraint and so did the trade unions. Public amenities, distribution of incomes, welfare effects of public finance, etc. had to take second place in Japan. It is only since the Social and Economic Development Plan 1967-1971, that those wider and in fact ultimate objectives are receiving some attention.

Government Assistance for Capital Formation

Government has always played an important role in the economic development of Japan by assisting capital formation, among other things. In its last stage the feudal Tokugawa Shogunate, as well as the *han* governments, started some Western-type factories. (*Han*, a province, was virtually a small state in itself economically and politically, except for the strong dependence on the *shogun*. There were over 250 *hans* headed by a feudal ruler, a *daimyō*). The shogunate and some *han* governments introduced ship-building and cannon casting for national defence reasons.*

In under-developed countries it is often suggested that government entrepreneurship should step in to compensate or to replace shy and weak private entrepreneurship; however, usually where good private entrepreneurship is scarce, so is the public one. Entrepreneurship is not just the big money, nor is it just a number of brilliant ideas which after a period of cogitation fall suddenly from a fertile brain, in or out of government service. Entrepreneurship usually involves years of "on the job experience" plus a flash of creativity. Thus concentrating enterprise in the hands of government is justified only if the private entrepreneurs are shy because of lack of experience, or the minimum

* Yasuzō Horie, "Modern Entrepreneurship in Meiji Japan", in *The State and Economic Enterprise in Japan*, ed. Lockwood, pp. 183-184.

economic size of the enterprise exceeds the resources of small men, *and if* the government service has attracted the cream of educated or trained manpower. In Japan all those conditions seem to have been met. The Japanese public servants came mainly from the *samurai* class who, in comparison to the rest of the population, were very well educated and well motivated. Horie writes: ". . . their cultural heritage and social environment were much the same as that of the business leaders."†️ Consequently it was easy for the public servants to adopt the role of leaders in business and also for the businessman to accept this relationship. The Meiji Government started a large number of state-owned enterprises. Almost immediately after the Restoration the new government set out to build railways and a telegraph system. Further, in that age of free private enterprise in the West, the Japanese Government was eclectic and pragmatic on many points. Thus the government started coal mines, built and operated iron foundries, shipyards and other factories *to pioneer* production of cement, paper, glass and other products. It was also the government that introduced mechanical silk-reeling, and spinning in the cotton industry. However, important as this form of leadership came to be, the Meiji Government was not doctrinaire about it. Indeed, it is only in retrospect that those activities can be seen as State pioneering of industrialisation. In fact the government responded pragmatically and flexibly to the various needs felt at the time, such as providing "hardware" for the military, trying to increase exports, or even trying to increase government revenue. However, when the large profits did not materialise, and when it became obvious that private enterprise could take over, in 1882 the government (motivated by its financial needs for building up the navy and the army) gave up the policy of owning enterprises and sold many of them to private businessmen.

All the same the initial step was not futile. In the first decade after the Restoration, the odds were against starting private enterprise: the risks loomed very large, and the small businessmen of the period were only too conscious of their limitations in knowledge, capital and experience. Thus the State was moderately successful in modestly piloting such ventures, without doctrinaire delusions of infallibility. The government later followed up the policy by various means of support to the private enterprise imitators.

Other forms of assistance were given by the government which bought textile machinery and then sold it on easy, interest-free instalment terms over ten years. The Japan Railway Company was exempt from the land tax, and in 1881 its shareholders were guaranteed dividends of 8 per cent p.a. in order to facilitate the flotation of stock.

† Horie, in *The State and Economic Enterprise in Japan*, ed. Lockwood, p. 206.

In other cases the government assured the firms of purchases of their output. This admittedly created some abuses—it created a special class of "privileged businessmen" (*seishō*), who lent money and sold goods to the government. However, this political patronage was one of the forms of assistance to industry which could not have been given through tariffs, because until the end of the century Japan was forbidden by the "unequal treaties" to impose tariffs. This restriction about tariffs was not without its good points. In that period of free trade Japanese industries which were grossly uneconomic (except for food growing) were generally sifted out and allowed to die. Thus, for example, uneconomic cotton growing disappeared entirely in that period.

Indeed, we could mention at this stage that Japan seems to have a peculiar ability to turn any of the limitations imposed upon her into an advantage. For instance, as is well known, Japan is extremely short of raw materials of any kind. Geographers usually consider this a disadvantage, but the fact is that the Japanese have turned this lack of domestic sources (which if available might have been not very economic) to their advantage, because Japanese industry is not compelled to buy expensive and/or inferior domestic materials but can buy from *the* cheapest source *in the whole world*. To give only a few examples, Japan buys Australian sugar, butter, cheese, and so on, at a much lower price than the Australians have to pay at home. In 1968 Australian cotton growers sold raw cotton to Japanese textile manufacturers at a lower price than they charged domestic textile manufacturers.

The preceding paradoxical advantage is shown even more clearly with respect to a country that discovers some natural resource which for reasons of its quality, location or domestic factor costs is not *the* cheapest in the world. For example, this has happened in Australia, where the recent discoveries of oil (which for various reasons will be substantially dearer than the imported oil) will tend to impoverish the country for many years because the oil could be obtained at a lower "opportunity cost" from abroad, but the government compels the country to use the dearer domestic oil.

Another Japanese limitation is an extreme shortage of land, especially flat land. As a result heavy industry often had to be located over reclaimed sea area. This location of industry, plus the fact that the vast majority of raw materials is imported have been turned to an advantage by building specialised giant ships (which reduces cost of transport) and by unloading coal and iron ore *directly* from the ship into the blast furnaces (which reduces handling costs).

The peace treaty prohibits the maintenance of Japanese armed forces (actually there is a small, high quality "Self-Defence Force"). This is saving Japan very large sums of money every year in defence expenditures, and in this atomic age she is defended even better than if she relied solely on her own expensive forces. In addition, although she is an ally of the U.S.A., she has been exempted from all the burdens of the involvement in the Korean and Vietnam wars (unlike the other allies).

Japan was compelled by the U.S. Occupation Government to abolish the monopolistic *zaibatsu* and to establish competition in the market. At first she complied reluctantly because from an economic viewpoint the large business concerns were not all bad. But as the order had to be carried out, the Japanese Government complied, dissolving the biggest ones, and establishing, according to the foreign instruction, laws and the Fair Trade Commission to enforce competition. Later Japan managed to preserve the newly established competition, while gradually re-assembling like a jig-saw puzzle the old industrial groupings in a new, superior form: the *keiretsu*. (This is discussed in detail in Chapter 7.) As a result Japan has the advantages of competition or "excessive" competition (which the Japanese *economists* agree helps economic growth) and the advantages of very large enterprises which give important economies of scale.

Efforts to Adopt Modern Civilisation

The feudal system of the Tokugawa Shogunate prescribed a specific social status and economic function for every social class, but it was not a completely rigid system. Young farmers or merchants' sons were occasionally adopted into the *samurai* class. Conversely, some *samurai* occasionally gave up their noble rank in order to engage in the more profitable occupation of a merchant. All the same the restrictions were there and the occupation of a merchant was not respected—those factors seriously hampered social mobility. The Meiji Government liberalised the whole system in a series of decrees, to increase social mobility in order to make better use of ability and in particular to remove barriers against commercial activity. Thus the guilds were abolished in 1868, the full freedom to choose any occupation was given in 1871-1872, farmers as from 1872 were freed from the compulsion to grow rice, and could grow what they thought profitable.* Thus the Meiji Government succeeded in removing the stigma of an inferior status from business-men (a strange phenomenon, common however to all under-developed traditional societies), and thereby provided important incentives for modern economic growth.

Soon after the Restoration the government also published two pamphlets on how to organise a joint stock company. The government also gave advice and economic assistance for the establishment of banks dealing in foreign exchange (1869), and "trading companies" (*tsusho kaisha*)

* Horie, in *The State and Economic Enterprise in Japan*, ed. Lockwood, p. 200.

to specialise in foreign trade. Small Japanese manufacturers would otherwise have faced extreme difficulties because of lack of knowledge of languages, foreign customs and markets, and the outside world in general.

The government determined to introduce modern Western civilisation as quickly as possible and, as has been shown earlier, was one of the first few countries in the world to introduce universal modern education. The system had Western content in sciences, but purely Japanese content in "moral education". This educational effort must have been harder for her than for the other countries. She did not yet have modern science teachers. The government imported a large number of foreign teachers, and sent abroad at considerable expense many government servants and young scholars. In choosing this technical advice, it appears that Japan deliberately spread her sources of supply very wide. Possibly she was afraid of relying on any one nation because of fear of colonialism. Also she wanted to be selective and to take the best, or what she thought to be the best, models and so the army patterned itself on Germany, the navy on the United Kingdom, medical education on Germany and so on. The Japanese seem to respect power and achievement and that has possibly influenced their choices. Among the numerous countries drawn upon for expertise, quantitatively in terms of the number of experts, the heaviest use was made of the United Kingdom, Germany, U.S.A., France, China, Italy, Holland and Austria (in that order of degree of concentration, which also is roughly the ranking of the countries in terms of national power in those days). During the period 1876-1895 the overwhelming majority (over 43%) of foreign experts came from the United Kingdom, yet Koichi Emi is of the opinion that the United States and Germany had greater influence on the formation of modern Japan.† Foreign experts were employed by both the central and local governments, and by all government ministries. In terms of the type of skill they ranged from mathematicians, engineers, to almost any occupation like "leather dressers" and shoemakers. (Leather shoes, leather and Western-type shoemakers did not exist in pre-Restoration Japan as there were hardly any cattle in the country and slaughter of animals was illegal.) However, the foreign teachers did not stay in Japan very long. According to Koichi Emi in the period 1876-1885 there were 2447 foreign employees in Japan, but in the period 1886-1895 the number declined to 1469. He estimates the total salary bill for foreign experts employed by both the central and local governments rose from just over 200,000 yen in 1868 to 1·5 million yen in 1874 (which at the time was equal to as many U.S. dollars). After 1874 the salary bill declined very rapidly as the foreign personnel were replaced by Japanese

† Koichi Emi, *Government Fiscal Activity and Economic Growth in Japan 1868-1960*, Kinokuniya Book Store, Tokyo, 1963, pp. 114-124.

staff who had been trained abroad in the meantime. The salary rates of the foreign personnel were extremely high. Koichi Emi says that they were ten times as high as those for the Japanese. In the long-run most of these foreigners made an important contribution, but the immediate and direct results were often not very satisfactory. This was not only because some of them were obviously ill-chosen. Koichi Emi quotes Yoshito Hosino to the effect that the poor guidance by the foreign experts, and the bureaucratic inefficiency of the Japanese managers, caused the early failings of industrial development. Kenzo Hemmi made a more profound observation on this matter. He said that the English agricultural experts tried to apply English agricultural techniques directly to Japanese conditions and "failed completely".* The Germans, however, made a detailed study of the Japanese conditions, taught the basic principles, and were more successful. Hemmi draws the general lesson here that there are no ready-made foreign agricultural techniques that can be imported by the under-developed countries, though some basic theory can be transplanted. Probably much the same is true though less strongly for importing foreign manufacturing techniques.

While the foreign experts were coming to Japan, the opposite stream of young Japanese went abroad with and later also without government assistance to acquire modern know-how. Already in the last decade of the shogunate the leaders of the Satsuma clan sent abroad about 20 young men secretly, against the shogun's prohibition. After the Restoration this became a stream. Koichi Emi estimated that total government expenditures to facilitate adoption of modern civilisation amounted to almost 6 per cent of the Ordinary Current Account of the central government during 1868-1872—a rather high figure which declined to just over 1 per cent towards the end of the century.†

High Saving Ratio

Although this factor is discussed at the end of the list of growth factors, this does not denote its relative importance. Indeed it would be difficult to rank the factors of growth.

Since Japan has raised herself by her own boot-straps it is clear that the Japanese have made a tremendous saving effort. They provided out of the unconsumed, often meagre income, all the resources needed for the development of the country. The Japanese were able to save a great deal when they were very poor, and now that they are becoming prosperous they are saving a higher percentage of income than any other nation. "The average rate of saving (private and public) as a

* Hemmi, pp. 9-10.
† Emi, p. 123.

percentage of G.N.P. increased from 9·8 per cent in 1906 to 23-25 per cent during World War I. It then declined, but again since 1925 has shown an increasing trend and reached a level in excess of 30 per cent in 1960."‡ In the sixties gross savings in Japan rose to nearly 40 per cent of G.N.P., of which 50 per cent is by companies, 30 per cent personal and 20 per cent by the government.* This fact is sometimes "explained" by an adjective: the Japanese are very thrifty. When a further explanation appears needed some writers add another adjective: the Japanese are frugal. But both statements mean the same thing and do not reveal much. The question really is *why* are Japanese thrifty, frugal, or whatever the word is? Dr. Saburo Okita† and Professor Shinohara§ listed some factors inducing the Japanese to save so much:
—An inadequate social security system.
—Consumption lag in a rapidly growing economy.
—The housing shortage and absolute shortage of housing land.
—The wage system with a substantial bonus payment once or twice a year, which is liable to be saved as it comes at the end of the period.
—An increasing share of property income accruing to the higher income group which has a higher saving ratio.
—The "forced saving" caused by monetary expansion ("overloan" to business).
One could add to this list the increasing stress put on university education in the post-war period, which has been forcing parents to save more and more for the high educational costs, and the under-developed state of consumer credit.

Active Policy of Importing Foreign Know-how

The economic development of Japan owes much to an energetic policy of introducing foreign technology and know-how under various patent and licensing arrangements. This introduction of specific types of know-how has been active throughout the last 100 years, but has been especially high in the post-war period. The business demand for foreign technology has been so high in the post-war period that the government passed a law in 1950 to control it through licensing of purchases of foreign know-how. This was partly in order to control the balance of payments which was very weak at that time, and partly to control and to check possible abuse of this type of transfer to make other kinds of money

‡ E.P.A., *Econometric Models for Economic Plan 1964-1968*, Government of Japan, Tokyo, p. 10.
* Okita, *Rapid Growth*.
† Saburo Okita, "Savings in Japan", *Economic Development and Cultural Change*, Chicago, October, 1957.
§ Miyohei Shinohara, *The Role of Savings in the Japanese Economy*, mimeographed paper 1965.

transfers. However, the Japanese Government has had a positive attitude to bona fide purchases of foreign know-how, and indeed guaranteed future remittances of foreign currencies to make the purchases easier.

As a result foreign technology was introduced (in Japanese-owned companies) in a vast range of industries, such as petro-chemicals, synthetic resins, synthetic fibres, electronics, atomic energy, automation technology, motor cars and many others.

In order to make the assimilation of foreign technology effective and quick, the Japanese Government gave the industries assistance in various forms, such as import controls, partial exemption of income tax, special depreciation, and exemption from tariffs on the plant and equipment used. All of these protective measures were *temporary*, unlike in many other countries where they became permanent props, thus robbing the management and workers of incentive to make the industry self-supporting. The large inflow of foreign technology, and the temporary nature of some protective arrangements against import of goods and against the entry of foreign enterprises induced many Japanese "infant industries", such as synthetic fibres, electronic products and motor cars, to grow up. But it has to be stressed that in fact those Japanese "infant industries" have had from the start at least a *potential* comparative advantage. As has been pointed out earlier, the Japanese labour force is highly trained and highly educated.

The volume of the know-how flow is revealed by the patent royalties payments. In 1968 alone Japan paid to foreign countries US$298 million, and received for her own know-how US$31 million.*

Since 1949, when the Government introduced a system for assisting introduction of foreign know-how (by guaranteeing foreign exchange for the purchases) and until the beginning of 1969, Japanese industry signed 9,856 contracts with the advanced countries, which cost Japan US$1,463 million,† for the purchase of foreign technology.

The Modernisation of Japan

As the examples of several countries with poor natural endowment (for example, Japan and Switzerland) show, poverty is essentially a cultural problem rather than purely a problem of natural endowment. Cultural patterns of nations are usually very rigid. The whole educational system in many countries (perhaps, in fact, in all countries) often aims at a rigidity of the cultural system! Cultural patterns are changed in many countries only after centuries, or thousands of years, when the

* H. Kanamori, "Conditions and Problems in Japanese Export Industry Development", *Inter-American Development Bank Meeting of the Board of Governors*, Guatemala, April, 1969.
† *The Japan Economic Journal*, 25 March 1969.

country experiences some profound shock, internally or externally applied. When a country which inherited an ancient system of cultural values is faced with modern civilisation and technology developed elsewhere, it can either abandon quickly many of the old cultural values, or try in a hopeless effort to reject modern civilisation. There is no other alternative because generally the old cultural values and modern technology are incompatible. Many under-developed countries have in fact consciously and unconsciously been trying to reject modern civilisation, as Japan did during the Tokugawa Shogunate. But the visit of Commodore Perry and the spread of the imperialism of some European nations in Asia shocked Japan out of her complacency. The consequential political, social and economic revolution was produced by the upper classes. The *daimyō* and the *samurai*, who overthrew the shogunate and restored the emperor to effective power, had both national and private reasons for their dissatisfaction. They saw the ineffectiveness of the late shogunate in standing up to foreigners, and the danger of Japan becoming a colony of the "barbarians". Privately, they had grounds for discontent because the style and the way of living imposed upon them by the *shogun* impoverished them and pushed many of them into debt. As a result many *samurai* although socially superior to the merchants were in an inferior economic position. These two types of discontent not only produced a political revolution but also were conducive to the growth of entrepreneurship and a grand economic effort. Many *samurai* became entrepreneurs. It should be noted in passing here that the merchants in Japan on the whole were too conservative to play the role that the merchants played in the Industrial Revolution in England.

These social forces induced Japan to concentrate on economic (and military) growth. To this day Japan has set economic growth as its highest objective and few other nations give it such a high priority.

CHAPTER TWO

Public Control of Economic Activities

In one form or another public control of economic activities in any country is virtually as old as the market system itself. Although many discussions of public control of industry are put in black-and-white terms, economic life is so complex that this is like putting oneself alternatively into two different straitjackets. Although some writers have caricatured the philosophy of Adam Smith and of nineteenth century England as examples of unlimited licence for the market forces, in fact Great Britain did then have public controls (though limited). Earlier Adam Smith was aware of some of the weaknesses of the market system. For example, he was concerned about the "propensity" of businessmen to form monopolies (and if he had faced an economic system so strongly permeated with monopolistic structures as are countries today, he would undoubtedly have favoured control of monopoly). Further, Adam Smith is on record as favouring the government taking over some fields of economic activity where the market system could not be expected to operate effectively, such as education or public works. All the same, in the circumstances of his day he was enthusiastically in favour of the market forces being given a free rein, because he saw clearly that the then ubiquitous system of government controls was ineffective even in terms of its own narrow objectives, not to mention that it often choked legitimate business activity.

Briefly, the issue of public control versus a free market and the sovereignty of the consumer is essentially an issue of the mixture of both that should exist in a particular economy in a particular historical phase. Whether an economy should have more or fewer controls depends in the first instance on how many controls it already has. (One should expect on *a priori* grounds that even in the most favourable case at some stage a sort of "diminishing returns" from the application of further controls would be likely to occur.) The issue also depends on the current state of *the public management arts* (which include economic theory of control, the statistical knowledge of the economy and data processing gadgets). Further, it depends on the quality of public servants (the would-be controllers) compared to the quality of the private businessmen, and also on the chosen goals of the two classes. Thus one would approve of economic controls and general government intervention in the Japanese economy in the Meiji period, because private businessmen were for several reasons unable to take up the true lead of economic development, and the bureaucrats and the remarkable political leaders were better equipped, better educated and had superior goals. The same argument, however, would not apply to President Sukarno's Indonesia. Similarly, in post-war Japan the case for government action is entirely different *in nature* from that in the older days.

Government control of the economy can be classified in several ways. These classifications are interesting because they all reveal something about the nature of controls, their effectiveness and their side effect. A government can influence the national economy in several distinct ways:

—Taking steps to maintain competition in the market.

—Consultation with the business community and "public relations" with the consumers.

—"Indicative" planning.

—Fiscal and monetary controls.

—Legislation and government regulations with legal sanctions.

—System of administrative controls where certain actions are penalised and others rewarded, or where some actions are subject to administrative permits.

—Imperative planning.

—Complete government control (not necessarily a direct one) over certain sections of the economy, such as nationalisation of an industry.

Another division of government controls is into macro-economic, and micro-economic ones. Macro-economic controls are directed towards influencing such economic aggregates as the level of total money incomes, that is, the level of economic activity, employment or unemployment rates, the price level, balance of payments, etc. Although some attempts at such controls were made even in the ancient past, on the whole they were only moderately successful until the appearance of the Keynesian theory of macro-economics in the 1930s, and its application mainly since the last War. Micro-economic controls on the other hand involve only particular industries or economic activities (even though a vast range, or even all the industries may be controlled). In this case the government influences a particular industry or economic activity, by encouraging or discouraging it financially or otherwise, by channelling it into particular lines, or by influencing the nature of the product, its price and its conditions of production or sale. Such micro-economic controls have been operated for numerous (often non-economic) ends, and have been more common than macro-economic controls.

When the government has decided on the nature of the desired change, that is, its goal (and this is often not a simple matter) it has to make another decision about the instruments to be used for implementation of the policy.

The instruments of control are extremely numerous, but can be divided into two broad categories:

direct controls, where specific categories of economic enterprises are ordered, permitted, or forbidden to take particular steps; and

indirect controls, where the controlling body does not give direct orders to the business community, but creates such a situation in the economy by fiscal and monetary controls that the community will be *induced* to take a particular action because the altered market conditions will render the old behaviour uneconomic.

In normal, peace-time conditions the indirect controls are far preferable to direct controls for several reasons. To begin with they are more acceptable to the governed because the indirect controls resemble the "rule of law", whereas the direct controls degenerate only too easily into the "rule of man", with the attendant evils of corruption, oppression, arbitrariness and inefficiency. In addition, the indirect controls are more flexible, and in fact show greater respect for the consumer's choice.

Central Planning in Japan *

The idea of economic planning has evoked numerous controversies, at least some of which would have been avoided if the term had been well-defined. "Economic planning" is often used to cover various kinds and degrees of government intervention, or even limited influence, in the economic system. The attempt here is to remove some of the confusion existing in Western literature about the nature of Japanese planning. In addition it will be demonstrated that if the heterogeneous concept of planning is broken down into well-defined categories, general agreement about the merits of *some* forms of planning is likely.

The essence of "economic planning" is that a central planning body first views the nation's resources and wants both in detail and as a whole to ascertain what they are, and what they should be. This body then tries to influence the allocation of resources both at macro- and micro-economic levels, as well as the distribution of the product, so as to maximise the welfare of the nation. The foregoing definition implies that where an economy is viewed and "planned" *only* in terms of Keynesian aggregates like total employment, incomes, saving, investment, etc., this is not "planning". Similarly, sporadic and *ad hoc* acts

---

* This section is the reprinting by kind permission of the Editor of *The Economic Record* of an article by this writer: "Economic Planning in Japan", *Economic Record*, June 1969.

of intervention by the government even in macro-economic matters, no matter how widespread, are not considered as planning, if they have not emerged as an interdependent set of policy recommendations from a systematic and quantitative overview of the economy. Thus although the governments of the U.S.A., or of Australia, have always controlled the national economies to a degree, those economies have never been planned.

Further, it is always necessary to qualify the term "planning" by a suitable adjective to indicate the nature of the plan's implementation. Economic plans may be *imperatif* or *indicatif*. "Imperative planning" refers to planning of the Soviet type, where the plan is in the nature of a set of commands with all the sanctions at the government's disposal. However, the term "indicative planning" is much less clear. France and Japan are usually referred to as the countries with "indicative planning". The writers using this term usually proceed to discuss the implementation† of these "indicative plans" and list various instruments of direct and indirect government intervention. But the word "indicative" itself should suggest that there is no implementation of the plan other than through the "announcement effect" which may or may not be strong according to the circumstances and the country. Those writers believe that under "indicative planning" the government carefully watches the provisions of the plan and the actual developments in the economy, and regulates and directs the economy at the micro-level by a combination of such devices as specific fiscal and/or monetary measures, that is by economic rewards or penalties. The facts of the case are that the two countries usually referred to as having indicative planning, France and Japan, do not now control their economies in that way (though in the immediate post-war period they were highly-controlled, but not planned, economies).

Planning the private sector is intended to offset various imperfections in the market mechanism. In addition, it is intended to co-ordinate the private and the public sectors.

The main imperfections of the uncontrolled market mechanism are: economic instability, a very unequal distribution of incomes, sometimes an "insufficient" rate of capital formation, monopoly, and last but not least, the inability of the market mechanism to allow for "externalities". Most of those evils except "externalities" can be checked without planning. The single entrepreneur, even if aware of the existence of "externalities", will not take them into account in his decision making. This is so because the external economies and costs that the firm bestows upon others are not compensated. The classical cases quoted in this respect are the beekeeper and the orchardist, and the factory air

---

† Cf. Norman Macrae in "The Rising Sun", *The Economist*, 27 May 1967.

pollutants and residents nearby. Less picturesque, but not less important, are what might be called "quasi-externalities", where joint or at least co-ordinated economic decisions of various firms would be best. For example, the establishment of an industry in a new area necessitates the availability of a sizeable electric power plant and, on the other hand, it would be foolish to set up a power plant if there were no industry nearby. Here the service to others is not quite an "externality" because it is charged for. All the same it could be called a "quasi-externality", because of the two-way dependence of one industry upon the other. The development of any single industry involves various important "quasi-externalities" such as the increased demand for building materials, municipal services and social facilities for the population that will concentrate nearby.

A modern type of "externality" arises from the fact that most modern industrial undertakings have a very large optimum size relative to the market available. In such circumstances the normal competitive free market behaviour in any country leads to a number of firms establishing separate plants which are far too small for economic operation and which are not fully used. A national economic plan can ensure that under such circumstances the plants that are set up are of optimum size and have a reasonable chance of running to capacity. In Japan the national plan sets up a desirable target for the whole petro-chemical industry and the competing oligopolists have some very broad guidance. (They can, and sometimes do, ignore the plan and only the market will reward them or punish them for this.) In addition there are industrial councils in many industries, both with and without government representation, which decide the current optimum size for a plant, and the government then sanctions such recommendations (in the petro-chemical industry the minimum permitted capacity for a plant is 300,000 tons output p.a.). The competing industrial groups can each set up plants of that size if they think that there is sufficient market at home or abroad. Alternatively they are induced to combine their efforts in a jointly owned company, or they agree to co-ordinate their investment programs to avoid plants of uneconomic size and levels of production. The companies co-operate in such efforts under the umbrella of the plan not so much to avoid competition, but to make it more effective. The argument for such co-ordination is even stronger when a few domestic producers of a similar product intend to establish plants in a small foreign market.

In all cases of "externalities" and "quasi-externalities", national planning permits the "internalisation" of those "externalities". When those problems are "internalised", the particular problems created by the growth of one activity are resolved by a suitable response in another part of the private or public sector. This means that "indicative planning" anticipates problems and bottlenecks and assists in their solution before they lead to heavy costs. Since gestation periods of investment acts are nowadays very long and the investments are large, any mal-adjustments must be very expensive. It is true that business firms could carry out surveys of the particular industries or the whole economy, and they could also make forecasts. Indeed, they are now doing this to an increasing degree. But such efforts cannot equal a central plan. Firstly, many "externalities" can be allowed for only through collective action. In addition, planning or forecasting the level of the whole economy carried out individually must be much more expensive, and much less satisfactory than planning by a central body, which has wide representation from industries, government departments and universities. The need for such advisory national "planning" arises from the fact that the business man acting individually and if planning at all, does it in a very narrow field and cannot see, or allow for, many important wider effects and connections. If all the firms prepared their own longer-range plans and did it well, the sum of the individual plans would often point to the advisability of alterations in the individual plans. The rational plan of action for an individual firm, or the nation, is dependent not only on the apparent availability of factors of production and the level of costs. It is also vitally dependent on what the other decision makers will do. From this inevitably follows a strong argument in favour of indicative planning: within limits, forecasts of collective behaviour have a sub-stantial element of self-validation in a country where they are respected. Even if the plan was built on inaccurate assumptions as to what the individual decision-makers intended to do, an internally consistent plan with some desirable objectives would have a good chance of being implemented.

Individual firms, having made separate market studies, may find that the state of the market in respect to both the supply of inputs and the demand for outputs does not warrant any expansion of the firm. This assessment may be fully correct within that framework, but if a respected planning body sets up a target for, say, 10 per cent expansion, it may be easily attained both individually and collectively, except, of course, for the external sector. In the external sector such a wishful-thinking policy will not work. Here the planners have to take the facts of foreign supply and demand as given, but they can recommend defensive steps to the monetary and fiscal policy-makers. In the framework of a com-prehensive plan embracing both the private and the public sectors, it must be easier to forecast effectively the balance-of-payments pressures, and to identify the industries with and without growth potential.

Only an enthusiast would believe that the central planning body would correctly solve all problems arising out of "externalities" and "quasi-externalities", or even that it would perceive all problems in time. How-ever, for the above reasons, the planning body will do the job better, assuming that its members are not of an inferior intellectual calibre compared with the average business executive. That, in essence, is the argument for indicative planning.

The next problem is to decide which sectors economic planning is to cover. In the past all advocates of planning dwelt exclusively on the numerous and real imperfections of the operation of the *private* sector. The proposal to correct and co-ordinate economic activities was to deal with the private sector. Needless to say, it was valuable to list the areas where the unaided private sector gave non-optimal solutions, but to exempt the public sector from any scrutiny was inconsistent, to say the least. The public sector is just as full of inconsistencies and of vested interests of a sort, and it needs co-ordination even more. It needs to be co-ordinated within itself, and then it needs to be co-ordinated with what the private sector is doing. It would be possible to give an almost endless list of lack of planning, inadequate co-ordination and schizo-phrenic decisions in the public sector of any country, even one which is supposed to be well governed. We are all aware of apparent sudden shortages of various goods and services and the consequential "crash programmes" to provide, for example, schools, universities, electricity, water, city transport, or to recruit teachers from emergency training or from abroad. Every such "crash programme" is uneconomic and demon-strates lack of planning in the preceding period. Further, we are all aware of how often absurdly uneconomic railways, when owned by the government, are given assistance to compete with economic road trans-port. Even within government departments there are numerous cases where the Ministry of Something not knowing (or knowing) what the Ministry of the Other Affairs is doing, takes exactly the opposite measures or duplicates the effort. In the United Kingdom there were some years ago (perhaps still are) no less than five entirely separate and non-co-operating government intelligence agencies. Not only did this have the disadvantage of excessive cost but as the agencies did not "exchange notes", the accuracy of the information depended on whether the agency approached was the best informed. In another English speaking country the Department of Forestry was planting large areas of a particular tree to prevent erosion, while the Department of Agri-culture was spreading a virus to kill that tree because it encroached on pasture land. The unfortunate thing in this case was that the virus, being spread by insects and birds, could not be confined to any single area. To take another kind of situation, the government will sometimes sub-sidise a commodity like milk or bread to assist the ordinary family, and at the same time collect a tax on soap! Or in countries with government monopolies of tobacco or alcohol, one government agency would advertise the products and another would provide hospital facilities to treat cancer and alcoholism.

Of course, the public servant is liable to err like any other mortal, but the point here is that many of those errors and much of the waste through duplication are caused by lack of co-ordination in the public sector. What is often ignored is the fact that governments are not monolithic bodies with a single set of interests and objectives. In fact, as soon as a government department is set up it develops its own set of goals and vested interests, mainly directed towards national interest, but strongly coloured by the particular expertise of the staff. Ultimately those actions are more or less subconsciously influenced by the personal interests of the staff (which includes both the private gain of the staff in the narrow sense, as well as their intellectual "interest").

Greater co-ordination of the public sector by some planning body, both inter-sectoral and inter-temporal co-ordination, within the public sector and within the whole economy, is badly needed. Of course, some attempt is usually made by a government department, sometimes the Treasury, or the Budget Office, to produce some sort of inter-departmental co-ordination. However, since budgets are made up on an annual basis, there is no inter-temporal co-ordination, and as there is no plan-forecast for the private sector there is an inadequate dovetailing of the public and the private sectors.

But even if some better system of co-ordination in the public sector is established, the problem there will still be bigger than in the private sector. This is so because in the private sector a single criterion—profitability compared to the rate of interest—determines whether a firm, a product or a process will survive. In the public sector there is no such simple criterion, and no such automatic sifting mechanism for allocation within the sector, and complementing and assisting the private sector. Consequently it would appear that the public sector needs planning more than the private sector! This is the old view of planning turned upside down.

PLANNING THE PRIVATE SECTOR

In Japan both the private and the public sectors are co-ordinated by the national economic plan. Indeed, it is possible to say that the public sector is much more planned than the private sector, and certainly there is an attempt to co-ordinate the public sector to fit it into the requirements of the private sector.

There are two opposing views in works published in the West as to the nature of the Japanese economic planning in the private sector: Norman Macrae, the deputy editor of the *Economist*, says: "First, the Japanese like to say that theirs is an unplanned, free enterprise economy. But in our western terms it isn't. It is, in your correspondent's view, the most intelligently dirigiste system in the world today."

As if this were not enough, he continues: "The ultimate responsibility for industrial planning for deciding in which directions Japan's burgeoning industrial effort should try to go, and for fostering and protecting business as it moves in those directions, lies with the government."

The preceding are not statements out of context. Elsewhere he speaks of: "the most successful sudden economic growth . . . of all time . . . implemented by a bureaucracy . . . the most mathematically-minded on earth . . . anybody who knows Japan will be aware that investment intentions in Japan were given a sharp push in the right directions by the official planners. . . ."*

Diametrically opposed to the view of Macrae is Shigeto Tsuru, a Japanese economist, in a paper called "Formal Planning Divorced from Action: Japan".† Tsuru's main point is exactly what the title of his paper says. In particular he says that the private sector of the Japanese economy is governed by "price mechanism resting on free enterprise", and that the government's position is "maximum respect for private initiative and the minimum resort to any kind of centralised planning". Similarly, but even more strongly, Toshio Shishido, the Administrative Councillor of the Planning Bureau, the Economic Planning Agency (E.P.A.), writes of the public sector as the "controllable sector" and the private sector as the "non-controllable sector".‡ Like some other writers he speaks of the plan's targets as "guide-posts" for private enterprise. This term, however, can be ambiguous and it certainly has misled some Western observers. The main issue is how much pressure, if any, is there that the "guide-posts" be followed? Speaking of the implementation of the plans, Tsuru says:

> Theoretically speaking, implementation of the policy objectives set forth was certainly within the capabilities of the government. In fact, a stranger who studies the Japanese scene from outside might suppose that the Economic Planning Agency, possibly under the strong leadership of the Prime Minister, could serve as a co-ordinating administrative body looking after the progress of the plan's implementation so far as these policy objectives are concerned, with a power to suggest needed measures and appropriations as the occasion demands. Theoretically such a supposition is warranted because Japan's administrative structure as it exists today permits this to happen if the Prime Minister decides to exercise his leadership in this direction. But the facts of the case are otherwise.§

Given these two widely differing views, where does the truth lie? It will be shown that Macrae is almost completely wrong and that the true position is much closer to the view of Shigeto Tsuru. But Tsuru

---

* Macrae, *Economist*, 27 May 1967.
† Tsuru in *Planning Economic Development*, ed. Hagen, pp. 119-149.
‡ Toshio Shishido, *"Economic Planning in Japan"*, mimeographed paper, Economic Planning Agency.
§ Tsuru in *Planning Economic Development*, ed. Hagen, pp. 142-143.

has gone too far. He and *some* other Japanese economists say that the Japanese economic plan is just a forecast, and, as it happens, not a very accurate one at that. Although appearances could lead us to take such a view, in fact the position is not so simple. Of course, any economic plan must be based on a forecast. The Japanese plan "forecasts" how the private sector and the public sector *would behave* if each business and government department carried out extensive research studies at both micro- and macro-levels considering all important economic factors and potentialities both at home and abroad, and after that proceeded to optimise its behaviour. Thus the plans are forecasts of what the optimal behaviour of the Japanese economy as a whole and in parts would be. Are they therefore plans or are they mere forecasts? The difference between a plan and a forecast is that a plan is a "forecast" not necessarily of the actual state in the future, but of what is the most desirable and still feasible state of affairs. In other words the plan contains a normative element, and is at least an act of advice, or an act of will.

In general, the normative element in the plan is accompanied by sanctions of varying degrees of intensity. The nature of various plans, and in particular the nature of Japanese economic planning, is revealed by an examination of the intensity of those sanctions. In the Soviet Union, for example, the sanctions for the economic plans include absolutely the whole range of instruments of power at the disposal of the government. In Japan the only sanction for both the private sector and the public sector is the moral or psychological one, based on respect for the intellectual quality of the plan and the planners. An Occidental might think that the influence of the plan is therefore negligible. The impact of the plans, however, is increased by several facts peculiar to Japan. First, Japan is probably the most patriotic and the most disciplined country in the world. Thus advice coming from the national plan adopted by the government would command respect and attention, though not necessarily compliance. The business community have a high (and well-founded) respect for the intelligence, education and general expertise of the Japanese public servants (and therefore of the Economic Planning Agency personnel).* This again increases the impact of the plan on the Japanese economy.

Briefly, in Japan the execution or implementation of the plan rests solely on the "announcement effect" of the plan, and the Economic Planning

---

* The situation in this respect differs in some countries. In France the public servant is both well-qualified and respected. No doubt this facilitates French "indicative" planning. In the U.S.A., the U.K., Australia and New Zealand the business man often has contempt or at best tolerance for the public servant, although in the latter two the average public servant at the executive level is probably superior to the average business executive in respect to education and intellect. In some under-developed countries, on the other hand, many of which are keen on planning, public servants are of lower calibre than businessmen.

Agency acts as a consultant, and not as a director. That the "announce-ment effect" of the Japanese plans is substantial and that it has been growing in strength is shown by the growth of private planning in the private sector and the fact that the private planners use E.P.A. plans as the basis for their own plans. According to a sample survey†　of 200 representative large firms, in 1952 none of the firms included in the sample had any plans of its own. In 1961 as many as 87% had their plans, and among those firms with long-term plans, 84% used the E.P.A. plan "as an important basis". Further, the respect of the private business community for the work of the E.P.A. is shown by the fact that at any time about 60 employees of private firms are on secondment from industry to the E.P.A., as trainees for about two years, with salary paid by the private business. A substantial number of business firms is on a waiting list to send their employees to the E.P.A.

Apart from the "announcement effect" of the plan another result is a substantial "learning effect" from the extensive process of making up the plan. The plan is formulated through innumerable meetings in many committees consisting of the E.P.A. permanent staff, full-time delegates (for two years or so) from various government departments, business representatives and some university professors. These commit-tees never vote,‡ but continue discussion until some sort of consensus has been reached. This means that every aspect of the plan is thrashed out in its micro and macro aspects in the context of the domestic and foreign conditions in order to make the plan internally consistent and acceptable to all important participants. In some years more than ten different drafts had to be prepared. It is obvious that the learning process must be great. The big-business representatives (who always have univer-sity degrees) learn about the wider implications of their own firm's behaviour, as well as learning something of value for the firm itself. The small firms, which are still numerous in Japan, are represented by their associations. Although this indirect participation may in itself be weak, the small firms' behaviour as subcontractors to the big firms is influenced by the latter who are directly involved in the planning. The government representatives and the university men learn more about the concrete practical problems of the business man. The partici-pation of business representatives in such committees for a few years

---

† Tsunehiko Watanabe, "National Planning and Growth in Japan", in B. G. Hickman, editor, *Quantitative Planning of Economic Policy*, The Brookings Institution, Washington, 1965.

‡ However, when a plan is completed and submitted to the government for approval, all cabinet ministers sign it, with some quite minor amendments, if any. The Diet as such does not approve the plan, though its members can influence the plan during its formulation, and, of course, will criticise it after-wards in the Diet. This differs from France where the plan is voted on in Parliament.

must surely have a great effect on the business world by making it more alert to the coming pattern of demand, the growing products, industries or markets, the latest technological processes, and generally the wider, national issues involved in various alternative modes of business behaviour.

It should be pointed out, however, that the "announcement effect" can work to make the plan effective, or can go counter to some objectives of the plan. Generally, where the plan coincides with private interest it will be followed, but if it goes against private interest it may be ignored unless the business community is very public-spirited. It is a fact that the Japanese business community, like the average Japanese, is extremely conscious of its obligations to the country, so that it will often follow a course of action that would not maximise private gain,* but needless to say there are limits to this. The important fact is that, on the whole, the Japanese plans prescribe a course of action for the business world that is in their long-run interest. Here, therefore, is another important difference from the Soviet type of planning. Japanese planning is essentially formulated to assist the business units in their endeavours, and obviously does not need any elaborate official implementation, except for the general Keynesian type of policies.

The Japanese plans after the War were not very sophisticated until perhaps the "Doubling National Income Plan 1961-1970" or the "Economic and Social Development Plan 1967-1971". Indeed, from a theoretical point of view those early plans left much to be desired, although they were broadly on the right lines as they stressed: the economic growth potential inherent in the availability of large numbers of skilled workers; the importance of balancing external payments; the importance of developing basic industries such as coal and electric power; and the desirability, in the Japanese conditions, of developing heavy industries and chemical industries.

It is true, of course, that all of these points, except perhaps the first one, were quite obvious without any statistical study. However, in the pessimistic mood after the War, the growth potential arising out of the skilled labour force was not obvious to many. The magic power which our age ascribes to statistical calculations, although only partly deserved, probably played a big role in pushing the Japanese economy into growth. Those early plans postulated G.N.P. growth of about 5 per cent p.a. This figure from today's standpoint sounds very modest, but in those days it was most daring because there was a general fear of the future,

---

* The following facts provide evidence for this statement: Japanese employers do not dismiss their workers when the firm is making losses, nor do they dismiss old or inefficient workers before the due retirement age. Japanese "trading companies" add a higher mark-up to prices of imported goods than to the prices of exported goods, in order to assist the balance of payments, though this could perhaps be due to different levels of competition in the two markets.

and a doubt whether Japan could ever regain her standard of living of 1930-1934.†

Therefore, whatever the faults of the early plans, they gave a most useful impetus to growth. In recent years, when actual growth rates have often exceeded 10% per annum, the planners have attempted to dampen the exuberant rate of growth, which caused a rapid rise in the cost of living and pressure on the balance of payments. They tried to do this by deliberately understating the expected, or planned, rate of growth. They felt that if they published the actual expected rate of growth, say 10%, the "announcement effect", together with the particular type of competitive behaviour of Japanese firms, would push the rate of growth to say 15%, because Japanese firms try at least to maintain their existing share of the market and, where possible, to increase it. The problem here arises from the fact that although the Japanese economy is highly competitive (and the Japanese ascribe their fast growth rate to that fact) it is a different competition from that of the Western countries. It is a *market-share* competition in which increasing the firm's market share ranks as a higher goal than profits!* Where the official plan persistently envisages a lower rate of growth than that actually achieved, and where conforming to the plan does not appear to the business man to coincide with the interest of his company, this aspect of planning has some limitations. One of the reasons for private planning by such businesses as banks (where the official overall plan and its breakdown might be considered as adequate in coverage), is that the official plan is "political", in other words it now deliberately understates the growth rate.

In the early days of Japanese planning the situation was different. Then in the climate of existing public and expert opinion, the planners were bold enough to predict a 5% growth rate. In those conditions to announce a faster rate of growth, even had it occurred to them, would have been inexpedient insofar as it might have destroyed the plan's and the planners' credibility. But since the Japanese growth momentum has been firmly established by facts, the planners' underestimation must be intentional (as they claim it now is). Even allowing for this reservation about the official rate of growth, and the growth of scepticism, some "announcement effect" of the official target cannot be ruled out, because the official target denotes the growth rate above which the Bank of Japan will start introducing a very drastic monetary squeeze. So it pays the business man to respect the official plan figure.

The Japanese plans provide less detail in micro-planning than is

---

† Cf. the view of E. A. Ackerman, an economic geographer on the staff of the American occupation authorities, *Japanese Natural Resources*, in *Essays on Japanese Economy*.

* E.P.A., *Economic and Social Development Plan 1967-1971*, p. 56.

generally believed. It is true that the Japanese planners provide sectoral targets, but an examination of the official plans reveals that the break-down does not go very far. The targets that are published are, in fact, semi-aggregates. As can be seen from the table reproduced below the entire Japanese economy is broken down into twenty sectors.

Table 2.1. Gross Output by Industry—in 1960 Prices (billion yen)

	Industry	Calendar years			Average annual rate of increase %	
		1960	1965	1971	1965/1960	1971/1960
1.	Agriculture, forestry and fisheries	3,138·3	3,403·1	4,032·9	1·6	2·9
2.	Mining	393·0	458·9	588·2	3·1	4·2
3.	Food and kindred products	3,338·9	4,467·9	5,989·4	6·0	5·0
4.	Textiles	1,956·6	2,473·1	3,260·9	4·8	4·7
5.	Pulp, paper and allied products	666·0	1,088·3	1,972·4	10·3	10·4
6.	Chemicals and allied products	1,530·6	3,127·4	6,249·4	15·4	12·2
7.	Primary metal industry	3,215·5	5,934·8	9,983·3	13·0	9·1
8.	Fabricated metal industry	582·6	986·7	1,819·1	11·1	10·7
9.	Machinery, except electrical	1,640·1	2,881·6	5,524·3	11·9	11·5
10.	Electrical machinery	1,427·1	2,296·4	4,683·1	10·0	12·6
11.	Transportation equipment	1,362·1	3,280·4	7,322·7	19·2	14·3
12.	Other manufacture	3,816·8	6,361·2	10,726·5	10·8	9·1
13.	Construction	3,181·5	5,461·7	10,438·8	11·4	11·4
14.	Electricity, gas and water	653·2	1,096·1	1,853·1	10·9	9·1
15.	Wholesale and retail trade	2,489·2	4,046·7	6,774·4	10·2	9·0
16.	Real estate and ownership of dwellings	619·1	917·9	1,111·8	8·2	3·2
17.	Transportation, storage and communication	1,803·7	3,125·3	5,377·9	11·6	9·5
18.	Financing and insurance	906·3	1,673·3	2,628·4	13·0	7·8
19.	Services	3,384·4	4,862·7	7,282·6	7·5	7·0
20.	Unallocated	943·9	1,859·8	3,034·6	14·4	8·5
21.	Total	37,048·8	59,803·3	100,653·9	10·0	9·1
	Primary industry (1)	3,138·3	3,403·1	4,032·9	1·6	2·9
	Secondary industry (2-13)	23,110·7	38,818·4	68,558·2	10·9	9·9
	Tertiary industry (14-19)	9,855·9	15,722·0	25,028·2	9·8	8·1

Source: E.P.A., *Economic and Social Development Plan 1967–1971*, p. 178.

It is obvious that the amount of detail, that is the extent of the breakdown, is inadequate for any firm even to think that it has any mandatory figure for output, or for any public, or semi-public institution like some banks, to exert pressure on any single firm to induce it to conform to the plan's target. There just is not any firm's target there! It is true that the E.P.A. does make a more detailed industry classifica-tion involving sixty sectors, but these figures are never published, although a firm could ask for a particular sectoral target in it and would informally be given the required figure. Moreover even this unpublished classification is not sufficiently detailed to exert significant pressure on any single firm. It certainly could not be used for official enforcement because it has such broad categories, such as natural textiles, chemical textiles, products of coal, products of petroleum, metal products, machinery, electrical machinery, railway transport, road transport, etc.

Why are there no detailed targets? The simple and obvious answer is that detailed targets or the detailed forecasts are much more difficult to make for various reasons. As our knowledge of statistical forecasting techniques grows and as computers develop, it may be possible to make fairly *detailed* forecasts. At present, however, there are substantial advantages in forecasting aggregates only. For instance, if we take an aggregate of ten industries and forecast the growth rate of the aggregate we are much less likely to be substantially wrong than if we forecast the growth rate of each single industry. This is so because the more industries that are included in the aggregate, the greater is the probability that errors leading to overestimation will cancel out the errors giving rise to underestimation. Thus if the forecast is only for the aggregate, its error expressed as a percentage of the aggregate will be smaller. In a sense this gain of accuracy is purely "statistical" but since planners are human and are especially sensitive to criticism (just because of the under-developed state of forecasting), it is not surprising that they tend to refrain from publishing detailed targets. In any case this factor is especially important where the implementation of the plan is dependent upon voluntary acceptance—in any truly indicative planning system. But there is also a real advantage to the economy in this approach in that an aggregate target that is reasonably realistic will be useful to some decision-makers outside and inside the group, while it will not positively mislead them quite so much as a detailed target would be liable to do.

PLANNING OF THE PUBLIC SECTOR IN JAPAN

The public sector in Japan is planned with a view to guiding, stimulating and assisting the private sector. But in the very process of preparing a plan for the public sector numerous conflicts between the aims and attitudes of various government departments have to be resolved in some rational manner: through discussion, instead of political power.

The role of the public sector in Japan has changed a great deal since the end of the War. Immediately after the War until about 1955 "the public sector played a leading role in rehabilitating [the Japanese] economy from war damage, until the functions of market mechanism could be restored".* In that period, there was wide government use of direct controls over the private sector, especially with respect to the production of basic commodities and services such as rice, coal, electric power, steel and transport. Those controls, however, were operated at the departmental level without any definite regard for the various

* Shishido.

economic plans that were prepared by various institutions. This was so partly because Japanese government departments have traditionally had considerable power of their own and have retained a good deal of it even under the post-war democratic constitution. But partly it resulted from the obvious generalities of the terms of the early plans, by methods that did not inspire much confidence, and by agencies that at first had neither executive power nor much prestige. The early plans were not even formally announced to the public.† They were mainly used as background material for formulating economic policies, or for negotiating with the U.S.A. At the same time, the particular government departments, such as the Ministry of International Trade and Industry, the Ministry of Finance, or the Ministry of Construction, had their own strong and cherished ideas, and operated direct controls according to their own lights, often not even paying much lip service to the national plans.

In the fifties, however, two factors emerged. Firstly, the market mechanism regained its functions, and direct government controls were largely abolished. Secondly, economic plans prepared by the E.P.A. acquired a substantially higher level of sophistication. Thus the national economic plans began to play a larger role and more notice of them was taken in the private sector. They also began to spell out in detail the economic policies in the public sector for a decade or so. The first national plan which specified economic policies in the public sector was the "Doubling the National Income Plan" published in December 1960. Mr. Toshio Shishido of the Planning Bureau of the E.P.A. said: "The cumulative sums of investment in the public sectors during the planned period, were indicated and classified according to purposes, while the projections of production, exports and imports for the private sector were much more roughly made."‡

Considerable difficulties were encountered in formulating the plans for the public sector. Various ministries have their own priorities, pet ideas and policies. Co-ordinating those policies in a long range plan did not prove easy. Although all of the ministries no doubt agreed about the great importance of building up social overhead capital, some had different priorities for parts of the public sector. The Ministry of Finance, which is responsible for the annual government budget, would not agree to the inclusion of annual figures for public investment, even for five years, arguing quite correctly that this would deprive it of any fiscal control over the economy. All the same everyone agreed that it was very desirable to have a long range investment plan. In a compromise the plan for the public sector shows only the figures for the entire period, in most areas ten years, in a few cases five years. A ten-year period is a

† Shishido.
‡ Shishido.

good choice, as it should cover both the upswing and the downswing of the cycle, thus allowing the annual budgets to play a compensatory role, while the general public investment program over the whole period would not suffer.

Although the plan for the public sector is prepared after the fullest consultation of all ministries, this does not mean that all of them would be equally happy about the details of the plan. In fact, two ministries, the Ministry of International Trade and Industry (M.I.T.I.) and the Ministry of Finance, happen to be the most influential in preparing a plan because of their statutory duties and their expertise and prestige.

However, the execution of the plan in the public sector is left entirely to the separate ministries and they can strongly influence the speed with which the particular aspects of the plan are implemented. Each ministry prepares its own program of investment for a number of years. At this stage some influence of the national plan is assured by the fact that each program has to be approved by the Diet which attaches to the bill a clause requiring the ministry to "consult" with the Director-General of the E.P.A., though it is not quite clear exactly what "consultation" means.

THE PLANNING PERIOD AND MACHINERY

The official planning period in Japan varies in several ways. Some plans have been officially announced for a period of ten years—the "Doubling the National Income Plan 1961-1970"—or for five years, in the cases of the "Medium-Term Economic Plan 1964-1968", or the recent "Economic and Social Development Plan 1967-1971".

The planners frankly admit that any plan is essentially and of necessity based on an extension of past trends and past relationships. Therefore, no matter how sophisticated the method, a plan would have reasonable predictive power for only a very brief time after the period on which the calculations are based. Because of this fact as soon as a plan is constructed, work starts on adjusting the data and even the conceptual basis of the predictions. It is usually found in Japan that a ten-year plan becomes obsolete within a few years of its commencement, in this case partly because the plan gives the Japanese economy so strong a stimulus that the aggregate targets are quickly surpassed. Though some Westerners write as if the Japanese Economic Planning Agency, or the government, intervened in some persuasive, though not coercive, fashion whenever targets are undershot or overshot, this is not so. Indeed, it is exactly the other way round. If the private sector's performance diverges from the plan, it is the plan that will be given the push; a new plan will be prepared. This system is called "rolling plans". In the process of preparing the new plan the planning system will accept the latest trends as a starting point.

Formally, the machinery to draft a new plan is set in motion by a request from the Prime Minister sent to the Chairman of the Economic Deliberation Council.

The Economic Deliberation Council is an advisory but politically influential body which decides the broad, or macro-economic policy objectives, such as the "optimal" rate of growth. It consists of part-time members, paid purely nominal fees, and chosen from the important company presidents, academic economists, representatives of various government departments and some consumer and trade union representatives. Broadly speaking the E.D.C. is dominated by businessmen, but academics have

Chart 2.1.
THE ORGANISATION CHART OF THE JAPANESE PLANNING MACHINERY

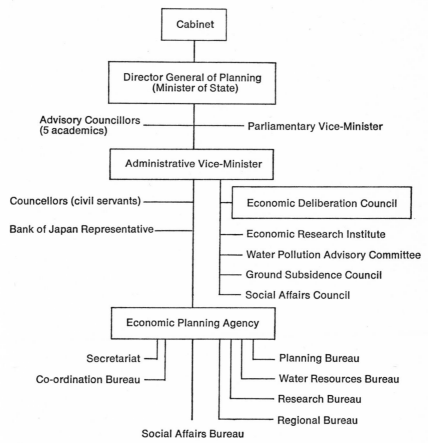

Source: E.P.A. Government of Japan.

considerable influence because of their prestige as scholars. There are thirteen committees and subcommittees of which the Econometric Methods Committee, consisting of academics, is perhaps the most important.

The actual day-to-day planning work is done in the Economic Planning Agency, and in particular in its Planning Bureau which is, in fact, a small planning agency.

If one leaves out of consideration the early post-war plans which were prepared more for political than economic reasons by various institutions, the interest concentrates on the plans prepared by the E.P.A. The first in this series is the "Five Year Plan for Economic Self-Support 1956-1960". This was an unsophisticated forecast. It used the "Colm method"* which relied on a projection of the population of the working age, multiplied by productivity growth which was taken by assumption to equal the pre-war Japanese growth of 3·5 per cent per annum. Having obtained a forecast of the G.N.P. in this way, the plan then provided its breakdown into production indices for fourteen industry groups. The plan envisaged a growth of G.N.P. of 5 per cent per annum—the actual growth rate turned out to be 10 per cent per annum.

The next plan was the "New Long-Range Economic Plan 1958-1962". This plan started with the assumption of three possible rates of growth and attempted to work out their implications for balance of payments, degree of full employment, and availability of capital. The implications were worked out by a system of unintegrated functional relationships between the variables, and the following sets of possibilities were obtained:

Table 2.2. The Planning Concept of the New Long-Range Economic Plan 1958-1962

G.N.P. growth rate	Balance of Payments	Degree of Full Employment	Availability of Capital
5% (pre-war rate)	+	—	+
7%	—	+	+
9% (post-war rate)	—	+	—

Meaning of signs: + = favourable, or feasible result.
　　　　　　　　　 — = unfavourable, or inadequate result.
Source: E.P.A.

As can be seen, the most attractive rate of growth which emerged was 7 per cent per annum, but this had to be corrected because it would have given a balance of payments deficit. As a result the "optimal" rate

* Used by G. Colm, *The American Economy 1960*, National Planning Association, Washington, 1952.

of growth was chosen intuitively as 6·5 per cent per annum. This, it was hoped, would permit external balance and full employment. As it turned out, Japan's competitiveness abroad was much greater than expected and this allowed a faster rate of growth of G.N.P. In fact, the growth rate turned out to be 10·1 per cent per annum.

The next plan, the "Doubling National Income Plan 1961-1970" started frankly from a political base. The Prime Minister, Mr. Ikeda, decided that in view of Japan's actual growth in the preceding period it should be possible to double the national income by 1970. For this to happen it was necessary for the G.N.P. to grow at an annual rate of 7·2 per cent. This rate of growth was then taken as a starting point and the planners were asked to work out the implications. This time, however, there was some change of procedure. For each industrial sector there was a mixed committee composed of the E.P.A. staff, representatives of government departments and private business, and consultations were fuller. In addition, there was a more detailed break-down of industries. The structural equations used by the planners were still not integrated into any single model. Several alternative sets of policy variables fed into the equations yielded by "iteration" possible outcomes from which one "optimal" set was chosen. The sector targets had to be estimated on the basis of those equations because no input-output tables were available at that time. As it turned out, Ikeda's expectations were too conservative. In fact between 1961-1966 the Japanese economy grew at an annual rate of 9·5 per cent. Admittedly, however, the balance of payments was strained, and the cost of living went up at a very rapid rate.

The next plan was the "Medium-Term Economic Plan 1964-1968". In making this plan a significant departure was made from the old style of planning. This time a completely integrated econometric model and input-output tables were used. In addition, while former plans were set out only in real terms and were in fact supply-oriented, this plan and the current one are expressed in terms of current prices, and are therefore somewhat demand-oriented. This new approach was caused by great public concern about the rate of inflation—the new model gave the price implications of various growth rates and policy variables. However, each structural equation has its own deflator, which allows derivation of the targets in real terms as well. The present plan-making process* is the construction of a comprehensive structural model of the economy, that is, a system of interrelated functional equations gives the functional relationships between the dependent and the independent variables. These interrelationships are first inferred from economic theory. Then the parameters are estimated from time series data, mostly over the

---

* This section is based on: Committee on Econometric Methods, *Econometric Models for Medium-Term Economic Plan 1964-68*, 1965. The Social and Economic Development Plan 1967-1971 was constructed in a similar fashion.

preceding ten years, but in some equations over the last twenty years, while in the case of saving, government investment and residential-construction functions, the parameters are estimated from annual data between 1906-1960. In fact, there are five different models.

Chart 2.2 THE SYSTEM OF MODELS

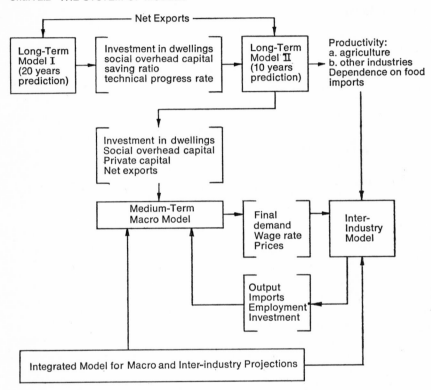

It is impossible in the compass of this chapter to present the structure of all the models. The structure of the simplest (the shortest) model is given below. Its characteristics resemble very closely the other models, with the exception of the Inter-industry Model.

Long-Term Model I

(a) Method of estimation: simple least squares.
(b) The model was solved by iteration because it contains non-linear equations.

(1) *Gross savings*
$$S^* = -1037\cdot7 + 0\cdot36738V + 457\cdot9\bar{z} \qquad \bar{R}^2 = 0\cdot963$$
$$(0\cdot013764) \quad (82\cdot2) \qquad \bar{S} = 185\cdot3$$

(2) *Personal residential construction*
$$\log_e I_h = -5\cdot6955 + 1\cdot2117 \log_e V \qquad \bar{R}^2 = 0\cdot814$$
$$(0\cdot088177) \qquad \bar{S} = 0\cdot314$$

(3) *Production function* (*capital stock requirement*)
$$\log_e \frac{V}{L} = -52\cdot438 + 0\cdot30185 \log_e \quad \frac{K_p}{L} + 0\cdot026489\bar{t}$$
$$(0\cdot25276) \qquad\qquad (0.0064602)$$
$$+ 0\cdot021199\bar{t}\bar{Z} - 41\cdot942\bar{Z} \qquad \bar{R}^2 = 0\cdot975$$
$$(0\cdot0070938) \quad (13\cdot886) \qquad \bar{S} = 0\cdot064$$

(4) *Private replacement investment*
$$R_p = 10\cdot9 + 0\cdot34347I_p - 263\cdot3\bar{Z} \qquad \bar{R}^2 = 0\cdot688$$
$$(0\cdot035233) \quad (46\cdot2) \qquad \bar{S} = 93\cdot3$$

(5) *Investment allocation*
$$I_g/I_p = \beta$$

Identity equations

(6) $\qquad S^* = I_p + I_g + I_h + \bar{B}$

(7) $\qquad K_p = K_{p-1} + I_p - R_p$

Notation

Figures in brackets indicate standard error of parameter.

$\bar{R}^2$ = Coefficient of multiple determination adjusted for degrees of freedom.

S = Standard error of the equation.

A bar on a variable denotes an exogenous variable.

V : Gross national product, in 1960 yen, thousand million.

L : Employment in thousand persons, based on "population Census".

S* : Gross saving excluding changes in inventories, in 1960 yen, thousand million.

I_p : Gross fixed investment by private enterprises, in 1960 yen, thousand million.

I_g : Gross fixed investment by government, in 1960 yen, thousand million.

I_h : Gross personal residential construction, in 1960 yen, thousand million.

$\bar{B}$: Net exports of goods and services, including factor payments, in 1960 yen, thousand million.

$\bar{\beta}$: Ratio of I_g to I_p

K_p : Private capital stock, undepreciated, excluding dwellings, in 1960 yen, thousand million.

R_p : Private replacement investment, in 1960 yen, thousand million.
$\bar{Z}$: Dummy variable, zero in pre-war and unity in post-war period.
$\bar{z}$: Dummy variable, unity in 1906-1919, zero otherwise.
$\bar{t}$: Time, in calendar year starting from 1960.

The method of estimating the parameters varied with the models and the equations, for example in the two Long-Term Models (the intermediate tools of plan-making) it was "simple least squares" whereas the Medium-Term Macro Model (one of the two final tools of plan-making) relied mainly on "limited information-maximum likelihood", and to some degree on "two-stage least-squares" methods.

Where functional relationships shifted, due to such events as wars, dummy variables of various kinds were used. Wherever possible, the equations are linear to make simultaneous solution of the model possible. Where non-linear functions cannot be avoided (in the price, wage and employment equations in the Medium-Term Macro Model) they are in a separate "block" which is solved by iteration, year by year, after which the rest of the model is solved simultaneously by a computer.

The final macro-target projection is made by the Macro Medium-Term Model.

The model contains variables of three broad categories: *data variables* (such as the value of world trade, Japan's population, etc.); *policy variables* (interest rate, income tax rate, indirect tax rate, etc.); *target variables*, also called endogenous variables (G.N.P., employment, prices, etc.).

How are the models used? The forms of functional relationships of the variables obtained from the time series data are used for projection into the future in the Macro-Model. That is, they are given new data variables (estimated separately) and are then fed with a large number of alternative sets of policy variables in a series of policy simulation exercises carried out by a computer. The computer solves the model simultaneously giving a different set of target variables for each set of policy variables. These simulation exercises provide a double service:

(a) They throw up a number of alternative outcomes for the target variables over the (future) planning period, according to the policy variables used. The planners then have to choose, through a political decision, which set of all the simulated outcomes is the most attractive, or "optimal". The model cannot indicate a choice because conflicting objectives have to be evaluated. Even for the E.D.C. the choice is not easy because, for instance, a particularly high rate of growth is wholly attractive to the representatives of the business community, but only partly so to the other members of the E.D.C. who are concerned about the consequential high rate of inflation and the balance of payments pressures.

(b) As the time of the plan period passes the discrepancies between the target figures and the actual outcome can be examined by the same model to obtain clues as to what was responsible for errors in the targets. In this case the performance figures which are actually achieved by the economy are put in place of the target variables and the model then suggests roughly where the responsibility may be—in the policy variables or the structural parameters. This allows continuous updating and improvement of both the "inputs" to the model and the model itself. The Medium-Term Macro model gives the choice of the "optimal" solution, that is the optimal set of macro-economic targets and the set of policy variables required for it. In the next step the target macro-economic aggregates which have been obtained (the G.N.P., consumption, government current expenditures, private investment in producer durables, private building construction, government investment, exports and imports), are fed into the Inter-industry Model, which is a set of input-output tables, to obtain a breakdown of those aggregates into broad industry-sector targets. While current government expenditure is put into the macro-model as a policy variable chosen from the simulation results, the *total* of government *investment* is decided by the (Long-Term) Model where government investment is "hooked" to private investment on the basis of the relationship of the two over the period of 1906-1960. But the government itself decides the allocation of the total investment figure among various ministries, and over the years within the plan period.

It will be appreciated that in the present planning process disputes may arise: when the structural equation forms of the model are estimated, either because of theoretical disagreement among the econometricians, or even from the business representatives because certain proposed functional equations or their parameters may have particular policy implications; when the range of policy variables for simulation exercises is chosen; or when the optimal set of policy variables and the aggregate growth rate are chosen in the light of the simulation results.

It will be clear that the present mode of plan-making has deprived the business community of some of the influence it used to have under the old, less mathematical method. The business men still have substantial influence in the E.D.C. when the "optimal" rate of growth is chosen, though even there they apparently did not have their way when the target rate of growth for the last plan was chosen, because since publication they have criticised it for being too low. In any conflict the staff members of the E.P.A. tend to have less influence than the others: more precisely, their influence rests only on their persuasive power, because they cannot easily resign. The academics have more power in that while they also have prestige, they can resign with relative impunity from the E.D.C. or the E.P.A. Indeed in recent years two professors did resign to register their protest about the plan-making process.

THE COST OF DRAFTING THE PLAN AND THE PLAN'S EFFICACY

Theoretical objections to planning have sometimes been raised in the West on the grounds of the "cost of obtaining information" relative to its value, and there is no doubt that in "imperative" planning, or any planning with official implementation, the "cost of information" must be so high that even accurate and good planning might easily be uneconomic. Therefore it is interesting to discuss the cost of Japanese planning and its usefulness. Here, however, the cost position is quite different from the "cost-of-information" argument. The total expenditure on E.P.A.'s own staff salaries and fees in the Japanese fiscal year 1967 was 629 million yen (less than U.S.$2 million) and other current expenditures were 1,077·5 million yen* (U.S. $3 million).

At that time there were 550 personnel involved directly in planning of which about sixty were "trainees" from private industry (paid by private industry). About two-thirds of the remaining 490 were permanent E.P.A. staff members and about one-third representatives (for two years or so) of various government departments.

It is clear that the cost of national planning Japanese style is not very high, representing a fraction of the cost of an average university in the West. And in this context it has to be borne in mind that a substantial part, if not all, of that cost is offset by the fact that the existence of government planning substantially reduces the expenditures on private planning by business firms, insofar as they use the E.P.A. plans. In Japan large private industry units and all major banks do make their own plans on the basis of the government plan. (In the West there is also a strong trend for *private* industry planning even where, as in the U.K., *public* planning of the mid-sixties failed.) Indeed, in the world of big business, imperfect competition, large scale of operation and long gestation period of investment projects in the present age, private planning by big firms is inevitable. In those conditions private industry must plan whether it likes it or not. When conditions were closer to pure competition and production units were small, it did not matter if a firm planned or not, because it could always assume that its own actions would not affect significantly the market.

The fact that private firms use the official plan in their own planning suggests that the official plan is useful in some sense. But how useful, or rather how good is the official plan? It is impossible to say with certainty how good any country's planning is. To know the effects of planning, we would have to know and compare the economy's actual performance both with and without planning. That will never be possible. We can, of course, compare the plan's targets or predictions with the actual turn-out of figures. In an "imperative" type of planning system one could, perhaps, say that if the plan were not realised the

* Source: Economic Planning Agency.

planning must have been bad, but there may be all sorts of complications. The plan may undershoot or overshoot the actual development because of some "acts of God". And even when an imperative plan is exactly realised it does not necessarily mean that planning was good. It is possible that the plan did not aim high enough, or that the planners were just lucky. If the "imperative" plan is exceeded one wonders whether this is good (because its over-fulfilment in some areas is bound to create problems in other areas) and also one may wonder whether the plan was not too modest.

In the case of the Japanese planning system, with implementation relying on the "announcement effect", the problem of evaluation is even more difficult. The plan is built on an assessment of objective factors that influence the economy, but the targets announced by the plan are themselves "objective" factors that will affect the actual turn-out. Thus in setting up official targets the planners ought to consider what effect the announcement of the targets would have on their implementation. In other words the planners might deliberately announce targets other than those they really expect to be reached.

Some comparisons of the targets and the actual performance have been made by two Japanese economists.* They show that actual G.N.P. was higher than the target level in each year of the planning experience. However, as the comparisons are in money terms, they are not very satisfactory because of price movements. However, they also make a comparison of the actual and predicted growth *rates* in *real* terms. It then appears that, except for 1958 and 1962, the actual growth rates in real terms greatly exceeded the forecast. In the early post-war period when there was a big pool of unemployed labour, both the target and the actual growth rates were very high and close to each other. Later in the early fifties when growth was slow (for Japan), the forecast target rates underestimated the actual growth rates, possibly because of a pessimistic general outlook in Japan at that time. But from 1959 onwards the plans grossly underestimated the actual growth rate—in 1959 the actual growth rate was 14·3 per cent compared with a predicted 5·2 per cent, and in 1961 it was 14 per cent compared with a predicted 6·5 per cent. In particular the plans underestimated the Japanese export performance and the private investment rate. The fact that the foreign trade was underestimated is not surprising; forecasting foreign trade is notoriously difficult. The fact that private investment was underestimated may be due to the very effectiveness of Japanese planning, in the sense that growing targets provide a powerful stimulus to Japanese firms which keep increasing their share of the market even with full knowledge that this may reduce their profits.

* (a) Shishido.
  (b) Watanabe.

In September 1969 the Japanese Government decided to ask the E.P.A. to prepare a new economic plan for 1971-1976. The Social and Economic Development Plan 1967-1971 became out of date. In that plan, Japan's economic development rate was to be kept at just over 8 per cent p.a., because it was feared that otherwise balance of payments deficits might develop. In fact Japan discovered that owing to various favourable (to Japan) developments in the world economy, the Japanese G.N.P. could grow at the rate of 14·3 per cent p.a. in real terms and Japan could still accumulate vast holdings of foreign exchange, instead of losing them. This obviously called for a new, bolder approach to the targets and to other economic policy issues. Japan can now enter upon fuller liberalisation of foreign capital inflow and can relax her restrictions on Japanese investment abroad. But the new plan will still have to deal with the high rate of price inflation, reflected recently not only in the retail price index but also in the wholesale price index.

On 2 April 1970 the Government announced the "New Social and Economic Development Plan 1971-1976". The planned growth rate of G.N.P. in real terms is lifted in this new plan from the former 8·2 per cent p.a. to 10·6 per cent p.a. for the five fiscal years beginning 1 April 1971 and ending 31 March 1976. For the Japanese Fiscal Year 1975/6 the new plan envisages a *per caput* income of 1,000,000 yen (U.S.$2,778). The plan is based on estimates that the world trade will grow annually at 7·5 per cent, but Japan's exports at 14·7 per cent p.a.! Japan's foreign exchange reserves at the end of the period are expected to be U.S.$6,000 million.

Most Japanese economists probably believe that planning has helped stimulate economic growth to some degree, but since they cannot prove this they state the case in a mild fashion. Their views range from seeing the plans as conservative forecasts to ascribing them an important role.* One thing seems to be certain: national economic planning has come to stay in Japan and has encouraged large firms to make their own plans.

Government's Influence
Over the Economy Outside the Plan

From the post-war period until the 1950s the Japanese Government maintained a widespread system of *direct* controls over the economy. Since then the market mechanism has taken over the control, subject to a pervasive, though diluted, system of government prods and checks.

* Cf. Moriguchi: "The rapid economic growth and the accompanying structural change characterised by heavy industrialisation and mobilisation of human resources from primary to secondary and tertiary industries should not be considered as an entirely natural development of the free market economy. I believe that the government's orientation and encouragement through its economic planning have played a significant role in it."

Since direct controls were removed (except for imports of some important foodstuffs) the main burden of the macro-economic control fell onto the monetary policy. Fiscal policy in Japan was in fact inactive until 1965, except that it aimed at a budget surplus. These two forms of control are so complex, however, that they will be dealt with in separate chapters.

Besides the above controls the government uses the following instruments:

  (i) Measures to ensure competition.
 (ii) Legislative control of particular industries.
(iii) Easy credit from government financial institutions for selected industries.
 (iv) Depreciation allowances for specified industries.
  (v) Two-way consultation between government and industry.
 (vi) Quantitative import controls and tariffs.
(vii) Government buying shares in some "infant industries", such as the aircraft industry, to assist them.
(viii) Public relations measures.

MEASURES TO ENSURE COMPETITION

The American Occupation Authorities imposed upon Japan in 1947 the Anti-Monopoly Act, which was one of the strictest laws in the world. Prior to that Japan had never had any control of monopoly, and indeed encouraged cartels. In 1948 a supplementary control, the Trade Association Act, was passed to check restrictive practices. By 1949 it became obvious that the rigid requirements of the Anti-Monopoly Act were an obstacle to post-war reconstruction especially when dealing with foreign domiciled business. Therefore the Act was amended to permit in certain circumstances interlocking of directorates, one company holding shares in other companies (with a limit), mergers which did *not* have to obtain prior approval, though they did have to obtain a subsequent approval, and to allow shipping lines to enter into "shipping conferences". In all these cases the Fair Trade Commission has the duty to check "unfair business practices".

With a typical adaptability, after independence (1952) Japan retained the principle of the law on monopoly and the Fair Trade Commission, but amended and softened their application, to obtain the benefits of both competition and monopoly. Because of a recession caused by a fall-off in the off-shore American purchases for the Korean War in 1953 the Anti-Monopoly Act was relaxed to allow:

(a) "depression cartels" for industries in great difficulties;
(b) "rationalisation cartels" (coal, machinery, fertilisers, non-ferrous metals, and textiles);
(c) resale price maintenance under certain conditions.

The formation of a *"depression cartel"* is permissible only to entrepreneurs in manufacturing, but not in services and retailing. Further, it
is subject to some conditions. There must be an extreme breakdown in
the balance of supply and demand so that: the price of the commodity
is below the average cost of production; a large proportion of businesses
may eventually have to leave the industry; and it is impossible to remove
the difficulties by rationalisation. In addition the cartel must not "unduly"
injure the interests of the consumers and related entrepreneurs, and the
entry into, as well as the exit from, the cartel must not be "unreasonably"
restricted.

Rationalisation cartels may be approved in manufacturing, where this is
necessary to carry out rationalisation of the industry (that is, improvement of technology, quality of goods, or reduction of cost). But the
conditions are stringent. The cartel agreements may restrict only: technological aspects, kinds of products, utilisation of facilities for storage of
raw materials or products or their transportation, or utilisation or purchase of by-products, waste, or scrap. Output volume of sale and sale
price *must not* be controlled by the cartel. In addition, there must be no
danger that the cartel would harm the interests of consumers.

Resale price maintenance, which is forbidden in general, was permitted
by Notification No. 11 of the Fair Trade Commission, as of 1965, in
cosmetics, hair dye, toothpaste, soap, liquor, caramel, drugs, cameras,
shirts, and published matter including records (these last two were
exempted by the Resale Price Maintenance Act).

THE FAIR TRADE COMMISSION

The Fair Trade Commission was established by Section 27 of the Anti-
Monopoly Act. It is a body with great statutory powers and a substantial
degree of independence. It has quasi-judicial and quasi-legislative powers.
Although the Commission is administratively attached to the Prime
Minister's Office, the Chairman and the four Commissioners perform
their duties independently with the status of their position strongly
guaranteed by the Act. Appointment of the Chairman or a Commis-
sioner is made by the Prime Minister with the consent of both Houses
of the Diet, and the appointment or dismissal of the Chairman is attested
by the Emperor. The Commission has a Staff Office with a personnel
number of 277 fixed by the Act.

The Staff Office has five local branches in Sapporo, Sendai, Nagoya,
Osaka and Fukuoka.

Enforcement of the anti-monopoly rules is carried out in two ways:

Administrative procedure. The Fair Trade Commission after investiga-
tion of suspect acts may initiate hearing procedures with the defendant,
and finally may order him to eliminate the violation of the Act. The
defendant has a right of appeal against the decision by instituting a

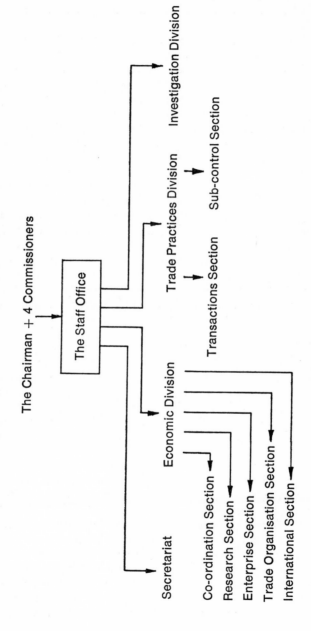

Chart 2. 3   THE STRUCTURE OF THE FAIR TRADE COMMISSION

suit in Tokyo High Court. However, the Court is bound by the Commission's decision if it was supported by substantial evidence. Any person who fails to comply with the decision is liable to be fined or gaoled.

Criminal procedure. Where a violation of the Anti-Monopoly Act has occurred (excluding merger, and "unfair business practices") the Fair Trade Commission may file on indictment with the Procurator-General and the Tokyo High Court then deals with it as a criminal case.

Any person who has suffered losses from monopolistic practices is entitled to claim indemnification for damages without need of proving the existence of wilfulness or negligence on the part of the violator, after the Fair Trade Commission found violation of the Act.

In recent years, however, the operation of the Anti-Monopoly Act *in respect to mergers* has been virtually suspended because the government decided that the economies of large scale operation outweigh the monopoly dangers arising out of large units. In fact the Ministry of International Trade and Industry often recommends mergers to private industry, and the Fair Trade Commission, after consultation with the M.I.T.I., often permits the particular proposed merger (though the other provisions of the Act about unfair practices would still apply).

LEGISLATIVE CONTROL OF PARTICULAR INDUSTRIES

A number of industries are controlled by the following Acts of the Diet:

> Petroleum Industry Law
> Electric Utility Industry Law
> Gas Utility Industry Law
> Transportation Law
> Mining Law
> Coal Mining Industry Law
> Cotton Textile Industry Law
> Machine Industry Promotion Law
> Electronic Industry Promotion Law.

The operation of the controls under these Acts is vested in the powerful Ministry of International Trade and Industry. The controls differ in scope between industries but, for example, the Gas Utility Industry Law gives very extensive powers to M.I.T.I. This law aims ". . . to preserve the safety of the general public by regulating the operation of gas supply, with a view to protect the interests of the customers, to promote sound development of gas utility, and to prevent public danger arising out of the production and supply of gas". (Article 1.)

Article 2 stipulates that any person who wants to operate a gas utility must obtain a licence from the Minister of International Trade and Industry. The Minister at his discretion may later cancel the licence

(Article 14.2) or change its terms. When granting the licence the Minister must be satisfied that: there is sufficient demand for gas; the capacity of the proposed plant is adequate; there is no excess gas supply capacity in the area; the applicant has sufficient funds to operate; and that the proposed plant is essential and adequate for the public interest. (Article 5.)

The gas tariffs and other supply conditions, and their subsequent changes, must be submitted to the Minister for approval. (Article 17.) The Minister may order the gas plant owner to repair, rebuild or transfer the plant when public safety so requires. (Article 28.) The Act even provides for ministerial approval of the chief engineer's qualifications and for the dismissal of the chief engineer on the request of the Minister.

As can be seen from the preceding example the statutory powers of M.I.T.I. over the *specified* industries can be very extensive. The other industries, which are not subject to the specific Acts of Diet, are controlled or influenced in more subtle ways through consultation and persuasion.

Government Financial Institutions

The Japanese Government established a number of semi-governmental financial institutions to assist some sectors of the economy not sufficiently provided with credit by the private banks.

The Export-Import Bank. This bank was established as the Export Bank of Japan in 1950 in a rather special set of circumstances. The Japanese economy was then undergoing a drastic domestic deflation which made it hard for would-be exporters to obtain funds. At the same time an expansion of exports was the most vital single policy objective, and that objective had to be achieved in a deteriorating world trade situation (recession in the U.S., and 1949 devaluation of sterling). In this situation the Export Bank of Japan was established to promote exports, especially of heavy machinery, to the developing countries on a deferred payment basis. Later, as a result of the outbreak of the Korean War, shortages of essential raw materials appeared in the world markets and in Japan. In order to assist Japanese industries in obtaining essential raw materials, in 1952 the bank's name was changed to the Export-Import Bank of Japan and the bank was also assigned the task of lending to Japanese importers the money for advance payment of the commodities designated by the government. In fact any substantial use of the import credits came as late as 1957 and after. Further, the import credits have never represented more than a minute proportion of export credits. Two raw materials, copper and coal (in that order), stand out as almost the only assisted commodities. The practice and the law until 1953 were that the Export-Import Bank of Japan lent

money only to Japanese firms and gave only supplementary finance—
where private banks also lent a proportion of the needed funds. In 1953
the Export-Import Bank Act was again amended: to permit it to grant
credit abroad for investment purchases, where Japanese equipment is
used; the maximum duration of loans was extended from five to ten
years; and the Bank was empowered to lend without the necessity of
private bank participation.

In 1957 further amendments allowed: relaxation of the conditions of
the loans; lending to foreign governments for investment purposes considered conducive to the expansion of the foreign country's trade with
Japan; financing of technical services abroad not in connection with
exports of machinery; and removal of the term restriction on loans.

The most recent amendment to the Export-Import Bank Act in 1964
permitted credit granting to the developing countries which were unable
to repay their debts to Japan due to foreign exchange shortage and
allowed the Bank to guarantee loans granted by commercial banks.

As a result of those changes, the Bank that originally began only as an
instrument of fostering exports, came to be a leading agency for the
Japanese government's foreign assistance programme. The Export-
Import Bank has played its most important role in assisting Japanese
exports, especially heavy industry products. So far it has financed about
60 per cent of the deferred-payment exports from Japan.*

It is noteworthy that the ratio of deferred-payment exports to total
exports is still increasing. In view of greater competitive pressures in the
world markets and shortages of funds in the developing countries, it
would appear that competition has moved into the terms of sale. Between
1950-1965 the Export-Import Bank of Japan lent the "developing
countries" the equivalent of U.S.$1,408 million for their purchases of
ships, rolling stock, machinery, etc. It lent $1,264 million to the
"developed countries" and $313 million to the "communist bloc".

The Export-Import Bank of Japan is fully owned by the Government.
Its President and Vice-President are appointed by the Prime Minister.
The President appoints the other members of the Board of Directors
(not more than 6), which operates in constant consultation with the
Government and private business. The capital of the Bank initially
came from the Government grant of U.S.$42 million in 1952 and sub-
sequently from annual loans from the (Government) Post Office Savings
Bank, and the (Government) Post Office Life Insurance Fund. In
addition the Bank may borrow from the other institutions of the
Government of Japan, and from foreign banks and other foreign financial
institutions (Article 39 of the Export-Import Bank Act).

The Japan Development Bank. This Bank was set up in 1951. Article 1

* Government of Japan, *The Export-Import Bank of Japan: Its Role and Functions,*
  p. 23.

Table 2.3.   Export-Import Bank of Japan. Credit Commitments by Type of Credit

Type of Credit	Fiscal 1966 (A) Amount mil. yen	%	Fiscal 1965 (B) Amount mil. yen	%	Increase in 1966 over 1965 (A-B) mil. yen
Export	201,744	71	145,762	71	55,982
Overseas Technical Assistance	1,614	1	2,760	1	−1,146
Import	6,895	2	2,673	1	4,222
Overseas Investment	13,650	5	8,211	4	5,439
Direct Loans	59,194	21	46,429	23	12,765
Total	283,097	100	205,834	100	77,263

Source: The Export-Import Bank of Japan, *Annual Report* 1966-67.

Table 2.4.   Export-Import Bank of Japan. Export Credits Commitments by the Product in the Japanese Fiscal Year 1966.

Product	Credit in mil. yen	% of total
Ships	143,853	71
Aircraft	1,841	1
Vehicles and Rolling Stock	4,835	2
Electric Machinery	2,487	1
Communication Equipment	274	0
Textile Machinery	6,412	3
Steel Products	4,254	2
Other Industrial Machinery	37,688	19
Durable Consumer Goods	100	0
Total	201,744	100*

* The percentages do not add up to 100 because of rounding.

Source: The Export-Import Bank of Japan, *Annual Report* 1966-67.

of the Japan Development Bank Act says that the purpose of the Bank is "to supplement and encourage the credit operation of ordinary financial institutions by supplying long-term funds in order to promote economic reconstruction and development."

The Development Bank's capital initially amounted to 10,000 million yen (U.S.$28 million) provided by Government and as of 31 March 1966, was equivalent to U.S.$650 million. The Bank's principal sources of funds are:

(a) its own capital and reserves;

(b) funds borrowed from the Japanese government;
(c) funds (U.S.$313 million) borrowed from the World Bank;
(d) external bond issue on the American and European capital markets
       (five issues amounting to U.S.$100 million).

Cumulative net earnings of the Development Bank amounted by March 1966 to the equivalent of U.S.$615 million, of which U.S.$451 million was paid to the Japanese Government, and the remainder U.S.$164 million was put into reserves.

The Bank has been lending to electric power companies, marine transportation, iron and steel industries, coal mining, machinery, petrochemicals, synthetic fibres, automobile, electronic and atomic power generation industries, and for the development of new domestic technology. Recently it has also lent to international and domestic airlines, private railways, the tourist industry and the distribution system. The Bank lends only for sound projects to large private industry and with part-participation of private financial institutions. Regional development loans for less developed areas of Japan have increased recently. All loans and guarantees given by the Development Bank have a maturity of more than one year and the Bank does not compete with private financial institutions. The standard interest rate used to be 8·4 per cent,

Table 2.5.   Japan Development Bank. Outstanding Loans and Guarantees in Yen and Foreign Currencies by Industry.

Loans	1967		1966		Increase 1967/1966
	Thousands US $	% of total	Thousands US $	% of total	Thousands US $
Transportation	1,093,812	34	897,874	31	+ 195,983
Electric power	1,069,606	33	1,054,848	37	+ 14,758
Mining	252,542	8	224,475	8	+ 28,067
Chemicals	185,590	6	172,247	6	+ 13,343
Metals	150,177	5	159,477	5	− 9,300
Machinery	123,068	4	111,721	4	+ 11,347
Hotels	74,273	2	69,078	2	+ 5,195
Other	261,289	8	190,913	7	+ 70,376
Total Loans	3,210,357	100	2,880,633	100	+ 329,724
Guarantees : (in foreign currencies)					
Electric power	195,512	49	214,442	57	− 18,930
Atomic power	85,596	21	45,626	12	+ 39,970
Air transportation	118,894	30	116,580	31	+ 2,314
Total guarantees	400,002	100	376,648	100	+ 23,354

Source : The Japan Development Bank, Annual Report for the year ended 31 March 1967.

which was reduced to 8·2 per cent in Ocober 1966 (Japan has high interest rates in the domestic market). However, certain Government (Ministry of Finance) designated industries, such as electric power, ocean shipping and coal mining were charged lower interest rates.

The preceding table shows that although the total of Development Bank loans outstanding in 1967 was fairly high (U.S.$3,210 million), many of those loans are tied up for lengthy periods and the increase in the total outstanding from 1966 (U.S.$330 million), which is a rough indication of new lending capacity, is quite small. Consequently this government financial institution, like the others, could not be easily used for any strict national economic plan implementation. Implementation of a national economic plan must involve the availability of a system of highly flexible instruments whereby an industry which undershoots the target is given a quick and temporary energising shot in the arm, and an industry which overshoots the target is temporarily checked. However, aside from temporary and ever-changing discrepancies between the national economic plan and the actual performance of the economy, there may be some areas where the government may decide (in a political decision) that a particular sector may need long-term assistance because it is an "infant industry" such as the aircraft industry in Japan. Assistance may also be given to a "decaying industry" such as coal mining on social grounds, that is, to avoid undue hardship. The government may also pick certain industries as being in some sense "basic". In all those

Table 2.6. Japan Development Bank. Sources of Funds Acquired and Loans Granted in Year Ended 31 March 1967.

Sources of Funds:	1967	1966	Loans Granted to:	1967	1966
	mil. US $	mil. US $		mil. US $	mil. US $
Previous profits put to reserve	32·7	29·7	Transportation	299·8	277·5
			Electric power	60·5	54·7
Repayment of principal	284·4	250·7	Mining	52·3	50·4
Net borrowing from:			Chemicals	26·2	37·0
Japanese Govt.	289·5	262·5			
I.B.R.D.	− 17·7	− 16·5	Metals	12·7	9·4
Bonds sold in US $	− 4·5	16·7			
			Machinery	42·5	30·8
All other sources	− 1·0	− 8·0			
			Other	89·3	75·1
Total	583·4	535·1	Total	583·4	535·1

Source: The Japan Development Bank, *Annual Report* for the year ended 31 March 1967.

cases government financial institutions do exert a substantial but fairly rigid long-term push.

How is the broad lending policy of the Bank determined? Each year the Ministry of Finance prepares a "Fiscal Investment and Loan Programme". Among other things this Government program outlines the allocations to be made from governmental special accounts to certain Government agencies and corporations like the Development Bank. After the "Fiscal Investment and Loan Programme" has been set up and the Budget approved, the Economic Planning Agency drafts a "Basic Policy for Employing Government Funds for Investment in Industrial Equipment and Facilities" for the Cabinet's approval. This "Basic Policy" describes *in very broad terms* the general objectives to be held in mind by various Government agencies. The Development Bank, however, has a considerable freedom in interpreting the "Basic Policy", and its officers are emphatic that they take no orders from the Economic Planning Agency (neither, of course, does the Ministry of Finance).

Government Assistance to Small Business

As will be shown in Chapter 7, Japan has a very large small business sector, the efficiency of which is very far below that of the advanced sector. This feature is probably not unique to Japan, though it may present itself in a sharp form there. At any rate, the Japanese Government is very conscious of the deficiencies of the small business sector and is trying very hard to assist it to reach higher levels of efficiency. This assistance takes the following forms:

(a) The Smaller Enterprise Agency activities.
(b) Organised Activities of Small Businesses.
(c) Direct Financial Aid from the Government.
(d) Government Institutions for Supplementary Financing of Small Businesses.
(e) Preferential Treatment in Taxation.
(f) Technical Guidance.

The Smaller Enterprise Agency. This Agency (about 160 officials) is a section of the Ministry of International Trade and Industry. It plans and carries out government measures for small businesses and supervises the operations of government financial institutions and other government organisations related to small businesses.

The Government tries to assist the small businesses in *their organisation* by setting up common facility co-operatives and commercial and industrial associations.

Direct Financial Aid from the Government. In accordance with the Small Business Modernisation Aid Law (No. 115 of 1956) the Government offers two types of interest-free loans to small businesses for modernisation of equipment, and developing superior structure, co-operatives or common facilities.

These Small Business Modernisation loans are available through the local government, but half the funds come from the General Account of the central Government, and half from the local governments. The maximum amount of an Equipment Modernisation Loan is three million yen. The total outstanding loans of this type as of 31 March 1966 were almost forty-five billion yen. The loans for purposes of reorganisation have an upper limit of half the amount needed by the borrower.

GOVERNMENT INSTITUTIONS FOR FINANCING OF SMALL BUSINESSES

The Small Business Finance Corporation was founded in 1953 for short-term (about five years) loans to small businesses when they cannot borrow in the market. The funds of the Corporation came from the original Government grant, loans from some Government funds (such as the Post Office Savings Bank) and proceeds from sales of Government-guaranteed corporation bonds on the open market. The total of these loans outstanding as of March 1966 was 364 billion yen. A large proportion of this was for equipment in manufacturing. As of 31 March 1966 the Corporation's loans represented 11 per cent of the total loans to small businesses. The upper limit on a loan is thirty million yen. These loans must be repaid within five years and interest charge is 8·4 per cent p.a.

People's Finance Corporation. This Corporation was founded in 1949 to assist individual persons and small businesses with small loans. The capital was provided by the Government. The limit on any loan is three million yen. The loans must be repaid within five years and the interest rate is 8·4 per cent p.a. On 31 March 1966 the total of these loans outstanding was 275 billion yen.

Shoko Chukin Bank ("Central Bank" of Industrial Co-operatives). This Bank was set up in 1936 as a co-operative financial institution to finance all co-operative efforts of small businesses. Its capital consists of roughly equal contributions by the Government and the affiliated co-operative associations. For its lending operations the Bank borrows from the Government, from small businesses (by deposits) and issues of bonds on the open market. On 31 March 1966 the total of the loans outstanding was 503 billion yen.

The Central and Local Government Credit Guarantees. Where a small business has an inadequate collateral security there are two types of government sponsored (and government financed, up to 90%) institutions that can give help:

(a) *Credit Guarantee Associations* (about fifty of them all over the country). The total of their guarantees amounted to 492 billion yen on 31 March 1966.

(b) *Small Business Credit Insurance Corporation.* This was set up in
    1958 by the Government. On 31 March 1966 the insurance cover
    amounted to 594 billion yen, and in addition it had loans amounting
    to twenty-five billion yen.

Small Business Investment Companies. These were established in 1963
in Tokyo, Osaka and Nagoya. They are designed to facilitate stock issues
by small businesses in the financial market by *accepting and holding*
their bonds and shares for a certain period of time. Part of the capital
of these three companies was provided by the central Government, part
of the local governments and the rest by local banks, security companies and similar institutions.

Preferential Treatment in Taxation. Small businesses, subject to corporation tax and corporate business tax, have lower tax rates up to a fixed
level of income.

Small businesses, with less than 100 million yen capital and employing
fewer than 1,000 workers in any designated industry, if purchasing
machines in a rationalisation process, are entitled to a special depreciation
in the first year of one third of the price of any machine, *in addition* to
the ordinary depreciation. Further, there are some temporary reductions
in the municipal property taxes on some equipment.

Guidance on Management and Production Techniques. Local governments provide free management diagnosis by hiring qualified small
business consultants. The costs are covered in part by the central
Government and in part by the local governments.

Local governments have established thirty-seven industrial research
institutions all over Japan. These public institutions disseminate the
results of their studies among the small businesses. In some areas they
also provide experimental facilities to small businesses.

The Nippon Institute for the Improvement of Small Enterprises. In 1962
this Institute for training personnel was established with government
funds.

FINANCIAL ASSISTANCE TO FARMING, FORESTRY AND FISHERIES

Farms, forestry businesses and fishermen often have difficulties in obtaining credit in the open market because they are small and often do not
have any suitable collateral security. Two types of financial aid are given
indirectly by the central government. Subsidies are given by the Department of Agriculture to prefectural governments which pass the subsidy
on to the farmers. In recent years, however, there has been a tendency
to use low-interest-rate loans as a means of assistance, rather than pure
subsidies.

At the grass root level assistance to producers is provided by an agricultural co-operative which exists in every rural community. These
agricultural co-operatives are so-called "general-purpose" ones. They

deal with credit, purchasing, selling and joint utilisation of facilities. They accept farmers' deposits and also make loans to farmers. All the funds which the local co-operative does not wish to use at the time are paid to a prefectural co-operative which is essentially a prefectural federation of the lower level co-operatives. These prefectural co-operative federations also give loans to the local co-operatives that are in a special need of funds. The prefectural federations pay their idle funds into the Central Co-operative Bank for Agriculture and Forestry, which co-ordinates the loanable funds at the prefectural level. The Central Co-operative Bank for Agriculture and Forestry issues "Agriculture and Forestry" bonds in the capital market, which increases the disposable funds of the Bank.

Although this co-operative financial system grants many loans every year, there are limitations to the assistance granted because those co-operative institutions have to protect the interests of the co-operative depositors. Thus they have limits on the amount lent and the period of the loan. They cannot lend to farmers of poor credit standing, and have to charge a fairly high interest rate. To mitigate these limitations the Government grants interest-rate subsidies for loans given by the co-operatives, and provides special loans to farmers out of its own funds. This is called "the special credit system". It has five distinct institutions.

The Agricultural Improvement Fund System. This is a fund for modernisation. Each prefecture has a *Special Fund* (from monies contributed by both the central and the local governments), which lends monies free of interest. This is necessary because the farmer modernising his techniques runs big risks. The Fund also lends monies to individual farmers through agricultural co-operatives or to farmers' associations. The outstanding loans under the Agricultural Improvement Fund System amounted to 8·5 billion yen at the end of March 1966.

The Agricultural Modernisation Fund System. In this case it is the agricultural co-operative organisations which grant the loans at a reduced rate of interest because of a subsidy and a guarantee by the central and local governments. Also since 1963 the "local (commercial) banks" have been included in this system. The farmer then pays only 6 per cent and in some cases 5 per cent interest, thanks to the government subsidy. At the end of December 1966 the loans outstanding under this scheme amounted to 204 billion yen.

The Natural Disaster Loan System. In case of damages to productive enterprises, agricultural co-operatives give credit at a reduced interest of 6·5 per cent to restore the capital asset. Where the loss is more than 50 per cent the interest rate is only 3 per cent p.a. The interest subsidy is then granted by the Central Government, prefectures or rural communities. At the end of December 1966 the outstanding loans of this type amounted to 29 billion yen.

The Settlers' Fund. In this case long-term loans are granted to settlers from a "Government Special Account for the Settlers' Fund". For productive purposes the interest rate is 3·65 per cent p.a., and for the settler's house 5 per cent p.a. At the end of March 1967 the outstanding loans amounted to 37 billion yen.

The Agriculture, Forestry and Fisheries Finance Corporation. This is a Government financial institution to provide long-term and low interest rate loans for maintenance and improvement of productivity in the industries involved, where loans from other sources, even the cooperatives, would not be forthcoming.

The Corporation's resources are confined to the funds provided by the Government. Its budget must be submitted to the Diet for approval and its profits must be paid to the National Treasury. At the end of March 1967 the Corporation's capital amounted to 168 billion yen.

There are also other Government financial institutions, such as: Hokkaido and Tohoku Development Finance Corporation, Local Public Enterprise Finance Corporation, and Medical Care Facilities Finance Corporation.

Depreciation Allowances. The Government, or more precisely the Ministry of Finance, has listed a number of industries which can depreciate their capital expenditures more quickly than under the normal arrangements. Such Accelerated Depreciation amounts to an interest free loan of the amount of tax, otherwise chargeable in the first few years, for the period of acceleration (assuming that the tax rates have not changed either way in the period). The most privileged group of industries can depreciate 50 per cent of machinery and equipment in any one of the first three years. The less privileged group can depreciate 10 to 50 per cent in any of the first three years. In addition there is a *wide variety* of various tax concessions for designated industries or activities, including some *additional* depreciation, in excess of 100 per cent of cost. The terms for eligibility for the various tax concessions and the nature of concessions are explained in Chapter 3. Here it should be noted only that those tax concessions could not be used for the implementation of the Economic Plan of the E.P.A. when the targets are overshot or undershot, because the concessions are fixed for long periods of time by the Minister of Finance or by an Act of the Diet. Thus, though they give a *long-term* push they are not used for short-term intervention.

THE TWO-WAY CONSULTATIONS BETWEEN THE GOVERNMENT AND PRIVATE BUSINESS AND PUBLIC ENTERPRISES.

Two-way consultations are extremely numerous in Japan. Here we shall mention only a few of the more organised forms of consultation.

The Industrial Structure Council. The connections of this Council are revealed by the following charts.

Chart 2.4 THE POSITION OF THE INDUSTRIAL STRUCTURE COUNCIL

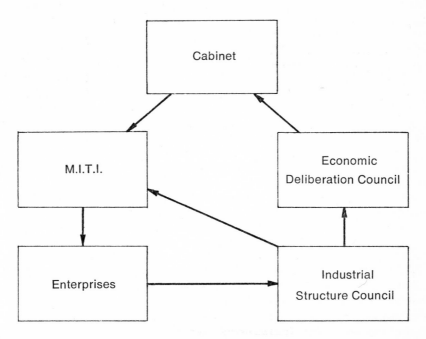

The Industrial Structure Council consists of 120 men—academics, businessmen, bankers and M.I.T.I. officials. They meet in M.I.T.I. offices. This Council would discuss major mergers, such as that of the Yawata Iron and Steel Company and the Fuji Iron and Steel Company, in the Steel Sub-Committee of the Heavy Industry Committee, and then make recommendations to the Government.

GOVERNMENT—PRIVATE INDUSTRY CO-OPERATION COMMITTEES

These Committees exist for the petrochemical industry, synthetic textiles industry and the ammonia industry. In this case the Committees do not advise the government, but the government is an important participant. For example, the M.I.T.I. will suggest the standards for starting a new enterprise. In the petrochemical industry, it would insist that the minimum size for any new plant must be 300,000 tons of output per year. M.I.T.I. would also suggest that self-finance must be used as far as possible.

If some firms are unable to meet those standards they are encouraged to make a collective effort with a few companies jointly setting up a large new plant. One of the most important reasons for this approach is that in modern industries (especially these three) the economies of large

Chart 2.5 ORGANISATION CHART OF INDUSTRIAL STRUCTURE COUNCIL

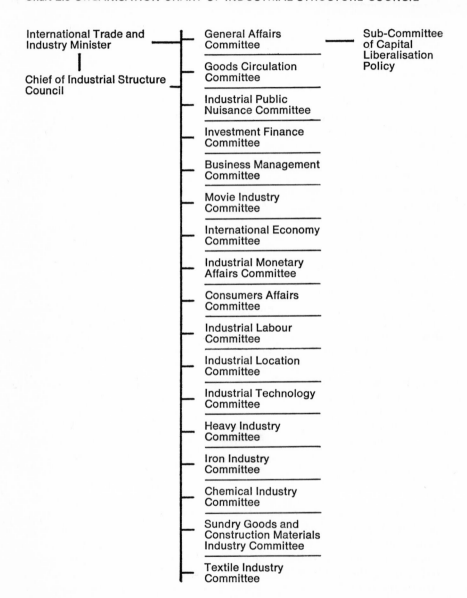

International Trade and Industry Minister

Chief of Industrial Structure Council

General Affairs Committee

Goods Circulation Committee

Industrial Public Nuisance Committee

Investment Finance Committee

Business Management Committee

Movie Industry Committee

International Economy Committee

Industrial Monetary Affairs Committee

Consumers Affairs Committee

Industrial Labour Committee

Industrial Location Committee

Industrial Technology Committee

Heavy Industry Committee

Iron Industry Committee

Chemical Industry Committee

Sundry Goods and Construction Materials Industry Committee

Textile Industry Committee

Sub-Committee of Capital Liberalisation Policy

scale production are enormous. If a large number of small enterprises competed with each other (as they do in many countries) they would all be uneconomic. In this case the Japanese Government deliberately accepts some domestic restraints on competition in order for the industry to be more cost-competitive both at home and abroad. In any case, competition between the giant Japanese companies is more vigorous than between the small (and uneconomic) but numerous enterprises in many other countries. Indeed, in Japan the business community still complains about "excessive competition".

JETRO. This is a popular name used even in Japanese. The abbreviation (though not a consistent anagram) stands for Japan External Trade Organisation, a title which is also used in Japan. The official name in Japanese is *Nihon Kaigai Bōeki Shinkō Kai*, the strict translation of which is Japan Overseas Trade Promotion Organisation. This organisation is a mixed Government-private business organisation which does market research, gives consultation services and produces good public relations for Japan abroad. It has Trade Centres in fourteen major cities of the world.

The Export Conference. This is a domestic organisation to promote exports. It has mixed membership of government and private industry. Each year it fixes a national aggregate export target. Its industrial sub-committees then fix targets on a commodity basis.

Japan Factory Plant Export Association. This association gives technical advice on overseas development projects and export promotion of heavy machinery.

Perhaps the most important two-way consultation is the very close contact of M.I.T.I. with the business community. M.I.T.I.'s functions are:

(a) Protection of "infant industries".
(b) Reorganisation of declining industries (such as coal mining and cotton-spinning).
(c) Assistance to small businesses.
(d) Control of *monopolistic competition* (a problem in any country), through: control of capacity expansion, and the minimum plant size; and assisting mergers to obtain economies of large scale production.

Direct Controls

These used to be ubiquitous until about 1955, but at the beginning of 1970 they were confined only to import controls on about 100 tariff items—mostly foodstuffs such as meat, grains and dairy products, and a few manufactured goods. These import controls are scheduled to be reduced to thirty items by the end of 1973. In addition there are strict capital inflow controls which are gradually being dismantled and are scheduled to be removed by 1972.

Appendix I

Selected Tables from the "Economic and Social Development Plan 1967–1971"

Gross Value Added (at Market Prices) by Industry – in 1960 prices (billion yen)

Industry	Calendar years			Average annual rate of increase (per cent)	
	1960	1965	1971	1960–1965	1965–1971
1. Agriculture, forestry and fisheries	2,102·6	2,178·4	2,441·1	0·7	1·9
2. Mining	261·0	306·2	393·8	3·2	4·3
3. Food and kindred products	691·8	1,015·6	1,357·7	8·0	5·0
4. Textiles	433·1	546·3	701·5	4·7	4·3
5. Pulp, paper and allied products	159·1	299·6	621·9	13·5	12·9
6. Chemicals and allied products	450·5	1,050·5	2,417·6	18·4	14·9
7. Primary metal industry	607·0	1,063·2	1,676·2	11·5	7·9
8. Fabricated metal industry	238·1	408·8	764·7	11·2	11·0
9. Machinery, except electrical	538·5	959·6	1,869·7	12·0	11·8
10. Electrical machinery	433·1	684·3	1,364·1	9·6	12·2
11. Transportation equipment	421·8	1,017·3	2,291·4	20·0	14·5
12. Other manufacture	1,455·6	2,561·4	4,536·4	12·0	10·0
13. Construction	1,004·8	1,616·4	2,791·9	10·0	9·5
14. Electricity, gas and water	416·2	685·0	1,108·2	10·5	8·3
15. Wholesale and retail trade	1,912·4	3,024·1	4,889·4	9·6	8·3
16. Real estate and ownership of dwellings	526·0	777·6	938·4	8·1	3·2
17. Transportation, storage and communication	1,223·6	2,070·6	3,485·5	11·1	9·1
18. Financing and insurance	656·6	1,196·1	1,848·0	12·7	7·5
19. Services	2,578·1	3,577·2	4,998·6	6·8	5·7
20. Unallocated	285·0	724·4	936·0	20·5	4·4
21. Total	16,394·7	25,762·3	41,432·2	9·6	8·2
Primary Industry (1)	2,102·6	2,178·4	2,441·1	0·7	1·9
Secondary Industry (2–13)	6,694·4	11,528·9	20,786·9	11·7	10·3
Tertiary Industry (14–19)	7,312·9	11,330·6	17,268·2	9·2	7·3

Note: Gross value figures for the industries listed are at "market prices", that is including indirect taxes (less subsidies).
Source: E.P.A., Economic and Social Development Plan 1967-1971, p. 179.

Employment by Industry
(thousands of persons)

Industry	Calendar years			Average annual rate of increase (per cent)	
	1960	1965	1971	1960–1965	1965–1971
1. Agriculture, forestry and fisheries	13,446·8	10,783·0	8,440·0	−4·3	−4·0
2. Mining	577·6	352·0	244·9	−8·7	−5·9
3. Food and kindred products	1,236·3	1,718·9	2,311·2	6·6	5·1
4. Textiles	1,264·3	1,346·8	1,602·4	2·0	2·9
5. Pulp, paper and allied products	304·7	376·4	509·9	3·8	5·2
6. Chemicals and allied products	472·9	526·2	522·6	2·2	−0·1
7. Primary metal industry	530·3	615·2	737·6	3·8	3·1
8. Fabricated metal industry	611·7	856·0	1,142·0	6·8	4·9
9. Machinery, except electrical	805·1	1,040·7	1,522·6	5·4	6·5
10. Electrical machinery	699·9	956·7	1,269·4	6·8	4·8
11. Transportation equipment	708·9	987·3	1,364·1	6·2	5·5
12. Other manufacture	3,410·7	4,150·8	4,732·8	3·3	2·2
13. Construction	2,773·2	3,367·0	4,171·9	3·0	3·6
14. Electricity, gas and water	255·0	305·0	340·4	4·0	1·8
15. Wholesale and retail trade	5,654·8	6,799·0	7,942·0	3·7	2·6
16. Real estate and ownership of dwellings	95·9	216·0	512·5	7·9	15·5
17. Transportation, storage and communication	1,966·1	2,613·0	3,225·4	5·6	3·6
18. Financing and insurance	774·0	1,005·0	1,093·2	6·1	1·4
19. Services	6,800·8	8,448·0	9,373·4	3·3	1·7
20. Unallocated					
21. Total	42,389·0	46,463·0	51,058·2	1·9	1·6
Primary Industry (1)	13,446·8	10,783·0	8,440·0	−4·3	−4·0
Secondary Industry (2–13)	13,395·6	16,294·0	20,131·4	4·0	3·6
Tertiary Industry (14–19)	15,546·6	19,386·0	22,486·7	4·5	2·5

Source: E.P.A., *Economic and Social Development Plan 1967-71*, p. 180.

Japan's Gross National Product – *in 1960 prices* (*billion yen*)

Item	Fiscal years		Average annual rate of increase (per cent)
	1965	1971	
Private consumption expenditure	13,384·4	20,125·5	7·0
General government current expenditure	1,910·8	2,488·5	4·5
Gross general government fixed capital formation	2,507·6	4,668·3	10·9
Gross private investment in producers' durables	4,510·8	7,772·1	9·5
Private residential construction	1,260·8	2,467·3	11·8
Change in inventories of private enterprises	434·9	1,238·5	—
Change in inventories by general government	71·4	12·1	—
Exports and factor income from abroad	3,802·6	7,197·0	11·2
Commodity exports	3,307·9	6,491·7	11·9
Service exports and factor income	494·7	705·3	6·1
Less: Imports and factor income paid abroad	3,220·1	5,768·5	10·2
Commodity Imports	2,347·1	4,437·3	11·2
Service Imports and factor Income	873·0	1,331·2	8·6
Gross National Product	24,663·0	40,200·7	8·5

Source: E.P.A., *Economic and Social Development Plan 1967-1971*, p. 167.

CHAPTER THREE

The Japanese Fiscal System and Policy

The Budget

In principle the fiscal operations of any government are revealed in the national budget. In fact, however, the matters are usually more complicated. In a strict sense, the national government's accounts *are* revealed in the national budget. In Japan this is called the *General Account Budget*, referred to as the "budget". But there are also other "Accounts".

Table 3.1. General Account Budget Revenue, Japanese Fiscal Year 1969.

Description	million yen	% of total revenue	
Tax and stamp receipts:	5,738,124	85·2	
Income tax	1,900,572	28·2	55·8
Corporation tax	1,858,031	27·6	
Inheritance tax and gift tax	96,671	1·4	
Liquor tax	567,050	8·4	
Sugar excise tax	39,078		
Gasoline tax	431,033		
Liquefied petroleum gas tax	7,386		
Commodity tax	300,184		
Playing cards tax	661		
Stock Exchange tax	4,579		28·0
Securities transaction tax	15,573		
Travel tax	9,476		
Admission tax	13,734		
Customs duty	311,544	4·6	
Tonnage tax	4,638		
Stamp revenue	177,914		
Monopoly profits	245,898		
Receipts from Government enterprises and properties	2,862		
Receipts from the sale of Government properties	18,841		14·8
Miscellaneous receipts	216,491		
Public bonds	490,000	7·3	
Carried-over surplus	27,395		
Total	6,739,574	100	

Source: Budget Bureau, Ministry of Finance, *The Budget in Brief*, 1969, p. 67.

Table 3.2.   General Account Budget Expenditure, Japanese Fiscal Year 1969

Description	million yen	% of total expenditure
Social security		
1. Public assistance	182,964	
2. Social welfare	88,454	
3. Social insurance	467,679	14·0
4. Public health service	122,004	
5. Measures for the unemployed	85,862	
Total	946,963	
Education and science		
1. National Government's share of compulsory education expenses	384,152	
2. Transfer to the National Schools Special Account	229,733	
3. Promotion of science and technology	91,672	
4. Public school facilities	36,092	12·0
5. School education assistance	48,923	
6. Scholarships on loan basis to students	15,181	
Total	805,753	
National Debt	278,839	4·0
Pensions and other		
1. Pensions for civil servants	29,427	
2. Pensions for veterans and dependants	212,763	
3. Administrative expenses	3,046	4·0
4. Aid to war-bereaved families and families of the unrepatriated	22,494	
Total	267,729	
Local allocation tax transfer	1,333,339	19·8
National defence	483,810	7·2
Public Works		
1. Erosion and flood control	203,478	
2. Road improvement	497,222	
3. Harbours, fishing ports and airports	98,105	
4. Housing	79,431	
5. Public facilities	47,989	
6. Improvement of conditions for agricultural production	162,323	17·8
7. Forest roads and water for industrial use	28,087	
8. Adjustment works	6,900	
9. Disaster reconstruction	78,727	
Total	1,202,262	
Promotion of foreign trade and economic aid to under-developed countries ("economic co-operation" in Japanese)	95,547	
Assistance to shipping	15,240	2·9
Assistance to small business	43,084	
Agricultural insurance	41,526	
Transfer to the Foodstuffs Control Special Account	300,100	4·5

Table 3.2. Continued

Description	million yen	% of total expenditure
Transfer to the Industrial Investment Special Account	78,100 ⎫	
Miscellaneous	757,282 ⎬	14·2
Reserves	120,000 ⎭	
Grand total	6,739,574	100·4*

*Note: Total exceeds 100 because of rounding.
Source: *The Budget in Brief*, 1969, pp. 68-71.

Table 3.1 shows that direct taxes, such as income and corporation tax, contribute more than a half of the budget revenue in Japan, whereas various outlay taxes represent only 28 per cent of the total revenue. Such proportions are not common in the world. There is a very recent trend in Japan to try to shift more of the tax burden from incomes to commodities, in order to encourage savings and investment, and generally to give incentives for risk-taking and effort. Customs tariffs revenue in 1969 represented only 4·6 per cent of the total revenue. However, this fairly low figure does not tell us much. The low percentage in theory could be due to the prohibitive height of the tariffs, or to the very low level of tariffs or to the reliance on non-tariff protective devices. In fact it is the other protective devices, import controls in particular, which are relevant here.

Some of the more noteworthy features of Table 3.2, showing the budgetary expenditure pattern, are the low level of expenditure on defence and the high level of subsidisation of domestic food production through the "Transfer to the Foodstuffs Control Special Account". It should be noted that food production is *in addition* very heavily protected from imports.

In addition to the General Account Budget in most countries there are other important institutions with *some* fiscal powers. In Japan there are forty-two *Special Account Budgets* (see Table 3.3).

Table 3.3. Special Account Budgets, Japanese Fiscal Year 1969.

Description	Million yen Revenue	Expenditure
I. Special Accounts for Government Enterprises:		
Mint	7,931	7,931
Printing Bureau	18,994	16,384
National Forest Service	174,979	174,979
Specific Land Improvement	37,169	37,169
Alcohol Monopoly	9,094	7,092
Harbour Improvement	88,777	88,777

Table 3.3 Continued

| Description | Million yen | |
	Revenue	Expenditure
Postal Service	626,749	626,749
Postal Savings	419,894	333,188
Road Improvement	553,501	553,501
Flood Control	194,767	194,767
II. Special Accounts for Insurance:		
Welfare Insurance	1,509,547	864,008
Seamen's Insurance	42,146	27,784
National Pensions	278,482	159,739
Agricultural Mutual Aid Reinsurance	45,204	45,204
Forest Insurance	1,891	1,891
Fishing Boats Reinsurance	10,306	10,306
Reinsurance of Loans to Fisheries	1,994	1,994
Export Insurance	22,705	22,705
Machinery Instalment Credit Insurance	1,516	1,516
Wooden Boats Reinsurance	422	422
Reinsurance of Compensation for Motor-car Accidents	198,524	198,524
Postal Life Insurance and Postal Annuity	575,919	304,308
Labourer's Accident Insurance	187,167	187,167
Unemployment Insurance	230,887	230,887
Earthquake Reinsurance	2,404	2,404
III. Special Accounts of Management:		
Precious Metals	22,964	22,964
Foreign Exchange	27,523	27,523
National Schools	276,372	276,372
National Hospitals	99,727	99,727
Opium	1,000	1,000
Foodstuffs Control	5,846,418	5,846,418
Special Measures for Establishment of Farms	3,523	3,523
Motor-car Inspection and Registration	3,871	3,871
IV. Special Accounts for Public Investment and Loans:		
Trust Fund Bureau	682,894	682,894
Industrial Investment	114,789	114,789
Finance for Settlers	8,283	8,283
Finance for Urban Redevelopment	7,765	7,765
V. Special Accounts to consolidate funds:		
National Debt Consolidation Fund	1,817,770	1,817,770
Reparations and Other Special Foreign Obligations	14,609	14,609
National Property Special Consolidation Fund	10,260	8,180
Allotment of Local Allocation Tax and Transferred Tax	1,451,711	1,451,711
Coal Mining Industry	88,453	88,453
	15,718,901	14,575,248

Source: *The Budget in Brief*, 1969, pp. 72-73.

The list suggests the general functions of those Special Accounts. Such Special Accounts are established where an administrative function is performed conjointly with a commercial function of one kind or another. These Special Accounts are usually financed in part from the national budget, but in addition they obtain their own funds from borrowing in the market, fees, charges and other receipts. It is because these institutions have substantial revenue of their own that they must be included in any overview of the fiscal operations of a country. (The same principle applies to the "Government-affiliated Agencies" discussed later.)

Two of these Special Accounts should be singled out for comment. One is the Industrial Investment Special Account which is the main agency for handling the issue of Japanese Government bonds abroad. The Trust Fund Bureau, attached to the Ministry of Finance, collects surplus funds accumulated by the Post Office Savings Bank and the Post Office Insurance Agency, and allocates them to various public institutions. All these Special Accounts are under the direct control of the relevant Ministry.

In addition there are fourteen "Government-affiliated Agencies" (which resemble in essence the "public corporations" of the United Kingdom).

Table 3.4.   Government-affiliated Agency Budgets, Japanese Fiscal Year 1969

Description	million yen	
	Revenue	Expenditure
Japan Monopoly Corporation	783,001	556,106
Japanese National Railways:		
Profit and Loss Account	1,100,080	1,100,080
Capital Account	541,493	541,493
Construction Account	381,848	381,848
Nippon Telegraph and Telephone Public Corporation:		
Profit and Loss Account	886,598	886,598
Capital Account	638,321	638,321
Construction Account	587,000	587,000
People's Finance Corporation	41,989	42,525
Agriculture, Forestry and Fishery Loan Corporation	47,448	49,073
Small Business Finance Corporation	53,432	51,607
Hokkaido and Tohoku Development Finance Corporation	12,480	11,494
Public Enterprises Finance Corporation	25,784	26,074
Small Business Credit Insurance Corporation	14,985	19,250
Medical Care Facilities Finance Corporation	7,978	8,050
Environment Sanitation Finance Corporation	6,849	6,675
Japan Development Bank	103,406	77,836
Export-Import Bank of Japan	53,016	54,477
	5,340,518	5,093,894

Source: *The Budget in Brief*, 1969, p. 74.

These are public institutions, as are the Special Accounts, but are set up where it is desirable to give the institutions full freedom from day-to-day control by government departments for the sake of flexibility, speed and efficiency.

The executive government also prepares the *Fiscal Investment and Loan*

Table 3.5. Fiscal Investment and Loan Programme in Fiscal Year 1969
(thousand million yen)

Source of Funds: Destination of funds	Industrial Investment Special Account	Trust Fund Bureau	Fund of Postal Insurance	Funds raised by public offering of bonds and borrowing	Total[1]
Special Accounts[2]		28·9	9·6		38·5
Government-affiliated Agencies total:	64·2	1,345·9	99·4	212·8	1,722·3
Japanese National Railways		133·0	32·0	125·0	290·0
Nippon Telegraph and Telephone Corp.				10·0	10·0
Housing Loan Corp.		174·8	16·4		191·2
People's Finance Corp.		173·0	15·0		188·0
Small Business Finance Corp.		159·0	20·0	20·0	199·0
Agriculture, Forestry and Fishery Finance Corp.		138·6	7·0		145·6
Japan Development Bank		205·0			205·0
Export-Import Bank of Japan	63·5	282·0			345·5
Others[3]	0·7	80·5	9·0	57·8	148·0
Public Corporations total:	20·0	353·5	85·9	292·0	751·4
Japan Housing Public Corp.		78·8	10·0	146·0	234·8
Pension Welfare Public Service Corp.		48·0			48·0
Metropolitan Subway Public Corp.		10·5	5·0		15·5
Japan Highway Public Corp.		63·7	44·8	68·3	176·8
Metropolitan Expressway Corp.		13·0	13·6	26·6	53·2
Han-Shin Expressway Corp.		9·0	9·5	19·2	37·7
Water Resource Development Public Corp.		10·4		3·9	14·3
Overseas Economic Co-operation Fund		27·6			27·6
Others[4]	20·0	92·5	3·0	28·0	143·5
Local Governments (local government bonds and borrowings)		349·6	110·0	62·0	521·6
Specific Companies, etc. total:	4·3	12·0	14·6	7·8	38·7
Central Bank for Commercial and Industrial Co-operatives		7·0	3·0		10·0
Electric Power Development Co.		5·0	11·6	2·4	19·0
Others[5]	4·3			5·4	9·7
The Ryukyu Government		4·0	0·5		4·5
Grand Total	88·5	2,093·9	320·0	574·6	3,077·0

Notes: 1. These agencies and institutions carry on their works with revenue sources, adding their own
      funds (such as retained profit) to funds raised through the FILP.
    2. This includes Urban Redevelopment Fund S.A., National Hospitals S.A., National Schools
      S.A., Fund for Settlers S.A., Specific Land Improvement S.A., and Postal Services S.A.
    3. This includes Medical-care Facilities Finance Corp., Public Enterprises Finance Corp.,
      Hokkaido-Tohoku Development Finance Corp. and Environment Sanitation Finance Corp.
    4. This includes Employment Promotion Public Corp., Public Nuisances Prevention Agency,
      Private School Promotion Association, Japan Railway Construction Public Corp., Coal
      Mining Area Rehabilitation Public Corp., etc.
    5. This includes Japan Air Lines Co., Tohoku Development Co., and Nihon Aeroplane Man-
      ufacturing Co.

Source: *The Budget in Brief*, 1969, pp. 75-76.

Programme (F.I.L.P.). While all the preceding budgets must be approved by the Diet this "program" does not require such approval. It is submitted only for reference, but is in fact very important as it estimates the total public capital available from various governmental institutions and outlines their broad disposal.

Finally, in any assessment of the impact of the fiscal system on the economy it is necessary to consider the fiscal operations of the *local governments*. In Japan local autonomy has traditionally been strong and it is perhaps because of this that quantitatively the local governments' budget is virtually equal to the budget of the national government. (It is doubtful if there is another unitary, non-federal country in the world with that ratio of national to local expenditures.) Although all levels of local government in Japan have their elective legislative assemblies which approve their own budgets, they do this subject to rigid central government limitations on the revenue side, but have a greater degree of autonomy for expenditures.

Each year the national government drafts the *Local Finance Plan* which estimates the main revenues and the broad categories of expenditure of the local governments. This is presented to the National Diet for reference, but the Diet does not vote on it. The local governments use this Plan as the basis for their budgets.

The Budgetary Process

The fiscal year in Japan runs from April 1 to March 31 and is named by the year in which it begins.

The Budget Bureau of the Ministry of Finance prepares the budget proposals each year on the basis of departmental proposals sent to the Ministry of Finance not later than 31 August of the preceding year. The Ministry of Finance makes a draft budget a little before the end of December, in line with the *Outlook and Basic Policy on the National Economy* prepared by the Economic Planning Agency and the "General Budget Principles" prepared by the Cabinet. This draft budget is submitted to the Cabinet for approval by the Finance Minister. The Cabinet usually makes some adjustments and approves the budget at the end of the calendar year. Through the Minister of Finance, the Cabinet submits the budget to the House of Representatives in January. The Minister of Finance introduces the draft budget in the "Financial Speech". It then goes to the Budget Committee for detailed discussion. Afterwards the Diet must approve the budget, but in this the House of Representatives is decisive. However, the House of Representatives can alter the draft budget, but if it increases the total amount the Cabinet has a right to comment on it.

When it appears that the budget will not be approved by the Diet before the beginning of the new fiscal year, a provisional budget is presented to the Diet. When the proper budget is passed, the measures taken under the provisional budget are absorbed into it.

When large unforeseen expenditures during the existing budget are necessitated by such events as natural disasters, wage increases for public servants, or deficits in the Special Food Control Account (caused by unexpected increases in the output of subsidised domestic foodstuffs), "*supplementary* budgets" are submitted to the Diet. Since the 1968 fiscal year attempts have been made to allow for such deficiencies in advance through an "integrated budget".

Chart 3.1.   THE BUDGETARY PROCESS IN JAPAN

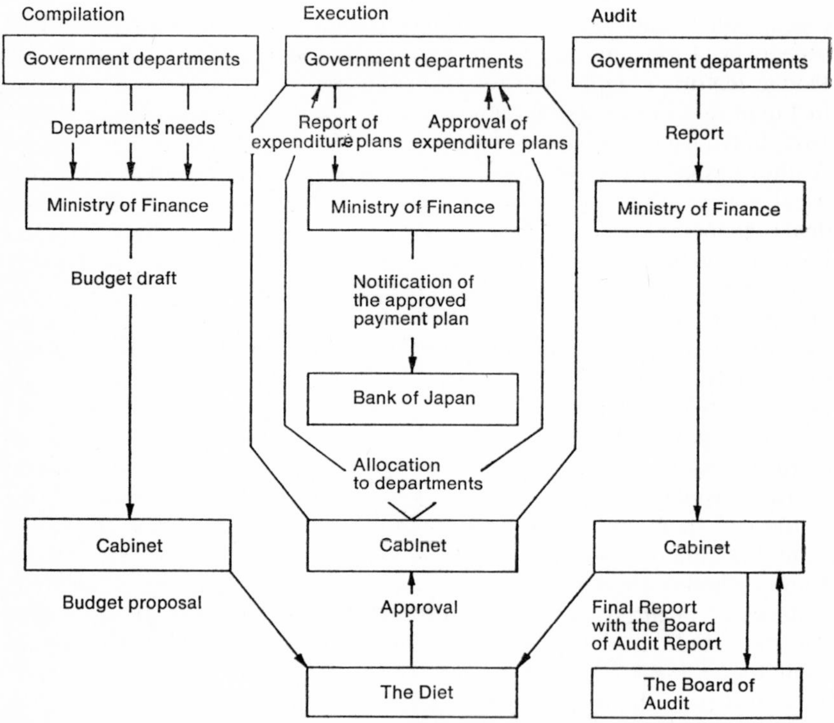

Public expenditures involve three stages:
(a) Incurring liabilities in accordance with the budgetary allocation to departments.
(b) Expenditure Plan. Payment is controlled through the quarterly *Expenditure Plan* prepared by each department for the Ministry of Finance. The Ministry of Finance compiles the total Expenditure

Plan having considered the seasonal availability of Treasury funds, the conditions in the money market and the circumstances of expenditure, and submits it to the Cabinet for approval. Then the Ministry of Finance gives the ministries and the Bank of Japan the details of the approved Plan.

(c) Actual payment by the Bank of Japan.

For important and large public expenditures such as public works, each Ministry also prepares a *Plan of Incurring Liabilities* which is then submitted to the Minister of Finance. The Minister of Finance approves the Plan and notifies the ministries and the Board of Audit.

General Fiscal Policy

Fiscal policy may be operated to achieve macro- and micro-economic objectives. From the end of the war (or more precisely since the 1949 Dodge Reform) until 1965, macro-economic fiscal policy was dormant in Japan, but in fact the budgets had a strong deflationary bias.

Joseph Dodge, an American banker, recommended to the Occupation Authorities what one would expect a banker to recommend—a "sound fiscal policy", that is, a balanced budget. At the time Japan had a great deal of unemployment and as economists generally consider a rigid balanced-budget policy at all times to be unsound, the Japanese Government did not like the Dodge prescription. Being subordinate to the Occupation Authorities who accepted the recommendation, the Japanese had to accept it too, and had to learn to live with it. This they did remarkably well. A deflationary balanced-budget *fiscal* policy was pursued, but its deflationary effects were offset by an expansionist *monetary* policy. Each year the Bank of Japan created vast sums of credit for the "city banks", which in turn expanded their credit creation to the business community. The latter borrowed so extensively that in the end their own capital represented only a small proportion of the capital obtained on loan from the banks.

Some orthodox-thinking Japanese came to consider the "highly-geared" finances of business firms unsound, but the policy was in fact the only one that could lead to growth of employment and economic development *under the circumstances*. In addition, because businessmen over-borrowed from the trading banks, and the latter had over-borrowed from the Bank of Japan, the Japanese monetary policy became extraordinarily effective when a "squeeze" was applied. (If the United Kingdom had some of this "unsound financial position" in business firms and trading banks its monetary policy would have been much more effective.)

The Japanese have managed to extract another advantage here. Under the circumstances of a rapid growth of the level of activity and incomes (the latter due conjointly to the high level of unemployment at the outset and the subsequent generous credit expansion), Dodge's "balanced-budget" principle led in fact to a super-balanced budget, even though the tax rates were occasionally reduced. The very rapid growth of employment and of income levels meant that large numbers of new taxpayers appeared every year and that the old taxpayers were steadily and rapidly moving into the high income tax rates. Thus government receipts each year were much bigger than estimated and the surpluses were shifted forward to the subsequent year. Automatically increasing tax revenues and the consequential budget surpluses meant that consumption levels were kept down, because under the circumstances the burden of high tax receipts fell on to the private income earners and consumers. This released resources for capital formation. The business firms did not then have much taxable income because their expansion was starting, profits were to come mainly in the future, and with the spurt of capital formation much of the business profit was deductible under the normal (and special) depreciation allowances. Thus the super-balanced budget did not curtail their activities. The fact that the *monetary* policy was expansionist not only made the crazy *fiscal* policy tolerable, but encouraged capital formation because trading bank credit is used almost totally for capital formation (and hardly ever for consumption). This is another example of how the un-doctrinaire, pragmatic Japanese approach extracts advantages out of disadvantageous positions. Dodge and the Occupation Authorities had the cake (locked up) and the Japanese managed to eat it (by investing the resources).

After 1955 Government expenditure began to rise rapidly. By then Japan had regained and overtaken the pre-war level of income. The Government rapidly increased expenditures on public works (the infrastructure) and on social security, while the rate of increase of tax revenues was not so high in the early sixties. As a result the possibility of an open budget deficit arose. The Government resolved the matter very simply to the satisfaction of those Japanese who swallowed the "sound-budget" policy of Dodge, and of those who saw the need for higher Government spending. Some of the General Account Budget items were transferred into the Fiscal Investments and Loans Programme, which was financed from the Post Office Savings Banks and the Post Office Insurance funds. This allowed the General Account Budget to remain in balance and in fact allowed Government expenditure to increase. This sleight of hand disarmed the simple adherents of the so-called "sound budget". In fact, however, the operation was almost identical to a "budget deficit", seen without the distortion of dogmatic spectacles. In the General Account Budget there have always been some items in the nature of capital expenditure. In the simple dogma of a balanced budget it is the *current* expenditure that is to be financed by ordinary revenue and not by borrowing. If the Government had expanded the General

Account expenditure to finance the expanded programme, it would have had to borrow through the issue of bonds. This act would have been opposed by those who accepted the Dodge fiscal ideas. By shifting some of the expenditures into the pure capital programme, called the Fiscal Investments and Loan Programme, the Government released the funds in the General Account Budget for *any* type of expenditure. The significant feature here is that the expenditure items shifted into the Fiscal Investments and Loan Programme have to be financed too, but there the "sound-budget" adherents would accept such financing as funds collected by the Post Office Savings Bank and the Post Office Insurance. In point of fact, however, there is *no difference of principle* between the Government raising funds through the issue of bonds, or through "borrowing" from depositors in the Post Office Savings Bank. In both cases the Government borrows funds and spends the money on some goods and services which are scarce, and in conditions of full employment, other things being equal, this contributes to inflation. Particularly under conditions where the Bank of Japan and the trading banks were flooding the economic system with funds, it was entirely immaterial whether the budget was "balanced" or not, and how the funds were obtained by the Government *from the market. What did matter* was whether in a given year the Government was taking a bigger or smaller percentage than before of the available limited supply of goods and services—of the G.N.P. More precisely, if the Government increased its total expenditures (including those of its agencies) in a year more than the G.N.P. increased, then its action could be considered inflationary. Conversely if it increased its purchases by a lower percentage than the G.N.P. growth, its action would be deflationary.

In 1965, due to the necessity of introducing a supplementary budget, a deficit appeared in the General Account. *At that stage* it was too embarrassing to try to shift some expenditures out of the General Account. The Government then issued short-term bonds in the market. The fact that they were "short-term" was meant to make the operation of deficit-covering more acceptable, though it was really of no consequence.

The budget for 1966 introduced an open "deficit" and covered it by the issue of *long-term* government bonds. To make the idea more acceptable they were called "constructive bonds" as opposed to "deficit-covering bonds", but again the concepts rested on (deliberate?) confusion. Bonds are always "deficit covering", and if bonds are issued and their proceeds are spent by the Government, no one can be certain what they were spent on, unless he knew which items of expenditure would have been cut if the bond finance had not been available. The 1965 supplementary budget and the 1966 ordinary budget were the first attempts in post-war Japan to break with the Dodge philosophy of the balanced budget and to introduce compensatory Keynesian financing to lift the country from the depressed levels of economic activity (created by an excessive monetary squeeze applied in order to protect the balance of payments). Again the method of financing did not matter, except for its minor effect on the private sector assets. What did matter was that the Government purchased more goods and services than it otherwise would have done. This increased the level of aggregate demand and therefore raised the level of economic activity.

During 1966 and the first months of 1967 the level of economic activity picked up, and partly as a result of this the balance of international payments began to deteriorate. To check this, the Bank of Japan applied a monetary squeeze on 1 September 1967 by raising its official discount rate by 0·365 per cent p.a. Shortly after, on 5 September 1967, the Government decided to postpone expenditures on public works of 311 thousand million yen until the following year.* However, during the second half of 1967, Government expenditures exceeded regular receipts by 590 thousand million yen,† mainly because of large deficits in the Food Control Special Account which supports the price of the domestically grown food. As a result of this and of the fact that business firms reacted to the domestic monetary squeeze by borrowing abroad, the liquidity of the economy was rather high. In January 1968 the Bank of Japan felt it necessary to increase its discount rate again by 0·365 per cent p.a. and to tighten the "window control" of its lending. This was especially necessary as in December 1967 the Government had introduced a supplementary budget substantially increasing expenditures. Briefly, the fiscal policy went against the monetary policy.

It is now recognised that fiscal operations have a high degree of "rigidity" and, in fact, are subject to a rigid upward bias of expenditures, because of the power of some pressure groups. Because of this lack of flexibility in the fiscal policy, it is probable that in future the burden of *restrictive* economic policy will fall on the monetary policy, and the burden of *expansionist* policy will be divided between fiscal and monetary policies.

In the budget for 1968 the Government made some attempts at disinflation because it was afraid that world trade conditions would deteriorate and competition would increase as a result of the British devaluation of 1967 and the U.S. attempts to improve its balance of payments. In fact, however, neither the fiscal restraint nor the world trade deterioration materialised (world trade actually grew by a very healthy 10 per cent). The Japanese General Account Budget and the Fiscal Investment and Loan Programme for 1968 showed restrained

* Keidanren, *Economic Picture of Japan 1968*, Keidanren, Tokyo, p. 70.
† Keidanren, p. 70.

increases, smaller than the increase of G.N.P., but the issue of bonds by local governments for public works was so large that it offset the mildly disinflationary nature of the first two sectors of the public finances.‡

It should be added that in 1967 the Government attempted to cut expenditures by introducing a plan to reduce the number of public servants by 5 per cent by 1971. All these attempts at economy, however, are frustrated by the seemingly inexorable rise in several important categories of public expenditures such as social security, public works, Food Control Special Account deficits and wage increases for public servants. These increased expenditures were normally voted in the supplementary budgets towards the end of the year. To put a check on them and to have a fuller budgetary control, in 1968 the principle of a "comprehensive" or "integrated" budget was introduced to preclude any subsequent increases in expenditures. The 1969 fiscal operations were fixed at moderately increased levels—the increase in Government expenditures (including public institutions and local authorities) would rise just over 12 per cent, whereas the projected growth of the G.N.P. is over 14 per cent.* Thus the fiscal system would be mildly disinflationary.

Table 3.6. Current Government (including local government) Revenue and Expenditure as Percentage of G.N.P. in Selected Countries in 1968†

Country	Revenue % of G.N.P.	Expenditure % of G.N.P.
Sweden	48·1	37·4
Norway	41·6	35·3
Netherlands	40·7	35·5
France	37·7	34·5
Austria	37·5	31·7
U.K.	37·4	33·3
West Germany	37·1	32·6
Denmark	37·0	31·4
Canada	35·2	30·3
Belgium	33·6	33·4
Italy	33·2	31·8
Australia	31·1	27·2
U.S.A.	30·0	28·7
Switzerland	26·8	22·4
Spain	21·4	17·1
Japan	20·6	14·4

† Note: Australian figures are for fiscal year 1967-68, all other figures for calendar year 1968.

Sources: a) Data for all countries except Australia are reprinted from *O.E.C.D. Observer,* February 1970.
b) Australian figures are calculated by the author from basic data in: Commonwealth Bureau of Census and Statistics, *Australian National Accounts: National Income and Expenditure,* 1968-69, pp. 27, 33 and 63.

‡ Keidanren, p. 70 and pp. 73-74.
* *The Budget in Brief,* 1969, p. 10.

Table 3.6 shows that the burden of taxation in Japan is extremely light compared to the advanced industrialised countries. Further, it shows that current account government expenditures (expenditures on the operation of the State machinery and social welfare) are at the very low level of 14 per cent of G.N.P. In other words, in Japan the State deliberately absorbs a very low proportion of the nation's yearly resources, for what might be called "public consumption". This fact, together with the public's high propensity to save (or low propensity to consume), means that a high proportion of the resources made available each year is devoted to capital formation (private or public). The fact that the Japanese Government can run a modern state with so low a level of expenditures (in terms of percentage of G.N.P.) is suggestive of very high efficiency in the administrative machine and good economic sense of the political leaders, though no doubt it also reflects the lower level of social security benefits. The fact that Japan has built up quite a substantial navy on a defence budget a fraction of that of most countries suggests that the Japanese Government is run very efficiently in the sense that little is spent on administration and what is purchased is purchased cheaply with less waste than elsewhere in the world.

To sum up this discussion, it can be said that although the restoration of an active fiscal policy has not been particularly effective, the crude legacy of Dodge has recently been abandoned and the principle of compensatory public finance has been firmly introduced.

The Japanese Tax System

Broadly speaking according to the place of assessment for tax there are four categories of taxes in Japan.

I. Taxes on income:
   (a) National: Income Tax (personal income), Corporation Tax (corporation income).
   (b) Local Government Tax: Prefectural Inhabitant's Tax, Enterprise Tax, Municipal Inhabitant's Tax.
II. Taxes on property:
   (a) National: Inheritance Tax, Gift Tax.
   (b) Local Government: Automobile Tax, Light Vehicle Tax, Mine Lot Tax, Property Tax, City Planning Tax.
III. Taxes on consumption:
   (a) National: Liquor Tax, Sugar Excise Tax, Gasoline Tax, Commodity Tax, Playing-cards Tax, Travel Tax, Admissions Tax, Local Road Tax, Liquefied Petroleum Gas Tax, Customs Tariff, Monopoly profit of State-owned monopolies.
   (b) Local: Prefectural Tobacco Consumption Tax, Local Entertainment Tax, Eating Drinking and Lodging Tax, Municipal Tobacco

Consumption Tax, Light-Oil Delivery Tax, Electricity and Gas Tax, Bathing Tax (hot springs).
IV. Taxes on Transfer of Goods:
   (a) National: Securities Transactions Tax, Registration and Licence Tax, Stamp Tax, Stock Exchange Tax, Tonnage Tax, Special Tonnage Tax.
   (b) Local: Real Property Acquisition Tax, Automobile Acquisition Tax, Timber Dealing Tax, Hunter's Licence Tax, Hunting Tax, Mineral Products Tax.

The following discussion will deal only with the more interesting features of Japanese taxes. The space in this book obviously would not allow full description* and analysis.

INCOME TAXES IN JAPAN

Japan was one of the pioneer countries in the world in introducing progressive income tax in 1887. (The U.K., for example, introduced progressive income tax in the twentieth century.) At the beginning the Japanese income tax had such modern features as a basic exemption and progression of the tax *rates* as the size of income grew.

Income tax in Japan consists of Personal Income Tax computed on a *calendar* year basis and a Corporation Tax computed on a *fiscal* year basis. The rates of income tax are progressive, starting at 9·5 per cent for low income and rising gradually to 75 per cent for the very high incomes' top *segments*. In principle the following sources of income are included for assessment of the income tax due:

1. Interest income.
2. Dividend income.
3. Real estate income.
4. Business profits.
5. Employment income.
6. Retirement income.
7. Timber industry income.
8. Capital gains.
9. Occasional income.
10. Miscellaneous income (including income in kind).

In fact, however, some of the sources of income are subject to specific concessions.
Income Deduction Concessions. Employment income, retirement income and timber industry income are given the right of special personal, basic exemption (which is not uniform but increases slightly within a range

---

* The interested reader will find full details of various taxes in: *An Outline of Japanese Taxes*, Tax Bureau, Ministry of Finance, Japan.

with the increase in income). Other income is not eligible for this concession. Life insurance premiums paid by the employer are not treated as income of the beneficiary. Life insurance premiums paid by the income-earner are income-deductible for tax purposes, up to a limit. So are the premiums for fire and accident insurance on the taxpayer's house and household goods. There are exemptions for wife and dependants and for medical and dental expenses. An interesting feature is that a resident taxpayer who is physically handicapped or has physically handicapped dependants can deduct a fixed sum from his taxable income. "Casualty" and "accident" losses due to earthquake, for instance, or theft, are income-deductible in excess of 10 per cent of income. Similarly, a sum can be deducted from the taxable income of a widow or working student. People over 65 years of age can also deduct a sum from their taxable income, but not if their income exceeds 5,000,000 yen. It should be mentioned that the Japanese income tax system shows here a few features superior to the provisions in most Western countries in that it allows tax concessions for the handicapped, casualty, accident and theft losses, working students, and that the age tax concession is not given indiscriminately but only to the people with moderate and low incomes. In order to assist the domestic timber industry, income tax provisions make several special concessions for incomes earned in that industry.

Capital gains are subject to income tax but with reduced force. In particular, capital gains have to be divided into "short-term" (realised within three years from purchase) and "long-term". The taxpayer deducts (at the time of writing) 300,000 yen from the capital gains (but from the "short-term gains" *first*) and then the taxable capital gains will consist of the balance of "short-term capital gains", plus one *half* of the "long-term gains" (subject to the *prior* deduction of up to 300,000 yen, if unused under short-term gains).

The final effect of these provisions varies according to the nature and size of capital gains. A taxpayer who had only "long-term" capital gains would be able to exempt a little over a half of his capital gains from normal income tax rates. Viewed as a capital gains tax, this is a rather high level. It is true that the pressure of the high tax level in this case is alleviated for the seller of a house or business premises, plant, or equipment, if he buys a replacement for them (within a year or an approved period). In these cases no capital gain is deemed to exist, to the extent that the new asset did not cost less than the sale value of the old. Emigrants from Japan who realise a capital gain on the sale of their assets qualify for a substantial special deduction from the gain. For other beneficiaries of capital gains, however, the standard concessions do not reduce the heavy rates of income tax sufficiently, and the arrangements probably do produce a good deal of distortion in the business behaviour of the would-be beneficiaries of capital gain (which is against the principles of a good tax). In particular, the great difficulty for the Japanese Government in reorganising agriculture through amalgamation of small, but often part-time-tilled farms must be due in no small degree to the existence of a very heavy capital gains tax. The owner of a small farm might be tempted to sell to his neighbour, but the inclusion of the capital gain in one year's income would have a strong discouraging effect. In fact, *by implication* this effect is recognised because an owner of land selling it for *housing development* (subject to some conditions) is eligible for 3,000,000 yen special deduction from the capital gain.

Credits Deductible from the Tax Itself. Dividend income (which has already been subjected to Corporation Tax) is deductible at the level of 15 per cent of the dividend income, subject to a few limitations. Foreign income taxes, *subject to specific limitations*, may be deducted from the Japanese income tax assessment, or, at the option of the taxpayer, may be treated as a cost, deductible from the Japanese income.

The cost of scrapping specific machinery and equipment in designated industries with special programs of improving industrial structure and strengthening the international competitive power of Japan is deductible from the income tax itself at 10 per cent of the cost of the new equipment. *The annual increase* in research and development expenditures over that in 1966 is deductible at 25 per cent of the cost.

Saving for house purchase held under a contract at a financial institution is partly deductible from the income tax—4 per cent of the amount saved with a maximum of 10,000 yen.

CORPORATION TAX (COMPANY INCOME TAX)

The rates and other conditions of corporation tax differ from those of the personal income tax. In 1968 the *general* corporation tax rate was 35 per cent. This looks lower than in most Western countries, but companies pay two other taxes on profits: Prefectural Enterprise Tax and Municipal Inhabitant Tax. For smaller companies the Corporation Tax rate was 28 per cent, and for that part of corporate income paid out as dividends the rate was generally 26 per cent. The low rate of tax on company profits, and in particular the lower rate on profits of smaller companies, compared to the relevant personal income rates tended to give a privileged tax treatment to this form of business organisation over unincorporated businesses. As a result in the post-war period Japan has experienced a vast switch of businesses into the company form.

In recent years Japan has tried to equalise the treatment of the two forms of business organisation. Thus, for example, companies which are owned mainly or substantially by family members are called "family corporations" and are subject to an additional tax. Co-operative businesses and non-profit organisations are subject to the lowest tax rate— 23 per cent. This explains in part the large number of co-operatives in farming. In addition, corporations are also subject to *Local* Residence Tax, and *Local* Enterprise Tax.

Various Special Tax Concessions

TAX CREDITS

(a) Income tax withheld (paid at the source) on interest, dividends, etc.
(b) Foreign income tax paid by a Japanese company is deductible against Japanese Corporation Tax.
(c) Tax credit in a specified amount for improving Internal Funds/ External Funds ratio of a corporation (reduction of the degree of "over-borrowing", or excessively "high capital-gearing").
(d) Special tax credit for scrapping old equipment in specified industries at 10 per cent of the cost of new equipment.
(e) Special tax credit for corporate merger.
(f) Any *increase* in research and development expenses over the largest expenditure at any preceding accounting period is deductible from corporation tax at 25% or 50%.

Prior to 1964 income derived from exports was exempt from income and company taxes, but in that year the concession was withdrawn under the pressure of G.A.T.T. (General Agreement on Tariffs and Trade) which considered the concession as an export subsidy. But in order to stimulate visible and invisible exports the Government introduced new measures of assistance.

Accelerated depreciation for enterprises deriving income *from overseas transactions*. The cash value of this is no more than the interest imputable to the tax payable in the first few years if the acceleration of depreciation were not allowed, and that is payable in the subsequent years (when the depreciable amount is exhausted earlier due to the acceleration).

The Overseas Market Development Reserve. The "cost" of overseas market development may be deducted from income into a "reserve" before tax assessment if a corporation derives income wholly or partly from "overseas transactions" which are defined as: exports of goods; sale of goods to an exporter; processing of goods on order of an exporter; or large-scale repair of ships paid for directly or indirectly in foreign currencies. The deductions into the "reserve" are not permanent. After five years the value of the deductions is returned into taxable income in equal annual instalments over a five-year period. This means that this concession resembles accelerated depreciation in essence (but not the amounts). Small and medium-sized enterprises can make this deduction into the "reserve" at a higher rate.

Overseas Investment Loss Reserve. A company may, under specified conditions, transfer into the "reserve" income up to a half of the cost of acquisition of foreign investment. The sum involved flows back into the taxable income from the sixth to the tenth years after the deduction.

Stock Transactions Loss Reserve (similar to the preceding).

There are several expenditures or losses where the cost or part of the cost is treated as an expense—the amount is *not* shifted back into taxable income at a later stage. This category includes: structural improvements for small and medium sized enterprises, structural improvements in specified textile industries, certain railway expenditures, afforestation expenditures, drought reserve, unusual risk reserve, default loss compensation, security transactions responsibility reserve, commodity transactions responsibility reserve, and reserve for losses caused by repurchase of electronic computers by the producers or dealers.

Depreciation Allowances Over-and-Above the Ordinary Depreciation.*
In addition to the ordinary depreciation allowances (100% of cost over a period of years), Japan grants Special Depreciation which allows the company in the approved cases to deduct more than 100 per cent of the cost of capital asset. These *additional* Special Depreciation allowances are granted by the Ministry of Finance after consultation with the relevant Ministry (such as M.I.T.I. or Agriculture and Fisheries). Because these allowances are given to specific categories of industries and can be withheld, and because the firm, plant or equipment has to be designated by the Ministry of Finance, the government has potential power over the industry. This must be persuasive even if the government does not specifically attempt to use the power for the purpose of enforcing its wishes in other matters.

Other categories eligible for *additional* depreciation are:

(a) Special depreciation on improved machinery, etc., in its first year of use: a third, fourth or tenth of cost.

(b) Special first-year depreciation in "under-developed districts", and coal mining areas: a third of cost on equipment, a fifth of cost on buildings.

(c) Special depreciation, one third of cost, on *designated* capital investment of small and medium-sized enterprises, fishing vessels and warehouses belonging to voluntary sales chains.

(d) Special depreciation of half of cost on machinery owned by members of commercial and industrial co-operatives which carry out the small and medium-size industry Improvement Program.

(e) Special first-year depreciation, one third of cost, on the machinery

---

* Tax Bureau, Ministry of Finance, *An Outline of Japanese Taxes*, Government of Japan, 1968, pp. 80-82 and 90-91.

recognised by the appropriate Ministers as required for "commercialisation" of new technological ideas.

(f) Special depreciation on the *fixed assets* of a corporation deriving income wholly or partly from specified overseas transactions in goods and services.

(g) Special depreciation on houses newly built for rent, 200 or 300 per cent of the ordinary depreciation for the first five years.

(h) Special depreciation for the first five years of 200 per cent of the ordinary depreciation on newly acquired business buildings.

(i) Special depreciation of 100 per cent of the ordinary depreciation for the first five years on the facilities for the storage of crude petroleum.

(j) Special depreciation for afforestation expenses.

(k) Special first year depreciation of one third of the ordinary depreciation on facilities of the associations of small and medium-size enterprises for the purpose of modernisation and job-training for the members of the association and members' employees.

(l) Special depreciation of monies paid to research associations.

DOUBLE TAXATION AGREEMENTS

In view of the present international spread of private foreign investment, the problem of double taxation has acquired great importance. Japan has concluded Agreements for the Avoidance of Double Taxation and the Prevention of Tax Evasion with Respect to Taxes on Income with the following twenty countries: the United States, Sweden, Norway, Denmark, Pakistan, India, Singapore, Austria, the United Kingdom, New Zealand, Thailand, Malaya, Canada, France, West Germany, Brazil, Ceylon, Belgium, the United Arab Republic and Australia.

THE OTHER NATIONAL TAXES

These taxes* have been listed in Table 3.1 and on the whole they are self-explanatory and do not differ very much from the corresponding taxes in other countries. It should be mentioned that some of the Japanese sales taxes have a protective element. For example, the commodity tax *rate* on motor-cars goes up with the size of the car, and liquor tax rate on whisky goes up with the quality of whisky. In both cases this differential tax rate discriminates against the foreign supplier, because foreign cars that would be imported are usually larger than the Japanese cars, and foreign whisky is usually dearer.

Local Government Finances

In most countries, writings on public finance barely mention local

* For details of those taxes the interested reader may consult *An Outline of Japanese Taxes*, Tax Bureau, Ministry of Finance, Japan.

government finances. This attitude is probably never excusable, and it would certainly be wrong in the case of Japanese public finances where local government expenditures *equal* the expenditures of the national government.

Local autonomy in government has a long tradition in Japan. At present there are two levels of local government: prefectures and municipalities.

There are forty-six prefectures, of which forty-two are called *Ken* (ordinary prefecture), one comprises metropolitan Tokyo and is called *To* (Metropolis), one comprises all of Hokkaido and is called *Do* (Circuit), and the two large cities of Osaka and Kyoto form two prefectures called *Fu*. The chief executive officer of the prefecture is the governor and the legislature is an assembly of representatives elected for four years. The prefecture administers the police force, public works such as roads and waterways, public health, some social security provisions, labour administration, high schools, some universities, libraries and public housing.

The ordinary prefectures and Hokkaido consist of cities, towns and villages. Tokyo consists of twenty-three wards which are only subdivisions of the *To* government; Kyoto and Osaka have no subdivisions. The chief executive officer of the city, town or village is the mayor or head. Cities, towns and villages also have their legislative assemblies, which administer elementary and junior high school education, roads, water supply, sanitation, fire control, some social security provisions and administration of harbours.

LOCAL GOVERNMENT REVENUE

For the fiscal year 1969 the estimated revenue of all local government bodies in Japan was 6,640 thousand million yen. Of this sum only 42 per cent was raised by local taxation.

Local taxes. Each year the Diet passes the Local Tax Law together with the Budget. This Law determines the kind of taxes and their "standard rates" for the local authorities. In the case of some taxes, the local authorities are allowed to impose tax rates below or above the "standard rate" within defined limits. It is only here that the local government has some measure of independence in the matter of collecting revenue. These local taxes, the prefectural taxes, and the city, town or village taxes, will be considered later on.

Local government borrowing. This source of local government revenue represented 4·4 per cent of the total revenue in 1969. However, local government borrowing is permissible only for the construction or acquisition of a specific property such as a water works, school or hospital. In addition, it requires the specific approval of the Ministry of Finance and the Ministry of Home Affairs. Borrowing through the issue of local government bonds can be from the public, the Trust Fund Bureau (of the Ministry of Finance), the commercial banks, and the Public Utility Finance Corporation (which also guarantees the repayment of loans from the banks).

Miscellaneous revenues. These consist of various charges such as public utility charges, fees, receipts from sale of assets, profits from organised sports and lotteries. Most of these, especially the public utility charges and education fees, are very inelastic sources of revenue. In fact, many of the public utilities are run at a loss. The total of the miscellaneous receipts represented 4·8 per cent of total local authorities' revenue in 1969.

Transfers from the national government comprise the rest of local authorities' revenue. In 1969 they represented 47·2 per cent of the total local government revenues. The national government subsidises the local government in three ways. One is through transferring a share (32 per cent) of the receipts from the *national* income tax, corporation tax and liquor tax, to the local government. That share of the taxes is called the *Local Allocation Tax* (or *Local Grant Tax*) although the taxes are essentially national taxes. The Local Grant Tax consists of two components: the "ordinary grant" available from the beginning of the fiscal year, and the "special grant" given to the local authorities towards the end of the fiscal year—in February, to meet the financial needs that were not foreseen. The transfer of the receipts from the Local Grant Tax to local authorities is in the form of general purpose grants, differentiated in amount with respect to various local authorities. They are intended to reduce the differences in the needs and resources of various local authorities. To determine the specific share of the Local Grant Tax for each local authority, the national government first estimates the "*basic revenue*" for each prefecture, city, town or village.

This is taken to be 80 per cent of the hypothetical revenue of a prefecture and 75 per cent of a city, town or village, assuming that they all collect their own taxes at the "standard rates". (This means that if any local authority decides to collect lower or higher local taxes than the standard rate, the amount of the transferred Local Grant Tax given to it will *not* be affected.) Then the national government estimates the "needs" of each local government if each were to provide facilities and services of a certain standard. The "needs" are estimated through specific formulae aiming at a uniform standard of service in all local authority areas. In other words, the length of roads in each area determines the amount of the grant for improvement or construction of roads, and the area of the roads determines the grants for maintenance, but these quantities are further adjusted by a coefficient according to differences in snow fall and traffic density. The difference between the "needs" thus estimated and the "basic revenues" of each local authority is then filled by the differential grant from the Local Grant Tax. In practice, the various local authorities find that their actual total revenues sometimes vary from the estimates, especially as some taxes, such as the enterprise tax and the corporation residence tax, are very sensitive to fluctuations in the level of activity. This is resolved in part by varying the rates of those two taxes, and the remaining discrepancy is made up two years later in the amount of the national grant from the Local Grant Tax to the local authority.

In the Fiscal Year 1969, this portion of the three national taxes (national income tax, corporation tax and liquor tax) earmarked for the local government represented almost 21 per cent of the total local government revenue.

Local Transferred Tax consists of three elements: the local road tax, the liquefied petroleum gas tax and the special tonnage duty. The local road tax is a petrol tax collected for convenience with the same national tax directly from the refineries. Like the national tax it is devoted entirely to construction and maintenance of roads. The liquefied petroleum gas tax is also a transfer—half of the receipts of the national tax. The transferred portions of the road tax and liquefied petroleum tax receipts are paid into the "Special Account for Allotment of Local Allocation and Transferred Tax". They are then allocated among the prefectures and the six largest cities in accordance with the length and the width of their roads.

The special tonnage duty is collected by the national government (together with its own tonnage duty) from port-entering ocean-going vessels and is given to cities, towns, and villages which are responsible for the operation of ports. The sum total of these transferred funds represents a little over 1 per cent of local government revenues.

The national government grants local authorities a variety of *subsidies*, such as a "Grant for Redemption of Special Enterprise Bonds" (issued by local authorities to finance certain public enterprises), "Special Grant for Traffic Safety Measures" (on the basis of density of population and the number of accidents), and a number of other subsidies for specific purposes like social security, science promotion, or half the cost of public school teachers. The total of all these subsidies is a very substantial sum and represents over 26 per cent of the total revenues of local authorities. Thus the total of the tax monies flowing from the national government to the local governments in 1969 represented over 57 per cent of all local government revenues.

In addition, with funds from the Treasury Investment and Loan Programme, the national government buys more than half of the bonds issued by local authorities to cover the expenses of public works like disaster relief and school construction.

PREFECTURAL TAXES

Prefectural Inhabitants Tax (or Prefectural Residence Tax). This tax is levied on both individuals in residence and companies with offices in the prefecture on 1 January. It consists of two elements: *per caput* tax (individuals and companies) and a levy on income. The rates of tax vary, but in 1968 the capitation fee was 100 yen p.a. for individuals, 600 yen p.a. for small companies, and 1,000 yen p.a. for companies with a capital of more than 10 million yen. The levy on income of individuals was 2 per cent for incomes below 1,500,000 yen, and 4 per cent above. The standard prefectural levy was 5·8 per cent of the national corporation tax.

Enterprise Tax. This tax is levied on companies and individuals in businesses other than newspapers, radio, publishers of textbooks, forestry, farming, fishing (with family labour only) and mining. This is a tax on income. For companies in 1968 there were three rates of 6, 9, and 12 per cent, according to the size of income. However, in the case of electric power, gas, and insurance companies this tax changes its nature and falls on gross receipts at a flat rate of 1·5 per cent. For individuals the tax rate varies from 3-5 per cent of income.

Real Property Acquisition Tax. This is payable on purchase of real estate. The rate in 1968 was 3 per cent of the appraised value (which has a tax-free exemption of 1,500,000 yen in the case of newly built homes).

Motor-car Acquisition Tax. This is at 3 per cent of the cost of acquisition (new or second-hand) and is payable by the buyer.

Tobacco Consumption Tax. This is payable by Japan Monopoly Corporation at 10·3 per cent of its sales to retailers.

Local Entertainment Tax. The operators of amusement and sports facilities charge a percentage of entrance fees (30 per cent for golf and 10 per cent for others) by adding it to the fee.

Eating, Drinking and Lodging Tax. These expenditures in an inn or hotel attract 15 per cent tax for food, drink or entertainment, when the bill per person exceeds 3,000 yen, and 10 per cent when the daily lodging charge is over 1,200 yen. If the daily charge is less than 1,200 yen no tax is payable.

Motor Vehicle Tax. This is an annual tax varied according to the size and the kind of vehicle. A large private vehicle has the highest tax rate.

Mine Lot Tax.

Hunter's Licence Tax.

Hunting Tax.

Light-Oil Delivery Tax. The person receiving light-oil pays the tax.

TAXES COLLECTED BY CITIES, TOWNS AND VILLAGES

Municipal Inhabitant's Tax. This tax is collected on individuals and companies. It has two elements: a *capitation fee* for individuals varying from 200 to 600 yen according to size of city, town or village; and from 2,400-4,000 yen according to the capital of the company. There is also an *income tax* for individuals varying from 2 to 14 per cent according to the size of income, while companies pay 8·9 per cent of the national corporation tax.

Property Tax. This annual tax falls on the assessed value of land, buildings and depreciable business assets (but not vehicles). The "standard" tax rate is 1·4 per cent, and the maximum permissible rate is 2·1 per cent.

Light Vehicle Tax.

Tobacco Consumption Tax. This is similar to the prefectural one, but the tax rate is 18·1 per cent of sales by Japan Monopoly Corporation.

Electricity and Gas Tax. This tax is 7 per cent of charges, with an exemption for "heavy users" of electricity—"heavy users" are those with over 5 per cent of the production cost spent on electricity.

Mineral Products Tax. The standard rate is 1 per cent of the value of the minerals.

Timber Delivery Tax.

Bathing Tax. This is levied on the users of hot springs for the purpose of improvement of tourist facilities.

City Planning Tax. Cities, towns and villages may collect not more than 0·2 per cent of the appraised value of land and buildings.

Other taxes. Subject to permission of the Local Government Minister, cities, towns and villages may collect a variety of taxes, such as dog tax, advertisements tax (Osaka, Kyoto and Kobe), and a tax on gift certificates issued by department stores.

CHAPTER FOUR

The Central Bank and Monetary Policy

The Bank of Japan

The Bank of Japan stands at the apex of the whole financial structure of Japan as a controlling agency. Directly or indirectly it has a very great influence on the system. It is, however, subject to control by the Minister of Finance. The Bank of Japan was originally established in 1882 (on the pattern of the National Bank of Belgium). It has since been reorganised many times. Legally it is a joint stock company in which the Government holds 55 million yen shares, and the public 45 million yen, but shareholders' meetings are not held and shareholders have no say about the policy of the Bank. The shareholders have a right only to a dividend with a maximum of 5%: the rest of the profits go to reserves and/or to the Treasury.

The Bank of Japan is administered by an executive board consisting of the Governor, Vice-Governor and several directors, auditors and advisers. Since 1949 policy is determined by the *Policy Board* which is the highest organ of the Bank. The Policy Board consists of seven members: the Governor, one representative of the Ministry of Finance, one of the Economic Planning Agency (neither of the last two have voting rights) and four members appointed by the Cabinet with the approval of both Houses of the Diet, from city banking, local banking, commerce industry and agriculture. The Government has wide legal supervisory powers over the Bank of Japan, but the Bank has always informally had a close connection with the Government so that statutory controls have never been invoked. Apart from the Tokyo head office, the Bank has thirty-one branches in large cities and thirteen local offices as well as representatives in New York, London, Paris, Frankfurt and Hong Kong. Like any other central bank, the Bank of Japan is:
(a) the sole institution authorised to issue bank notes,
(b) the Government's bank,
(c) the bankers' bank,
(d) an institution with wide monetary control powers.
The basic function of the Bank of Japan as a central bank is to

contribute to fast and healthy development of the economy through its monetary policy. In any economy there are many independent decision makers at the production, distribution and consumption levels. In a private enterprise system all of them make their decisions substantially in isolation (and even in a "command economy" there is an element of this). Consequently in the absence of regulating agencies the sum of individual economic acts would often be so high, or so low, that the economy could not accommodate it without substantial overall changes which would produce many very undesirable side effects. Of course, ultimately the market mechanism would produce a new equilibrium *on its own* by changing the relative prices of goods, labour, capital (interest rates), and money (the foreign exchange rate). The new prices would be in effect signals to the buyers and sellers to vary demand or supply according to the price change. But a change in the price of goods or foreign exchange is upsetting in numerous ways because all economic interrelationships are expressed using the common yardstick of price which is in money terms. It is most undesirable that this common yardstick should change unless there are overwhelming reasons (mainly based on rigidities in some areas of the economy). For those reasons, all governments, even the most devoted to free enterprise, attempt to keep the yardstick as stable as they can. This, however, involves some controls over the individual decision makers. A regulating body issuing instructions with penalties and rewards attached is an example of *direct* or *physical control*. There are two types of *indirect* controls: monetary and fiscal. They operate indirectly through the market mechanism—for example, the producers, consumers or importers who might be inclined to buy too little, or too much, are induced by actions like a change in the price of goods, or capital or foreign exchange, or change in taxes to reduce or increase their purchases of particular goods or to change the total of their expenditures as desired.

Realising the great importance of money in the economic system, and knowing that under the modern conditions a commercial bank creates or destroys money whenever it grants a loan or accepts a repayment, it then becomes obvious that some agency is absolutely necessary to regulate this creation and destruction of money. Especially in Japan, where fiscal policy was in disuse between 1948 and 1965, the monetary policy carried the whole burden of control and has been particularly important.

ISSUE OF BANKNOTES BY THE BANK OF JAPAN

The Bank of Japan has the exclusive right to issue bank notes in Japan. (These bank notes are then lent either to government or to commercial banks.) The total issue of these bank notes is not tied in any way to gold or to foreign exchange holdings. There is no legal obligation to convert the banknotes into gold or foreign currencies. But there is at any time an *upper limit* fixed by the Minister of Finance above which bank notes may be issued only with his special permission and subject to financial penalties. In October 1966 the maximum permissible note issue was 2,450 billion yen and penalty for excess issues at the rate of 3% p.a. The Bank of Japan can *sell* the notes only against silver, gold, foreign currencies, government securities, bills of exchange, and bonds and debentures, or *lend* the banknotes on the collateral security of the bills and bonds and debentures. In the case of assets other than gold, silver and foreign exchange, there are *individual** maximum amounts fixed by the Minister of Finance, but not published.

THE BANK OF JAPAN AS GOVERNMENT'S BANK

The Bank of Japan holds all the funds of the government, lends money to the government against bills and bonds, and handles the Treasury in-and-out payments. In addition it handles the flotation, servicing and retirement of government debt and the transactions of the Foreign Exchange Special Account. The Foreign Exchange Special Account is a government account which holds the country's foreign currency reserves, other than the working balances of the authorised foreign currency banks. The Bank of Japan is the agent of the Minister of Finance for buying and selling of foreign exchange from and to the authorised foreign currency dealer banks.

THE BANK OF JAPAN AS BANKERS' BANK

It accepts deposits from the following financial institutions: city banks, local banks, trust banks, long-term credit banks, The Foreign Exchange Bank, mutual loans and savings banks, credit associations, the National Federation of Credit Associations, the Central Bank for Commercial and Industrial Co-operatives, the Central Co-operative Bank for Agriculture and Forestry, securities finance companies, securities companies and call-loan dealers.

These deposits are then used by the owners to settle "clearing" balances, remittances and call-loan transactions.

In addition the Bank of Japan lends in various ways to most of the financial institutions. Here the Bank of Japan emerges as quite different from the other central banks. Usually the central banks lend only as a last resort, but the Bank of Japan lends substantially to *the city banks* on a regular and permanent basis. (See Table 5.4.) Thus it has provided vast funds for the economic development of Japan by assuring the city and the local banks of adequate liquidity, which has induced the creation of a *multiple* expansion of credit. The Bank of Japan lends

---

* Economic Research Department, The Bank of Japan, *The Bank of Japan: Its Organisation and Monetary Policies*, Tokyo, November 1969, p. 6.

in the following ways: by discounting of commercial bills and export trade bills; by lending on the security of government bills and bonds. government-guaranteed bonds, local government bonds, company debentures, bank debentures, bills and promissory notes; and by overdraft (which is not used at present).

The Bank of Japan also affects the liquidity of the financial institutions through purchase from and sale of securities to them. The purchases and sales of monetary silver and gold are made by the Precious Metals Special Account, and foreign exchange is handled by the Foreign Exchange Fund Special Account, both of which are Government institutions for whom the Bank of Japan is only an agent.

Instruments of Monetary Control of the Bank of Japan

THE BANK RATE

It is clear that lending policy—the terms on which various loans or discounts are made—affect the behaviour of the borrowers or would-be borrowers.

One of the important terms for loans is the interest rate, or the "Bank Rate" in this case. Since the Bank of Japan grants several types of loans it therefore has several Bank Rates, in fact, seven of them.

Table 4.1.   The Bank Rates of the Bank of Japan as at end October 1966.

		% p.a.
1.	Discount rate on commercial bills (the "basic rate")	5·475
2.	Discount rate on export trade bills	4·015
	Interest rate on *loans* secured by :	
3.	Export trade bills	4·380 or more
4.	Import trade bills (the special rate discontinued in 1960)	5·840 or more
5.	Government securities, designated local government securities, company bonds, and other securities	5·840 or more
6.	Other collateral (e.g. promissory notes)	6·205 or more
7.	Interest rate on Bank of Japan overdrafts (overdrafts not used nowadays)	6·570

Source: *The Bank of Japan: Its Organisation and Monetary Policies*, March 1967, p. 9.

Whenever only the terms the Bank Rate, or the 'basic Bank Rate" are used in Japan, it refers to the discount rate on commercial bills. Usually the Japanese interest rates expressed *per annum* have several decimal points, because in Japan the established practice is to express interest rate *per diem* per 100 yen. (The recent exception to this rule is that since September 1969 the Bank of Japan has used Western notation.) In this system the smallest current unit of money would be too large therefore old smaller units are used. They are *sen* = 1/100 yen, and *rin* = 1/1,000 yen. Thus when the Japanese say that the rate of interest is 1 *sen* it means 0·01 yen times 365, which equals 3·65 per cent p.a.

Usually the basic Bank Rate in Japan goes up or down by only one *rin* (1/10 of *sen*), which expressed in per annum terms means 0·365 per cent. The remarkable fact here is that such small alterations are usually sufficient to produce a change in the Japanese business climate, whereas changes of 2 or 3 per cent produce little effect in the United Kingdom! This shows how sensitive the Japanese commercial banks are to changes in the bank rate, partly because of their "overloan" condition and partly because they know that the Bank of Japan means business and if necessary would use a bigger stick without hesitation. The Bank of Japan would be ruthless if needed, partly because the Japanese appreciate the economic facts of life better than most people, and partly because since 1949 the burden of the aggregate (Keynesian) control of the economy has been almost entirely left to monetary controls and fiscal aggregate controls were not used at all until 1965/6.

The effectiveness of the Japanese Bank Rate changes is further enhanced at the second level of borrowing, that is, by the business world from the commercial banks, owing to the fact that (in 1958) Japanese commercial banks agreed to change their lending rates in sympathy with the changes in the Bank Rate.

CONDITIONS OF BANK OF JAPAN LOANS

The Bank of Japan also influences the borrowing by the commercial banks in other ways. In the first instance it determines rates of interest for securities which are eligible for the discount facility, and for those which can be used only as a collateral for loans. The export trade bills denominated in yen against an irrevocable letter of credit enjoy the lowest cost of discounting. These export trade bills in Japan can be of two types: export *advance* bills, drawn by the producer to finance the purchase, manufacturing or processing of export goods; and export *usance* bills, which are drawn by the exporters on the foreigners to collect payment for goods shipped (also against an irrevocable letter of credit).

Until 1966 import trade bills enjoyed a *slight* preference in the rate of discount over the general bills. In the post-war period until 1969, the Bank of Japan policy was to have as much of the short-term financing of Japan's trade as possible handled abroad, that is, discounting of bills was done in London and New York, because Japan was short of capital and short of foreign exchange. In 1969 the Bank of Japan has encouraged —but with an upper limit—the Japanese commercial banks to discount usance bills. This is called the "yen shift", and has been motivated by two factors. Firstly the cost of discounting bills in London and New York has risen to record levels as the U.K. and the U.S.A. increased their measures to defend their currencies. Secondly, the balance of payments of Japan has recently shown large surpluses, and while welcomed by Japan, they are so large that they are embarrassing internationally. Such surpluses are a good argument for the U.S.A., the U.K. and the international organisations like G.A.T.T. or the I.M.F. to press Japan for reduction of trade barriers, in particular for removal of import controls, and/or for upward revaluation of the yen. By reducing the extent of short-term borrowing abroad the "yen shift" in financing "usance" credit prevents Japan's international reserves from rising.

THE BANK OF JAPAN LOANS MAXIMUM LIMITS

Since 1962 the Bank of Japan has occasionally imposed maximum limits on *its* loans to those city banks whose "overloan" position is too high. The maxima are not rigid, in the sense that they can be exceeded, but in such cases the borrowing banks have to pay a penal rate of interest equal to the Bank Rate plus 3·65 per cent p.a. (1 *sen* per 100 yen *per diem*).

THE BANK OF JAPAN DISCOUNT "WINDOW OPERATIONS"

These "operations" have usually been in the nature of guidance and advice on the lending policy of the would-be borrowers from the Bank of Japan. The Bank of Japan stresses that the guidance is purely quantitative, not qualitative, that it aims solely at the limitation of the total of loans to the public by a bank and does not aim at any directional shift in loans. The name "window guidance" comes from the fact that such guidance would be given only if a financial institution came to "the window" to ask for loans or rediscount facility. The implication is that if a financial institution did not ask the Bank of Japan for such assistance it would also escape "window guidance". Needless to say, the nature of the "window guidance" changes as the level of economic activity changes. Before 1966 the "window guidance" advice to banks was not to exceed a specified rate of increase in lending. In June 1966 this "window guidance" was abandoned (rather late in fact) because the danger of inflation had passed and the country was in a recession and needed stimulation of credit. The "window guidance" is a purely one-sided instrument of restriction. It is used as a support or substitute for increasing the Bank Rate when it is considered that a further increase in the Bank Rate would be impossible or undesirable because of the side effects. The Bank of Japan uses the Bank Rate in preference, because it is afraid that financial institutions might resort to hidden loans (something like a "black market credit") which could not be controlled by the "window guidance", but which would be checked by a higher Bank Rate and some other instruments of control.

THE "OPEN MARKET OPERATIONS"

"Open market operations" are sales or purchases of securities (in most countries government securities) in the *open market* by the central bank with the objective of *indirectly* affecting the liquidity of the commercial banks and thereby their credit-granting capacity. The private buyer of securities from the central bank pays with a commercial bank cheque (or cash withdrawn from a commercial bank) and when the cheque reaches the central bank the cash reserves of the respective commercial bank are reduced. Conversely, a purchase of securities by the central bank in the open market leads ultimately to an increase in the cash reserves of the commercial banks. Since the cash reserves of a commercial bank determine its credit policy (and since under the "fractional cash reserves" system there is a multiplication effect) this is an important instrument of monetary policy.

The Bank of Japan also uses "open market operations" to influence the level of economic activity, but there are some peculiarities about it in Japan.

Firstly, the Bank of Japan Act authorises the Bank of Japan to buy and sell commercial bonds and bills, as well as government bonds and bills. Between 1962 and 1965 the Bank of Japan had to use commercial "securities" in those operations because the government was not borrowing in the market (not issuing the bonds). Further, the sales by the Bank of Japan were made *directly* to the banks and were subject to a repurchase agreement at prices fixed in advance. Since February 1966 when government bonds became available, the Bank of Japan has introduced four changes:

(a) Only government bonds will be used.

(b) The purchase is outright (but still dealing directly with the financial institutions).

(c) The purchase is on the basis of market prices just before the financial institution is asked to sell.

(d) Securities companies have been added to the list of institutions asked to sell. The list is now: city banks, local banks, long-term credit banks, the specialised foreign exchange bank (the Bank of Tokyo), the National Federation of Credit Associations, mutual loans and savings banks, and those securities companies that maintain deposit accounts with the Bank of Japan.

It can be seen that the Japanese variety of "open market operations" hardly deserves the name. In the first instance it is not in the "open market", secondly it is not subject to market forces. The financial institutions in fact have to be *instructed* by the Bank of Japan: "Sell securities to us", or "Buy securities from us". Thus the device has more affinity to the administrative variation of the minimum statutory deposits.

In January 1966 the Bank of Japan, as an agent for handling government borrowing, had decided to sell *short-term* government securities to the call loan dealers instead of absorbing and holding them itself. The Bank of Japan publication *The Bank of Japan: Its Organisation and Monetary Policies* (1966, p. 12) erroneously mentions this as an "open market operation" (Japanese style), when actually it was a pure *fiscal* operation, or rather assisting the fiscal operation of the government. As an open market operation in a period of recession, as it was, it would have been an upside down, a counter-productive policy. In a recession the point for the central bank engaging in an open market operation is to purchase securities (not to sell them!) with newly-created central bank money in order to increase the liquidity resources of the financial institutions, hoping that they will lend more, and thus help revive business. Selling short-term government securities to "call-loan" dealers in January 1966 and as long as the recession lasted was a policy to do exactly the opposite of the aim of "open market operations". That selling reduced the liquidity of the "call-loan" dealers and thereby tended to produce a cash stringency for all the financial institutions that borrow from the call-loan market. (The fact that the government would spend the money makes no difference here. Under the previous arrangements short-term government securities were purchased and held by the Bank of Japan and the government also spent the money. Clearly, that was more expansionist a policy.)

THE RESERVE DEPOSIT REQUIREMENT SYSTEM

This method of monetary control was first suggested in the inter-War period by Keynes. It was later adopted by New Zealand, the U.S.A. and gradually other countries. Its essence is that the central bank requests specified financial institutions to deposit specified amounts or proportions of cash in frozen accounts. These frozen minimum deposits are varied as the economic conditions change. Japan passed an Act of Diet in 1957 authorising the Bank of Japan to operate the system, which came into use in September 1959. It should be noted at the outset that in Japan the system was introduced under quite different circumstances than in the U.S.A., New Zealand or Australia. In those countries at the time there was so much excess liquidity in the banking system that most of the other available methods of monetary control would not work. In the U.S.A., for example, the excess liquidity of the commercial banks was so high that if the U.S. Federal Reserve Board wanted to produce a monetary squeeze by open market operations, it would have had to sell all its security holdings and the banks would still have had excess liquidity, and still have been able to expand credit. The position was similar in New Zealand, Australia and some other countries, but *not* in Japan. There the commercial banks are at the opposite extreme. They are perennially short of liquidity and the city banks are always in debt to the Bank of Japan. Under such circumstances all the preceding conventional methods of control are fully adequate. Thus the introduction of the new device was essentially an act of imitation. At present the new method can be used to restrict the operations of those financial institutions that never borrow from the Bank of Japan, though all institutions that are asked to make stated minimum deposits can also be reached directly by the Japanese-style open market operations. When the securities market has broadened, indirectly they will be reached by the Western style of open market operations.

The financial institutions that are obliged to observe the minimum deposits are city banks, local banks, trust banks, Japanese branches of foreign banks, long-term credit banks, the specialised foreign exchange bank (the Bank of Tokyo), and those mutual loans and savings banks and credit associations whose deposits exceed 20 billion yen.

Table 4.2.   Minimum Deposit Requirements as at 16 July 1965.

Institutions	Time Deposits %	Non-time Deposits %
All Banks:		
Deposits of:		
more than 100 billion yen	0·50	1·00
20 – 100 billion yen	0·25	0·50
20 billion yen or less	0·25	0·50
Mutual Loans and Savings Banks and Credit Associations:		
Deposits of:		
more than 100 billion yen	0·25	0·50
20 – 100 billion yen	0·25	0·50

Source: *The Bank of Japan: Its Organisation and Monetary Policies,* March 1967, p. 14.

The Act of Diet which authorised the Bank of Japan to operate the variable minimum deposit requirement set an upper limit to these compulsory deposits at 10% of the customers' deposits in the financial institution. The Bank of Japan must obtain approval of the Minister of Finance for changes in the required deposits. If a financial institution's daily average deposit with the Bank of Japan during a month falls below the required deposit, the institution pays a penal interest charge which is calculated on the amount of the deficiency and the number of business days in the month. The rate of interest is the "basic" discount rate for commercial bills at the end of the month *plus* 1 sen per 100 yen per diem.* This fine is paid to the Bank of Japan which passes it on to the Government Treasury.

* The following two publications of the Bank of Japan in English contain errors in this matter, no doubt due to faulty translation: *The Bank of Japan: Its Function and Organisation,* 1964, p. 46; and *The Bank of Japan: Its Organisation and Monetary Policies,* March 1967, p. 15.

CHAPTER FIVE

The Commercial Banks and the Short-term Financial Market

The banking system of Japan as it is today started from an imitation of the English system. In the course of development it has acquired so many peculiar Japanese characteristics and has adopted some Continental European features, so that the similarity to the British system has virtually disappeared. As a result the financial system of Japan differs from that

Table 5.1.   Financial Institutions in Japan.

Institutions	The number of institutions as at the end of 1968	Operating funds trillion yen as at 31 March 1968
I. *Central Bank* (The Bank of Japan)		
II. *Commercial Banks:*		
† * (a) City banks	13	14·9
† * (b) Local banks	62	9·8
† * Long-term credit banks	3	3·7
† * The specialised foreign exchange bank (Bank of Tokyo, customarily considered a "city bank")	1	0·7
Foreign banks	16	
* Trust banks	7	5·3
III. *Financial Institutions for Small Business:*		
† * Mutual Loan and Savings Banks	71	4·5
† Credit Associations	520	4·5
† * National Federation of Credit Associations	1	0·4
* The Shoko Chukin Bank (Central Bank for Commercial and Industrial Co-operatives)	1	
Credit guarantee corporations	51	
Credit Co-operatives:		
(a) Credit Co-operatives	543	1·1
(b) National Federation of Credit Co-operatives	1	0·09
Labor Credit Associations:		
(a) Labor Credit Associations	46	0·2

Table 5.1. Continued

Institutions	The number of institutions as at the end of 1968	Operating funds trillion yen as at 31 March 1968
(b) National Federation of Labor Credit Associations	1	0·04
IV. *Financial Institutions for Agriculture, Forestry and Fisheries:*		
* Central Co-operative Bank of Agriculture and Forestry	1	1·4
Agricultural Co-operatives:		
(a) Agricultural Co-operatives	6,868	3·5
(b) Credit Federations of Agricultural Co-operatives	46	2·1
Fisheries Co-operatives:		
(a) Fisheries Co-operatives	1,694	0·1
(b) Credit Federations of Fisheries Co-operatives	34	0·1
V. *Government Financial Institutions:*		
* Trust Fund Bureau Special Account (Postal Savings and Postal Transfer, etc. 17,042 P.O. branches)		
* Japan Development Bank	1	1·1
* Export-Import Bank of Japan	1	0·9
* People's Finance Corporation	1	0·4
* Housing Loan Corporation	1	0·7
* Agriculture, Forestry and Fisheries Finance Corporation	1	0·6
* Small Business Finance Corporation	1	0·5
* Hokkaido and Tohoku Development Corporation	1	0·1
* Local Public Enterprise Finance Corporation	1	0·3
* Small Business Credit Insurance Corporation	1	0·05
* Medical Care Facilities Finance Corporation	1	0·8
* Environmental Sanitation Business Finance Corporation	1	
VI. *Others:*		
Life Insurance Companies	20	3·3
Non-Life Insurance Companies	21	0·6
Short-term Credit Brokers (call-loan brokers)	6	0·9
Securities Companies	593 until 1968, now 277	
* Securities Finance Companies	3	0·2
Credit Card Companies	8	

Notes: 1. The institutions with a cross are required to keep a variable minimum deposit with the Bank of Japan (for the purpose of monetary control).

2. The institutions with an asterisk keep an account with the Bank of Japan (for their own convenience).
3. 1 trillion = 1 million million.

Sources: *Fuji Bank Bulletin*, March 1969, pp. 39-40.
The Bank of Japan, *The Japanese Financial System*, March 1969.

of all other countries. It is a mixture of government and private institutions, where some of the institutions are more highly specialised than anywhere else. At the top of the financial system is the Bank of Japan. Its most important function is direct and indirect control of the monetary situation in the country (and that means a great deal). In addition it is the Government's bank.

The other financial institutions can be divided into two categories: privately owned financial institutions and government-owned financial institutions. (The latter have been discussed in Chapter 2.)

In Japan the banking system is extremely well developed. In fact, it is better developed than in many European countries. Every town or village has either a proper bank branch or at least an agricultural co-operative which receives deposits from the public. It is estimated that there is one financial institution for every 500 households in Japan.*

"Commercial Banks"

In 1968 there were seventy-six "commercial banks" in Japan. They are of the branch-type as in the United Kingdom, not unit-type as in the United States of America. Many of them are huge. According to a compilation of the *American Banker* in 1966 there were twenty Japanese banks among the 100 largest banks in the non-communist world. Japanese "commercial banks" can be divided into fourteen *City Banks* including Bank of Tokyo (specialised foreign exchange bank customarily included among "city banks") and sixty-two *Local Banks*.

The terms "commercial banks" or "trading banks" are not used in Japan. Their approximate equivalent in Japan is called either "city bank" or "local bank". The difference between the two is not easily seen and is often confused. It is usual in Japan to say that the "city banks" have their head offices in large cities and operate on a national scale. They include the Fuji Bank, the Sumitomo Bank, the Mitsubishi Bank, the Sanwa Bank, the Tokai Bank, the Dai-Ichi Bank, the Mitsui Bank, the Nippon Kangyo Bank, the Kyowa Bank, the Daiwa Bank, the Bank of Kobe, the Hokkaido Takushoku Bank, and the recently established Taiyo Bank (from a reorganised Nippon Soyo Bank). The Bank of Tokyo is also considered a city bank. On the other hand, it is said that the sixty-two "local banks" have their offices in provincial cities and operate in neighbouring areas. It is usually claimed that the "local banks" are small and the "city banks" large.

None of those criteria in fact defines the true differences between the two kinds of banks, because some city banks have their head offices in the same provincial cities as the local banks do, and some local banks

* Economic Research Department, Bank of Japan, *Money and Banking in Japan*, 1964, p. 85.

are equal in size to the city banks (although their *average* size is about one tenth of that of the city banks). The true difference lies in the nature of the majority of customers of the banks and therefore also the nature of the business. City banks lend more than half of their total loanable funds to large business enterprises. More than 60 per cent of their deposits come from large corporations, and time deposits of individuals represent only a quarter of their total deposits.* The rapid growth of the Japanese economy in the post-war period has been led by large enterprises. As they have had to undertake a vast investment program, it follows in view of the under-developed capital market that they would impose large demands for funds on the city banks, and at the same time would provide relatively small deposits. This means

Table 5.2.   The Balance Sheet of Commerical Banks (End of 1968)
(in billions of yen)

	City banks	Local banks
Assets		
Cash and near money	2,164	960
(Cheques and bills)	(1,850)	(722)
Deposits with others	341	250
Call money lent	32	364
Securities	3,261	1,730
(Government securities)	(374)	(179)
(Local government securities)	(374)	(166)
(Public corporation bonds)	(398)	(295)
(Bank debentures)	(809)	(450)
(Industrial bonds)	(633)	(495)
(Shares)	(673)	(145)
Loans and discounts	15,712	8,876
(Discounts)	(5,582)	(2,929)
(Loans)	(10,130)	(5,946)
Foreign exchange	1,597	23
Total	26,335	13,320
Liabilities		
Deposits	18,047	11,295
(Current deposits)	(2,410)	(1,303)
(Ordinary deposits)	(2,750)	(2,055)
(Deposits at notice)	(1,952)	(789)
(Time deposits)	(9,890)	(6,299)
Borrowed money	1,811	53
(Due to the Bank of Japan)	(1,355)	(37)
Call money borrowed	1,033	14
Foreign exchange	888	12
Reserves	1,182	943
Capital	431	124

Source: *The Japanese Financial System*, p. 31.

* *Money and Banking in Japan*, p. 120.

that the city banks in this period have been perpetually short of funds and in debt to the Bank of Japan and the call-loan market. As a result the city banks are always in the so-called "over-borrowed" condition. This, incidentally, makes them particularly sensitive to such central bank monetary controls as an increase in the bank rate and the "window control".

On the other hand, the local banks deal mainly with small enterprises and individuals. They lend mostly to small enterprises, and moreover a half of the total local bank deposits comes from individual persons, of which three quarters are time deposits. This means that much of the business of local banks is similar to savings bank business. As a result, unlike the city banks, the local banks tend to have an excess of investable funds over the investment outlets. Consequently they rarely borrow from the Bank of Japan, and indeed often provide short-term loans on the call-market (much of which goes to the city banks). This also means that the local banks are immune from the (unfavourable) direct effects of an increased bank rate, or a stringency in the call-market (though they are not immune from other controls, such as open market operations or minimum reserve requirements).

The nature of the business of the commercial banks is readily seen from the bank balance sheet (Table 5.2). The commercial banks (city and local) were originally intended to operate as short-term credit institutions. However, the rapid growth of industry has caused a large demand for long-term capital, at the same time as an under-developed state of the capital market (as well as lack of a sufficient volume of savings) virtually compelled the Japanese commercial banks to become long-term lenders to a substantial degree. The Japanese government respected the conventional (and arbitrary) old English conception that commercial banks should lend only for short periods, both in the pre-war period when it established "special banks", and in the post-war period when it encouraged the establishment of the three long-term banks. But despite this even now the commercial banks lend a substantial proportion of their loanable funds on a long-term basis and, unlike Western banks, they also buy commercial bonds and shares (which can be viewed as a provision of long-term capital).

BANK DEPOSITS

There are the following kinds of bank deposits in Japan:
Current deposits correspond to the cheque accounts in the West. This facility together with the cheque use is expensive for the banks to operate and therefore these deposits yield no interest, but in Japan there is no charge for that service. The Japanese banks are selective about allowing customers to open this kind of account (because of the possibility of abuse).

Ordinary deposits, like the current deposits, are payable on demand, on presentation of a passbook and a personal seal. (Personal seals are frequently used as a means of identification in Japan, because *Kanji* characters do not lend themselves to individualised signatures as easily as the Latin alphabet does). Ordinary deposit accounts can be opened quite easily by any person or business. This deposit serves to collect temporary surplus funds of individuals and enterprises. Although the single ordinary deposit accounts fluctuate, the total does not and, in fact, shows a steady growth. In addition these deposits are inexpensive for the banks to handle. As a result the banks pay $2 \cdot 19$ per cent interest *per annum*, or, as the Japanese put it, $0 \cdot 6$ *sen* per 100 yen *per diem*.

Circular deposit is a special type of a savings account which has the convenience that the money can be withdrawn at any branch of the bank in the whole of Japan. The interest yield is the same as for the "ordinary deposit" ($2 \cdot 19$ per cent p.a.). Because of its convenience, especially for travellers, it has become very popular.

Deposit at notice requires two days' notice for withdrawal, and there is a minimum amount for depositing. This yields $2 \cdot 555$ per cent p.a. (or $0 \cdot 7$ *sen* per 100 yen *per diem*) and is almost entirely used for surplus funds of business firms.

Time Deposits are made for fixed periods: a three months' deposit yields 4 per cent p.a.; six months yields 5 per cent p.a.; and one year yields $5 \cdot 5$ per cent p.a. The deposit may be inscribed in a pass book, in a certificate of deposit in a particular name, or in a bearer-form certificate. In the latter case the only identification of the holder is the personal seal registered with the bank. The depositor may designate a specific maturity date.

Automatic Renewal Time Deposit is a one-year account with an arrangement for automatic renewal of the principal and the interest.

Instalment Deposits are for customers who would like to have a specified sum at a specified date for such things as educational expenses, travel or furniture. Regular instalments are made and interest is paid at the rate for time deposits for the period of the instalment held by the bank.

Deposits for Tax Payments yield $2 \cdot 92$ per cent p.a. ($0 \cdot 8$ *sen* per 100 yen *per diem*), which is exempt from personal income tax and stamp duty, provided the deposit is used for tax payment only.

Bank Credit Card Service is given by some banks to the holders of one-year time deposits amounting to no less than 50,000 yen. The credit card can be used for purchases at leading department stores. This offers in some respects as good a facility as a cheque account, while the deposit funds earn $5 \cdot 5$ per cent p.a. interest.

Deposits in Foreign Currencies can be made by certain categories of persons and institutions (diplomatic missions and their personnel, insurance companies, airlines and shipping companies) on approval of the Japanese Ministry of Finance.

The preceding list of deposit facilities offered by Japanese commercial banks is much larger than in the West. Western commercial banks offer usually only two kinds of deposit facility, the cheque account (subject to fees) and the savings account usable only at the office where it is held.

Non-residents of Japan can hold three types of account:

Non-resident Free Yen Accounts. (Current Account, Ordinary Deposit, Deposit at Notice and Time Deposit.) The "Free Yen" funds are fully convertible into any currency. Deposits in this form can be made from funds transferred to Japan, from other Free Yen accounts, and from proceeds of goods imported to Japan (but not services sold in Japan).

Non-resident Yen Deposit Accounts. These funds have limited convertibility into foreign currencies, but can be used freely in Japan (except for payment into the Free Yen accounts). Monies from investments in Japan, receipts from the Japanese national and local government agencies, and monies from other Non-resident Yen Deposit Accounts may be paid into this type of account.

Non-resident Non-convertible Non-transferable Accounts. Funds which cannot be paid into the Free Yen Accounts, or even the Yen Deposit Accounts, such as monies earned in Japan, can be paid into an account at a Japanese bank for purely internal use in Japan.

BANK BORROWING FROM THE BANK OF JAPAN

Borrowing from the Bank of Japan and from the short-term money market comprises the next type of commercial bank liabilities. One of the characteristic features of Japanese commercial banking is the heavy, regular, and apparently permanent dependence of the "city banks" on loans from the Bank of Japan and from the short-term money market. In the West the central bank acts as a lender only occasionally, and as the last resort, but in Japan it acts primarily as a regular supplier of funds, though when the market is tight it will act as the last resort lender for some institutions. This permanent and heavy dependence of the city banks on the Bank of Japan is called the "over-loan" condition (but should be called "over-borrowed" condition). This condition, together with the concomitant low liquidity level of Japanese banks has existed in Japan since before the last War. Japanese general economic policies and circumstances have created a steady high level of demand for capital in the economy. The Japanese say, rightly in a way, that the capital market has been under-developed and therefore could not supply enough funds, so that the full and excessive strain fell on the commercial banks. This explanation is inadequate. Although the Japanese capital market has been under-developed, this cannot be said about the Japanese banking system for many decades past. Apart from the widespread commercial banking offices throughout the country, there are numerous widely spread co-operative banking institutions and government financial institutions with the Post Office Savings Bank system. Thus unless the savers had an extremely high liquidity preference, that is, preferred to keep their funds in tins and unless the banks made no attempt to offer them inducements to part with liquidity, the savings of the country would flow to the banks. Indeed, the more under-developed the capital market has been, the more these funds should increase.

The true explanation of the state of "overborrowing" of the commercial banks in Japan must therefore lie in a whole set of circumstances and policies which have created a level of demand for savings that has been higher than the supply of savings. In this situation the Bank of Japan and the commercial banks stepped in and provided the missing money. Such a policy would, of course, tend to have inflationary effects, but not where there are unemployed (or under-employed) resources, as has been the case in Japan until lately. The Japanese monetary policy, in fact, applied one of the Keynesian principles: saving does not have to precede investment in conditions where there is unemployment, but investment acts financed from bank-created money can precede savings. Then as the unemployed resources are used up, the required savings arise at the same rate from the newly created incomes (according to the multiplier principle to the full amount of the investment made with the newly-created money). The remarkable fact is that the Japanese introduced that policy several years before Keynes published his book, and have continued it with great success until today. Although such policy is obviously fraught with inflationary and balance of payments pressures, in Japan it has not produced very strong unfavourable by-product effects except during the War. However, in the present conditions, where an excess of labour, however defined, has disappeared, the Bank of Japan has been trying to curb this commercial bank reliance on central bank credit. Commercial bank borrowing from the Bank of Japan takes the following forms:

(a)   rediscounting of *domestic* commercial bills (commercial bills are widely used in Japan for domestic payments);

(b)   rediscounting of export trade bills;

(c)   borrowing on the security of export trade bills, government securities, and even on the security of company bonds and securities (as a rule the central banks in the West do not lend on the security of company bonds or shares);

(d)   borrowing on overdraft.

The interest rates on these types of loans in general vary according to the policy of the Bank of Japan, but they also vary for the type of loan, that is, rediscounting export trade bills is cheaper than rediscounting domestic trade bills (in order to assist exports), loans on *the security* of trade bills carry a higher rate of interest than the rediscount rates, and the interest rate on overdrafts is the highest, usually about 7 per cent per annum.

The Main Categories of Bank Assets of Japanese Commercial Banks

Loans are the largest single asset of the Japanese commercial banks. They represented 40 per cent of total assets of city and local banks at the end of 1968. Next in size are discounted bills which were 21 per cent of total assets. Then come securities, which were 13 per cent of total assets. In Japanese banking, unlike in the West, securities held by banks include not only government bonds and public corporation bonds, but also the debentures issued by other banks, industrial bonds and even ordinary shares in private industry. At the end of 1968 the following percentages of total assets of city and local banks were in the form of various securities: government and government-guaranteed bonds, 4·5%; other bank debentures, 3·2%; industrial bonds and shares, almost 5%. Japanese commercial banks also grant overdrafts, but since the War these represent only a small fraction of the total of loans.

Finally, the "city banks" hold a substantial amount of foreign exchange, as working balances only, because the bulk of national foreign exchange reserves is held by the Foreign Exchange Fund Special Account which is a government institution. It should be noted that the local banks which do not have Foreign Exchange Licence A cannot hold foreign exchange.

The Role of Commercial Banks in Japan

The Japanese commercial banks, especially the city banks, have played an outstanding role in the rapid economic growth of Japan in the post-war period. Indeed, without the vast credit expansion by these banks the great economic growth would hardly have been conceivable.

As Table 5.4 shows, between 1946 and 1968 bank advances rose 290 times. However, the banking system cannot expand credit unless it has an adequate liquidity base. The question is then: what enabled the banks to expand credit on this vast scale? The liquidity base of the banks and the "fringe banks" can be expanded by surplus in the balance of payments; by government borrowing from the Central Bank and spending the money; by the Central Bank buying assets in the domestic market; and finally by Central Bank lending to domestic institutions.

In the period under consideration the first two factors played a negligible

Table 5.3.   The Structure of Principal Interest Rates (End of 1968).

			Interest rates
Bank Rates	Discount	Commercial bills	5·84
		Export trade bills	4·015
	Secured loans	Export trade bills	4·38
		Government securities, etc.	6·205 or more
		Others	6·57 or more
Interest Rates on Deposits, etc.	Banks and mutual loans and savings banks	Ordinary deposits	2·19
		Time deposits (1 year)	5·5
	Post offices	Ordinary savings	3·6
		Time savings (1 year)	5·0
Lending Rates of Banks, etc.	Trust banks	Loan trusts (5 years)	7·27
	Standard rates of banks	Discount of commercial bills eligible for rediscount by the Bank of Japan	5·84
		Discount of and loans on commercial bills corresponding to the above in credit worthiness	
		More than 3 million yen	6·022
		3 million yen or less	6·387
	Bank loans secured by other bills or discount thereof	More than 3 million yen	7·665
		3 million yen or less	8·03
	Average interest rates on loans and discounts	All banks	7·377
		City banks	7·045
		Local banks	7·625
		Long-term credit banks	8·322
		Mutual loans and savings banks	8·457
Call Money Rates	Unconditional		7·665
Average Yields to Subscribers of Securities	Short-term Government securities		5·710
	Long-term Government bonds		6·902
	Government-guaranteed bonds		7·139
	Local Government securities		7·441
	Bank debentures (discount)		6·022
	Bank debentures (interest-bearing)		7·3
	Industrial bonds (top grade A)		7·628

Source: *The Japanese Financial System.*

Table 5.4.   Credit Creation by the Japanese Banks.

Year	A Bank Advances (other than those by Bank of Japan) *million yen*	B Bank of Japan Loans and Discounts to the banking system *million yen*	$\dfrac{B}{A}$ =%	Bank of Japan Government bonds holdings *million yen*
1946 average	118,160	49,621	42	34,700
1947　　 „	136,843	43,906	32	145,800
1948　　 „	246,159	54,238	22	247,700
1949　　 „	494,431	77,792	16	188,600
1950　　 „	820,526	123,251	15	136,700
1951　　 „	1,241,180	179,502	14	126,000
1952　　 „	1,808,130	241,134	13	286,100
1953　　 „	2,391,795	307,490	13	314,300
1954　　 „	2,830,895	365,477	13	483,500
1955 end of year	3,195,800	319,000	10	553,600
1956　　 „	4,066,100	139,900	3	586,700
1957　　 „	5,024,400	551,900	11	387,200
1958　　 „	5,812,900	379,900	6·5	536,000
1959　　 „	6,802,800	337,900	5	644,800
1960　　 „	8,182,600	500,200	6	569,100
1961　　 „	9,770,100	1,284,500	13	287,700
1962　　 „	11,494,600	1,285,100	11	378,300
1963　　 „	14,562,600	1,155,600	8	346,000
1964　　 „	16,829,700	1,110,400	7	760,900
1965　　 „	19,217,900	1,627,700	8·5	930,000
1966　　 „	22,046,000	1,741,200	8	638,100
1967　　 „	25,323,000	1,515,100	6	1,144,000
1968　　 „	29,032,800	1,563,200	5	1,434,100

Sources: *Japan Economic Yearbooks* 1955, 1963, 1964-5, 1969.
　　　　Statistics Department, The Bank of Japan, *Hundred-Year Statistics of the Japanese Economy,* 1966.
　　　　Bureau of Statistics, Office of the Prime Minister, *Monthly Statistics of Japan,* May 1969.

role in increasing the liquidity position of the financial institutions. The balance of payments was strained most of the time (until quite recently). Under the Dodge Line there were budget *surpluses,* that is the Government was in fact *repaying* old debts—it was only in 1965 that the Government started to borrow. Thus between 1948 and 1965 fiscal operations tended to reduce liquidity. Therefore, as Table 5.4 shows, the liquidity base of the Japanese financial institutions was expanded only thanks to the vast direct lending by the Bank of Japan to the commercial banks. The loans by the Bank of Japan to the financial system between 1946 and 1968 increased thirty-eight times (while the advances of the other financial institutions rose 290 times). This ratio of increases was more than adequate in view of the fact that financial institutions hold only fractional cover for their deposit liabilities, and increase their credit creation by a multiple of the increase of their liquid resources.

Purchases of securities by the Bank of Japan, which is the other way of increasing the liquidity of the financial system, did not show any clear trend until 1964. Since then, however, they have doubled.

In addition to the growth in bank advances shown in Table 5.4, the banks' purchases of company debentures, shares, and national and local government bonds were rising at a similar rate although in smaller absolute amounts, that is, from 1·9 trillion yen at the end of 1961 to 5·2 trillion yen at the end of 1967,* thus again providing additional funds mainly to the private sector. If the banks had not created that vast increase in money, the economic growth would have been choked, because foreign trade transactions could not possibly produce such surpluses, and foreign investment would have been quite unlikely on such a scale. A vast credit expansion by the banking system is, of course, nothing novel, but what is remarkable here is that in Japan it has produced all the favourable results and very few undesirable effects. In most countries that have ever tried credit expansion on a similar scale, it has produced all the undesirable effects and little economic growth. The peculiar Japanese outcome has been partly due to some Japanese institutions and substantially due to the skilful, un-doctrinaire Japanese fiscal and monetary policies and perhaps above all due to the Japanese restraint in consumption even though average consumption per person was at a low level and even though rising incomes enabled consumers to demand more goods.

At this stage it is necessary to elucidate only the process of this credit creation. The favourable investment climate has produced in Japan a large demand for investable funds. Those funds just did not exist when the development was about to start. Most of the time the Japanese entrepreneurs did not approach the capital market because it could not cope with demand of that size. The commercial banks, who create "money" in the process of lending, could have performed the task only if their liquidity had allowed it. The liquidity problem of the commercial banks was solved by two means. First, the banks consciously allowed their liquidity ratios to run down to very low levels (compared to the usual liquidity levels in the U.S.A., the United Kingdom or Australia). They did this because they were sure that in a bank liquidity crisis the Bank of Japan would provide immediate assistance. Second, the commercial banks, especially the "city banks", which were under pressure from the large-scale firms (where most of the economic growth occurred), asked the Bank of Japan for additional liquidity, and the Bank of Japan provided it *on a regular and semi-permanent basis.* (See

---

* *Japan Economic Yearbook*, 1968, p. 220.

Table 5.4). The outcome of this process has been the "over-borrowed" condition of the city banks and to a much lesser extent of the local banks, and the "over-loan" condition of the city and the local banks, which means that the ratio of loans and bills to deposits and bank debenture issues plus own capital is very high.

Table 5.5. Indicators of "Over-loaned" Position of All Banks.

End of year	Loan to deposit + debentures ratio		Ratios of liabilities[1]		(In per cent) Ratio of borrowings from the Bank of Japan[2]	
	All banks	City banks	All banks	City banks	All banks	City banks
1955	89	91	3	7	1	1
1956	92	94	6	10	3	4
1957	100	107	12	19	10	15
1958	96	101	9	14	5	9
1959	93	98	8	14	4	7
1960	93	98	8	14	5	8
1961	96	103	13	22	11	18
1962	96	105	12	22	9	16
1963	96	102	10	19	7	12
1964	96	104	12	21	5	9
1965	93	99	10	19	5	9
1966	92	97	9	17	6	10
1967	93	99	8	16	4	8
1968	91	96	7	15	4	8

Notes: 1. Ratio of liabilities

$$= \frac{\text{Borrowed money} + \text{Call money borrowed} - \text{Call money lent}}{\text{Deposits}^* + \text{Bank debentures} + \text{Borrowed money} + \text{Call money borrowed} - \text{Call money lent}} \times 100$$

2. Ratio of borrowings from the Bank of Japan

$$= \frac{\text{Borrowings from the Bank of Japan}}{\text{Deposits}^* + \text{Bank debentures} + \text{Borrowings from the Bank of Japan}} \times 100$$

*excluding cheques and bills.

Source: *The Japanese Financial System*, p. 22.

In traditional Anglo-American practice and theory, commercial banks are to concentrate on short-term credit. An old English banking adage is: "To be successful, a banker must know the difference between a bill and a mortgage." In Japan, however, commercial banks have always lent large amounts for long periods, that is, for fixed capital not only for working capital. At the end of 1966, for example, 7·6 per cent of the city banks' and 11·3 per cent of the local banks' loans were formally granted for fixed capital investment, that is for long periods. In fact it is understood that a very high proportion of *short-term* loans will be renewed, so that they are *de facto* long-term loans as well. In addition, the Japanese commercial banks provide long-term capital through large purchases of debentures. They buy about 40 per cent of the debentures issued by the Long-Term Credit Bank which lends money for fixed capital, and they purchase over 50 per cent of the bonds issued by companies.

The relative ease of obtaining bank finance and the relative difficulty of obtaining capital from stock exchanges has led to the extremely "high-geared" capital composition of the typical Japanese company, in other words to its excessive reliance on short-term liabilities. The Japanese companies find borrowing from banks both cheaper and more convenient than obtaining capital through bond or share issue. According to the Social and Economic Development Plan 1967-1971 the average equity capital ratio for Japanese industry is only 20 per cent.* This "over-borrowed" condition at the commercial bank and company levels is often deplored in Japan—the Social and Economic Development Plan 1967-1971 repeatedly brands it as undesirable.† Yet it is over-looked that it is this very "over-borrowed" condition of the commercial banks and business firms that renders the Japanese monetary control so extraordinarily effective. Of course, it would be possible to reduce commercial bank dependence on loans from the Bank of Japan and companies' dependence on commercial bank credit, and still maintain the efficacy of monetary control. However, it should be mentioned that in recent years the underlying economic conditions have changed.

In the present, altered, circumstances the case for the Bank of Japan supplying liquidity to trading banks so generously as in the past is not so strong. Unemployed labor has been absorbed. From now on the orthodox principle—for every act of investment there must be a prior act of saving—holds with one qualification only. The total creation of the volume of money, apart from offsetting the changes in its velocity of circulation, must not exceed the increases in the output due to increases in the number of workers and productivity. Since productivity increases have recently been over 12 per cent p.a., and the labor force has increased 1 per cent p.a., an annual increase of 13 per cent in the volume of money would be justified. However, this would keep the economy very tight-stretched.

Foreign Exchange Banking Business

In Japan foreign exchange banking is concentrated in:
(a) the specialised foreign exchange bank, that is, the Bank of Tokyo;
(b) the authorised Foreign Exchange Banks Class A (all the city banks except the Kyowa Bank and the Hokkaido-Takushoku Bank);
(c) the Authorised Foreign Exchange Banks Class B—in this category

* *Money and Banking in Japan*, p. 89.
† For example, see pp. 50-55.

belong fifty-five of the other banks: two city banks without A licences, two long-term banks without A licences, certain local banks and all trust banks.

(d) Tokyo branches of foreign banks (Class A licences). There are sixteen of them with over forty branches.

The Bank of Tokyo was established under the Foreign Exchange Bank Act of 1954 as a joint stock bank specialising in foreign exchange. (It inherited the tradition and the personnel of the old Yokohama Specie Bank which also specialised in foreign exchange business.) It has twenty-eight branches in the main centres of Japan and a large number of offices all over the world, about fifty of its own offices and many affiliates. The Bank of Tokyo performs all normal banking activities, but its main business is related to financing international trade. The numerous branches both at home and abroad give it supreme advantages in carrying out international transactions. Some Japanese commercial banks which could perform their own foreign transactions avail themselves of the facilities of the Bank of Tokyo. As a result it handles the largest proportion of the foreign exchange business of Japan. In addition it acts for the Japanese Government in handling foreign bond issues, payments of war reparations and economic aid.

In 1962 the Foreign Exchange Bank Act was amended to allow the specialised foreign exchange bank to issue debentures (in Japan) as a means of increasing its yen funds.

Foreign Exchange Authorised Banks Class A are allowed to conclude "correspondent bank" contracts with foreign banks, open accounts with foreign banks and hold foreign currencies needed for foreign exchange operations, open and receive letters of credit, buy export bills, settle import bills, handle bills for collection, buy and sell "spot" and "forward" foreign currencies. They are required, however, to hold a certain fixed percentage of specific foreign currency liabilities in the form of liquid foreign currency assets as minimum reserves.

Class B banks as a rule are not permitted to make any business arrangements with foreign banks, but have to use the facilities of Class A banks. In 1966, however, three Class B banks were authorised to conclude correspondent contracts with a limited number of foreign banks.

Foreign Exchange Markets

At present there are two foreign exchange markets in Japan, the main one in Tokyo, and a small one in Osaka. The holders of foreign exchange are confined to:

(a) The Government through the *Foreign Exchange Fund Special Account* (where the bulk of international currency reserves of Japan is held).

(b) Bank of Japan.
(c) The authorised foreign exchange banks.
(d) Exceptionally, the "general trading companies", insurance companies, shipping companies, and certain other companies engaged in international transactions may hold foreign exchange, subject to permission by the Minister of Finance.

Individuals and firms not falling under one of the preceding categories must sell foreign exchange to foreign exchange banks within ten days of acquisition. Foreign exchange banks hold only as much foreign exchange as they need for their business and sell the balance to the Foreign Exchange Fund Special Account.

Under the Foreign Trade and Foreign Exchange Control Act, Japanese banks can accept payments from abroad only in the "receivable currencies", as designated by the Minister of Finance. At present the designated "receivable currencies" are: U.S. dollar, pound sterling, Canadian dollar, Swiss franc, West German mark, Swedish krona, French franc, Dutch guilder, Belgian franc, Italian lira, Austrian schilling, Danish krone, Portuguese escudo, Australian dollar and Japanese yen. But the Foreign Exchange Fund Special Account can hold only gold, U.S. dollars and pounds sterling as "reserve currencies" (the Japanese call them "the currencies to be concentrated"). The Foreign Exchange Special Account buys and sells these two reserve currencies without limitation at the request of the exchange banks at the specified rates of exchange (which are called "the Minister of Finance concentration rates"). Foreign exchange banks buy and sell foreign currencies at the request of their customers, and also on their own to correct their over-bought, or over-sold positions. In the case of the two reserve currencies ("concentration currencies") the corrective transactions can be carried out between the exchange banks themselves or with the Foreign Exchange Special Account. But in the case of the other "receivable" but not "concentration" currencies the adjustments of the exchange positions if not effected in the domestic market cannot be effected through the Foreign Exchange Special Account. However, since those "non-concentration", "receivable" currencies are freely convertible into U.S. dollars or pounds sterling *in foreign markets*, the exchange banks can convert these currencies into the "concentration currencies" and then adjust their position by a sale to the Foreign Exchange Special Account.

The value of the yen is fixed under the I.M.F. arrangements at 360 yen = 1 US\$. (The rate on 1 April 1970.) The Japanese Foreign Exchange Special Account is always ready to sell "spot" U.S. dollars when they reach a level $0 \cdot 75$ per cent above parity, and buy them when they fall $0 \cdot 75$ per cent below parity. This facility sets the upper and the lower limits to the fluctuations of the external value of the yen (like the gold export and the gold import points did under the old Gold Standard). In fact, however, usually the inter-bank spot rates fluctuate well within those limits.

Government Control Over Banks
and the Trend Towards "Liberalisation"

Government controls over the financial institutions are effected through the rules of the Bank Act and other specific Acts, and through administrative guidance.

Setting up or closing down a bank, opening a branch, change in its capital, merger, and holding of an outside position by a bank officer all require the approval of the Minister of Finance. Further, if a bank has committed an illegal act or if there is deterioration of the bank's position which would threaten the depositors' interests, the Minister of Finance may give the bank any orders he considers necessary.

The "administrative guidance" is otherwise merely advice, and essentially aims at the protection of depositors and restriction of competition between the strong and the weak institutions. For this protective purpose the Director of the Banking Bureau of the Ministry of Finance fixes the minimum or maximum ratios, such as the ratio of current expenses to current income (maximum), the ratio of the total of loans to deposits (maximum 80 per cent), the ratio of quick assets to deposits, and so on. Contrary to the opinions usually held by foreigners with some Japanese experience about the power of "administrative guidance", the banks often do not observe those ratios; for example, the ratio of loans to deposits has been *persistently* held above the recommended maximum of 80 per cent. The government has not applied any sanctions, indeed the Bank of Japan has equally persistently aided and abetted the banks in their behaviour by lending money to them.

The structure and operation of the Japanese financial system are undergoing an examination by the Monetary System Research Council set up by the Ministry of Finance. This Council is examining the "administrative guidance" and other controls of the financial system. It is also examining the trend to mergers of various financial institutions, as well as changes in their character. In particular there is the important issue whether the commercial banks should be formally allowed to encroach on the field of business which has so far been largely reserved for the long-term banks. At present there are two main distinctions between these banks. The commercial banks are not allowed to accept deposits for a longer basis than one year, whereas the long-term banks issue debentures (with a limited life, five years for example). The commercial banks would like to be able to accept deposits from the public for two to three years. They would be able to offer higher interest rates on them and thus attract some of the funds now going into the bank debentures of the long-term banks. In addition, the commercial banks would like to be able to issue "certificates of deposits", which would also compete with debenture issues by the long-term banks. These changes would be serious for the long-term banks because the commercial banks have a far larger network of branches and if put on equal deposit-collection footing would gain superiority.

The other difference between the two sets of institutions is that the commercial banks nominally at least cannot lend for long terms, whereas long-term banks, and "trust and banking corporations" do lend long-term. In fact, of course, the commercial banks do lend for long-term. As the Monetary System Research Council reported, 24 per cent of the total loans given in 1968 by the commercial banks were in fact for terms longer than one year through the device of extending short-term loans.* The commercial banks want to have this practice legitimised and extended. Further attacking the preserves of the long-term banks, they argue that all "indirect financing" (that is, financing other than through the Stock Exchanges) should be only for about three years and any longer-term financing should come from "direct financing" from the Stock Exchanges. The commercial banks are motivated by the fact that they have been losing their former share of the banking business.

The long-term banks oppose any change and argue that the commercial banks should be confined to their traditional functions and that the long-term banks efficiently perform the task of collecting savings and supplying long-term capital, in some areas at least more efficiently than the Stock Exchanges would.

In the Japanese financial system in general there is a trend towards liberalisation of the rather extensive system of Ministry of Finance controls. Until recently the Ministry of Finance restricted competition among financial institutions in order to assist the weaker elements. Thus it controls the setting up of branches, sets the maxima for interest rates and dividends, and so forth. At present the Ministry of Finance is relaxing its controls to allow greater competition and the survival of the fittest.

This trend has exposed the weaker and smaller financial institutions. Generally, those banks whose main customers are large enterprises have been doing better because the large enterprises have produced the mainstream of economic growth and high profits. The banks associated with smaller enterprises have fared less well, and probably the quality of their management has gradually slipped.

These trends will produce mergers—some have already occurred such

* *Japan Economic Yearbook*, 1969, p. 43.

as the new fourteenth city bank called the Taiyo Bank which arose out of a merger in 1968.

Financial Institutions for Small Enterprises

Small enterprises in Japan have many peculiar problems and difficulties (see Chapter 7). In particular their capital equipment is inadequate, and access to capital is very difficult. For these reasons the government has created a number of governmental financial institutions (see Chapter 2) and has encouraged the establishment of private enterprise financial institutions solely for supplying credit to small enterprises.

The usual definition of a small enterprise in Japan is one employing less than 300 workers. About half the loans to small enterprises comes from the "commercial banks" and half* comes from specialised institutions such as the mutual loan and savings banks, credit associations and credit co-operatives, and, of course, the government-owned Small Business Finance Corporation and the People's Finance Corporation.

MUTUAL LOAN AND SAVINGS BANKS

There are seventy-one mutual loan and savings banks in Japan and they have about 2,569 offices. Some of the larger banks are similar in size to the city banks. They are established under the Mutual Loan and Savings Bank Act of 1951, but their origin is in an indigenous institution called *mujin* (savings—instalment loans). The essence of *mujin* business is similar to that of the building societies in the West. The customer (member) agrees to pay a fixed sum regularly for a stated period. During that period he can qualify for a loan (bigger than his instalments) by drawing lots or by bidding for a loan. There is also a variety of pseudo-*mujin* where no money pool is organised, no drawing or bidding is used, and where the management by its own decision grants a loan on application after a certain number of instalments has been paid.

The mutual loan and savings banks in addition do most of the normal commercial banking business, except foreign exchange business. They are, however, under the following special legal restraints: they can open branches only in their region so that the funds collected are employed in that same region; they are not allowed to lend any customer more than 10 per cent of his capital and reserves, or 30 million yen, whichever is lower; and like the commercial banks, they must maintain a minimum Statutory Deposit with the Bank of Japan.

CREDIT ASSOCIATIONS

Credit associations appeared in the Meiji period but their present form was influenced by two Acts of Diet. The Act for Co-operatives and

* *Money and Banking in Japan*, p. 150.

Small Businesses of 1949 was intended to organise all kinds of small *business* activity in co-operatives. Some of the co-operatives that grew out of it were purely *financial* institutions, which in addition to dealing with members, accepted deposits from outsiders. Consequently there arose the problem of regulating the new credit co-operatives to protect the outsider depositors. This led to the 1951 Credit Association Act.

Credit associations are non-profit financial co-operative organisations who perform business similar to that of commercial banks except that they are to finance co-operative or individual-owned small enterprises. The Act imposes some restraints in that they can lend only in their locality, and only to members (except that they can lend local authorities and other financial institutions up to 15% of the total of loans to members plus deposit-secured loans). They may accept deposits from members and non-members. The maximum interest that they can pay on deposits is $0 \cdot 1$ per cent higher than the maximum for banks. They must maintain a minimum reserve (for safety of depositors) of $1 \cdot 8$ times the sum of the total of 10 per cent of their time deposit liabilities, and 20 per cent of their other deposit liabilities, in the form of: cash, deposits with other financial institutions, call loans, government-guaranteed bonds, bank debentures and other financial assets. Finally, they must not lend to any one member more than 20 per cent of his own capital, or 30 million yen, whichever is the lower.

At present there are about 520 of these credit associations. Membership is confined to small businesses (less than 300 employees) or persons residing or working in the locality. Almost all members are business proprietors. The credit associations are growing very rapidly.

The Credit Associations Act of 1951 allowed voluntary establishment of federations of credit associations. In fact there is only one such institution called The National Federation of Credit Associations. Its function is to improve the efficiency in the use of funds available to individual credit associations where regional surpluses or regional deficits arise. The Federation accepts deposits from its members (the individual credit associations), the national and local governments and some non-profit institutions. In addition, it receives surplus funds of credit associations as "short-term funds".

CREDIT CO-OPERATIVES

These are those old credit co-operatives established in 1949 under the general Act for Co-operatives of Small Businesses, that in 1951 chose not to avail themselves of a somewhat wider franchise under the specific 1951 Credit Associations Act, and the numerous subsequently established credit co-operatives. Their main difference from the "credit associations" is that they cannot accept deposits from non-members (except for the relatives of members). Credit co-operatives make loans and discount bills for members. In 1954 the credit co-operatives formed the National Federation of Credit Co-operatives, whose function is similar to the National Federation of Credit Associations.

Credit co-operatives, like credit associations, have experienced a very rapid growth, faster than that of the banks.

THE CENTRAL BANK FOR COMMERCIAL AND INDUSTRIAL CO-OPERATIVES

This is not a central bank in any accepted sense, but solely a bank for co-operatives, and industrial and commercial associations. It has about 15,000 member organisations. It was first established in 1936 and reconstituted after the War. More than a half of its capital has been provided by the government, which has empowered it to issue debentures which are its main source of funds. Debentures can be issued up to twenty times the bank's capital and reserves. The bank accepts deposits from member associations and the constituent members of the associations and can lend to those bodies. It is subject to much more control by the government than any other bank, but the government provides, together with bond subscriptions, about a quarter of its funds. The bank charges over 9 per cent p.a. interest on loans. This high interest reflects the general high price of credit in Japan.

DEVICES TO IMPROVE THE CREDIT STANDING OF SMALL BUSINESSES

There are fifty-one Credit Guarantee Associations in Japan. They are usually organised by local authorities with membership from various banks and other financial institutions. These associations guarantee the repayment of loans to small enterprises and make the payment in case of default. Funds for that purpose are obtained from grants by local authorities and grants and loans from the Small Business Credit Insurance Corporation. They operate under the Credit Guarantee Association Act of 1953.

The Small Business Credit Insurance Corporation was established by an Act of Diet in 1958, which converted the former Small Business Credit Insurance Special Account, a government office, into a corporation. The capital of the Corporation is supplied by the government. Its function is to give an automatic risk insurance to any credit guarantee association. If a small business borrower defaulted on a loan guaranteed by a credit guarantee association the association pays the debt and then the Small Business Credit Insurance Corporation refunds 70 per cent of the money to the credit guarantee association. This is intended to give credit guarantee associations an incentive to give guarantees on the loans to small enterprises, but also to induce some care in the choice of loans to be guaranteed. At the end of 1962 the paid-up capital of the Small Business Credit Insurance Corporation was

19·4 billion yen, of which 8·1 billion yen was for insurance purposes, and 11·3 billion yen for loans to the needy credit guarantee associations.

Financial Institutions for Agriculture, Forestry and Fisheries

Financing agriculture, forestry and fisheries is a difficult task in all countries. Ordinary banks do not like to lend to those industries for numerous reasons such as their low profitability (in countries like Japan), high risks, bankers' lack of familiarity with the industry, small size of an average loan, lack of a satisfactory (reasonably liquid) collateral security and difficulty for the banker in overseeing such activities. Before the War the Hypothec Bank of Japan lent partly to agricultural, forestry and fishery industries. After the War the Hypothec Bank shifted its activities to small industrial and commercial activities. Then the provision of credit for agriculture, forestry and fisheries was taken over by co-operatives. Each of these three industries has *multi-purpose* co-operatives at the village or town level, credit federations of the co-operatives at the prefecture level, and at the top the single Central Co-operative Bank of Agriculture and Forestry.

In addition, the government-owned Agriculture, Forestry and Fisheries Finance Corporation lends a good deal of money to those industries and looms large as a supplier of credit in forestry. The commercial banks and the other ordinary financial institutions also lend to these industries and they are important in fisheries and forestry (both relatively small borrowers) while they hold a very small share of loans to agriculture, which is relatively a big borrower.

Producer co-operatives are widely spread in Japan. Every village and town has at least one agricultural co-operative. The co-operative performs many tasks, such as buying, selling, mutual assistance, collecting deposits and instalment savings from its members and lending money to members. However, the *forestry* co-operatives do not collect deposits and their loans are only agency service, handling the loans from the Agriculture, Forestry and Fisheries Finance Corporation.

The Central Co-operative Bank of Agriculture and Forestry arose in 1943 out of the former Central Bank for Industrial Co-operatives. It has 26 branches all over the country and it is comparable *in size* to a "city bank". It collects deposits from member organisations and also from affiliated organisations and municipalities. In addition, like the long-term banks, it issues bank debentures, interest-bearing and discount debentures. The Bank lends primarily to member bodies but with the approval of the Minister of Agriculture, Forestry and Fisheries it can make loans (usually short-term) to outsiders. Interest charges vary according to the borrower and the duration of the loan.

Consumer Credit

Consumer credit is still not well developed in Japan (and this in part explains the high propensity to save), but it has been developing in the 1960s (See Table 5.6). Broadly speaking, consumer credit falls into four categories: a *charge account* where credit is given by the retailer; *instalment purchase*, with credit given either by retailer or by a third party, a financier; *consumer loans*, where credit is given by a third party, a bank; and the *credit card* system.

Charge accounts and instalment purchases are not common in Japanese department stores or large shops, though small shopkeepers give credit. Consumer loans by banks were started in Japan in 1964, and are not yet widely available. As of 1967 only 9 per cent of Tokyo families had ever used consumer loans.*

Table 5.6. Consumer Credit in Japan
Outstanding balances, in million yen

End of	Instalment Consumer Credit granted by:		Non-instalment Consumer Credit	Total
	Financial institutions	Producers or dealers		
1955	0	38,600	75,700	114,300
1956	0	54,800	83,400	138,200
1957	0	72,900	83,100	156,000
1958	100	86,200	87,200	173,500
1959	100	94,000	87,700	181,800
1960	200	120,000	104,600	224,800
1961	500	160,600	114,300	275,400
1962	800	204,500	126,000	331,800
1963	11,900	279,200	140,700	431,800
1964	32,500	347,100	151,000	530,600
1965	35,600	455,500		
1966	43,900	508,000		
1967	65,900	591,000		

Sources: a) *Kinyu Journal*, November 1968, p. 37.
      b) E.P.A. *Statistical Data for Hire Purchase*, Industry Bureau, Kigyo Kyoku, M.I.T.I., May 1969.

Table 5.6 shows a fairly rapid growth of various forms of consumer credit in nominal terms in the 1960s in Japan. However it should be noted that it was a growth from a very low base. Personal loans by financial institutions for consumption purposes began in a rather nominal way in 1958 (total U.S.$277,778) and increased to $183 million in 1967, which is still very small as it does not amount to two dollars *per caput*. Similarly, total consumer credit (personal loans plus hire

* Koichi Tanouchi, "The Credit Card System in Japan", *Hitotsubashi Journal of Commerce and Management*, April 1968.

purchase) started to grow from a low base in 1950s and when one allows for the fall in the value of money (and a rise in incomes) it has shown only a moderate growth rising fourfold in money terms from U.S.$317 million in 1955 to U.S.$1,473 million in 1964.

Table 5.7. Hire-purchase Sales of Various Goods as Percentage of Total Sales in 1967.

Commodity	Number of Stores (Firms) involved	Hire purchase transactions (mil. yen) A	Total of retail sales (mil. yen) B	$\frac{(A)}{(B)}$ %
Total	95	89,396	178,102	45·1
Sewing Machines	46	29,708	52,517	56·6
Manual Knitting Machines	46	11,322	14,190	79·8
Electric Home Appliances	45	21,811	78,036	27·9
Beds	16	11,820	12,359	95·6
Furniture	6	15	1,457	1·0
Musical Instruments	13	5,103	14,056	36·3
Bedclothes	8	1,859	3,410	54·5
Watches and Jewellery	3	148	1,711	8·6
Other	33	7,609	20,367	37·4

Source: Firms Section, *A Survey on Hire Purchase in the Registered Stores*. ("Toroku Warihu Hambai Gyosha Zittai Hokoku") September 1968, p. 15.

As Table 5.7 shows, by 1967 the dependence of consumer durables sales on hire-purchase had become very high. The reader may be puzzled by the very high degree of hire-purchase financing in Japan of sales of beds, manual knitting machines, and even bedclothes. The explanation is that those goods are purchased mainly by the lower socio-economic groups. This is obvious in the case of, say, manual knitting machines or even sewing machines. The case of beds looks at first most peculiar. In Japan one might think Western beds would be a luxury, as the Japanese normally sleep on "the floor", or rather on special *tatami* mats. However, *tatami* mats can be used only in homes with wooden floors. Many people in lower income groups are now housed in municipal-owned flats made entirely of concrete and in those circumstances beds are a necessity. Bedclothes, together with the other goods just mentioned, are the typical wedding gifts from the relatives among the lower income groups. Those relatives usually purchase the gifts on hire-purchase. Hire-purchase is common only among the working class; among higher social classes it carries a stigma.

The new device, likely to lead in future to a cashless society, is the *credit card*. This system combines the advantages of a cheque and automatic very short-term credit (till the next month's salary comes).

Under this system on presentation of his membership card the consumer obtains automatic credit from all the retailers associated with the particular credit card company, without any check on his credit-worthiness when he is making his purchases.

The credit card system in Japan is only at the beginning of its growth. It began only in 1960 and now a large proportion of shops in large cities carry the plaques of various credit card companies. In 1969 there were eight credit card companies in Japan (and one about to appear):

(a) *The Japan Diners' Club*, established in 1960, capital US$278,000.

(b) *The Japan Credit Bureau*, established in 1961, capital $US583,000.

(c) *Osaka Credit Bureau*, a small local organisation.

(d) *Himawari*, a small organisation.

(e) *Diamond Credit*, established by Mitsubishi Bank in 1967, capital US$277,778.

(f) *Sumitomo Credit Card Service*, established by Sumitomo Bank in 1967, capital US$277,778.

(g) *The Million Card Service*, established by Tokai Bank in 1968, capital US$277,778.

(h) *Hokkaido Credit Bureau*, established in 1968.

(i) In 1969 six large commercial banks: Fuji, Mitsubishi, Dai-Ichi, Nippon Kangyo, Taiyo and Saitama, planned to establish a new credit card company.

Apart from general world-wide factors, such as greater convenience for the growing numbers of middle class consumers and for the retailers, and the competitive element of attracting business, there have been some special local factors leading to the introduction of the credit card system in Japan.

The immediate, though not fundamental motive for founding the credit card system was the aim by the Japan Travel Bureau (the largest private tourist agency in Japan) to assist foreign visitors to the 1964 Tokyo Olympic Games and to encourage them to travel in Japan by making it easier. The Japan Travel Bureau was joined by the Fuji Bank and the American Diners' Club.

The need for a device such as a credit card has been great in Japan because personal cheque use is very rare and very few individuals have cheque accounts, but many have savings accounts, especially at the Post Office Savings Bank. In the earlier post-war years when the banks' lending powers were overtaxed, the banks did not try to attract personal or consumer loan business, but now the situation is changing and the city banks, which are losing their share of the financial market to the "fringe banks", are entering the race in a new form. In this way they get a footing in a new and growing business, and they also familiarise the general public with the facilities and use of the commercial banks, so that some of the credit card company members may become customers of the sponsoring bank. This effect would arise from the fact that the accumulated credit card amounts are settled through the bank.

One month after the establishment of the Japan Diners' Club, the Sanwa Bank was joined by Nihon Shimpan (the biggest consumer finance company in Japan) in the establishment of the Japan Credit Bureau. Nihon Shimpan itself was founded in 1951 to lend to consumers who could not pay cash, but as the prosperity of Japan grew and more and more consumers were able to pay cash, it decided to enter the new and promising "infant industry". As the customers of Nihon Shimpan have always been from the lower income class and a lower sociological group (the higher social groups were too class-conscious to use such an organisation), the management of Nihon Shimpan wanted to reach the middle class through the credit card system. Similarly, the Osaka Credit Bureau was later founded by the Sanwa Bank and the Osaka Shimpan.

At the beginning of 1968 there were about 110,000 credit card holders in Japan (Japan Diners' Club 26,000, Japan Credit Bureau 40,000, Osaka Credit Bureau 35,000, and Himawari 8,000).* The growth in the popularity of the credit card system has been so fast that towards the end of the same year, that is, by 7 October, the number of card holders with Japan Credit Bureau alone was 300 per cent higher than the total of the credit card holders with all the credit card companies at the beginning of the year. By 7 October 1968 the six largest credit card companies had 775,000 card holders, which means that in less than one year the growth in the number of the credit card holders with all credit card companies must have been well over 700 per cent.

Table 5.8.   Membership of Six Largest Credit Card Companies as of 7 October 1968.

	The Japan Diners' Club	Japan Credit Bureau	Diamond Credit	Sumitomo Credit Card Service	The Million Credit Card Service	The Hokkaido Credit Bureau
Card holders	60,000	350,000	150,000	100,000	100,000	15,000
Retailers	6,000	25,000	11,000	8,000	16,000	1,000

Source: *Kinyu Journal*, November 1968, p. 41.

The main obstacle to further development of the credit card system in Japan is the lack of a universal credit-worthiness intelligence system such as exists in U.S.A. or Australia. The particular credit card company must do its own research and assessments, and that is both expensive and unsatisfactory. As a result the Japanese credit institutions

* Tanouchi.

tend to use the social status of the applicant rather than any past-debt-repayment record.

Table 5.9.   The Japanese Criteria for Assessing Credit-Worthiness of Individuals.

I Class	II Class	III Class	IV Class
Executives of Companies listed on the Stock Exchange	Senior Managers of Companies listed on the Stock Exchange	Junior Managers of Companies listed on the Stock Exchange	Workers of at least ten years seniority in big business.
Top Govt. officers	Presidents of medium-sized companies	Senior Managers of medium-sized companies	
University Professors	Lawyers	Presidents of small companies	
Chartered Public Accountants	Doctors	Teachers	
	Top-flight actors and actresses		

Source: Tanouchi.

How does the Japanese credit card system work?

An individual applies to a credit card company to become a member. If his credit-worthiness is good according to the criteria in Table 5.9 he obtains a credit card which will be honoured by retailers who are members of the credit card company. To become a member of the credit card company system and display the card credit company's sign-board, a retail business has to pay the credit card company a membership fee (J.C.B. 50,000 yen; J.D.C. 51,000 yen); the Japan Diners' Club requires in addition a deposit of 50,000 yen as an entry fee. Both the credit card companies require the retailer to pay a service charge which varies between 4-10 per cent of the value of sale according to the credit card company, and according to the nature of the retailer's business (night-clubs, bars, inns and similar businesses pay at the top level). In the case of department store sales to foreigners under the credit card system, the store has to pay a slightly higher service charge.

At the beginning of 1968 the Japan Credit Bureau had about 3,300 retailers on its member list, but by 7 October had increased the number to 25,000 retailers, and Japan Diners' Club has had a growth from 2,500 to 6,000 retailers in the same period. The more retailers the credit card company has on its membership list, the more money it is likely to obtain from its charges and the more attractive the service will be to the potential and the actual holders of the credit cards.

The consumer who holds a credit card obtains goods or services by presenting the card and signing the invoice or bill. The retailer sends a copy of the signed bill to the credit card company which totals the various bills received between the fifteenth of the previous month and the current month and automatically instructs the bank to pay the total amount on the signed invoices minus the service charge into the account of the retailer. Payments are made at the end of the current month and on the fifteenth of the next month in the case of J.D.C. and on the tenth of the following month at J.C.B. The credit card company then asks the credit card holder to pay the total value of the outstanding invoices into his account at the bank by the ninth of the following month, and the money will be drawn upon on the tenth. If the money due is not paid by the ninth the credit company automatically charges interest on it. It is easy to see that the system has advantages to all parties involved. The credit card company obtains profits. The bank induces the public to become bank customers. The retailer increases his sales. The consumer has the safety and convenience of a cashless system plus, in fact, credit for a period of twenty-two to twenty-five days (depending on when the purchase is made relatively to the settlement days).

The Call-loan Market

The call-loan markets have evolved to allow financial institutions to adjust their liquidity positions. The financial institutions in their operations face a conflict of desire for liquidity and desire for profit. Subject to statutory or conventional liquidity requirements or sudden changes in their cash position, the financial institutions have evolved a fine art of liquidity adjustments, and the call-loan market is the instrument of quick adjustment. The institutions that have temporary excess cash lend it (directly or indirectly) to the institutions that are temporarily short of cash. In Japan there are six kinds of call loans:

Half-day loans. Morning loans are repaid at the time of bank Clearing Settlement (1.00 p.m. Monday to Friday, 11.30 a.m. Saturday) and afternoon loans are repaid at the close of the business.

Overnight loans. These are repaid the next day before the Clearing Settlement.

Unconditionals. These are made for two days in the first instance, but are then repayable on one day's notice.

Undecideds are "unconditionals" which may be recalled by the lender the next day if he is in need.

The term loans are for a fixed period of a week or more.

The over-the-month loans are recallable after the second day of the following month.

Call-loans are given against collateral security. From the time of the Dodge Report until 1965, the Japanese Government did not issue bonds. As a result other "securities" including all "commercial paper" came to be used as collateral.

On theoretical grounds one would generally expect short-term rates of interest (especially those on call-loans) to be very low because the capital risks or interest rate risks due to a possible change in the market interest rates are very low in such short periods. In fact, owing to the persistent "over-loan condition" of the city banks, the call-money rates are usually high and are liable to be even higher than the Bank of Japan Discount Rate when "window control" is introduced. When the Bank of Japan announced its "window controls" on 21 June 1968, this was followed in three days by an increase in the call-market rates: the "unconditionals" went up by one *rin per diem* (0·365 p.a.) to 8·395 per cent p.a., and the "overnights" went up to 8·03 per cent p.a., while the Bank of Japan discount rate was 6·205 per cent p.a. (Note that not all "securities" are available for discounting at the Bank of Japan, but all are acceptable as collateral in the call-loan market.)

The Federation of Bankers' Associations of Japan fixes the maximum interest rate on call-loans. The supply of and the demand for call-loans change during the day as a result of Bank Clearing Settlements and the Remittance Clearing Settlements. They also vary during the month when the monthly tax payments are made or wage payments are made. During a financial squeeze the demand for call-loans increases. Those would-be borrowers who must obtain cash and cannot find it in the call-market

Table 5.10. *Average Amounts Lent and Borrowed by Various Institutions in the Japanese Call-Money Market (December, 1968).*

Institutions	Billion yen Lent	Billion yen Borrowed
City banks	1	988
Local banks	206	20
Trust banks	198	28
Mutual loans and savings banks, credit associations, The National Federation of Credit Associations	215	182
The Central Co-operative Bank of Agriculture and Forestry, credit federations of agricultural co-operatives	305	
Others	237	
Total	1,162	1,218

Source: *The Japanese Financial System,* p. 59.

have to go to the Bank of Japan. In the prolonged bank "over-loan" conditions, city banks have been persistently borrowing vast sums of money in the call-market, provided mainly by the local banks, trust banks, and mutual loan and savings banks. (See Table 5.10).

There are six companies authorised by the Minister of Finance to deal in the call-loan market. They accommodate the needs of those financial institutions that have temporary cash surpluses and those who have temporary deficits. (Sometimes, however, the lenders deal directly with the borrowers.) Briefly, the call-loan market consists of the would-be very short-term lenders and would-be very short-term borrowers, and the intermediaries, the call-loan dealers. The call-loan dealers operate under direct control of the Minister of Finance. They perform the following business operations:

Call-loan transactions. Before the War the call-loan dealers were mere go-between agents for the lenders and borrowers, but they are now dealers in their own right.

Discounting bills of exchange. The bill market is very small because Japanese banks do not like to part with their bills (which would reveal the nature of their dealings with various firms). Call-loan dealers invest a minute proportion of their funds in discounting bills.

Purchase and sale of government bonds. This is also a minor function for call-loan dealers but it is growing.

Some of the call-loan dealers also deal in foreign exchange.

The nature, and the relative importance, of the operations of the call-loan dealers is revealed by their balance sheet. (Table 5.11.)

As can be seen from the liabilities side of the above collective balance sheet, the capital structure of the call-loan dealers is "highly geared",

Table 5.11. *Assets and Liabilities of the Six Call-Loan Dealers*
(end of 1969)

Assets			Liabilities		
	Million yen	% of total		Million yen	% of total
Call-loans	1,499,607	84·0	Call-money	1,546,405	86·7
Cash and deposits with other institutions	437	—	Borrowed money for longer periods than "at call"	123,030	6·9
Securities	180,413	10·1	Own capital	442	—
Other	104,132	5·9	Other	114,712	6·4
Total	1,784,589	100·0	Total	1,784,589	100·0

Source: By courtesy of the Economic Research Department, Bank of Japan.

their own capital represents a minute proportion of their working funds. However, at their back stands the Bank of Japan, which will discount their bills and lend on collateral.

As has been seen in this chapter and will be seen in the next one, the Japanese banking system is possibly the best developed in the world, from almost any point of view—the variety of banking institutions, the variety of bank deposits and bank services, the country-wide spread of branches of financial institutions, and so on. This factor no doubt contributed to effective mobilisation of spare cash of the country to serve as a basis for credit creation and capital formation. The widespread existence of financial institution branches also tends to increase savings and that is important under any monetary standard as long as there is full employment. In addition, the well developed financial system assisted capital formation by making credit easily accessible.

One of the consequences of this high development of the Japanese banking system has probably been a discouragement of the capital market, in particular the Stock Exchange. The result is the prevalence of "indirect" over "direct" financing. Has this factor assisted or hindered the economic development of Japan? Clearly in general the answer depends on the relative economic quality of the decisions made by the bankers when lending or refusing money, and on the quality of the decisions of the private would-be shareholders who would have been buying shares (supplying capital) or refusing to buy shares in particular enterprises under the alternative system of direct financing. The answer to this question differs according to the particular circumstances of the country concerned. In many English-speaking countries, future bank managers are recruited from the high-school leavers who are "good at figures" and who have a good testimonial from a few ministers of religion. Although these men undoubtedly have their qualities there is no reason to think that they are economically more sophisticated, especially in wider issues, than the average would-be investor. In Japan, however, the bank managers or the decision-making personnel invariably have university degrees. This fact, together with the bankers' normal practical experience, would probably make their decisions on allocation of funds to the claimants superior to the decisions of the average investor. Thus it is probable that the prevalence of "indirect financing", which is often deprecated in Japan, has performed a good service for the country.

CHAPTER SIX

The Capital Market

The capital market in Japan consists of long-term credit banks, trust banks, the insurance companies, and the securities market.

Long-term Credit Banks

There are at present three long-term credit banks in Japan: the Industrial Bank of Japan, the Long-Term Credit Bank, and the Hypothec Bank of Japan. The Hypothec Bank of Japan was originally an agricultural mortgage bank, but is now an industrial long-term credit bank. All three are banks which raise most of their capital by issue of debentures (up to twenty times their total capital and reserves, whereas other companies can issue bonds only up to the value of capital and reserves). These debentures are issued in two forms, five-year interest-bearing bonds (over 7 per cent p.a.), and one-year "discount debentures", where the yield comes in the form of capital gain instead of interest rate (equivalent to over 6 per cent p.a.). The long-term banks also collect deposits from their borrower-customers, the national and local government and the companies for which they have floated bonds, but not from the general public and business community at large.

The long-term banks lend their available funds for long terms, that is, for fixed capital and long-term working funds. They also can supply short-term working capital but only within the limits of their deposits. They lend for housing and other consumer durables against the collateral of real property. The Industrial Bank lends mainly to big business and deals in foreign currencies (Class A Foreign Exchange Bank) and assists in Japanese investment abroad. The Long-Term Credit Bank lends to large firms but it cannot act on its own in foreign exchange business (Class B Licence in foreign exchange dealings). The Hypothec Bank lends mainly to medium and small enterprises.

Long-term credit banks play an important role as trustees for flotation of company bonds, and provide several services in that field.

The *relative* importance of the long-term credit banks and the city banks in the capital supply varies in opposite directions during periods of monetary ease and squeeze. During monetary ease and low interest rates, the business of long-term credit banks booms as they can easily issue their bonds because the city banks which normally buy the bulk of the long-term bank bonds find this profitable and feasible. During a monetary squeeze the bond issue market shrinks because the city banks find it necessary to restrict lending under pressure of large corporations and they restrict it where it hurts them least, that is, in the purchase of the bonds.

The long-term credit banks were established as private institutions under the Long-term Credit Bank Law of 1952 to replace the government "special banks" of the pre-war period which were closed down by the American Occupation Authorities. At the end of 1953 the long-term credit banks' loans to industry amounted to 8 per cent of the total bank loans and by the end of 1962 they had risen to 11·3 per cent.

The Trust Banks

The Japanese "trust business" has been modelled after the U.S. system, but it has undergone some local changes. The essence of "trust business" is that the trustor passes money or a property to the trustee with the instruction that the trustee administer it, or dispose of it for a specified purpose for the benefit of a designated beneficiary. At present the trust business is done by seven specialised banks and one city bank: The Mitsui Trust and Banking Company (established in 1924); The Yasuda Trust and Banking Company (1925); The Sumitomo Trust and Banking Company (1925); The Mitsubishi Trust and Banking Company (1927); The Nippon Trust and Banking Company (1927); The Toyo Trust and Banking Company (1959); The Chuo Trust and Banking Company (1962); and the city bank, The Daiwa Bank (1918).

Money trusts were most successful in the early history of the Japanese trust business. They were able to distribute higher yields than interest on bank deposits and as a result they grew so fast that by the middle of the 1930s they held similar status to the major commercial banks. The War, and the inflation and the drastic changes in property distribution in its aftermath, dealt severe blows to the trust companies. In 1948, to assist the surviving trust companies, the government allowed them to do ordinary banking business, changing their name to "trust and banking companies".

At present there are the following varieties of trust business in Japan: *Money trusts, and loan trusts.* Essentially these are savings put at the disposal of the trust and banking companies for *broadly* specified investment. Loan trusts differ from money trusts in that the contract, and

pooling of the loan trust funds, are uniform and the trust company
issues negotiable trust certificates. The funds collected are lent by the
trustee to large companies for long term. Money trusts and loan trusts
have a higher yield than any other kind of deposit.

Pension trusts. The Tax Law of 1962 gave a stimulus to these trusts
by giving tax concessions to funds set aside for company employee
pension trusts, provided that the money is held outside the company by
a trust bank or an insurance company. A peculiar Japanese feature is
that many company employee pension trust contracts are joint contracts
of several trust banks with one company. This stems from the fact
that many large Japanese companies do business simultaneously with
several banks.

Pension investment trusts, equity type. These allow investment of pension
funds in company shares as a hedge against inflation.

Securities' investment trusts. In this case there is a specific contract
between the trustor and the trustee about the employment of the funds
for the purchase of securities.

Real estate trusts. The trustee bank provides the management of the
real estate.

The trust banks provide a range of other trust services, such as money
claim trusts.

Nowadays trust banks also do general commercial banking business, and
perform a wide range of services connected with issue and purchase of
company bonds and shares.

Insurance Companies

Insurance companies play an important role in the Japanese capital
market. Their holdings of industrial bonds and shares amount to about
three-quarters of such holdings by all banks (including the long-term
banks). As a result stock operations of the insurance companies exert
a marked influence on the Stock Exchanges.

The government also runs numerous insurance services, some of which
aim at increasing welfare of vulnerable groups, others at assisting some
economic activities. The most notable is the Post Office Life Insurance,
oriented towards the lower income groups. The others are: Health
Insurance, National Health Insurance, Welfare Pension Insurance, Work-
men's Accident Compensation Insurance, Unemployment Insurance,
Seamen's Insurance, Export Insurance, Agriculture Mutual Relief Insurance, Forest Fire Insurance, and Small Business Credit Insurance. All
these institutions collect substantial funds and reserves, and their
surpluses are deposited with the Trust Fund Bureau (of the Ministry of
Finance) and are then used for the Fiscal Loan and Investment
Programme.

There are both life and non-life insurance companies. There are three kinds of life insurance policies in Japan: mortality assurance, where a fixed sum is payable into the estate of the insured person on his death; endowment insurance, where a sum of money is payable to the insured person when he has reached a certain age; and "old age" insurance, which combines the features of mortality assurance and endowment insurance.

Non-life insurance gives compensation for a range of undesirable economic contingencies such as fire, marine losses, transportation losses, accident losses and others.

The nature of the risks of the life and non-life companies determines their allocation of funds among various assets. Life insurance companies regularly collect substantial premium payments under conditions where the future contingency is usually many years in the future and where actuarian data can predict the future out-payments exactly. An individual's length of life is unpredictable but the average length of life of a large number of insured people is highly predictable. As a result life insurance companies can commit a very high proportion of their funds to very profitable long-term loans without any great risk. On the other hand the risks of non-life insurance business such as fires or natural disasters are highly unpredictable on both the individual and group levels. Although non-life companies try to spread the risks by world-wide sharing of the business through "underwriting", non-life companies must hold a much higher proportion of assets in liquid form. This difference between the two kinds of insurance companies is shown in their distribution of assets.

Japan has twenty life insurance companies, of which sixteen are "mutual

Table 6.1. *Distribution of Assets, Life and Non-Life Insurance Companies* (*31 December 1962*).

Assets	Life Insurance		Non-Life Insurance	
	billion yen	percentage of total assets	billion yen	percentage of total assets
Cash and deposits with financial institutions	5·3	0·5	49·6	17·4
Call loans	13·2	1·2	3·6	1·3
Securities	273·5	24·4	124·0	43·4
(Stocks)	(252·8)	(22·5)	(110·4)	(38·7)
Loans	689·1	61·4	45·4	15·9
Real assets	123·5	11·0	24·3	8·5
Other	17·6	1·5	38·6	13·5
Total	1,122·2	100·0	285·5	100·0

Source: *Money and Banking in Japan*, p. 180 and p. 184.

companies" and four are joint stock companies. In the case of a mutual life insurance company there are no shareholders—rather all insured persons are shareholders with equal voting power. In this case the company's profits are distributed between policy holders. In the case of the joint stock life insurance companies, some profits go to the shareholders and some profits go to the policy holders. In fact, however, there is very little difference between the two kinds of insurance companies.

The establishment of a life insurance company in Japan requires permission of the Minister of Finance. The other statutory requirements are so easily met that they are nominal: the capital must be 30 million yen or more, and in mutual companies there must be no more than 100 persons.

The disposition of the assets of a life insurance company is subject to legal constraints, aiming *only* at safeguarding the interests of the policy-holders (not as in some Western countries where the governments require life companies to hold a *minimum* percentage of their assets in government bonds). Thus the Japanese life company must not hold more than 30 per cent of its assets in company stock, and 20 per cent in real estate. The premium rates are subject to approval of the Minister of Finance. Life insurance companies employ more than half a million salesmen (some of them part-time).

There are twenty-one non-life insurance companies in Japan: nineteen of them are joint stock and two are mutual companies. They have several devices for dividing the risk (including re-insurance of the motor car insurance risks with the Japanese Government). Non-life insurance also requires a licence from the Minister of Finance, and is regulated by law.

The Securities Market

The securities market consists of the issue market and the trading (second-hand) market.

THE ISSUE MARKET

The issuing of company bonds and shares in Japan is reserved to "securities companies" which have the sole right of "underwriting" and issuing them (under the Securities Transactions Act of 1948). Government bonds, local government bonds and government-guaranteed bonds can be underwritten by banks. However, in both cases some of the securities are placed directly by the issuer into the hands of the holder. It is still rare for a Japanese company to make a public offer of shares. Instead the company issues new stock to the existing shareholders *at face value*, as "rights" (using the Western term). Public offers of shares are rare because of such factors as an under-developed Stock Exchange market in Japan, and the extremely well developed variety of banking institutions, which mean that companies resort to "indirect financing" (a Japanese term), where public savings are placed on time deposit with a bank and companies then obtain long-term loans from banks. Partly because using the Stock Exchange as a means of obtaining capital is rare, the usual charges for underwriting and issuing shares are excessively high in Japan, about 5 per cent of the sale value. This together with the Japanese custom of issuing new shares *at face value* makes the use of Stock Exchanges for new issues unecomonic. It is also unattractive to the existing shareholders because they have to share the improvements in the economic position of the company with the new shareholders. This would not be so if the new shareholders had to pay the market price and if the issues were made when market prices were booming. Then the new shareholders would be likely to subsidise the old. The Japanese appear to be unaware of this fact. They also believe that making public issues of shares "increases the number of unstable shareholders",* although there is no evidence that this is so, and under the circumstances this would not matter even if it were so. Those attitudes are gradually changing in Japan. On 11 October 1968, *Nippon Gakki* created an historic event by issuing six million shares for public subscription *at the market price*. At first the market reacted very unfavourably to this by producing a large drop in price of the *Nippon Gakki* shares, which later recovered because of the undoubted internal strength of *Nippon Gakki*. This development suggests that in future public issues of shares at market prices will become common.

Early in 1970 a number of companies issued shares, not at par value, but at "near market prices". Existing shareholders were still given priority in share acquisition. Again the shareholders protested by putting large volume of stocks onto the market. However, it will not take long for the public to get used to the new system.

The various categories of bond issues are somewhat different from share issues. Until 1965 the Japanese Government did not issue any long-term bonds. Its short-term bonds are the Foreign Exchange Account Bills (with which foreign exchange is purchased) and the Food Agency Bills (to subsidise the price of controlled foodstuffs until the budgetary funds arrive). Nominally, the short-term bonds are offered to the public, that is, to the banks. In fact, however, these short-term bonds are unattractive to the banks, which are always short of liquidity, and because the short-term bonds carry too low an interest rate. As a result the short-term government securities are bought by the Bank of Japan. Long-term government bonds are purchased by banks and other financial institutions because their rate of interest is more attractive. Local government bonds are mainly taken up directly by the financial institutions in

* *Money and Banking in Japan*, p. 238.

the district of the issuing local authority. The other type, the Government-guaranteed bonds, are issued by public corporations, some governmental financial institutions and government-assisted companies like the Japan Air Lines Company. The banks and the securities companies handle their sale and absorb the unsold bonds.

Private company bonds are issued through the securities companies. The bank debentures (interest-bearing, for five years, and discount debentures, for one year) are issued directly by the bank concerned, though the securities companies help to sell them.

In general, bonds are sold mainly to financial institutions, and their volume and terms of issue are controlled by the Ministry of Finance.

THE TRADING MARKET

The trading market in securities consists of two sections: Stock Exchanges, and "over-the-counter" markets and the "second sections" of the three major Stock Exchanges (Tokyo, Osaka, and Nagoya).

The Stock Exchanges deal primarily in the listed securities which are those listed by the respective Stock Exchange according to the rules of the Securities Transactions Act. There are nine Stock Exchanges in Japan in Tokyo, Osaka, Nagoya, Kyoto, Kobe, Hiroshima, Fukuoka, Niigata and Sapporo. The Tokyo Stock Exchange is by far the most important as it handles about 70 per cent of stock exchange trading in the whole country. The Stock Exchanges are incorporated bodies consisting of securities companies as members.

There are five types of transactions on the Stock Exchanges in Japan:

(a) The "same day" settlement.

(b) "Ordinary transactions", with settlement made on the fourth business day from the day of the contract. This is the most common type of transaction. It is also the only kind of transaction that the Japanese Government allows the foreigners to participate in.

(c) The "specified date" transactions. In this case a day within fifteen days from the contract day is agreed upon as settlement day.

(d) The "when-issued" transactions. Here the settlement day is the day when the issuing company issues the stock.

(e) The "margin transactions".

MARGIN TRANSACTIONS

These speculative transactions are considered necessary on any organised market to give the market "depth" (that is, to produce conditions where the entry of one buyer or one seller does not affect the price). Unfortunately, of course, they can give rise to speculative price fluctuations. The unemotional, rational view is that profitable, or correct, speculation is good for the whole economy, but of course speculators often commit errors.

Margin transactions are in effect transactions on credit (where the seller has no securities, and the buyer no cash) with a partial deposit called a "margin". The maximum life of a margin transaction in Japan is six months. Margin transactions in Japan are possible only with designated securities and only in the "First Section". The customer obtains the fixed margin from securities finance corporations and pays it to the securities company handling the sale.

Margin transactions were begun in 1951 to improve the market by giving it depth. The Japanese Stock Exchanges determine from time to time the level of the margin, for example when the share price trend was rising in September 1968 the margin was raised from 30 per cent to 40 per cent, while on 18 August 1969, the margin was reduced to bolster up the sluggish market.

THE OVER-THE-COUNTER MARKET

This is a somewhat more informal market. Originally it was transactions outside the Stock Exchanges, literally over the counter of the dealer, the securities company. As this informal market grew rapidly in 1961 the three major Stock Exchanges, Tokyo, Osaka and Nagoya, opened the "second floor", or the "second markets". The "over-the-counter" market deals in the securities that have not been listed, and the securities in "parcels" smaller than the minimum trading unit in the First Market.

Under the 1948 Securities and Exchange Act the principle of *free competition* was introduced in the Japanese Stock Exchange dealings after the U.S. pattern. Any company could become a dealer and/or a broker on the Stock Exchanges on registration. Under this system full trust was placed in the efficiency of the workings of free competition to produce desirable results. Under that system the Japanese Stock Exchanges and the volume of dealings showed a remarkable growth, and the number of securities companies dealing on the Exchanges grew to 593 from a very low number prior to the opening of the Stock Exchange in 1949. However, in the middle of the 1960s the stock prices fell drastically (for reasons initially not quite connected with the dealers, but mainly due to the domestic requirements of a balance of payments policy). This created a crisis in the securities market, and the crisis has been overcome only by the co-operation of the government, Bank of Japan, and securities companies and banks, which have established a share-price-support system. The government came to hold the view that the structure of the securities market contributed to the securities crisis, and it passed The Revised Securities and Exchange Act which became operative on 1 April 1968.

The main features of the new system are that the mere registration of dealers is replaced by government *licensing* (the intent is the elimination of incompetent dealers before they start business); along with this goes an increase in the "administrative guidance" given to the securities market. The objectives are to increase the social standing and reputation of securities dealers and to give more security to investors, but the means are substantial abrogation of free competition.

In future four distinct types of business would be separated and each would require a licence: for the securities company to deal on the Stock Exchange on *its own account*; to deal as a *broker* on behalf of the public; to underwrite issues of securities and sell them; and to handle the subscription and public sale of securities.

As a transition measure, many securities companies temporarily obtained licence for more than one function, and the "big four", Nomura, Nikko, Yamaichi and Daiwa obtained all four licences, but this will not be possible in future. This is undoubtedly a sound reform. The company that deals on its own account and also on behalf of a customer would often meet a conflict of interest, which is clearly undesirable.

The Investment Trust Act was also revised for more effective regulation of investment trusts which had contributed to the share price depression as the participants in the trusts cancelled their contracts.

In addition there were other reforms. Unofficial transactions outside the Stock Exchange of officially quoted stocks (*baikai*) have been forbidden in order to concentrate transactions on the floor of the Stock Exchange and thus help formulate genuine market price for shares. Also, a more complete compulsory disclosure system of company condition was introduced, and margin transactions in stock were improved.

The Bonds Market

After the War the Stock Exchanges in Japan were reopened in 1949. The dealing in shares developed very rapidly, but the trade in bonds and debentures was at best erratic. Until the last few years bonds and debentures were not bought by the general public for whom they were unattractive because the rate of interest fixed on them by the Government (about 7 per cent) was too low compared to other rates of interest (often below even the call-money rates). In addition the previous history of high inflation rates in the Japanese economy made them unattractive, because unlike shares they do not appreciate in capital value as inflation grows. In fact it is the financial institutions who buy bonds in Japan. Between 1959 and 1965 the financial institutions bought more than 80 per cent of all bonds issued.* There are two reasons why the financial institutions found bonds acceptable. First, in the case of company bonds, the bonds taken up by the banks often were a mere conversion of loans to companies, which had acquired such a long-term

* Robert Ballon, editor, *Doing Business in Japan*, Charles E. Tuttle Co., Rutland, Vermont, 1967, p. 106.

character that the bank felt safer in converting the loan into debentures. Second, bonds acquired most of the characteristics of a liquid asset for financial institutions (not the general public) in view of the fact that they can be used as a collateral security for borrowing from the Bank of Japan. They can also be used for sale to the Bank of Japan, when the latter engages in the "open-market-operations" (*direct* purchases from the banks). Having acquired bonds, the financial institutions rarely sold them in the market. For a liquid asset they gave a good return.

The other reason why the bond market has not yet developed was the fact that from the adoption of the "Dodge Line" in 1948, the Japanese Government did not issue any bonds until the second half of 1965 as a matter of policy.

As a result dealings in bonds on Stock Exchanges were so scarce that price quotations were suspended in April 1962. They were reopened at the beginning of February 1966 (by which time the call-money rates had fallen slightly below the bond rate, and substantial government bond issues appeared).

Securities Finance Companies

The Securities Finance Companies must be clearly distinguished from the Securities Companies. The securities companies are dealers in shares and bonds on one of the Stock Exchanges, while the securities finance companies provide them with loans of cash or of shares and bonds to facilitate dealings in shares and bonds. Thus the securities finance companies are almost pure credit institutions (except that they also lend shares and bonds). The securities finance companies are a Japanese innovation to allow "margin transactions" on the Stock Exchange, in view of the fact that Japanese banks would not finance such transactions. ("Margin transactions" are speculative Stock Exchange transactions which are generally considered necessary to establish well functioning Stock Exchanges). The speculative buyer of stocks borrows funds from a securities finance company for payment on the settlement day. This loan is made to him on the security of the stocks to be acquired. The security company also lends *shares and bonds* to the would-be speculative sellers of shares and bonds, in this case on the security of the proceeds from the sale. The securities finance company is therefore particularly well placed to provide for these two opposed needs. It really needs to cover only the difference between the value of stocks lent to the sellers and the amount of funds lent to the buyers.

The securities finance companies also make ordinary loans on very short-term securities, like ordinary financial institutions. The bulk of their funds are obtained on call-loans and loans from the banks.

The securities finance companies were established in 1949 to assist recovery of share prices, and their present form was acquired in 1951 when margin transactions were begun on the Stock Exchanges. There are now three securities finance companies, one for each Stock Exchange in Tokyo, Osaka, and Nagoya.

Securities Companies

Securities companies are Stock Exchange dealers and/or brokers. As dealers they buy and sell bonds and shares on their own account, and as brokers they act as agents for their customers. Securities companies also underwrite and float bonds and shares on the market and provide some ancillary services. Between 1948 and 1968 there were about 600 securities companies of which about one-third were members of one of the nine Stock Exchanges. The remaining two-thirds were not members, but dealt in the "over-the-counter" market, in shares not listed by the Stock Exchanges or in amounts smaller than the prescribed minimum trading unit for the Stock Exchanges. Four securities companies (Nomura, Yamaichi, Nikko, and Daiwa) have dominated the whole market by doing the bulk of the business. Since the 1968 reform which imposed the licensing system there are only 277 licensed securities companies.

Securities companies deal in the new issue market when underwriting and floating bonds and shares, and in the second-hand bond and share market. The underwriting of company shares and bonds is entirely reserved for securities companies under the Securities Transactions Act of 1948, but the underwriting of government script can be done by banks too. Until the resumption of government borrowing in 1965, government bonds were limited to local authority and public corporation borrowing and their total was therefore relatively small.

In the new issue market company *bonds* have been the main business of the securities companies, because Japanese companies prefer that method of obtaining capital. This is going to change in future.

Securities Investment Trusts

These are companies, associated with securities companies, which invest trust funds in specified securities for the benefit of the participants who hold beneficiary certificates. The subsequent profits (or losses) are then distributed among the holders of certificates. Securities investment trust funds are invested in company shares, debentures, government bonds, government-guaranteed bonds, bank debentures, deposits, money in trust, call loans, and so on. There are three types of investment trusts: unit trusts; open-end trusts; and bond trusts.

Two main features differentiate unit trusts from the open-end trusts. The unit trust's beneficiary certificates that are sold to the public in a customary one month period constitute a unit of trust, independent from other units. In the case of the open-end trusts there is no time limit for each trust but there is a value limit at which the trust is closed. Secondly, a unit trust has a fixed life of five years, although the holder can in fact sell his beneficiary certificates back to the securities company before the end of that period. On the other hand the open-end trust has an indefinite life but beneficiary certificates can be sold any time without any restriction.

The operations of securities investment trusts are regulated by the Securities Investment Trust Act of 1951, and controlled strictly by the Minister of Finance to protect the interests of the owners of funds. Securities investment trusts are a very important element of the capital market as they are larger investors than insurance companies.

The Collapse of the Stock Exchange Prices and the Support Schemes

The collapse of the Japanese share prices in 1964 and 1965 was caused primarily by credit squeeze begun by the Bank of Japan in 1961, relaxed in 1962 and resumed in December 1963 for the protection of Japan's balance of payments. However, once the squeeze had depressed the share prices and business expectations, the institutional weaknesses in the Japanese capital market dramatically accentuated the share price weakness. The result was a major crisis for many Japanese financial institutions.

Table 6.2 shows that the weighted Fisher's "Ideal" and the unweighted Dow-Jones share price indices were rising rapidly until the first big squeeze in 1961, dipped in 1962, resumed growth in 1963 (when the monetary squeeze was withdrawn), and in 1964 began an even more rapid fall. It is interesting to mention that the unweighted simple average of share prices started to decline about one year earlier. This means that the most important shares held their prices better but in the unweighted price average they were swamped by the falling mass of shares. The fall in share prices was accompanied by a sudden rise in the number of bankruptcies. Incidentally, it can be seen that the bankruptcy rate is a very insensitive indicator of the level of business activity. After a prolonged high activity and a high business "birth rate", an equally prolonged period of high "business mortality"* comes with a time lag and after some decline in the level of activity. The coincidence of the share price collapse with a sudden and large increase in bankruptcies, *both preceded* by a

---

* Similar features have been observed for New Zealand in: K. Bieda, "Bankruptcies in Depression and Boom", *Economic Record*, August 1957.

Table 6.2. Tokyo Stock Exchange Share Price Indices, the Volume of Transactions
on the Japanese Stock Exchange and the Number of Bankruptcies.

Year	Weighted Fisher's "Ideal" Index	Dow-Jones Type (Un-weighted, allows for issue of "rights") Index	Unweighted Simple Average of 225 share prices on First Market and 50 shares on Second Market Price in yen	Volume of Share Transactions in Japan billion yen	Number of bankruptcies (in excess of 10 mil. yen)
1953	34·68	390·90			
1954	29·30	340·79			
1955	32·97	374·00			
1956	44·85	485·33			
1957	49·19	535·57			
1958	51·70	571·97			
1959	75·49	821·52	146·39	5,589	
1960	97·35	1,116·62	167·58	9,334	
1961	112·10	1,548·94	187·39	9,807	1,102
1962	98·59	1,419·44	141·08	9,893	1,779
1963	108·20	1,440·61	127·27	8,234	1,738
1964	95·56	1,262·88	106·30	4,830	4,212
1965	91·68	1,203·16	99·56	5,783	6,141
1966	109·88	1,479·16	120·40	7,571	6,187
1967	110·48	1,412·01	113·43	6,281	8,192
1968	118·91	1,544·81	125·81	11,734	10,776
1969 January	136·98	1,792·15	151·45		
February	138·58	1,812·91	154·53		
March	139·90	1,796·69	155·98		
April	145·29	1,880·74	167·80		
May	151·00	1,939·32	175·68		
June	152·86	1,954·58	171·90		
July	149·91	1,927·67	166·42		
August	147·09	1,887·54	161·02		
September	155·41	1,990·94	171·72		
October	159·54	2,081·08	181·12		
November	164·96	2,160·56	197·96		
December	171·11	2,252·14	204·23		

Sources: a) Share price indexes: *Monthly Statistics of Japan*, May 1969 and January 1970.
b) Number of bankrupticies: *Japan Economic Yearbook*, 1969, p. 213.
c) Volume of share transactions: *The Japanese Financial System*, March 1969, p. 61.

Warning to the reader:
The official Japanese primary source of statistics, the *Monthly Statistics of Japan* gives to the three indexes names that convey virtually no meaning. The official companion volume, the *Supplement to the Monthly Statistics of Japan—Explanatory Notes 1969*, which gives a longer explanation, is in parts wrong and in parts ambiguous. For the correct names and description of the nature of these indexes see: Y. Taki, *Economic Indexes in Japan: Theory and Practice*, available only in

Japanese: *Nihon no Keizai Shisu*, Nihon Hyoronsha Publishing Company, Tokyo, 1969, pp. 129-130.

Author's notes on the share price indicators

None of the three share price indicators is ideal. The so-called Fisher's "Ideal" Index is here a "geometrical average" of two indices, Paasche's and Laspeyre's.

$$I = \sqrt{\frac{\Sigma P_n Q_o}{\Sigma P_o Q_o} \cdot \frac{\Sigma P_n Q_n}{\Sigma P_o Q_n}}$$

Since both Paasche's and Laspeyre's formulae have their errors, and since those errors need not have any systematic bias it follows that neither arithmetical average nor geometrical average will yield the right result. Since both Paasche's and Laspeyre's formulae are weighted ones (each particular share price is weighted by the quantity of shares) the "Ideal" Fisher's formula is also weighted.

The Dow-Jones index is essentially an unweighted price average of a parcel of shares, with an attempt to allow for the price effect of issues of "rights" (issues of shares at par value to the existing shareholders). Its nature is best shown by a simplified example.

Suppose there are only three shares on the market, that is those of Companies A, B and C and their *market* prices are: A $=$ 100 yen

$$B = 80 \text{ yen}$$
$$C = 70 \text{ yen}$$

Now Company A decides in Year 2 to issue "rights" (but B and C do not), one new share for each old share. Customarily they are issued at 50 yen each. If the company did not make any exceptionally high profits in Year 1, simple logic tells that the *usual* profits will have to be divided among twice as many "ticket" holders as before. Thus the price of the "tickets" (the shares) must fall (under assumption made). So the effect on the average price of A shares is:

$$\frac{100 \text{ yen} + 50 \text{ yen}}{2} = 75 \text{ yen, that is shares A fall by 25 yen because of issue of "rights".}$$

Dow-Jones average share price: $\dfrac{100 + 80 + 70}{3} = \dfrac{(100 - 25) + 80 + 70}{\text{coefficient X}}$

Solving the equation: $X = 2.7$

Thus Dow-Jones average share price in Year 2 is $= \dfrac{75 + 80 + 70}{2.7}$

The weakness of Dow-Jones share price average is that it is unweighted, so that say a ten per cent rise in the price of a share with a minute turn-over on the Exchange is equated with a ten per cent price rise of a share with very large turnover. The simple arithmetic *average* of the prices of the selected shares has the disadvantage of being unweighted. Its advantage it is claimed is that being an average price in yen (not an index) when related to the average dividend of the companies whose shares are in the average, it gives instantly the effective yield, and an index does not do that.

Briefly, there is no perfect price index and there never will be!

drastic monetary squeeze, explains the main immediate cause of the share price crisis.

For a number of years in the post-war period, until roughly 1968 or 1969, the rapid Japanese economic growth was subject to a severe constraint of the balance of payments. Severe pressures on the balance of payments developed, particularly in 1961, when Prime Minister Ikeda's Doubling the National Income Plan got under way. The announcement of the Plan induced (or increased) a rush of investment by private industry, and this naturally had an unfavourable immediate effect on the balance of payments, and in addition the wholesale price index started to rise at an alarming rate. Further, a survey of the investment programs of 150 leading enterprises made in May 1961 showed the intention to produce an even more dramatic investment increase, almost a half more than the preceding, already excessive one. Under those circumstances various authorities took action in July 1961. The Ministry of Finance, the Bank of Japan and the city banks made a common appeal to the business community to postpone at least 10 per cent of their total investment. Soon afterwards, the Bank of Japan increased Bank Rate by one *rin*, that is, the "basic Bank rate" rose from 1·8 *sen* to 1·9 *sen* (1·9 *sen* per 100 yen *per diem* equals 6·94% p.a.). Although in Japan an increase of the Bank Rate by 1 *rin* (0·365% p.a.) usually produces a contraction of the level of activity and imports, in this case it did not. As a restrictive measure the government therefore increased the required level of compulsory cash deposits against future imports, and introduced reductions of expenditures in its own finances. The Bank of Japan again increased the Bank Rates (the basic rate rose to 2·0 *sen* = 7·3% p.a.) and it increased the penalty interest rates for deficiency in the required minimum deposits. Later in October 1961 the minimum compulsory deposit requirement with the Bank of Japan by prescribed financial institutions was increased. (These Bank of Japan measures were called the "troika system", from the old Russian name of a three-horse carriage.)

Despite these pressures in 1961, large issues of company bonds and to a lesser extent of shares continued to be floated.

Finally, in October 1961 the various forms of monetary squeeze started to take effect. The wholesale price index not only stopped growing, but started to decline. Production was cut down in a number of industries, such as textiles, iron and steel, and paper. Thus a recession came in the end but for 1961 the Current Account of the Japanese balance of payments showed a deficit of over 1 billion dollars. In 1962 the delayed effects of the squeeze were so strong that the wholesale price index declined by about 7 per cent, and the Current Account of the balance of payments recorded a small surplus. In view of those changes the Bank of Japan reduced the "basic" Bank Rate by one *rin* in October and another one *rin* in November of 1962. Early in 1963 all the "troika" measures were withdrawn.

In 1963 the foreign trade account of Japan again turned unfavourable, and in autumn the Bank of Japan again started a monetary restraint including "open market operations", limiting its loans to city banks and increasing the minimum reserve requirements. In January 1964 "window control" was reimposed by the Bank of Japan, and in March the Bank Rate was raised by 2 *rin* from 1·6 *sen* to 1·8 *sen*. Further, the Government increased the level of the compulsory "import guarantee deposits" and the commercial banks were instructed to pay those deposits into the Bank of Japan.

The Price Index for the Tokyo Stock Exchange (based on the Dow-Jones formula), with the values of 16 May 1949 taken as 100 yen, rose rapidly as recovery proceeded and reached 471·53 yen on 27 December 1957 and then quickly soared to a peak of 1,829·74 yen on 18 July 1961. Then it began to fall. By that time the effective yield fell from 9·44% in 1954 to 3·24% which was extremely low compared to the very high interest rates in Japan at that time. Companies issued new stock under the old investment impetus and were stimulated by the record prices of stocks as well as Ikeda's Doubling the Income Plan. Until very recently, stocks have been issued at par (usually 50 yen a share) as "rights" to the existing shareholders, who could then sell them in the market making a large profit. The prospects of these vast capital gains with large "rights" issues further stimulated the rise of share prices until the speculative rise fed on itself. Large issues of company stock continued until 1962. But when share prices began to decline in July 1961 due to the monetary squeeze of that year, the excess supply of shares became accentuated, again through "speculative" behaviour, but in the opposite direction. The speculators were taking bets on further share price *falls* this time. Chart 6.1 shows how the real investment boom accelerated up to 1961 and how it collapsed under the conditions of monetary squeeze.

Because of the monetary squeeze some of the shareholders had to sell some shares to be able to buy the new "rights". Worse than that, many investment trusts which had become very popular were closed prematurely by the investors, so that investment trusts unloaded part of their holdings on to the falling market. (Investment trusts have never regained their relative or even absolute financial position.)

In that situation the securities companies (dealers in their own right and brokers) which had their own securities' holdings had an interest in preventing falls in securities prices. They decided to buy up the disgorged securities, but this made them highly illiquid and left them with excess holdings of securities. It is true that in the earlier period the securities companies had made large profits by buying shares when

Chart 6.1.   ANNUAL EQUIPMENT INVESTMENT OUTLAYS
              BY INDUSTRY 1955-1967

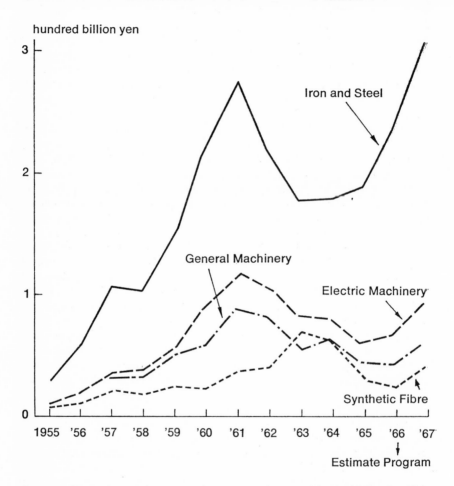

Source: Survey by the Japan Development Bank, quoted by Asahi Evening News,
          24 February 1968.

they were cheap, but they did this with borrowed funds, in particular
call-money, which became very expensive under the monetary
squeeze. Besides, the large profits became largely ephemeral paper
profits when the share prices dropped. The city banks first came to the
rescue of the securities companies in June 1962 and several times later,
by lending to the securities companies against the collateral of *bonds*.

At the end of October 1962, the share price index dropped again to 1,216·04, one-third below the peak price (1961). The city banks granted additional credit against the collateral of government-guaranteed debentures. This, together with new source of support—the insurance companies bought shares in a large way—temporarily reversed the market trend and in April 1963 the Tokyo Dow-Jones index regained the level of 1,634·37 yen. But the market was still basically weak and Japanese stock prices collapsed again in July 1963 when President Kennedy's message revealing the weakness of the U.S. balance of payments implied less favourable world trade conditions for the future. This time the position was serious. The securities companies which had been supporting the share prices (in order to preserve the value of their old holdings) were grossly overextended financially. Even one of the most famous and largest securities companies, the Yamaichi Securities Company, came close to bankruptcy. As an immediate step the Mitsubishi Bank, the Fuji Bank, and all the remaining city banks lent money to Yamaichi Securities Company, and to other securities companies. (The Mitsubishi Bank obtained a directorship on the Yamaichi Securities Company board for more effective control.)

In the end, on 18 January 1964, all the city banks, the Industrial Bank of Japan, the Long-Term Credit Bank and the "big four" securities companies established a share-price-support institution, the *Japan Joint Securities Corporation*. It has authorised capital of 10 billion yen, of which 2½ billion yen was paid in at once, and the paid-up capital later reached 30 billion yen, while the Bank of Japan lent the new institution about 100 billion yen. Two months later the Japan Joint Securities Corporation entered the market as a stock buyer to prevent the Tokyo Dow-Jones Index from falling below 1,200 yen level. In the course of its operations it gradually obtained the support of about 119 large financial institutions: local banks, insurance companies, and large and medium sized securities companies. The share price index continued to fall, however, because the operations of the Corporation were inadequate in size, and the securities companies, afraid of the future, were unloading their holdings on the market. When the index fell to almost 1,200 yen in January 1965 the second share-price-support institution, the *Japan Securities Holding Association*, was formed. This one was established by the securities companies themselves, though with the blessing of the Bank of Japan and a loan of 230 billion yen from it (through the Securities Financing Company). In this new institution the securities companies provided their share of capital in the form of shares which thereby became "shelved" or "frozen", and thus would not be dumped on the weak market.

In addition, the large loan from the Bank of Japan was used in part (50 billion yen) for a purchase of shares under a re-purchase agreement from the securities companies, at the outset, and the balance (182·6 billion yen) was used for absorbing shares thrown on to the market by the investment trust companies.

For support purposes the Japan Securities Holding Association acquired shares to the total value of 232 billion yen, of which 182 billion yen worth of shares were from investment trusts. The investment trusts were forced by institutional weakness to unload the shares. The sapping of the market's confidence in future share price trends by the credit squeeze triggered off cancellations of investment trusts contracts by the public. As a result, investment trust companies had to unload some of their share holdings on to the weak market to obtain cash.

The additional market support by the Japan Securities Holding Association was proving to be inadequate in view of the market pressures. In March 1965 the Tokyo share price index fell below 1,200 yen. This had a serious effect on securities companies, some of which, especially the Yamaichi Securities Company, were close to bankruptcy. On 21 May 1965 the Yamaichi Securities Company, unable to pay even interest on its borrowing, announced a reorganisation plan and stated that banks had agreed to a moratorium on interest payments. This announcement had a disastrous and immediate effect on public confidence and revealed another institutional weakness. It led to mass cancellations of the so-called "securities management contracts", which were comparable to a "run on a bank" for the securities companies. The securities management contracts are agreements between a securities company and its customers to hold and manage the customer's securities (mainly the one-year bank "discount debentures") with the right to use them while they are deposited. For this deposit or rather loan of the securities, the securities company paid the depositor a fee of one *sen* per 100 yen per day (3·65 per cent p.a.). The securities company then used the "borrowed" securities as a collateral when it borrowed cash in the call-loan market. Since the public that lent the securities did not obtain any collateral security, the panic cancellations were perfectly understandable when the securities companies revealed their own weakness. The situation for the whole financial structure became so serious that a week later the Bank of Japan decided to give full assistance to Yamaichi Securities Company under the Article 25 of the Bank of Japan Act: ". . . undertake any business necessary for maintaining and fostering the credit system." The next day the Minister of Finance gave his consent and over the next two months the Bank's loans to Yamaichi Securities Company to enable it to meet the demand for cancellation of securities management contracts reached 28 billion yen. Shortly after another company, Oi Securities, received a 5 billion yen loan from the Bank of Japan. The Bank of Japan felt compelled to lend to two securities dealers almost US$92 million.

These determined efforts by the Bank of Japan and the commercial banks, together with the general improvement in the level of economic activity, restored confidence in the stock market. But it should be noted that in this crisis the relaxation of monetary policy proved inadequate to restore a healthy level of economic activity and the "Dodge Line" of "balanced budgets" had to be thrown overboard (where it belonged). In the Japanese Fiscal Years 1965 and 1966 the Government of Japan produced deliberately substantial budget deficits to restore normal levels of economic activity. As one of the results of those policy steps, the Tokyo share price index picked up substantially by 1966. Incidentally, in September 1966 the Yamaichi Securities Company was reorganised and the new company adopted a plan for repayment of the rescue loans over the period of 18 years. Subsequently, the previous free entry into the business of dealing in securities was replaced by licensing system, but life being what it is, Yamaichi Securities Company, which got into difficulty partly because it had been both a broker and a dealer, still managed to obtain a double licence whereas many other securities companies failed to obtain any! The law on investment trusts was also revised.

As can be seen from Table 6.2, the recovery of share prices of 1966 has continued. In 1966 the Finance Committee of the Diet recommended that the Japan Joint Securities Corporation and the Japan Securities Holding Association should start disposing of the shares acquired in the price support program. However, in that year and in 1967, only a small amount of holdings was disposed of, because the market responded unfavourably. As from April 1968 a Stock Exchange boom developed in Japan partly because of a growing inflow of foreign portfolio capital. As a result, the Japan Securities Holding Association disposed of its holdings of shares (241 billion yen) by the end of 1968 and was dissolved at the beginning of 1969. The other support institution, the Japan Joint Securities Corporation, also got rid of a large amount of shares (112 billion yen worth) during 1968, and additional substantial amounts during the first half of 1969. But by the end of April 1969 the Joint Securities Company still had about 50 per cent of its peak holdings of shares on its hands.*

According to the *Nikko Monthly Bulletin* (March 1970) in 1969 the frozen shares amounted to 115,000 million yen, but at the beginning of 1970 were reduced to 40,000 million yen.

In the second half of 1969 the booming share market showed some hesitation and declines, and its future as well as the course of further liquidation of support stocks will be dependent on foreign capital inflow, which also started to show signs of hesitation due mainly to a general

* Bank of Japan, Special Paper No. 36, May 1969, p. 6.

shortage of cash and high interest rates in the world. Net foreign capital inflow to Japan was $56 million in 1967, $344 million in 1968 and $288 million for the first five months of 1969, but in July and August 1969 some foreign capital was leaving and this had a depressing effect on the market.†

Foreign purchases at the Japanese Stock Exchanges rose later and the share price index reached a record level in January 1970, and then declined in the first half of February 1970. The probable causes of this decline were an increase in the practice of companies' issuing new shares at "near market price" which induced many disappointed shareholders to sell out, and the restrictions imposed by the American Government in January 1970 on purchases of Japanese securities.

† *The Economist,* 30 August 1969, p. 55.

CHAPTER SEVEN

The Structure of Industry

The Japanese industrial structure is distinctive in several ways: Japanese industry (and even the economy as a whole) is said to have a dual structure, which is a term with several meanings and aspects. Broadly speaking, it is characterised by the co-existence of the modern and the traditional sectors. Some aspects of this general dualism can also be observed in cultural life, sociological phenomena, and even in consumption. There is also a high degree of separation of production from distribution in Japanese industry. Japanese producers of all kinds generally use the services of the "trading companies" for marketing their products and for market research.

The Japanese industry operates in conditions of keen competition. This is due in part to the very powerful anti-monopoly laws (and a powerful and independent enforcement agency, the Fair Trade Commission). The extreme competition is also due to the emergence of the *keiretsu* which in contradistinction to the former *zaibatsu* acquired a spirit and structure highly conducive to competition between the giant industrial-financial-commercial conglomerates. The *keiretsu* base their policy on the "one-set-of-everything" principle, meaning that each conglomerate tries to have a footing in the production of as many *different* products as possible. They compete strongly with each other in all spheres: price, quality, size of the firm, the share of the market, the level of investment and even the range of *different* industries linked together through the *keiretsu* network of relationships.

This very high level of competition is also evident among the single large firms which at first assessment may appear to be oligopolies, but on closer inspection turn out to be strange creatures, not yet admitted to the economic theory textbooks, which perhaps would be best called by the paradoxical name of "competing oligopolies".

The competition between the single-firm oligopolies and the multiple-firm oligopolies (as the *keiretsu* perhaps could be called) has reduced the costs, mark-ups and prices, but maintained profitability by increasing efficiency and the scale of operation. Indeed, the large firms and the *keiretsu* members do not try to maximise profits but fight to increase their share of the market. This business behaviour is called "excessive competition". The fight for the share of the market even extends to foreign economies. If one large firm or *keiretsu* establishes a business in Thailand, Taiwan or Korea, the other competing firms or *keiretsu* would attempt to do the same even if the local market in that country could not support more than one business. However, in such a case the Ministry for International Trade and Industry and the Industrial Structure Council would intervene to co-ordinate the general investment programmes of firms to avoid creating excess capacity. Although the "excessively competing" business executives and shareholders do not like this state of high competition, the present Japanese industrial system is probably quite a good way to obtain the best features of the two worlds of perfect competition and monopoly. The large oligopolistic firm can afford expensive research establishments, is organisationally better equipped to acquire and adopt foreign know-how, and has the resources to start any new enterprise at the optimum size. On the other hand the evils of oligopoly are held in check by the competition among oligopolists. Many Japanese economists see this high level of competition as one of the causes of the rapid advance of the Japanese economy, and the role of the large enterprises is universally acknowledged.

The fourth peculiar feature of the Japanese industry is its method of financing investment. Several large members of a *keiretsu* pool their financial resources, thus providing enough capital to start a new giant enterprise, which can reap all the economies of scale available.

The Dual Structure

The term "dual structure" was probably coined in 1957 by Hiromi Arisawa* and was immediately taken up by the Japanese "Economic White Paper" of 1957, and later this led to extensive discussion of the phenomena so named. Dual economic structure, of course, is not a phenomenon limited solely to Japan. Almost all countries which used to be traditional and have lately experienced rapid economic growth develop some features of duality, but rightly or wrongly the Japanese economists have persuaded themselves (and many Western scholars) that dualism appears in a particularly acute form in Japan.

Duality is usually seen in the pronounced differences in the operational methods of the traditional small scale firms and the large scale modern firms. Alternatively the duality is seen in the existence of an extensive

* Hiromi Arisawa, *Seisansei Hombu Soritsu 2-shunen Kinen-Koen*, March 1957.

sector of proprietor-run small businesses, and another quite different sector of large companies. There are also cultural, sociological, and even consumption dualities, which are all strongly linked.

The duality of the small and large scale industries manifests itself among other things in disparities in productivity, wage rates and other conditions of employment.

Duality is sometimes seen between the small scale agriculture and (large scale) manufacturing. This, however, is not as meaningful because technology and demand for the various factors of production in agriculture in a land-hungry country like Japan require different scales of operation and other characteristics than manufacturing.

Shinohara observes that during the Meiji period (1868-1912) what is now considered dual structure in manufacturing did not exist.* He shows that wage rates in small enterprises and in those employing 500 or more workers differed only slightly in 1909, but that there was a small rise in the wage differentials between 1909 and 1914. Extraordinarily large wage differentials arose in the Taisho period (1912-1925). Presumably during World War I, which gave a big stimulus to economic activity in Japan and especially to the growth of modern product industries, there was a great shortage of workers with modern skills, while workers with traditional skills were still plentiful. This would create the wage differentials between larger modern industries and smaller traditional

Table 7.1. Index of Wage Rate Differences Between Manufacturing Firms of Various Sizes (1958–1968). (Wage rate in the largest enterprises=100.)

Employees					
Age Group	Year	more than 1,000	500–999	100–499	30–99
20–24	1958	100·0	91·3	86·7	86·3
	1961	100·0	94·0	92·8	92·1
	1964	100·0	97·5	98·0	102·0
	1968	100·0	94·9	94·9	97·1
25–29	1958	100·0	91·7	83·1	76·0
	1961	100·0	92·7	89·6	83·9
	1964	100·0	98·2	94·4	95·0
	1968	100·0	94·4	93·8	91·4
30–34	1958	100·0	89·9	76·0	66·0
	1961	100·0	87·5	79·4	68·9
	1964	100·0	89·4	83·8	76·7
	1968	100·0	92·3	86·7	80·1

Source: *Nihon Kokusei Zue*, p. 105.

* Shinohara, *Growth and Cycles*, pp. 14-25.

industries. These large wage differentials have continued in the Showa period (from 1925). In the immediate two or three post-war years these wage differences were temporarily reduced by hyperinflation and a large fall in general living standards. They later rose until the sixties, though recently the differences have narrowed. A measure of the wage differences that have emerged is the fact that in 1957 the average wage in manufacturing firms employing four to nine workers was only 30 per cent of the average wage in manufacturing firms employing 1000 workers or more. Indeed, as the size of the firms (measured by the number of workers) increases the average wage for the group of industries invariably increases.†

Table 7.1 does not provide information for firms which employ less than thirty workers—if it did the difference shown between the wage rates would be even greater. All the same this table yields several conclusions: as a rule wage rates in the last decade have continued to be much lower in small enterprises than in large ones. The wage differentials have, however, been continuously narrowed in the last decade. (Compare the wage rate indices in any one of the three right-hand side columns, moving down the column for each age group.)

In view of the fact that there is a "wage for age" system in Japan with automatic wage increments as the worker gets older, it is interesting to compare the wage disparities between small and large firms for the three age groups. It is clear that the youngest age group (twenty- to twenty-four-year-olds) has had the lowest wage rate disparity and the highest age group (thirty- to thirty-four-year-olds) has had the highest wage disparity. This phenomenon can be explained by the fact that in this decade labour, particularly young labour, has become very scarce. This is due to a general demographic trend, and particularly in this decade is due to the sudden increase in the proportion of high school leavers going to tertiary institutions. This has reduced the current labour supply by postponing the entry of a large number of young people into the labour force for four years or more. As a result labour became so scarce that small firms were forced to compete more with large firms in recruiting high school leavers and tertiary education graduates. That this scarcity of young labour has been the cause of closing the wage disparity is strikingly demonstrated by the fact that in 1964 the wage disparity virtually disappeared *for the youngest age group.* The years around 1964, of course, had particularly low numbers of labour force entrants, since the industry was drawing then on people born during the War when the birth rate declined dramatically. Older workers could not alter their wage rates in the conditions of labour scarcity that developed *after* their recruitment, because of the Japanese principle

† Shinohara, *Growth and Cycles*, Table 9, p. 17.

of lifetime employment with the firm, which meant that the older workers could not reopen their wage contracts.

The preceding analysis prompts a prediction that as annual labour force increases are going to be smaller in the years ahead than they have been over the last decade, the result will be a gradual elimination of wage disparities between the small scale and large scale firms.

THE CAUSES OF THE EMERGENCE OF ECONOMIC DUALITY

Generally in a *traditional* society where capital accumulation, modern know-how and modern entrepreneurship are in limited supply, a rapid economic development must lead to some degree of dualism. Development cannot proceed in all sectors at once, but is of necessity uneven. Theoretically, there are three alternatives for a traditional society embarking on rapid economic development where capital is very scarce in relation to the labour force. One is to spread the new capital becoming available equally but thinly over all the workers seeking employment. According to the equi-marginal returns principle, this should bring the highest total return. However, in practice it would be necessary for a large number of technologies to be available, all with various *flexible* factor proportions—there must be "modern" machinery which has been designed to operate *with various degrees of labour intensity*. In fact this is not the case. There are roughly only two technologies available, both with *fixed* factor proportions: a modern one, developed in the pioneering advanced countries which is both capital and know-how intensive, and the traditional technology which economises on capital but is labour intensive. This second technology "suits" the developing countries because it does not demand many of the factors that they do not have in plentiful supply. But it does not give higher income, and above all is not growth-promoting. The feasible way out of this dilemma is to create a situation where the major part of the newly available capital flows into the modern sector, and the rest of the economy continues with the old ways. Gradually, as more capital becomes available, some elements of the traditional sector will be upgraded, though this will be slow because the modern sector will almost always continue to be insatiable for capital.

The third way out is to assist the spearheading modern sector to obtain enough capital (within reason) and to try to develop domestically for the traditional sector a half-way technology that is only mildly capital-intensive. This means the developing country must either actually design and produce this half-way technology, which is extremely difficult, or it must use second-hand equipment which as a rule is relatively labour-intensive and is cheap to buy. Second-hand equipment is labour-intensive in two ways. Firstly, the usual motive for designing a new machine or process is to save labour, that is, to replace labour by capital. Secondly, equipment that has already had some use will require more servicing, will have more breakdowns to repair and as a result becomes itself more labour intensive in an absolute sense. Thus equipment that becomes economically obsolete in the modern large scale sector where wages are high, but has still plenty of life, can be used in the small scale sector where wages are low and the obsolete labour-intensive machine is still economical. For this solution to be feasible, the existence of dual structure is an indispensable condition. As a result, at least in the early stages of economic development, the existence of a dual structure with duality in the wage rates is in fact an advantage.

Japan took advantage of some of the dual economy features she created as she developed. Unwittingly, perhaps, the government assisted the growth of duality in several ways. The Meiji government began a tradition of fostering and assisting the development of the banking system. Indeed, banks often enjoyed a privileged position so that in the twentieth century Japan emerged with one of the most developed banking systems in the world. (See Chapters 5 and 6.) It is a well-known fact that banks, especially large banks, in any country do not like lending to small businesses, but are closely linked to large firms. Thus large firms found it easier to develop their technological facilities, while the small ones had to get along with the traditional equipment. It was only quite late in the inter-war period and especially after the last War that the government created financial institutions for the small businesses. Similarly, the Japanese governments looked kindly upon large firms and until the American occupation never introduced any legislation against concentration or monopoly. This also assisted large firms and made it harder for the small firms.

Given the emergence of duality, Japan made full use of some features. Agriculture has been making substantial progress though until recently in a rather traditional way with little capital input. But when modern capital became available, it was used with local adaptations. First came the manually operated wheeled cultivator, followed by the little petrol-driven cultivator in the post-war period as wages and savings went up. Now, when wages are high, a Japanese-designed rice-planting machine has appeared. In the manufacturing sector, large scale industry made full use of the small-scale firms through sub-contracting and sold its out-of-date equipment to the low-wage sector where the equipment gained a new lease of life.

In many developing countries there have been attempts to abolish the duality in the wage structure by legislating a minimum wage rate. While of course such a step is desirable on social grounds, it is undesirable on economic grounds. If the small business sector has to pay the same wage rates as the advanced large scale sector, the half-way technology (mildly capital-intensive) will not develop, and the discarded second-hand equipment will become uneconomic to use anywhere in the economy. Since, however, it would be impracticable for the country to supply *all* its workers with the endowment of capital required by the modern technology, some workers will have to be wholly unemployed, or they will gather on the fringes of employment in the cities, picking up casual jobs at the standard rate, and then being unemployed again.

In this context it is interesting to note that the economic development of Japan and to some extent of the Soviet Union actually took advantage of duality, but the economic development of the United Kingdom in the nineteenth century did not rely on duality. In Japan the traditional sector of farming and small scale crafts has been a Cinderella of the economy until recently. In the Soviet Union the collective farmers' incomes have had no minimum, and the growth of capital intensity of their production methods, like their incomes, has lagged very far behind the privileged manufacturing sector. In the United Kingdom's industrial revolution, however, where the country gradually built up technologies *in concordance with the relative domestic factor endowment*, such duality had no cause to arise.

In Japan's economic development until quite recently duality has been unavoidable *and* desirable. (This, of course, is not to argue that the Japanese Government did not or should not have tried to assist the traditional, capital-poor sector as far as it could.) Indeed, in a typical undoctrinaire pragmatic way, Japan made full use of some features of the duality. The spearhead of technological and economic growth was provided by the advanced, capital-intensive, large-scale sector which obtained the cream of capital and skilled labour supply, thanks to various institutional arrangements such as banking practices, and the banks' direct links with large scale industry. The traditional, small scale sector looked after the unfortunate rest of the economy and even provided the country with some savings and a good deal of foreign exchange earnings. In particular the small scale low wage sector absorbed all the vicissitudes that the economy suffered. It could do that because it paid low wages and because it had a very high wage rate flexibility. The small firm sector served the useful function of maintaining almost full employment when capital was too scarce to employ all the existing labour in modern enterprises. It also absorbed the shocks arising out of changing world trade conditions and domestic fluctuations. The small firms which frequently have worked as sub-contractors to large firms have allowed the modern sector to expand or contract output as the market dictated, by simply increasing or decreasing the amount of sub-contract work. If business was difficult and sub-contracting work was falling, the wage rate in the small scale sector would rapidly fall to a low level. There would be *some* wage level at which the workers involved would be re-employed (almost exactly as the textbooks of the classical economists said) and the product of such very low wage labour would be sold abroad (if for Keynesian reasons it did not have effective demand at home). Of course, this last effect could not be reached by *all* countries, because all countries could not increase exports if demand were constant, but *some* countries could do it and Japan did. Thus the small sector not only solved the employment problem but also made substantial earnings of foreign currencies. Even as late as 1964 the small businesses provided between 30% to 50% of Japan's exports.*

Seymour Broadbridge gives a brilliant argument to show that duality is not all bad for economic growth. He argues that the onslaught of the modern ways can be too complete for economic growth to be fostered. This happens when all the traditional ways, including consumption patterns, are replaced. This full "demonstration effect" leads to strong demands for immediate consumption of the fruits of increased productivity and thus undermines the very basis of the increase. Broadbridge said: "To stimulate new wants is to provide a spur to growth; yet growth can only be rapid if the wants go largely unsatisfied." He argues that Japanese economic growth in the modern sector "rested upon a core of largely untouched social and economic relationships including consumption patterns which survived from the Tokugawa period".†

The interesting question here is why a nation which showed so much flexibility in technical, military and cultural matters, was so conservative in consumption. There is no satisfactory explanation for this phenomenon. Perhaps it was due to the combined effect of two historical accidents: incomes were unequally distributed in Japan; and the ruling class, obsessed with the necessity to catch up with the West, kept its own consumption down to traditional levels, thus setting an even stronger "demonstration effect" for the lower classes than the "barbarians" did.

Broadbridge merely says: "It was the government which received the demonstration effect and was determined to keep up with the Jones's . . ."‡

He also links§ the wage dualism with the growth of the *zaibatsu* between 1910-1940. However this may be a spurious connection: for his statement to hold it would be necessary to show that the *zaibatsu* were particularly prone to pass some of their profits on to the workers in the form of increased wages. If he succeeded in doing this the *zaibatsu* would have emerged with a much better standing than they have in the

---

* *Outline of Small Business Finance Corporation*, Small Business Finance Corporation, Tokyo, 1964, p. 8.
† Seymour Broadbridge, *Industrial Dualism in Japan*, Aldine Publishing Company, Chicago, 1966, p. 18.
‡ Broadbridge, p. 19.
§ Broadbridge, p. 12.

West at any rate. (The Japanese have never seen the *zaibatsu* as villains, as the Westerners have.) It is more likely that the various dualisms (including wage dualism) have been caused by the sectoral introduction of modern technology, and by the technology's requirements. The arrival of this technology coincided with the emergence of the *zaibatsu* and therefore it only looks as if dualism were caused by the *zaibatsu*.

THE CONTINUATION OF DUALISM

In a general way dualism is just coexistence of the old and new ways. In cultural life the dualism is now threatened, but one hopes that this dualism will always exist, as the preservation of the best of the typical Japanese culture contributes to the world's cultural heritage. In diet, clothing and housing the traditional content is overwhelmingly strong. Indeed, in these fields an unbiased observer would have to say that the modern Western ways are superior. When Western diet is made available and familiar to the Japanese, it is usually considered superior though it is very expensive in Japan (and even though it *may* bring its own problems such as overweight and cholesterol). Western style clothing is not only much cheaper but also more practical—it is universally adopted in Japan for work and the traditional dress is used mainly for special occasions. Housing is even more traditional than the Japanese diet and yet outside the three or four months of the year when the weather is equable, it is extremely uncomfortable in spite of its visual charms. In addition it is uneconomic because the Japanese house is built of such materials and in such way (it is never painted) that its life span is not much more than twenty years, while a good quality Western house could stand for centuries. In particular, central heating and air-conditioning do not go well with the Japanese-style house, and they are bady needed in (a prosperous) Japan.

The long-lived dualism of agriculture and manufacturing was unavoidable in the past if fast economic growth was to materialise, but now some of its aspects are an obstacle to further economic improvement. Until quite recently wages in agriculture were very much lower than in industry, capital intensity still is much lower, and the way of working and living was more traditional. However, in 1968 rural incomes (farming and non-farming) caught up to urban incomes, and the methods of production are rapidly becoming more capital intensive. All the same, agriculture still awaits major restructuring at the fundamental level. (See Chapter 8.)

Dualism is said still to persist in manufacturing and distribution. In view of the great economies of large scale production and distribution, the continued existence of small scale industry and its importance in terms of employment or even value added in production is puzzling at first sight.

Table 7.2. The Importance of Small Firms* in Various Industries (July 1966)

Industries	Number of Firms (A)	Small Firms (B)	$\frac{B}{A}$ (%)	Number of Employees in the Industry (1,000) (C)	Employees in Small Firms (1,000) (D)	$\frac{D}{C}$ (%)
Mining	2,253	2,139	94·9	265	87	32·7
Construction	45,449	44,875	98·7	1,838	1,426	77·6
Manufacturing	182,158	177,832	97·6	9,049	4,924	54·4
Trading	244,257	231,072	94·6	3,983	2,421	60·8
Transportation	19,283	18,376	95·3	1,469	730	49·7
Services	67,825	64,125	94·5	1,307	919	70·3
Others	20,869	19,833	95·0	1,377	628	45·6
Total	582,094	558,252	95·9	19,287	11,135	57·7

Source: *Nihon Kokusei Zue*, p. 413.

*Note: Small firms in this table are defined as follows:
   In mining, construction, manufacturing, transportation and others: firms with capital less than 50 million yen; in trading and services: firms with capital less than 10 million yen.

We have made estimates of the small firm share of the total value of manufacturing output. In these estimates "small firms" are defined as those employing less than 200 workers. (Statistical data were not fully available for the conventional division line of less than 300 workers.) The calculations show that in the post-war period of great economic growth and the spectacular growth of large scale industry, the relative share of the value of output held by small firms has remained virtually constant. In 1941 small firms held 46 per cent of the value of output; in 1963 it was 44 per cent; and in 1966, 44 per cent.†

Some nineteenth century European writers predicted the disappearance of small firms, yet they continue to exist in all countries, though the size of the largest firms in most industries has increased enormously. There are apparently many industries where there may always be some room for small firms, especially where mass-production is not possible because of individualised demands. Indeed, by increasing incomes, economic progress based on mass production techniques creates a demand for something that is different, individually produced "to measure", and such products are the preserve of small firms. In addition, there will always be some people who attempt to start business on their own with small capital. Since large firms do decline and die, the ranks of the large firms will always be replenished by the surviving successful small firms,

† Sources for basic data:
    (a) Industrial Statistics Section, Research Statistics Division, M.I.T.I., *Statistical Tables for Industry*.
    (b) Bureau of Statistics, Office of the Prime Minister, *Japan Statistical Yearbook 1968*, p. 184.

though it looks as if the emergence of *keiretsu* financing of new enterprises might severely limit this opportunity.

In Japan, as in some other countries, there have been other reasons why small firms persist, such as national shortage of capital; shortage of high quality entrepreneurship (which is particularly important in large enterprises); shortage of particular modern skills, though this factor is not now as operative in Japan; government assistance to small firms; lack of mobility of labour especially between the small and large enterprises; and assistance to small firms by the large companies which use them for sub-contracting.

Paradoxically, substantial reduction of economic discrepancies between agriculture and manufacturing has been easier than similar reduction between the small and large manufacturing enterprises. Under the "income-parity policy" the government has kept increasing food prices by drastic quantitative import controls and this, plus agricultural subsidies and special tax concessions, has increased the rural (farm and non-farm) incomes to the over-all national level. This process was assisted by the outflow of the labour force (mainly young people) from the countryside to the cities. Wage disparities coupled with the greater attractions of city life induced large shifts of labour from agriculture, especially when there was a high demand for labour in cities. The shift of labour from the countryside was easy because young labour is highly mobile and because given the small size of the farms, farmers have had industrial jobs on the side for a long time, so that the shift was not as large as it might seem.

Within the manufacturing industry itself, the upward mobility of labour from small scale to large scale firms is still very low even now, and indeed there is some movement in the opposite direction. There are four reasons for this: the principle of lifetime employment with a single firm prevents switching from small to large employers (but does not prevent a farmer's son taking a job in a city). Large firms do not engage older workers, but recruit only the cream of the high school leavers and tertiary education graduates. While the brightest sons and daughters of farmers upgrade themselves by entering large scale industry after schooling, the rest are rejected as not well enough qualified, and they go to small scale industry. The ranks of the self-employed and the employees in the small scale industries are continuously replenished by the former government servants and large scale industry employees who are retired very early in Japan. Some special occupations like police or the military retire at forty-five, the public servants ordinarily retire at fifty-five. In large scale industry employees are retired at fifty-five, though there is now a trend to lift the retirement age to sixty under the pressure of trade unions and labour shortage. (Improved life expectancy is used to rationalise the demand for later retirement. Although there are good arguments for later retirement, especially in conditions of labour shortage and undeveloped pension schemes, the argument resting on the increased life expectancy is entirely wrong. What has increased in all countries in the last few decades is the life expectancy *at birth*, but medical progress has not yet increased life expectancy from the age of fifty or fifty-five.) While some of the retired are given "temporary employment" at a *much* reduced pay, others are retired completely. As a result some of the former employees in large scale industry are compelled to search for work in the only outlet open—small scale industry and distribution.

In view of the preceding factors it is clear that duality is likely to continue as long as the present institutional arrangements continue. The small scale sector has to accommodate the rejects of the labour force and is generally unable to offer the young conditions and prospects which are competitive with those offered by the large scale sector, so that it attracts the less able or the less qualified. This makes the small scale sector less profitable and less able to compete financially for high quality manpower, thus perpetuating its inferior performance. In addition, the small scale sector is handicapped in competition for capital owing to bankers' preferences, in spite of the existence of numerous financial institutions set up by the government for small scale industries.

To keep matters in proportion it should be stated that most or all European countries would be found to exhibit wage and income dualism, capital dualism, and so forth, if they had statistics as comprehensive as Japan's, but it is perhaps probable that this dualism has been stronger in Japan.

Moreover it is necessary to keep in mind the Japanese definition of small enterprise. Until 1963 the small enterprises were legally defined—to determine eligibility for various types of assistance—as firms with less than 10 million yen capital (approximately U.S.$27,800) *or* not more than 299 employees. For distribution and services the maximum number of employees was set at fifty. Under the Small Businesses Basic Law of 1963 the limit of capital in manufacturing, mining, construction and transportation has been increased to 50 million yen (approximately U.S.$139,000), except for commerce and services where it was left unchanged.

Recently the Japanese Government expressed great fears for the small enterprises. In the *White Book on Small Enterprises* for the fiscal year 1968 it said:

> . . . at home, the accentuation of labour shortages eliminated low wages, the most important factor on which the existence of small enterprises depended. On the international scene the small enterprises have been directly or indirectly hit by increases in competition coming from the developing countries, the progress in the liberalisation of entry of foreign capital to Japan and the stronger internationalisation of the Japanese economy.

In 1970 the developed countries are to give tariff preferences to the "developing countries" (really the under-developed countries) for which Japan will not qualify. This will hurt her labour-intensive exports even more.

The Economic Planning Agency and the Japanese Government are concerned about what they consider inadequate response of the small scale industry to these challenges. In March 1968 the E.P.A. carried out a survey of 2,442 small manufacturing enterprises (10-299 workers) about their attitudes to the approaching greater internationalisation of the Japanese economy. The answers were:

Measures to cope with the problems of internationalisation
   have already been taken   12·3%
Such measures are not considered necessary   38·3%
Measures are considered necessary but have not yet been taken   49·4%*

The responding small scale firms suggested the need for obvious general improvements in production methods such as automation or increased labour productivity. Only 10 per cent favoured development of overseas markets, and only 1·6 per cent favoured establishment of overseas plants. However, the surveys carried out by the Osaka and Tokyo Chambers of Commerce on the attitudes to investing abroad revealed that

Table 7.3. *Numbers of Cases of Foreign Investment by Large and Small Japanese Enterprises, as of March 1968.*

Region	Total number of cases of foreign investment	Under Y100 million total	Number of cases by size of capital of investing enterprise			
			Small enterprises			
			Y50–100 million	Y30–50 million	Y10–30 million	UnderY10 million
North America	38	1	1			
Latin America	120	7	2			5
Southeast Asia	449	124	30	8	27	59
Hong Kong	44	13	5		3	5
Taiwan	135	54	11	5	10	28
Europe	22	3	3			
Near and Middle East	6	3	2			1
Oceania	31	1			1	
Africa	37	3	1	1		1
Total	703	142	39	9	28	66

Notes: Based on approvals of foreign investment in manufacturing only, as of 31 March 1968.
Source: *White Book on Small Enterprises for Fiscal 1968; Fuji Bank Bulletin,* June 1969.

* *Fuji Bank Bulletin,* June 1969.

Table 7.4. *Analysis of Direct Foreign Investment by Small Enterprises*

	Number of cases
By branch of industry	
Textiles	18
Machinery	12
Wholesale trade	8
Electrical machinery	7
Transportation machinery	6
Food processing	5
Chemicals	4
Ceramics	2
Other manufacturing	10
Other industries (including services)	3
By objective	
Utilisation of local labor	43
Development of new markets	28
New sales outlets	24
Exports of raw materials	15
Utilisation of local raw materials	11
In lieu of payment of receivables	9
Export of machinery and equipment	6
Defense of existing markets	4
Cost reduction of imports	4
Financial aid to subsidiary	2
Participation in management	1
By location of investment	
North America	14
Europe	7
Latin America	2
Oceania	3
Africa	4
Communist countries	2
Taiwan	34
Thailand	8
Republic of Korea	5
Philippines	3
Okinawa	3
Hong Kong	2
Singapore	2
Pakistan	2
Malaysia	1
Burma	1
Ceylon	1

Notes: 1. Based on ninety-four cases of foreign investment by seventy-five enterprises which are customers of the Central Bank for Commercial and Industrial Co-operatives.
2. Figures under "Objective" cannot be added because the same foundation may serve several purposes.

Source: Central Bank for Commercial and Industrial Co-operatives, Survey on Foreign Investment, 13 November 1968. *Fuji Bank Bulletin*, June 1969.

about 30 per cent of the canvassed firms were interested in it.† The striking difference in these surveys and the one carried by the E.P.A. may perhaps be explained by the nature of the questionnaire itself. The last two surveys almost suggested an answer.

As Table 7.3 shows, out of the total 703 cases of foreign investment by Japanese companies as of March 1968, 103 cases were small enterprises (capital under 50 million yen), which is rather remarkable performance, though the Japanese authorities do not think so.

CURRENT ECONOMIC DUALITY

Some writers place great importance on the differences of value added per worker in large and small industries. The value added reflects the intensity of application of *all* the factors of production, and since the application of capital in small scale industries is lower (for various, sometimes purely technological reasons), it is not surprising that if the *total* value added in both groups of industries is expressed per number of workers only (and no allowance is made to cover differing amounts of capital applied), then some substantial differences in value added per worker would emerge (as long as capital is productive!).

Those writers who conclude from statistics of value added per worker, or "wage" per worker, that the physical productivity of *the worker* is lower in small scale industries make also another error. The small scale industries are highly competitive and large scale industries are almost by definition oligopolistic or monopolistic. Therefore one would expect large scale industries to charge more per similar product, make larger profits, have higher value added per worker, and even pay a somewhat higher wage. But this would not mean that the *physical* productivity per worker in the *small* scale industries is that much lower than in the large scale industries. If the small scale industries formed a powerful cartel and restricted output, with their present technology, know-how and effort by the workers, the price of the product and the value added per worker could go up to any level! If the trade unions in the small scale industries were better organised, they could push their wages up. But would all these changes mean that the physical product available for the whole nation would be higher? On the contrary, elementary theory tells us that monopolistic or oligopolistic policy rests on *restricting* output.

Further, it must be noted that the large firms in Japan are often in the position of a monopsonist or oligopsonist in dealing with the subcontracting small firms. Again this implies that the large firms are able to strike more favourable price bargains. This will lead to lower profits and value added in small scale industries, but does it mean that the

† *Fuji Bank Bulletin*, June 1969.

physical productivity of the workers in small-scale industries is that much smaller? And if the small scale industries developed some countervailing power to nullify the monopsonistic power of the large firms, would the physical product available for the nation go up?

The usual Japanese statistics (such as the quoted Table 7.1) purporting to prove wage duality are not convincing enough even at their own level. The data are too aggregative and do not compare like with like. In particular the usual tables in Japanese literature show the weighted average "wage" for *all* company *employees* in the small scale sector and in the large scale sector, without regard to the existence of different ratios of males to females, university graduates to non-graduates, and high-school leavers to middle-school leavers in the small scale firms compared to these ratios in the large scale firms. Once we accept the probability that the large firms may employ fewer women than the small firms (which are mainly light industries) and given the fact that the average female wage in Japan is only half* of the average male wage, it is clear that any aggregate statistical table which does not handle male and female wages separately cannot prove the existence of wage duality, although, of course, it will show a "statistical" difference.

Exactly the same argument applies to the problem of different ratios of university graduates to non-graduates in the large and small firms. Of course, large firms will employ, *and will need to employ* more university graduates than small firms, and this again will push up the average "wage" in the large firms. In Japanese statistics "the wage" usually quoted includes payments to the ordinary workers as well as to the company lawyers, accountants, architects and business executives. Large companies will need those kinds of university graduates on their staff, whereas the small companies often do not need any accountants and obtain the occasional services of the other professions outside their own staff.

If the wages paid to similar categories of labour in small firms and in large firms were compared the difference would not be very large. Much of the remaining difference would still be explicable by the fact that even inside a single category of labour, such as university graduates, there would be differences of quality as the large firms attract and pick the best students from the best universities. (Universities in Japan, as in the U.S.A., differ a great deal in quality.) The large firms are able to pick the best of the labour force because they offer most scope for promotion, greater security in employment, are prestigious, have the reputation of being generous employers, and in fact probably are somewhat more generous.

The usual Japanese statistics involve still another conceptual confusion

---

* Division of Labour Statistics and Research, Ministry of Labour, *Yearbook of Labour Statistics 1966*, p. 54.

Table 7.5. Percentage Share of Value of Output in Manufacturing Produced by "Small Firms" by Industry in 1963.

Wood and timber	93%
Clothing	92%
Furniture	91%
Leather products	89%
Metal products	79%
"Other"	77%
Foodstuffs	72%
Textile materials	61%
Publishing or printing	61%
Ceramic and concrete products	59%
Pulp, paper and paper products	56%
Instrument making	50%
Machinery (excluding electric)	49%
Chemical products	33%
Non-ferrous metals	31%
Rubber products	30%
Steel	28%
Electric appliances	28%
Petrol and coal products	21%
Transport equipment	20%

Source for basic data : Research and Statistics Department, Ministry of International Trade and Industry, *Census of Manufactures*, Government of Japan, 1963.

in showing lower wages and lower profitability of small scale firms as an evidence of economic duality or backwardness of the small scale sector. Table 7.5, showing the share of the total output by value held by firms below 300 workers in 1963, demonstrates that small firms predominate in a special category of industries (as ranked in Table 7.5 by share of total output): wood and timber, clothing, furniture, leather products, metal products, unspecified "other" and processing foodstuffs. Most of these industries would have to be classified as industries where the scope for machinery is very limited and will be limited for a long time to come. Above all they are industries where competition from the low wage under-developed countries is the strongest. Thus it is not surprising that their profitability and wages are low. The conclusions from this table prove that the low profitability and wages in the small scale sector shown by aggregate statistics for manufacturing as a whole are due not only to low level of capital use, but also to the fact that they are the wrong industries for Japan given present conditions and wages. Thus any technological, and especially privileged financial and fiscal, assistance to those small firms has not and could not have been reducing the duality. In fact it has accentuated the duality, because some factors of production that would and should have left the sector were induced to stay.

Another conclusion stemming from Table 7.5 is that the usual Japanese aggregate all-manufacturing statistics purporting to show economic duality (in the sense of culpable, or remediable inefficiency in the small scale sector) are just irrelevant. To be relevant, to show duality in some meaningful sense, each industry would have to have separate statistics for wages, value added, and so on. If this were done the overall picture of duality would be much weaker.

Indeed, if one compiled "wage" statistics for the fully advanced countries of the West on the same basis as Japan does, it would turn out that the United Kingdom, Germany, United States, France, and probably all advanced countries have duality, in some cases larger than Japan. If one took Germany, for instance, the duality would almost certainly be higher than in Japan, simply because the average rural income in Germany is still *much* below the urban income, and in Japan the rural incomes caught up with the urban incomes in 1967. The same applies to France with respect to the urban and the rural incomes, relative urban and rural sophistication, and the use of capital and modern technology.

It is probable that there are very few countries that would not show features of dualism as Japan does. The main reason why most countries do not claim a dual structure is that they do not have nearly as much statistical data about their economies as Japan. They simply do not know the average wage in firms employing less than 300 workers, or in firms employing more than 299 workers, nor do they have any other data for the two groups. Only the primitive tribal countries, like Basutoland, are sure to have no economic dualism.

It would appear then that the extent of duality and its alleged uniqueness are exaggerated in Japan. It is almost certainly true that the vast amount of intellectual effort spent in compiling the statistics by statisticians and in analysing the duality by economists is excessive compared to the degree of duality. All the same the practical effects of this preoccupation with duality may have been desirable—the attention of the government and the financial institutions was attracted to the problems of small scale industries. Although the features of the duality in the post-war period may have been weak, the important fact is that the small firms employ the overwhelming majority of labour. Thus any technological up-grading of this vast sector through technical advice or provision of better access to finance is important, though there is a danger that assistance might slow down a natural shift of factors of production out of a sector that is no longer economic for Japan.

The General Trading Company

The Japanese "general trading company", *shoji kaisha,* or as it is often called, the *trading company,* cannot be defined in one sentence. It has multifarious purposes and activities. It is usually said to be unique to Japan, but there are three exceptions. There are two trading companies in West Africa—United Africa Company and the Swiss Trading Corporation—and *Société Général* in Belgium. All of them are much smaller in capital and volume of trade and very much simpler in the range of activities. These three trading companies, along with the Japanese trading companies, arose in the second half of the nineteenth century though it is difficult to say which was the first, especially as they developed gradually. (The Swiss Trading Corporation, for example, began as a Swiss mission to convert the "heathens" in Africa, but the missionaries gradually found trading more attractive.)

The general trading company is the result of carrying the principle of division of labour (specialisation) into the sales process. Historically and logically it originates from circumstances where there were many small producers who would have had extreme difficulties in trying to run their own sales and purchases, especially when distant or foreign markets were involved. The difficulties would have arisen because of lack of time, lack of knowledge of the markets, lack of knowledge of foreign languages and foreign business practices, and even lack of capital. The producers in the Meiji Japan were simply compelled to admit that buying and selling is a task for specialists, as they had no option at that time. The interesting fact is that in the inter- and post-war periods when many manufacturers reached enormous size, they have continued to use the services of a trading company. This is so because the trading companies developed a structure and activities which make their services attractive. One might think that as Japan's export products became sophisticated pieces of mechanical or electrical engineering, the intermediation of the general trading company would tend to bring a dilution or distortion, or just excessive delays in the two-way technical information passed between the market and the producer. But the trading company employs many thousands of staff (some foreign) many of whom are highly qualified scientists, engineers and economists. They are scattered all over the world, speak the local language, and provide better market research, inspection, and servicing than even a very large manufacturing company could do for itself.

The general trading company will sell anything anywhere. The numerous Japanese manufacturers rely on the general trading company to sell their products. Some very large manufacturers of products like cars and electronic equipment may establish their own sales agencies in the major countries, but in countries with a small market they will still use the services of a general trading company. The use of a trading company is a frequent practice for marketing producer equipment, the demand for which is scattered geographically and in time.

Small manufacturers are highly dependent on the services of a general trading company for marketing. The trading company will frequently buy the product from the small manufacturer and put its own name on it, thus accepting the responsibility for the product and providing the after-sale service.

The largest two trading companies, the Mitsubishi Shoji Kaisha, and Mitsui and Company (or Mitsui Bussan) have more than 100 branches each all over the world. Each employs about 10,000 people. Their annual sales in 1969 were at the rate of US$6 billion, which would give each of them the rank of one of the twenty largest trading *countries* in the world. Two other trading companies, Marubeni-Iida and C. Itoh, are expected to reach similar rank in the near future. The number of trading companies is in the thousands, but the "Big Ten" play an overwhelmingly large role in Japan's economy (and an important one in the world's economy). In 1969 they accounted for about 50 per cent of Japan's exports and about 60 per cent of her imports.

Table 7.6. The "Big Ten" Trading Companies (ranked by sales in 1966).

Rank	Trading Company	Sales U.S. $ mil.	Profit after tax U.S. $ mil.	Paid-up capital U.S. $ mil.	Total Assets U.S. $ mil.	Number of employees	Profit as % of sales	Profit as % of total assets
1	Mitsui & Company	4,932	10·3	37·8	1,876	9,649	0·1	0·4
2	Mitsubishi Shoji	4,803	12·0	62·5	1,515	7,546	0·2	0·7
3	Marubeni-Iida	3,832	2·9	43·0	1,246	7,391	0·1	0·2
4	C. Itoh	3,462	6·6	46·9	1,009	6,277	0·1	0·6
5	Toyo Menka	2,052	2·9	20·6	701	4,011	0·1	0·4
6	Sumitomo Shoji	1,753	4·1	19·4	629	4,446	0·2	0·6
7	Nissho	1,655	3·5	19·4	445	3,777	0·2	0·7
8	Nichimen	1,644	0·061	20·8	493	3,519	0·0	0·0
9	Toyota Motor Sales	989	11·8	33·3	489	2,621	1·1	2·4
10	Ataka & Company	979	3·2	16·7	334	2,389	0·3	0·9

Source: *The President Directory 1967,* President Diamond-Time Co., Tokyo.

Table 7.7   Profits of Japan's Ten Largest Trading Companies for October 1968-
March 1969 Period.

Trading Company	Profits after tax	In million yen Dividends	% Annual Rate Dividend
Mitsubishi	1,330,509 (1,187,875)	3,059 (2,700)	15 (12)
Mitsui	1,251,384 (1,116,394)	2,319 (2,167)	14 (14)
Marubeni-Iida	909,467 (870,451)	1,210 (1,193)	12 (12)
C. Itoh	827,177 (795,378)	1,268 (1,292)	12 (12)
Nissho-Iwai	626,180 (615,166)	921 (686)	12 (12)
Sumitomo	530,163 (471,164)	1,115 (1,014)	12 (12)
Toyo Menka	518,482 (484,483)	582 (520)	10 (10)
Nichimen	365,792 (350,377)	315 (202)	0 (0)
Kanematsu-Gosho	310,028 (298,216)	324 (314)	8 (8)
Ataka Sangyo	270,800 (248,338)	682 (630)	12 (12)

Note: Parenthesised figures are those for the previous six-month term.
Source: *The Japan Times*, 10 May 1969.

There are at least forty large trading companies with substantial foreign business. The many purely domestic general trading companies are called the *tonya*. There are various types of *tonya*. Some have their own manufacturing subsidiaries, some sell for cash, and some sell on credit. The *tonya* has a peculiar relationship to the retailer or another middleman between them which is quite different from Western commercial relationships. The *tonya* owner or manager and the retailer are like personal friends. The *tonya* must help the retailer in need. It owes him *ninjio* (humanity) and the retailer owes the wholesaler *giri* (obligation). The distribution system in Japan is excessively long, complicated and very expensive. Japan has an extraordinarily high proportion of salesmen in its labour force—every tenth Japanese of the actively employed *male* population is a salesman. In the whole world Japan ranks the fourth after Hong Kong (which is a special case because of the importance of "shopping tourists" in the "customs free" country), Venezuela and Uruguay.* Whether Napoleon was right or not in his day when calling Great Britain a "nation of shopkeepers", today Japan is the "nation of shopkeepers"! Western businessmen have difficulty understanding the Japanese distribution system, are often frustrated by it, think that their product is discriminated against, and generally think the whole system of distribution to be inefficient. The reasons for such an extensive distribution system with many middlemen are complex. Perhaps the system is partly a matter of habit and tradition; however, it is partly due to the fact that many Japanese retailers and small producers need assistance in the form of capital and storage facilities. Storage facilities

*U.N., *Compendium of Social Statistics: 1967*, pp. 500-512.

are scarce as land is very expensive or simply not available near the particular businesses. Many shopkeepers carry very little stock, which means that some trading company must perform that trading function and make frequent deliveries.

The large general trading company performs most or all of the following tasks: importing and exporting; domestic trading; and "triangular trading" which involves, for instance, the sale of Polish second-hand airplanes to New Zealand as the Sumitomo Shoji Kaisha did in 1968.† The Mitsubishi Shoji Kaisha had run up triangular trade to the value of twelve billion yen during the six months from October 1965 to end of March 1966. (Note: Japanese company accounts are made for six month periods.) Recently the large trading companies have experienced a spectacular growth in their third countries' trade. In 1969 the third countries' trade done by the major Japanese general trading companies amounted to 10% of their entire trade volume.‡ The largest part of the increase is due to the establishment of numerous Japanese joint ventures abroad by the general trading companies and by Japanese manufacturers. These joint ventures are sometimes located in the low-cost-of-production countries but are intended to sell a proportion of the output abroad. The trading company is well equipped to do such business. All the major general trading companies are preparing themselves for a further expansion of the triangular trade. In 1969 C. Itoh established special sections in its Tokyo and Osaka branches to handle triangular trade exclusively.

General trading companies also provide extensive and intensive market research all over the world. For example, the Mitsubishi Shoji Kaisha has about forty domestic branches and about sixty-five subsidiary companies, branches and representative offices abroad, in such countries as the U.S.A., Canada, Mexico, Colombia, Peru, Brazil, Chile, Argentina, France, West Germany, Italy, Iran, Thailand, Australia and others.

The trading companies act as credit dealers, providing credit to producers, dealers or the industrial users. They "buy" credit from a bank and then "sell" it at a slightly higher price to trade customers; the loans of the Mitsui Bank to Mitsui Bussan (the trading company) are at present at the level of U.S.$140 million. The Mitsui Bussan pays the Bank about 7 per cent interest, and it charges its customers 9 to 10 per cent. The Bank does not mind this because the general trading company, dealing regularly with its trade customer, is better placed to assess the risks and to supervise the loan.

Joint ventures or wholly owned commercial, mining or industrial enterprises abroad are organised by large trading companies. Mitsui trading company operates a large number of joint ventures in Canada, Mexico,

† *Asia Scene*, January 1969, p. 37.
‡ *Nihon Keizai Shimbun*, 5 August 1969.

Central and South America, Germany, France, Australia, Thailand, Ceylon, Malaya, Portugal and many other countries.

Trading companies also organise co-operative construction of complete plants abroad for foreign owners where several specialised producers (usually Japanese) have to co-operate, for example, a civil engineering firm makes surveys and prepares the land and roads, a construction firm puts up the buildings, one or more engineering firms supply the equipment, and still another firm starts the production until the locals can take over. They advise Japanese tenderers for contracts abroad on the likely competition and optimal tenders.

They organise what can best be called "private bilateral trade", where the general trading company supplies a complete plant or part of the equipment on credit and agrees to accept the products of that company in repayment. As a result the trading companies play a large role in the imports to Japan of such materials as crude oil, iron ore, coal, timber and so on.

They provide technical consultancy services for foreign customers in development projects. Joint ventures are set up by trading companies, which negotiate on behalf of a Japanese customer or customers with foreign governments and other foreign interests. In such negotiations the strength of the general trading company comes from the fact that it has full knowledge of conditions on the world-wide scale.

General trading companies also perform the following services: negotiating with the Export-Import Bank of Japan on provision of credit for financing exports or imports; setting up their own manufacturing subsidiaries in Japan or abroad, as opportunities are shown by market research; warehousing, domestic transportation and shipping; insurance; dealing in real estate; and establishing subsidiary companies for running department stores and chain stores.

The strength of the general trading company, apart from its own merits, has been derived partly from associations with a particular *zaibatsu* in the past and a particular *keiretsu* at present. However, the general trading company will take business outside the *keiretsu*, and it is claimed that some will even handle the business competing with the products of the *keiretsu* members, if such business is more profitable.

When a Westerner looks at a general trading company he is apt to think that the trading company creates even more new problems than it solves because the two-way communication lines between the producer and the ultimate buyer and user become very extended. The Westerner might be prepared to admit that the trading company might have some merits in the case of standardised products in international trade. But he would fear that where complex modern manufactured machines are sold, any intermediary (not to say intermediaries) would clog and distort the two-way communications between producers and users and would not be able to provide after-sale services. However, the Japanese general trading company has found a solution for this problem: it employs an army of engineers and scientists.

Most Japanese producers put a high value on the general trading company, make use of it, and expect a great future for it. However, some of the very large manufacturers, such as Honda, Nissan, Toyota and Canon Cameras, have made their own sales arrangements and do not use the services of any general trading company.

The "Zaibatsu" and the "Keiretsu"

THE ZAIBATSU

The word *zaibatsu* literally means financial clique (*gunbatsu*, military clique, *kanbatsu*, political clique). The origin of the *zaibatsu* as a monopolistic organisation is in the Meiji era. At least one of them is much older as a business firm—Mitsui is over 270 years old. The Mitsui and Mitsubishi family businesses were on the side of the Emperor in the revolution and the new political order favoured them. Mitsui in particular was a central figure in the Japanese economy in the Meiji period. These two were later joined by the Sumitomo concern. In time they came to be called the old *zaibatsu* and they have always enjoyed a high reputation among the Japanese (unlike in the West where for various reasons *zaibatsu* is a term of condemnation). In the inter-war period there arose new *zaibatsu,* some of which may not have been generally regarded as *zaibatsu* but would like to be so called. Each *zaibatsu* was usually rigidly controlled by a family, through the device of a "holding company" (the *hon sha*) which held a controlling block of shares in the subordinate companies. The subordination was complete—before the last War each new employee of any of the Mitsui companies had to sign a written oath of loyalty to *the head of the Mitsui family.* Thus there was a feudal element in the personnel relationships.

The *zaibatsu,* which were always very strong financially because of their mere size, took advantage of their position by buying out and absorbing smaller competitors. As a result they developed into very powerful monopolistic organisations which controlled the market in a number of commodities. Each *zaibatsu* specialised in a few categories of goods, but the Yasuda family *zaibatsu* (the Fuji concern) was a purely financial one controlling insurance and finance businesses. The Mitsui *zaibatsu* controlled paper, coal, synthetic dyes and much of the foreign trade. The Mitsubishi *zaibatsu* controlled heavy industry, shipbuilding, marine transportation and plate glass.

Until the post-war period the Japanese Government never discouraged large firms. In fact it assisted these monopolistic organisations. In the inter-war period the Japanese Government was not alone in these policies.

Facing shrinking markets during the Great Depression, many European governments including the British assisted cartelisation under the euphemistic name of "rationalisation of industry". In the preparation for and during the War the *zaibatsu* fully co-operated with the government and this, together with the facts that they were monopolies and were very powerful competitors with the American businesses, gave them a very bad name in the West.

After the defeat of Japan, one of General MacArthur's first steps was to dissolve the *zaibatsu*. The Economic Deconcentration Law issued by the Occupation Authorities declared as illegal all designated companies with large assets and many employees; engaged in inter-company activities different from normal supplying of products or selling of products to each other; exercising managerial control over other businesses; or enjoying near monopoly power.

Originally 257 companies in manufacturing and in mining, and sixty-eight companies in commerce and services were designated, but in fact only eighteen companies were broken up, including all the *zaibatsu*. The *hon sha* became illegal. Even the large trading companies were broken up into small companies. All the *zaibatsu* and other large companies were splintered into a large number of small companies. The Americans, with a large dose of emotional and what might be called "hind-thinking", decided to destroy the military power and the heavy industry of Japan "forever" in order to be safe. They also compelled the Japanese to include a clause in the new constitution forbidding any future Japanese government to establish any military forces of its own. However the economic costs of breaking up over 300 companies would have been too high, especially as the economic position of Japan was so desperate that the Americans had to provide economic aid. Consequently the decree was carried out only in respect of eighteen companies. Further, when Japan obtained independence after the San Francisco Peace Treaty of 1952, the new Japanese Government relaxed the restraints, although continuing to maintain very strict anti-monopoly laws. As a result many of the splintered companies soon came together by merging the component parts back into the old industrial or trading companies. The whole conglomerate *zaibatsu* groups arose again, but this time a different liquid was put into the old bottles.

(It is interesting to note in this context that in military matters the American Government is now trying to persuade the *unwilling* Japanese to remove the anti-military clause from the Japanese constitution!)

It is remarkable that the American Occupation Authorities restructuring of the Japanese economy never touched the large Japanese banks which were often close to the heart of the *zaibatsu*. In fact the large banks came to be protected by the Americans. The Occupation Authorities froze all large bank deposits held by the *zaibatsu* and the armament industry with the city banks. This was, of course, to the advantage of the large banks—they were freed from meeting their liabilities. It is true that these banks were going to lose much of the loans to the armaments industry, but even there the industrial company shareholders had to make good up to 90% of industry debts to banks. One could only speculate why deconcentration policy was not applied to banks and why they were given such privileged treatment.

THE EMERGENCE OF THE KEIRETSU

Whatever the emotional attitudes about business concentration might be, the hard facts of economic life are that large size confers many important economic advantages. It was because of these advantages that the American Occupation Authorities halted their program of deconcentration after the first step of dissolving the proscribed eighteen companies. It was because of these advantages of scale that the *keiretsu* emerged. A large business can reap the following economies of scale: in purchasing supplies on a large scale, in selling on a large scale, in obtaining finance, in obtaining credit, in production through a large plant, long "runs" of production for the product, and the ability to carry out expensive research and experimentation. Although some of these advantages are not available for a loose grouping like the *keiretsu*, many are. The literal meaning of the term *keiretsu* is "linked group" or "affiliated group". The very strong Japanese but American-inspired post-war anti-monopoly legislation and enforcement prevented the reappearance of the old *zaibatsu* with strong central control through the holding company. Instead much looser conglomerates emerged, with links dependent upon the mutual interest and convenience of the associated companies. However, what is striking is that the broken-up ex-*zaibatsu* companies, run by new executives (formerly only of middle rank in the *zaibatsu*) virtually all came together again like a jigsaw puzzle. The ties of tradition and of collective operation, which were the natural Japanese way of doing business, assured the re-emergence of the traditional industrial and financial groupings. But very great differences from the old pattern appeared in the new groups.

The first difference is that the *keiretsu* does not have any central control over the members: there is no holding company. The holding company is still illegal in Japan. The linking of the *keiretsu* group of companies which arises from mutual interest is formalised through mutual exchange of shares and the link of swapping directorates between the companies. Last but not least, there is a strong link provided by the institution at the centre of the *keiretsu* (a bank in the case of the *kinyu keiretsu*, and a substantial company in the case of the *sangyo keiretsu*) which gives advice and financial assistance in the form of credit to the affiliated members. The company at the centre of a *sangyo keiretsu* also purchases the output, or much of the output, of the smaller affiliated company.

The *kinyu keiretsu* (sometimes called *yushi keiretsu*), literally meaning "financially linked group", is only loosely linked. The shares in capital exchanged between the *keiretsu* bank and the *keiretsu* members do not give any strong controlling interest. The *keiretsu* member does obtain the bulk of its bank loans from the *keiretsu* bank and this is a substantial link only as long as the company is completely dependent on that source of finance. Any *kinyu keiretsu* member is free to leave the *keiretsu* in which case it sells the shares it holds in the bank and the bank sells the shares it holds in the company. No permission is needed, though as a matter of courtesy the company leaving the *keiretsu* is expected to notify the bank of its intention to sell the shares. Having left the *keiretsu* the company cannot, however, count on preferential credit allocation from the *keiretsu* bank. Since in the post-war period a practice has developed where large companies as a rule borrow simultaneously from more than one bank (because some companies are so large and have such large credit requirements that one bank would not be able to satisfy them), it follows that a company could leave the *keiretsu* relatively easily, if it felt that the *keiretsu* bank was not giving it a fair deal, and that some other bank would treat it better. It should be noted here that the Japanese banks do not mind if a customer borrows from another bank, indeed they encourage it.

The other link of the *kinyu keiretsu* is the trading company. It buys the supplies for the *keiretsu* members, sells their products and supplies them with loans it acquires from the bank. The members of the *keiretsu* do not have to deal through the trading company but they usually do. The trading company can sell the products of the outsiders, but there is some doubt what it would do when the outsider's product competes with the products of the *keiretsu* companies. Certainly the Mitsubishi Shoji Kaisha would not sell the product.

The *keiretsu* bank and the trading company exercise some influence over the associated companies' policies and appointments, but the member companies cannot exercise such influence in reverse. However normally the influence of the bank and the trading company is very limited unless the member company is in difficulties.

The matter of influence by the central company is substantially different in the case of the *sangyo keiretsu* (also called *kigyo keiretsu*) which is an industrially-linked group. In this case there are the credit links and exchange of shares but, in addition the central company will be the main or the only buyer of the products, and as a result the central company will have a substantial degree of control over its satellites. While a member of the *kinyu keiretsu* can leave the group easily, this is not so in the case of the *sangyo keiretsu*. Indeed the Japanese economists give some of the *sangyo keiretsu* the name of "*torasuto gata*" *keiretsu*, which means they are strongly linked organisations like trusts. In the case of some of these *sangyo keiretsu*, the master company belongs itself to a *kinyu keiretsu*; for example, Toshiba and Toyota belong to Mitsui *kinyu keiretsu*; Yawata Steel and Hitachi belong to Yasuda *kinyu keiretsu*. But in the case of some of the *sangyo keiretsu*, such as Nissan,

Chart 7.1 DIAGRAMMATIC REPRESENTATION OF THE MITSUI KINYU KEIRETSU AND ONE OF THE ASSOCIATED SANGYO KEIRETSU

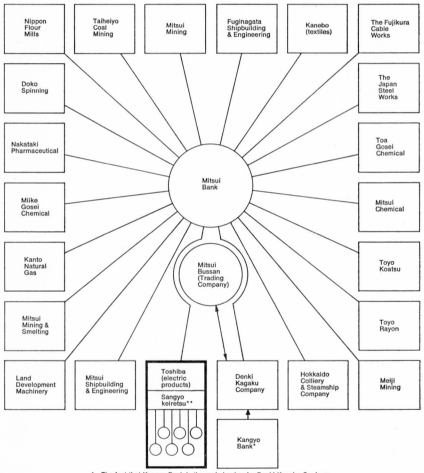

* The fact that Kangyo Bank is the *main* banker for Denki Kagaku Co. is an exception. It is more or less due to the wish of the Mitsui Bank. Denki Kagaku belongs to the Mitsui keiretsu because of its close links to the Mitsui Bussan. In general, the Mitsui keiretsu has looser ties than say Mitsubishi keiretsu.

** Not only Toshiba Co. has its own sangyo keiretsu. The other large companies also have formed their own sangyo keiretsu.

the master company does not belong to any *kinyu keiretsu*. Matsushita (National) belonged to the Sumitomo *kinyu keiretsu* until 1960 but is now independent.

The membership of the other kinyu keiretsu:

Mitsubishi keiretsu:
Mitsubishi Bank
Mitsubishi Trust and Banking Corporation
Nikko Securities Company
Tokyo Marine & Fire Insurance Company
Meiji Mutual Life Insurance Company
Mitsubishi Shoji Kaisha
Mitsubishi Real Estate Company
Mitsubishi Warehousing Company
Mitsubishi Heavy Industries Ltd.
Mitsubishi Electric Corporation
Mitsubishi Atomic Power Industries, Inc.
Mitsubishi Chemical Machinery Manufacturing Company
Mitsubishi Oil Company
Mitsubishi Steel Manufacturing Company
Chiyoda Chemical Engineering & Construction Company
Mitsubishi Metal Mining Company
Mitsubishi Mining Company
Yubetsu Coal Mining Company
Mitsubishi Chemical Industries Ltd.
Mitsubishi Petrochemical Company
Mitsubishi Monsanto Chemical Company
Mitsubishi Plastics Industries Ltd.
Mitsubishi Paper Mills Ltd.
Mitsubishi Edogawa Chemical Company
Mitsubishi Rayon Company
Mitsubishi Acetate Company
Mitsubishi Vonnel Company
Asahi Glass Company
Mitsubishi Cement Company
Kirin Brewery
Nippon Kogaku Kogyo K.K.
Nippon Yusen Kaisha (N.Y.K.)
Mitsubishi Economic Research Institute

"*Other companies*" (linked to Mitsubishi group, with foreign participation):
Mitsubishi Reynolds Aluminium Company
Yuka Badische Company
Caterpillar Mitsubishi

Mitsubishi Precision Company
Mitsubishi T.R.W. Company
Asahi Fiberglass Company

Sumitomo keiretsu:
Sumitomo Bank
Sumitomo Trust & Banking Company
Sumitomo Marine & Fire Insurance Company
Sumitomo Life Insurance Company
Sumitomo Shoji Kaisha
Sumitomo Real Estate Company
Sumitomo Warehousing Company
Sumitomo Coal Mining Company
Shionogi & Company
Daido Oxygen Company
Sumitomo Chemical Company
Sumitomo Metal Industries Ltd.
Sumitomo Light Metal Industries Ltd.
Kanto Special Steel Works Ltd.
Osaka Kinzoku Kogyo Company
Osaka Titanium Company
Koyo Seiko Company
Nihon Spindle Manufacturing Company
Nisshin Electric Company
Nippon Electric Industry
Sumitomo Metal Mining Company
Sumitomo Bakelite Company
Dai Nippon Pharmaceutical Company
Nippon Sheet Glass Company
Tohoku Metal Industries Ltd.
Nippon Aluminum Manufacturing Company
Nippon Stainless Steel Company
Sumitomo Machinery Company
Nippon Pipe Manufacturing Company
Nippon Electric Company
Sumitomo Electric Industries Ltd.
Teikoku Car and Manufacturing Company
Sumitomo Naugatuck Company
Sumitomo Chiba Chemical Company
Sumitomo 3-M Ltd.
Sumitomo Rubber Industries Ltd.
Tokai Rubber Industries Ltd.

"Others":
Sumitomo Atomic Energy Industries Ltd.

Sumitomo Joint Electric Power Company
Sumitomo Forestry Company
Sumitomo Construction Company
Nikken Sekkei Komu Company

Yasuda keiretsu:
Fuji Bank
Yasuda Trust and Banking Company
Shoei Silk Manufacturing Company
Niigata Ryusan K.K.
Showa Denko K.K.
Daiichi Cement Company
Japan Oxygen Company
Nippon Eternit Company
Nippon Oils & Fats Company
Nihon Cement Company
Nippon Kokan K.K.
Azuma Steel Works Company
Showa Aluminium K.K.
Nippon Hume Pipe Company
Oki Electric Industries Company
Toshiba Steel Company
Nippon Seiko K.K.

Dai-Ichi Bank keiretsu:
Kawasaki Steel Company
Fuji Electric Company
Ishikawajima Heavy Industries
Ishikawajima Harima Shipbuilding Company
Kobe Steel Company
Isuzu Motors Ltd.

Sanwa Bank keiretsu:
Teijin Company (synthetics) and a number of small companies

The composition of the members of the *keiretsu* just given shows conclusively that the *keiretsu* are very different from the former *zaibatsu*. To begin with they are not monopolies. In fact, they represent neither the case of "horizontal integration" (monopoly) nor the case of "vertical integration". They are a unique case of groupings of heterogenous industries. Each *keiretsu* tries to expand the set of heterogenous industries in the group.

CAUSES OF KEIRETSU DEVELOPMENT

The banks, having been spared and even in fact assisted by the Occupation Authorities, were the only source of substantial financial resources after the dissolution of the *zaibatsu*. They sponsored new enterprises both in terms of initiative and of financial assistance in launching new ones or expanding the existing ones. As a result many enterprises became dependent on a few large city banks, and these groups became the *kinyu keiretsu*.

The policy of developing *sets of heterogenous industries* by the large banks was the only road open in view of the very strict post-war anti-monopoly legislation and extremely strict enforcement of the legislation (though lately this has been slightly relaxed). The banks, prevented by law from establishing holding companies, and from inducing and financing take-overs of homogenous product firms ("horizontal integration" leading to monopoly) *had* to choose the path of what looks like another kind of horizontal integration (but technically is not called so) —the "one set of industries" principle.

For the executive officers of the splintered elements of the former *zaibatsu*, the long tradition of collective action as well as the general economic advantages of size and/or of collective action were sufficiently strong to propel them to work together as soon as Japan regained political independence. The splintered general trading companies came together and the Japanese Government, which always realised the importance of exports and of the general trading companies, allowed their reassembly after Japan regained independence. The industrial firms, dependent on bank finance, and on the trading company finance (which in turn is dependent on the bank) and on the selling and purchasing services of the trading company, found it natural and advantageous to fall into the orbit of the bank and the trading company.

As economic development picked up and various industrial firms grew in size and resources, the initiative and the power for setting up new enterprises partly slipped from the hands of the banks into the hands of the large institutions. As a result new enterprises are often sponsored by a large industrial firm or firms, or alternatively old but small and weak firms engaged in sub-contracting or supplying become attached to the large one when they obtain financial assistance or long-term orders for goods. This gives birth to a *sangyo keiretsu*, an industrially-linked group.

Chart 7.2 shows a very complicated *sangyo keiretsu* built on the initiative of a member of the Mitsubishi *kinyu keiretsu*, the Mitsubishi Petro-chemical Company, with co-operation of a few other Mitsubishi companies and other outside enterprises. It should be noted that the sponsor, in this case the Mitsubishi Petrochemical Company, itself was sponsored in 1956 by a Mitsubishi group of companies. This way of organising a firm is usually called "*keiretsu* financing".

Chart 7.2 shows the "backward and forward linkages" in the growth of the firms in this *sangyo keiretsu*. The Mitsubishi Petrochemical Company supplies some of the numerous products of cracking and molecular

Chart 7.2 AN INTERESTING CASE OF SANGYO KEIRETSU—THE MITSUBISHI PETROCHEMICAL GROUP

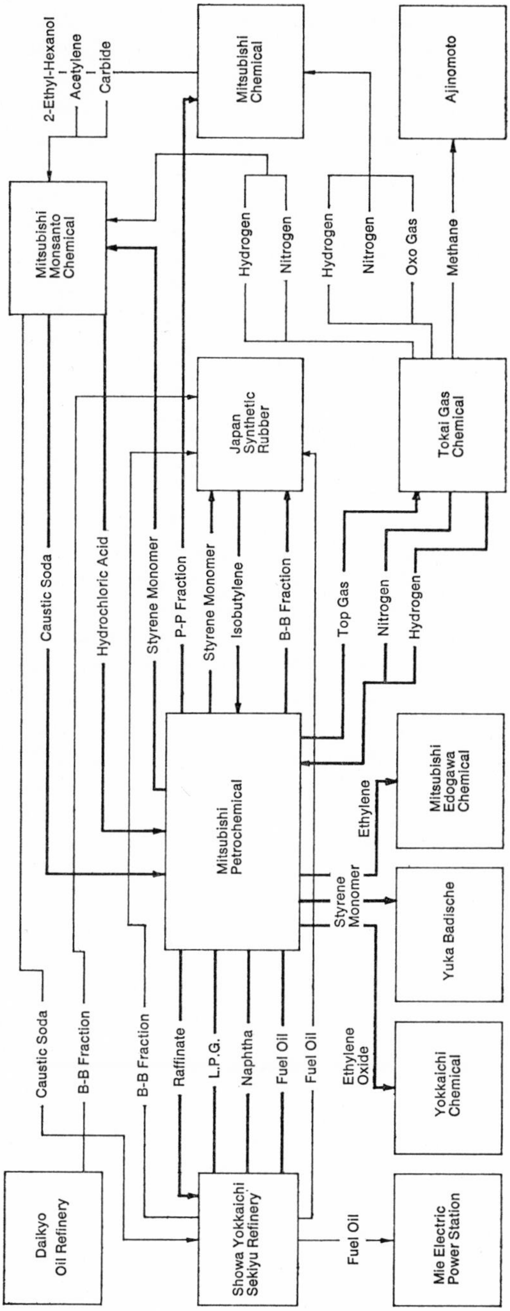

Source: Mitsubishi Bank.

restructuring of oil components to the members of the group, while at
the same time it buys some of their output. This, of course, is not
just "taking each other's washing", because the more finished products
as well as a proportion of the part-processed products are sold to the
outsiders in Japan (some of whom again are members of the Mitsubishi
kinyu(!) *keiretsu*), and abroad. This is just a case of mutually supported
growth in the group. The group, the *sangyo keiretsu*, and even more,
the *kinyu keiretsu*, gains as a result a high degree of self-sufficiency
in supplies of inputs, regularity of supply, removal of the high costs
of intermediaries' services and the cost of transport, because the companies of the Mitsubishi Petrochemical Company *sangyo keiretsu* have
all been located close together (at Nagoya) and are connected to
each other by pipelines. Thus one company's growth escalates the other
companies' growth and conversely. Briefly, the "externalities" or "backward and forward linkages" of growth are internalised in the *keiretsu*.
The price of this? No doubt the size and complexity of the *keiretsu* introduce enormous problems into the management of such loosely-structured
giants. Where the management is highly trained, as is in Japan, and
with the use of modern management and data processing techniques, the
problems may be solved at least to give a clear net advantage to
such groups.

How close are the financial and other ties in a *kinyu keiretsu*? The
conventional answer is that the bank's shareholdings of any company
cannot by law exceed 10 per cent and that in fact they are usually
well below that maximum limit. In addition, of course, in this system
there would be differences between the various *keiretsu*, for example
the Mitsui *keiretsu* is considered much looser in various ways than
the Mitsubishi *keiretsu*. The Japanese would say that the Mitsubishi
keiretsu executives have more traditional ties, or more collectivist spirit.
They are imbued with the ideas of the remarkable founder of the Mitsubishi business, Yataro Iwasaki, while the post-war Mitsui group executives are said to be more individualistic. It is difficult to measure these
factors. It is also difficult to assess qualitatively the financial ties in
the *keiretsu* system, although quantitative data are available. While
nominally no *single* company nor the bank can control any member
company of the *keiretsu*, there is substantial group control. Quantitatively, in fact, a group of fifteen of the largest companies of the
Mitsubishi *keiretsu* hold anything up to 31 per cent of the shares issued
by any *single* Mitsubishi company—in the Mitsubishi Shoji Kaisha (the
trading company) the fifteen largest Mitsubishi companies held 31·13
per cent of capital issued.*

---

* R. Ohashi, "Sociological Class Structure and Top Management in Post-war
  Japan", in *Contemporary Economy and Statistics, Essays in memory of 77th
  birthday of T. Ninagawa*, Yuhikaku Co., Tokyo, 1968, pp. 234-235.

It might appear that 31 per cent of the shares would not give control over the Mitsubishi Trading Company. But if one considers the fact that the other shareholders number in the thousands, and that many of them will not bother to attend shareholders' meetings, or will not take an active role if they do, or alternatively will often splinter into small groups thus cancelling each other's influence, it can be seen that 31 per cent could give effective control. It should be remembered that before the last War in the heyday of absolute family control of the *zaibatsu* through the holding company, the Iwasaki family held only 47·8 per cent of the shares of the holding company and it enjoyed complete control of the holding company and the whole Mitsubishi *zaibatsu*.

Further, in this evaluation of control the following two facts should be remembered: the four financial institutions of the Mitsubishi *keiretsu*, the Mitsubishi Bank, the Mitsubishi Trust and Banking Company, Meiji Life Insurance, and Tokyo Marine and Fire Insurance together provided in 1967 over 35 per cent[†] of the total *credit* obtained by the Mitsubishi Trading Company, and the rest of the loans were provided in small amounts by numerous other financial institutions. Secondly, the Mitsubishi Trading Company has a "highly geared" capital structure, that is, the shareholders' funds represent only 6 per cent(!) of the total capital.[‡] It follows then that the Company is extremely dependent on the four financial institutions. Thus it would not be surprising if it obeyed their wishes.

It is true that in other Mitsubishi companies the total shareholding of the fifteen largest companies is often below 20 per cent of the capital issued by the company, but in such cases the share of the *loans* provided to the company by the four financial institutions often goes up to 50 or 60 per cent (it is 57·7 per cent in the case of the Mitsubishi Real Estate Company) and thus the control of such companies by the four financial institutions is assured. Further, if the four financial institutions of Mitsubishi effectively control the trading company and the group's Real Estate Company, then they have additional power over the rest, as the "troublesome" companies could be given a cold shoulder by the trading company and/or the Real Estate Company, which would hurt.

Briefly, even if the shareholding in each of the member companies by the bank or the financial institutions is small, there are numerous other instruments of control at their disposal. In particular it may be a mistake to think that because much of the control appears to be by a group of the member companies over each single member, it is a diluted and weak control. In fact in social groups such group control almost invariably degenerates into individual control through manipulation of the group by one or two of the members. That this is at least potentially likely can be

† Ohashi, pp. 234-235.
‡ Ohashi, pp. 234-235.

seen from the fact that the *Kinyokai* (Friday meetings held on the second Friday of each month) of the top executives of the Mitsubishi group include only six top companies out of the total of thirty-two major companies in the *keiretsu*, and among these six companies are the bank, the trading company and the Real Estate Company.

The links between the members of a *keiretsu* are provided also by exchanging directorates. Although on the face of the matter it might appear that the exchange of directorates between, say, the Mitsubishi Bank and a member company would have symmetrical effect on the relative influence of the two institutions, this is not necessarily so. The two directors as a rule wield unequal power in their new positions. In addition, in some cases directoral appointments are not reciprocated.

The role of the *keiretsu* in the Japanese and the world economies is shown by the following figures. In 1966 the annual turnover of the twenty-eight main members of the Mitsubishi *keiretsu* alone (excluding its four financial institutions) was about 9 billion U.S. dollars, which means that it was larger than the G.N.P. of many sizeable countries. The annual sales of all the manufacturing companies of the Mitsubishi group total about 10 per cent of Japan's G.N.P. However, the Mitsubishi group's output has lately been rising at only half the rate of the G.N.P. The Mitsubishi Trading Company handles about 10 per cent of Japan's exports and about 15 per cent of her imports.

Table 7.8   Some Salient Economic Data about the Mitsubishi Keiretsu
(as of September 1967)

Unit: Million Yen ( ) Million Dollars

	Total Assets	Net Worth	Yearly Sales	Capital	Dividend %	Rank in own sector in Japan
			(Deposits)			
Mitsubishi Bank	2,543,550	58,870	1,775,984	36,000	9	
	(7,065)	(163)	(4,933)	(100)		3
Mitsubishi Heavy Industry	786,718	126,745	557,828	79,806	10	
	(2,185)	(352)	(1,549)	(221·6)		1
Mitsubishi Electric Corporation	252,626	59,639	233,162	43,200	8	
	(701)	(165)	(647)	(120)		3
Mitsubishi Atomic Power	3,593	1,558	1,190	4,000	—	
Industries	(9·9)	(4)	(3)	(11·1)		1
Mitsubishi Shoji Kaisha	795,230	36,670	1,033,240	22,500	12	
(trading company)	(2,209)	(101)	(5,647)	(62·5)		1
Mitsubishi Chemical Machinery	10,232	1,847	7,418	1,200	8	
Manufacturing Company	(28)	(5·1)	(20)	(3·3)		1
Mitsubishi Steel Manufacturing	30,942	5,361	17,404	4,767	—	
Company	(86)	(14)	(48)	(13·2)		3
Mitsubishi Oil Company	97,147	14,699	116,076	10,000	8	
	(269)	(40)	(322)	(27·7)		4
Chiyoda Chemical Engineering	37,244	3,979	27,587	2,700	10	
and Construction Company	(103)	(11)	(76)	(7·5)		1
Mitsubishi Metal Mining	79,904	19,412	80,334	10,000	10	
Company	(222)	(54)	(223)	(27·7)		2
Mitsubishi Mining Company	56,624	8,053	37,564	7,473	—	
	(157)	(22)	(104)	(20·7)		3

Table 7.8 Continued

Unit: Million Yen ( ) Million Dollars

	Total Assets	Net Worth	Yearly Sales	Capital	Dividend %	Rank in own sector in Japan
			(Deposits)			
Yubetsu Coal Mining Company	14,264	1,814	8,304	1,452	—	
	(39)	(5)	(23)	(4)		8
Mitsubishi Chemical Industries	158,128	33,571	120,274	28,402	10	
	(439)	(93)	(334)	(78·8)		1
Mitsubishi Monsanto Chemical	19,980	4,247	14,082	3,000	10	
	(55)	(11·7)	(39)	(8·3)		—
Mitsubishi Plastic Industries	22,723	3,725	18,506	3,150	—	
	(63)	(10)	(51)	(8·7)		—
Mitsubishi Petrochemical Company	94,472	20,654	13,600	5,000	12	
	(262)	(57)	(37)	(13·8)		1
Mitsubishi Paper Mills	50,024	8,692	30,218	5,600	10	
	(139)	(24)	(84)	(15·5)		6
Mitsubishi Edogawa Chemical Company	20,551	3,935	9,826	2,400	10	
	(57)	(11)	(27)	(6·6)		1
Mitsubishi Rayon Company	100,813	12,995	109,854	7,780	12	
	(28)	(36)	(305)	(21·6)		4
Mitsubishi Acetate Company	19,182	2,123	23,184	1,650	12	
	(53)	(5·8)	(64)	(4·5)		—
Mitsubishi Vonnel Company	18,180	2,775	15,668	2,250	12	
	(50)	(7)	(43)	(6·2)		—
Asahi Glass Company	97,925	43,184	70,132	21,600	14	
	(272)	(120)	(194)	(60)		1
Mitsubishi Cement Company	32,580	4,808	26,484	3,500	10	
	(90)	(13)	(73)	(9·7)		4
Kirin Brewery Company	113,760	37,743	223,650	23,014	15	
	(316)	(104)	(621)	(63·9)		1
Nippon Kogaku K.K.	14,573	3,790	14,864	2,400	10	
	(40)	(10)	(41)	(6·6)		2
Nippon Yusen Kaisha	144,053	15,803	89,924	14,600	6	
	(400)	(43)	(249)	(40·5)		2
Mitsubishi Estate Company	127,659	32,909	9,692	33,000	13	
	(354)	(91)	(27)	(91·6)		2
Mitsubishi Warehouse Company	12,233	4,693	11,810	2,000	10	
	(34)	(13)	(32)	(5·5)		1
Meiji Mutual Life Insurance Company	255,257	12,409	73,786	—	8	
	(709)	(34)	(205)			5
Mitsubishi Trust & Banking Corporation	355,103	23,740	241,007	10,000	9	
	(986)	(66)	(669)	(27·7)		1
Tokyo Marine & Fire Insurance Company Ltd.	119,644	27,550	77,031	13,500	11	
	(332)	(76)	(213)	(37·5)		1
Mitsubishi Reynolds Aluminum Company Ltd.	15,988	462	7,622	8,000	—	
	(44)	(1)	(21)	(22·2)		1
Total	6,500,902	638,455	6,097,305			
	(18,058)	(1,773)	(16,936)			

Year ended
March 1967

				(C)		
(A)	Mitsubishi *keiretsu* (excluding Mitsubishi Bank, Mitsubishi Trust & Banking Corp., Tokyo Marine & Fire Ins. Co., & Meiji Life Ins.)	2,827,772 (7,855)	505,628 (1,404)	3,562,420 (9,895)	(C)/(E)....9·7%	
				(D)		
(B)	All of Japan's top 618 companies	27,803,925	6,328,373	15,404,665	(D)/(E)....42·0%	
(A)/(B)	Share of Mitsubishi group	10·1%	7·9%	23·1%	(Gross National Product 36,661,400 million yen (E))	

Source: Mitsubishi Bank.

Mergers: The Trend to Concentration

Concentration in Japanese industry is not a new phenomenon and it has never been viewed by Japanese governments in such an unfavourable light as in the West. But the American-designed Act of 1947 for Exclusion of Excessive Economic Concentration produced the greatest breaking up of monopolistic organisations in the history of the world. The Anti-Monopoly Act of 1947 provided very strict laws against monopoly and a very strict enforcement system with a strong and independent Fair Trade Commission. However, already under the American occupation in 1949 an amendment of the Anti-Monopoly Act was passed. The Americans saw the rise of the Communist Party in China and wished to rebuild Japan as a countervailing power. The first amendment to the Anti-Monopoly Act was intended to facilitate rationalisation of management of industry, to aid in development of the Stock Exchange and to facilitate approved foreign investment in Japan. The total prohibition of companies holding other companies' shares was removed, provided that holding the shares did not create a monopoly situation. The Japanese companies wishing to enter into agreements with foreign companies were allowed to do so even if some restrictions on competition were involved. In 1952 the Small Business Stabilisation Act and the Export and Import Trading Act officially legalised cartels in specified cases of industries in difficulties. In 1953 when Japan became independent another amendment to the Anti-Monopoly Act was passed. It approved "recession and rationalisation cartels" and permitted industrial and commercial companies to hold each other's shares and to exchange directorships, provided that a substantial restriction of competition did not result. Resale price maintenance contracts became legal again. Companies were allowed to buy shares in other businesses provided that the result was not a holding company.

Very early in these developments the attitude of M.I.T.I. manifested itself unambiguously in favour of "rationalisation" of industry through cartels and mergers. Following the lead of the powerful M.I.T.I. the government subsequently tried to reduce the severity of the Anti-Monopoly Act in 1957 and again in 1962 by introducing amendments to make it easier to obtain Fair Trade Commission's approvals for cartels and mergers. However, the reaction of consumers, small businesses and the opposition parties was so strong on both occasions that the legislative attempts failed. M.I.T.I. then applied a new direct strategy. In 1966 it sent the Fair Trade Commission a memorandum* on the application of the Anti-Monopoly Act which referred to the industry's problems in connection with the proposed first step of liberalisation of direct

---

* Koujiro Niino, "Industrial Organization Policy and Economic Growth in Post-war Japan", *Kobe University Economic Review*, No. 14, 1968.

foreign investment in Japan in 1967. The memorandum then argued that:

(a) If some companies in an industry decide to regulate their investment programme by mutual consent such steps should not be treated as infringing the Anti-Monopoly Act, as long as the agreement does "not exert any substantial influence upon the relationships between the supply of and the demand for the product of the industry at present or in near future".

(b) Collective investment and control of excess capacity should be treated as under (a).

(c) In deciding on applications for permission of mergers, the Fair Trade Commission should consider not only the market share of the would-be merger company, the number of firms in the industry and the size ranking of the applicant companies, but also the capacity of the new company compared to the rest of the industry, the conditions of trade with other industries, competition with substitute and imported products, and the possibility of new domestic or foreign entrants to the industry.

M.I.T.I., with the support of the government no doubt, tried to persuade the Fair Trade Commission to be more tolerant in the application of the Anti-Monopoly Act. These legislative attempts, the memorandum and the clear attitude of the government were not without practical influence on the decisions of the Fair Trade Commission on particular mergers. The number of approved mergers grew rapidly from 381 in 1956 to almost 1,000 in 1963 and in the 1960s approvals came even for very large mergers with the after-merger capital of more than 10 billion yen.*

Among these large mergers there were several particularly remarkable ones which concerned restoration of the former companies broken up under the Act for the Exclusion of Excessive Economic Concentration, namely the mergers of Yukijirushi Milk Company and Clover Milk Company, and of Shinmitsubishi, Mitsubishinihon, and Mitsubishi Heavy Industry. Early in 1968 Yawata Iron and Steel Company and Fuji Iron and Steel Company applied to the Fair Trade Commission for permission to merge these two vast companies, former components of the broken-up Nippon Iron and Steel. When the Press reported the application, the Prime Minister, Mr. Eisaku Sato, the Minister for International Trade and Industry, Mr. Shiina, the Minister for the E.P.A., Mr. Miyazawa, and the Minister for Construction, Mr. Ohira, all gave public support and blessing for the merger application. After an examination of the application the Fair Trade Commission at first refused permission in May 1969. Public opinion, the Socialist Party and the academic economists were strongly against the merger (the latter signed a

* Niino.

statement condemning the proposed merger). The proposed merger, if approved, would establish a powerful precedent in favour of almost any merger. Not only was this an attempt to recreate a proscribed company, but also the size of the merger was exceptional. It would breach the rule that a merger company should not have more than 30 per cent of the market in its products. Yawata Steel was already Japan's largest steel producer, and the world's fourth largest. Fuji Iron and Steel was Japan's second largest, and the world's fifth largest steel company. A merger of these two giant companies would produce the second largest steel company in the world, after the United States Steel Company. Its output would be larger than that of the whole British steel industry.

For the Fair Trade Commission, however, the main objection was the fact that the new company would hold 70-90 per cent of the Japanese market in pig iron for casting (excluding pig iron for steel making), rail, tinplate and iron sheet. The two applicant companies pointed out that these four products together make up only 4 per cent of their total output, and began discussions about divesting themselves of some of their capacity in those products. Then somewhat unexpectedly on 29 October 1969 the Fair Trade Commission gave way and approved the merger on the condition that the two companies take steps to eliminate all possibilities of conflict with the Anti-Monopoly Act. The two companies concerned announced that the new combine would be called Nippon Steel Corporation. It is expected that if the recent Japanese steel expansion continues the combine will soon become the largest in the world.

One can only speculate on what pressures and persuasion were exerted upon the Fair Trade Commission by the government and industry. This decision will probably be of historical significance for Japan. It made a fundamental breach in the containing barriers of the Anti-Monopoly Act. It would now be very difficult for the Fair Trade Commission to refuse an application for any merger at all. Thus under the pressure of the government and the industry in general (even the competitors of Yawata Steel and Fuji Steel supported the application), the Fair Trade Commission gave in. Japan has unambiguously taken a stand: in the conflict between the economies of scale plus the dangers of monopoly against a sacrifice of economies of scale in order to maintain competition, the mixture of economies of scale and some dangers of monopoly won.

Mergers have been occurring like an epidemic all over the world in the 1960s but nowhere have they been as widespread and as numerous as in Japan. Merger is the considered Japanese answer to two separate problems facing Japanese industry.

One is increased competition in the world markets. The Japanese expect the mergers to lead to economies of scale and rationalisation and thus to lower costs which will allow Japanese firms to compete more effectively with foreign businesses.

The second problem is the typical Japanese fear that after liberalisation of foreign investment in Japan, which is expected to be completed under international pressure by 1972, the smaller Japanese companies will be exposed to take-overs by foreign companies which might have larger financial resources. Thus the Japanese Government and business hope that the large merged units will have enough financial strength and a healthy market position to enable them to withstand the expected onslaught of large international companies. The almost pathological fears of foreign investment (because it would not be easy for a foreign company to run a business in Japan), are partly due to excessive nationalism of the Japanese, and partly due to the expectation that the foreigners, who admittedly usually do not understand the Japanese ways of doing business, might introduce "alien" attitudes and methods into Japan. It is true that the foreign companies might attempt to do away with lifetime employment security, the wage-for-age system, the highly developed committee consultation system and might even change the general operation of industrial and labour relations. The Japanese are afraid that foreign-owned companies would be less amenable to "administrative guidance", and less likely to follow the recommendations of the national economic plan. The least analysable, therefore the worst sin, is that they would establish foreign "domination" of bits of Japan. In fact, the Japanese business world is moving to the Western ways anyway in gradually adopting the "wage-for-merit" system, administrative guidance and the Plan's recommendations are not always followed, and for the rest the foreign companies set up in Japan will not find it easy to compete with skilful Japanese management.

The Japanese fears of foreign investor invasion are grossly exaggerated, as are the hopes of some Western companies of easy, large profits. What matters, however, is the fact that these fears in Japan are strong. Thus for the sake of greater efficiency of merged large units, greater international competitiveness of Japanese goods abroad and at home, and Japanese enterprise at home, Japan is prepared to run some dangers of monopoly and M.I.T.I. is pushing mergers as hard as it can. There is hardly any branch of economic activity in Japan (except agriculture) that has missed this merger growth. Heavy industry has had its giant mergers: Ishikawajima Heavy Industries absorbed another machinery firm and a shipbuilding firm. In addition, it has established very close links with Tokyo Shibaura (Toshiba) by sharing company executives and swapping 10 million shares. The advantage of this link lies in tendering for construction of complete plants in under-developed countries, especially in Asia. I.H.I. provides the ordinary plant and Toshiba provides electrical equipment, all in one parcel. There is proposal of a similar link or merger in the Sumitomo *keiretsu*. Hitachi Ltd., Hitachi Shipbuilding, and a construction machinery company plan a merger. Mitsubishi Heavy Industries, which consummated a tripartite merger in 1963, is expanding into motor cars and chemical machinery. In the Dai-Ichi Bank *keiretsu*, the recent merger company of three heavy industry companies is already negotiating with an electrical company of the Furukawa group. Mergers already established, planned, or likely, include such industries as paper (the Oji group), motor cars, shipping, chemicals, textiles, aircraft, electronics, foodstuff processing, and many others. Mergers in manufacturing induce other mergers in distribution and even in banking. The mere private agreement between Yawata and Fuji steel companies induced a merger between two large "general trading companies", Nissho and Iwai, which both deal in steel and are both linked to Yawata and Fuji steel companies. There are prospects of mergers among other "trading companies": Sumitomo-Shoji, C. Itoh, Ataka & Company, and Marubeni-Iida.

The trend to concentration is also visible in retail distribution. There it shows itself in large gains in the volume of sales by department stores and supermarkets relative to the sales of small distributors; mergers between retailers; tie-ups of retailers, department stores and supermarkets with the "general trading companies" (Mitsubishi Shoji Kaisha concluded in 1969 a tie-up with Seibu Department Store); and tie-ups between retailers. A survey of 102 top-ranking retail enterprises revealed that fifty-one enterprises were interestd in tie-ups or mergers.*

There have been mergers in banking—in 1968 the new city bank, Taiyo Bank, was established from a bank merger. The Ministry of Finance supports mergers here because Japan still has a very large number of banks, and some of the banks, especially smaller ones, are inefficiently run. The Ministry of Finance sheltered the weaker banks in the past, but now would like the more efficient banks to expand their business, where necessary taking over the small ones. Even the large banks would like mergers because they are losing their former power in the economy. Some of the new merged companies are so large that even the biggest banks are losing their grip on them. The typical Japanese practice of large companies borrowing simultaneously from several banks reflects the fact that the present banks are too small for their giant customers. In the past the initiative for the *keiretsu*-financing of a new enterprise came from the bank, now it often comes from a large manufacturing company. Until 1968 bank mergers were restricted by banking legislation, but in that year the restrictions were relaxed by an amendment to the law on mergers or absorption of smaller financial institutions. The Ministry of Finance is considering introduction of

* *Nihon Keizai Shimbun*, 20 May 1969.

legislation to make it easier for large banks to merge, and Japanese banking circles are discussing numerous proposals of bank mergers. At the beginning of 1969 the Mitsubishi Bank (the third largest in Japan and the twentieth largest bank in the world) and the Dai-Ichi Bank (the seventh largest bank in Japan, and the thirty-third largest in the world) proposed a merger. This merger would make the new bank the fourth largest bank in the world after the Bank of America, the Chase Manhattan Bank, and the First National City Bank of New York. There has been speculation that the Fuji Bank (the largest in Japan and fifteenth in the world ranks) may link up with Mitsui Bank (the eighth largest in Japan and the thirty-fourth in the world), and that Sanwa Bank (the fourth in Japan and twenty-second in the world) may merge with Kobe Bank (the seventeenth in Japan and seventy-fifth in the world). If those large bank mergers go through they will in turn induce a new wave of mergers among the manufacturing and trading companies because these banks are important centres of the various *keiretsu*, and bank lending in Japan is accompanied by advice on how to run the client's company. Briefly, the existing general wave of mergers in the Japanese economy, and the stimulus given to further mergers by the recent approval of Yawata Steel and Fuji Steel may produce incalculable developments in the control and organisation of the Japanese economy.

Liberalisation of Capital Movements

JAPANESE INVESTMENT ABROAD

Under the Foreign Exchange and Foreign Trade Control Law of 1949 and subsequent administrative rulings, every case of Japanese investment abroad and each increase of capital must be individually approved by the Japanese Ministry of Finance which consults the other appropriate Ministries, especially the M.I.T.I. The application has to be submitted through the Bank of Japan and must provide a great deal of information about the project and its background. The formal application is normally lodged after satisfactory informal soundings of the authorities, and as a result no useful statistical data of refusals are available. There are no published criteria for approvals. It is understood that the authorities wish to make sure that the investment will result in a *short-term* gain in the balance of payments or that some major "national interest" is promoted. They consider expansion of exports to be desirable but not sufficient in itself to warrant approval. The authorities will want to satisfy themselves about the general local conditions in the host country and about the standing of the foreign partners. M.I.T.I. would want to make sure that where the foreign local market is limited not more than one Japanese firm makes the investment. Generally the authorities adopt a paternalistic attitude; they assess not only the national interest but also the interests of the applicant and they act on the assumption that they can assess both better than the applicant.

Japan joined the Organisation of Economic Co-operation and Development in 1964 and as a result would have been expected to adopt the O.E.C.D. Capital Movements Code, but the Japanese Government lodged full reservations about capital movements which thus temporarily exempt her from the obligations to make capital movements free. In recent years, however, Japan has been under powerful political pressure from the U.S.A. and the international organisations to liberalise her economy, that is, to remove governmental controls and allow the market to make the decisions. The early Japanese objections to full liberalisation of capital exports were justified by references to the weakness of the Japanese balance of payments. Since 1968 and especially 1969 when the Japanese yen showed a quite unexpected strength, the case for liberalisation of capital outflow has become very strong not only in terms of the international obligations, but also in terms of narrow national interest. In particular, the criterion that the investment bring a *short-term* gain in the balance of payments is now quite irrelevant, and indeed bad policy for Japan's interests.

Table 7.9.   Geographical Distribution of Japanese Subsidiaries and Joint Ventures Abroad, at end of March 1966.

Area	Amount mil. US $
North America	134·3
Central and South America	156·2
Asia	80·5
Europe:	19·9
Germany	(4·36)
Belgium	(3·33)
France	(2·92)
Italy	(2·62)
Portugal	(1·59)
United Kingdom	(1·29)
Luxembourg	(1·00)
Switzerland	(0·83)
Ireland	(0·71)
Spain	(0·41)
Netherlands	(0·35)
Greece	(0·20)
Lichtenstein	(0·04)
Malta	(0·22)
Africa	8·2
Oceania	5·5
Total	404·6

Source: O.E.C.D., *Liberalisation of International Capital Movements: Japan,* Paris, 1968, pp. 20–21.

Chapter 1, especially Table 1.12, gives some information about the value of the total Japanese investments abroad. It should be mentioned here that all foreign assets of the Japanese held in 1945 were confiscated by the victorious powers. New Japanese investments abroad did not appear until 1951 and between that year and 1965 Japanese businesses established 1,051 subsidiaries and joint ventures abroad, of which 484 were engaged in manufacturing and 446 in trading.*

Table 7.10. Geographical Distribution of Japanese Companies' Branches Abroad at end of March 1966.

Area	Numbers	Capital invested mil. US $
North America	63	6·526
United States	(61)	(6·472)
Central and South America	5	0·335
Asia	136	7·697
Europe:	40	2·287
Belgium	(1)	(0·016)
Denmark	(1)	(0·080)
France	(2)	(0·473)
Germany	(4)	(0·235)
Italy	(1)	(0·066)
Netherlands	(1)	(0·050)
Switzerland	(1)	(0·050)
United Kingdom	(29)	(1·317)
Africa	1	0·019
Oceania	0	0
Total	245	16·864

Source: O.E.C.D., *Liberalisation*, p. 21.

The main motive for approving these investments was not so much to allow the investor to make a profit on the investment project itself as to promote Japanese exports directly or indirectly by providing Japanese technical assistance which would subsequently lead to purchases of Japanese equipment or even whole plants, and to secure sources of materials for Japan from abroad.

The rather low average profitability of Japanese investment abroad—up to 1965 the highest average annual return was only 6 per cent†— suggests that either the Japanese authorities did not primarily look for direct profitability in approving the applications (a good excuse), or that they performed the usurped function of assessing profitability somewhat

* O.E.C.D., *Liberalisation of International Capital Movements: Japan*, Paris, 1968, p. 18. The discussion of Japanese regulations on capital movements draws heavily on this work.
† O.E.C.D., *Liberalisation*, p. 22.

poorly. However, an additional reason for low profitability was that much of the investment was very new in these years and consequently some of it would not yet have reached full profitability.

Because of balance of payments pressures the Japanese Government until recently gave permission for investing abroad only in special cases, but where the project was approved, the government took steps to assist it by organising the Overseas Investment Insurance Programme in 1956. The programme was sponsored by M.I.T.I. It covers both capital and earnings, but only equity investment is insurable. The insurance cover costs $0 \cdot 479$ per cent p.a. of the insured sum. The cover is good against losses from expropriation, nationalisation, or liquidation of the business because of war, civil war, riots or other disturbance, or because of foreign government interference making the operation of the business impossible.

Although various international institutions and the U.S. Government have been exerting pressure on Japan to liberalise her attitude to foreign investment *in* Japan, there is no published record of similar pressure on Japan to liberalise her controls on Japanese investment abroad. From a general economic standpoint of optimal allocation of resources on the world scale, the case for liberalisation is good and is equal in both fields. The lack of symmetry in the political pressures in the two fields is suggestive of the motives for the political pressures.

LIBERALISATION OF FOREIGN INVESTMENT IN JAPAN

The advantages and disadvantages of using foreign capital.

Foreign investment in a country may be equity capital (direct or portfolio investment), or fixed interest capital. Unfortunately it is not possible to draw a hard and fast line, even in theory, between direct investment and portfolio investment. In both these cases the foreigner holds some shares in the Japanese businesses. In principle the division line is defined by the following criterion: does the share held by the foreigner give him effective control over the company? If it does the foreign investment is called direct investment, if it does not it is called portfolio investment. To have effective control over a company, where the vast majority of shares is widely dispersed among numerous apathetic and uninformed shareholders, it is not necessary to have more than 50 per cent of the shares. It is not necessary to have even near half of the shares. For this reason various governments and many writers have fallen back upon a perfectly arbitrary division line of 25 per cent. If a single body holds more than 25 per cent of shares of a company, it is a case of direct (equity) investment; if the percentage is less then it is a case of portfolio investment. In theory one might say that the intention of the foreign shareholder would be decisive: if he wishes to exercise control over the company it is direct investment; if he does not wish to exercise control but merely to participate in profits, it is a case of portfolio investment. However, the statistician computing the data on investment cannot know the intentions of the investors which change with time. What began as a case of portfolio investment (in exchange for cash on Stock Exchange, or as shares given to the foreigners in exchange for know-how) for the sake of income only, may change later into a case of control or direct investment.

By the standards of the rest of the world, Japan (like the Communist countries) has made little use of direct foreign investment. (For details see Chapter 1.) Unlike many other countries Japan has been making *no* efforts to attract direct foreign investment, in fact quite the contrary! However she has made some use of foreign fixed interest loans, and has *tolerated* some portfolio investment within strict limits. Unlike the government of a country like Australia, the Japanese Government does not set up foreign investment promotion schemes, and does not offer incentive schemes or even information on investment opportunities. Neither do the Japanese banks display any more interest in attracting direct investment to Japan and they seem unwilling to provide information needed for direct investment, though they provide some information on portfolio investment. In international negotiations Japan has fought hard to retain her restrictions on entry of foreign equity capital for as long as possible. The remarkable feature of this is that Japan pursued that policy even when she was desperately short of capital *and* weak in her balance of payments. The main reasons here are that the Japanese fear foreign economic domination and are imbued with an extremely strong economic nationalism. They also have a sceptical attitude about the benefits from foreign investment.

Of course, it is true that foreign investment is a mixed blessing: to some extent the balance of its merits and demerits depends on the nature of the alternatives that the recipient country has, and to some extent it depends on the nature of investment. Where a country is desperately short of reasonable domestic entrepreneurial talent, like Puerto Rico has been, the case for encouraging foreign direct investment is very strong. (In the case of Puerto Rico direct foreign investment has made an outstanding contribution to the economic development, though in this case there has been a special feature in that the U.S.A. admitted duty-free the Puerto-Rican made goods of U.S.-owned enterprises.) Where a country is not so desperately short of domestic entrepreneurial talent, the case for direct foreign investment is much weaker. The free admission of foreign investment in countries such as Japan or Australia at an early stage does assist development, but it is also liable to suppress the nascent domestic would-be entrepreneurship. It may even have unfavourable effects on domestic saving, because the need for increasing domestic savings does not appear so urgent to the policy-makers and the public. As a result after some years of such economic development the G.N.P. will have risen but a great deal of the increase will accrue to the foreigners. As a further result much of the domestic effort is suppressed. Because of an active policy of assisting foreign investment in the motor car industry, for example, Australia will never in the next 100 years be likely to have a domestically-owned motor vehicle factory, because the existing number of assisted foreign manufacturers who have set up factories there is already too high, and also because any domestic would-be car manufacturer would not be even able to start in an overcrowded market against the competition of established manufacturers with the support of large overseas organisations. It is said that there is a learning process from foreign enterprises, but there are sometimes severe limitations on this gain to the host country. If an Australian does acquire some know-how in an American-owned car company in Australia much of the fruit of this will be reaped by the American company, and even if he resigns alternative employment will be in another foreign-owned company.

Briefly, although the foreign investment undoubtedly "adds" (in a narrow sense) to the productive facilities of the host country, that increase is not a measure of its advantages. The net advantage or disadvantage of foreign investment could be found only if we could compare the size of the economic growth due to direct foreign investment with the size of economic growth that would occur without foreign investment. That will never be possible. Thus the issue has to be judged in deductive terms: what is the effect of foreign investment on domestic entrepreneurship, on the spread of foreign know-how into the indigenous sector, and on the availability of capital, and how much of the fruit of the increased productive facilities accrues to the people in the host country? Of course, where the foreign investor ultimately follows his capital and settles permanently in the country of his capital's adoption, as was the case with the nineteenth century investment in the U.S.A., the benefit is clear. But in many cases, in particular in the case of Japan, this result is unlikely.

Where there is a reasonable supply of domestic entrepreneurship the case for direct foreign investment is weaker, because the other factors of production (know-how and the capital) can be obtained from abroad if necessary on more favourable terms than through direct foreign investment. With direct investment the foreigner must also fear the loss of capital through economic causes in an unfamiliar environment and through confiscation.

Japan has had plenty of domestic entrepreneurship and the government virtually excluded direct foreign investment. As a result local entrepreneurship (an important factor of production) has been completely protected from competition (but has not been protected quite so much when it came to the sale of the finished product of entrepreneurship, the saleable goods or services). Further, the Japanese Government has assisted and encouraged the import and acclimatisation of the foreign know-how. The foreign owners of know-how, fully aware that their entry as producers into Japan was impossible, must have been weaker in bargaining about the price of the know-how to be sold to a Japanese entrepreneur. Thus Japan nurtured its own entrepreneurship and obtained the know-how more cheaply. Further, the Japanese entrepreneur has been psychologically more prepared to try to adapt the foreign know-how to the local conditions, as well as to try to improve it generally, than a branch of a foreign parent company would have been. This would be so because contrary to general belief, the Japanese have never been *pure* imitators, and the manager of a foreign company branch abroad is likely to be complacent about his parent company's product (and he is often a second-rater who has been moved out of the head office) and therefore would not be well equipped to perform the task. In fact the Japanese entrepreneur has performed this task admirably. Japan also has solved its problem of supply of capital, but at a heavy cost to a few generations. In this last case, however, Japan may have carried determination to "do it itself" too far. Although her reluctance to draw on foreign equity capital may have been justifiable in the circumstances, the case for using more fully foreign fixed-interest capital has been very strong indeed. Japan has used some foreign fixed-interest capital, but she could have used more. (For details of fixed-interest investment see Table 1.12.)

The full use of foreign fixed-interest capital has many advantages in the development of a country like Japan, especially so in an age of world-wide inflation. Using mainly fixed-interest foreign capital protects the economy from falling under foreign control, which would occur with direct foreign investment. In an age of rapid inflation the real burden of servicing a foreign debt is automatically scaled down in the case of fixed-interest debt, but is not so reduced in case of equity investment (because in that case the foreigner's real asset appreciates in money terms at least as much as the general price level has gone up, and the dividends also rise at least as much).

In an economy with the growth of productivity as high as Japan's, the fixed-interest debt is quite easily serviced. Further, this method of financing reduces the concentration of the burdens of financing economic development on the shoulders of one generation. The alternative, a fully domestically financed development, requires one or two generations to make excessive sacrifices to compensate for the neglect of many generations.

LICENSING OF FOREIGN INVESTMENT IN JAPAN

Foreign investment in Japan is subject to permits issued by the Ministry of Finance under the Foreign Investment Law of 1950. Needless to say,

Table 7.11.   Origins of Foreign Investment in Subsidiaries and Joint Ventures in Japan between April 1950—June 1965.

Country	No. of Cases	Value mil. US $	No. of Cases %	Percentage of value held
U.S.A.	404	162·3	67·6	69·6
United Kingdom	51	21·6	8·5	9·3
Canada	15	8·4	2·5	3·6
West Germany	18	3·2	3·0	1·4
Netherlands	7	4·5	1·2	1·9
Panama	10	4·0	1·7	1·7
Venezuela	9	1·1	1·5	0·5
France	9	1·0	1·5	0·4
Switzerland	49	12·3	8·2	5·3
Saudi Arabia	1	6·9	0·2	3·0
Kuwait	1	6·9	1·2	3·0
Others	23	1·1	3·9	0·5
Total	597	233·3	100	100

Source : Ministry of Finance, Japan, quoted by O.E.C.D., *Liberalisation*, p. 33.

the permit is issued by the Ministry of Finance after fullest consultation with M.I.T.I. or other relevant ministry.

As can be seen from Table 7.9, in a four-year period only eighty-three new enterprises with *some* foreign ownership were allowed in the "sensitive" sectors of the Japanese economy. Of this total only forty-five cases were in manufacturing (on an average of ten and a half cases per year), and forty-four of the new manufacturing firms had less than 50% foreign shareholding. Table 7.9 shows clearly how sensitive the Japanese Government (M.I.T.I.) has been about foreign control of industry. As a result the Japanese economy emerges as the most domestically-owned in the world after the communist countries.

The basic criteria for dealing with applications for making foreign investments were stated in 1963 when Japan exchanged "memoranda of understanding" with the O.E.C.D. prior to joining the Organisation. The criteria are: "maintenance of full employment"; "internal and external financial equilibrium"; and "co-ordination of industrial development with special regard to small and medium enterprises" (protecting weak Japanese-owned small and medium enterprises from the entry of foreign competitors).

In practice joint ventures with the Japanese capital in control have a better chance of approval than any other form of foreign investment.

The licensing procedure and criteria differ for equity type and portfolio investments. In the case of subsidiaries and joint ventures in equity type investment the rules again differ from those applicable to branches.

Table 7.12. Authorisations of Foreign Direct Investment in "Sensitive" Sectors in Japan Between 1 July 1963 and 30 June 1967.

Investment	New Establishments	Capital Increases of Old Establishments
Totals	83	49
of which foreign participation		
up to 50% of the capital	(58)	(29)
above 50% of the capital	(25)	(20)
Of these directly engaged in		
manufacturing industries:	45	35
Chemicals	(21)	(6)
Machinery	(13)	(16)
Metal	—	(1)
Others	(11)	(12)
With foreign participation in		
manufacturing up to		
50%	44	28
51%	—	1
60%	1	—
62%	—	1
70%	—	1
75%	—	1
100%	—	3

Source: Ministry of Finance, Japan, quoted by O.E.C.D., *Liberalisation*, p. 31.

SUBSIDIARIES AND JOINT VENTURES

Foreign businesses wishing to establish subsidiaries and joint ventures in Japan have to apply on official forms through the Bank of Japan to the Ministry of Finance. The applications must supply a great deal of information on the entire project, its prospects, relevant contracts with third parties, and even on the activities of the parent firm at home and in third countries. The Ministry of Finance consults any other relevant Ministries, which attach their comments to the application. The file then usually goes to the Foreign Investment Council—a consultative institution under the wings of the Ministry of Finance. In the past the Foreign Investment Council consisted mainly of official members, but since February 1967 it consists of appointees of the Minister of Finance. The Council has only an advisory function and does not have to be consulted. The real decision is made by the relevant (the Japanese say: "the competent") Ministry, which in the case of manufacturing and trade is M.I.T.I. Article 20, Chapter VI, of the Law Concerning Foreign Investment (1950) allows the unsuccessful applicant the right of appeal and a public hearing, but so far not one appeal has been lodged because the applicants felt that it would be futile!

The formal submission of any application is customarily preceded by preliminary soundings by the would-be applicant with the relevant authorities, in the course of which he may be "advised" to submit information not asked for in the application blank. He may also be "advised" to make changes in the proposed project. Where Japanese partners are involved, as would almost invariably be necessary for practical operating reasons and to facilitate obtaining permission, the relevant Ministry may "advise" the Japanese partners to renegotiate the terms of the contracts with the foreign business.

Obtaining permission to invest in Japan is a lengthy process. Foreign businessmen claim that in past cases it has taken up to a few years. "Soundings" in particular are apt to be very frustrating to foreigners for several reasons. The administrators have an in-built reluctance to admit foreign investment. Foreigners usually do not understand the Japanese style of communicating thoughts (even if perfect Japanese, or say perfect English is available to both sides). Ambiguity is built into Japanese communication to avoid giving offence. The Japanese act collectively, and make decisions collectively. Consequently even the smallest matter cannot be decided by one man, but has to go to a committee or committees. In those committees the Japanese try to avoid taking a vote, but try instead to talk themselves gradually into a compromise. Such process is democratic in nature but slow. The Western businessman who would expect immediate decision on some matters, and a quick one on others, is therefore often frustrated.

Government "advice" to the would-be applicant is never written and it should be appreciated that solely oral communication carries many possibilities of misunderstandings, even if both sides have a perfect command of the language used. Western businessmen are also frustrated by the fact that even the final *refusals* of formal applications (and reasons) are given only orally (but approvals are given in writing).

The main criticism of the licensing system that foreign businesses rightly have is that there are no rules or criteria which would allow an interested party to know what kinds of projects the Japanese Government likes and what it dislikes.

At the beginning of August 1966 the official processing of applications was reformed and somewhat speeded up by unpublished "internal rules" laid down jointly by the Ministry of Finance and M.I.T.I. The officials of the Ministry of Finance have stated on this matter:

Applications for validation under the Foreign Investment Law in the matter of:

(a) conclusion or alteration of technical assistance contracts
(b) acquisition of stocks or proprietary interest in subsidiaries or joint ventures or
(c) acquisition of claimable assets arising from loans

are, as a rule, passed on by the competent Ministries to the Foreign Investment Sub-Committee of the Foreign Investment Council within one month after the applications have been filed with the Bank of Japan. [In the past this took about three months.]

The Sub-Committee meets every Wednesday and when it determines the desired modification of the content of an application it informs the applicant on the day after the meeting. Such notice is given verbally, and the reasons for the recommended modifications, if any, are also disclosed verbally. However, the resident party to the joint venture contract when transmitting by letter to the foreign would-be investor the nature of the oral recommendation may have its letter's content confirmed in writing by the Sub-Committee.

When the Sub-Committee deals with a case for which the relevant Ministries do not require modifications the applications are passed on to the next session of the Foreign Investment Council which meets once a month. Then unless the Council raises any objections the application is approved by the relevant Ministries without delay, usually in the afternoon of the day the Council meets.*

The Japanese Government claims that this new procedure has reduced the *average* period between submission of the application and approval from 135 to fifty-one days. However, this estimate does not include the period of preliminary "soundings" of the authorities.

BRANCHES

Permits are not required for the establishment of wholly-owned *branches* in sectors other than banking, insurance and public utilities, but they must be reported in advance to the Ministry of Finance and to M.I.T.I. through the Bank of Japan. However transfers of funds to any branch must be individually approved by the Ministry of Finance (applications through the Bank of Japan).

Government permission is also required for branches' arrangements with the parent company about intellectual property (patents, licences, trade marks, know-how and so forth), technical assistance, and acquisition of equity interest in Japanese companies.

LIBERALISATION OF CAPITAL INFLOW OF 1967

On 1 July 1967 the Japanese Government introduced the first step of capital inflow liberalisation. Two carefully picked and rather small categories of industries were lifted from discretionary control and will be "automatically" approved (on application) *subject to some conditions*, and a special provision was made for a *limited* "automatic" liberalisation of the listed industries not meeting these conditions. However, this liberalisation was somewhat hollow. Among the thirty-three industries included in the "Class One" were such industries as: "Western

* O.E.C.D., *Liberalisation*, p. 43.

restaurants, limited to those with a capital of fifty million yen or more", "laundry business, limited to linen supply service", tape recorders, cameras, "shipbuilding with docks of 200,000 d.w.t. capacity or more", and warehousing. "Class Two" included seventeen industries, such as some textile industries, travel agencies, the rest of shipbuilding, piano manufacturing and so on. It is perfectly clear that those are the industries where the Japanese enterprises have acquired so much know-how and are so well organised and geared for production that it would be dangerous for a foreigner to try to establish production in Japan. In any case, there are conditions attached to that "automatic" liberalisation.

Conditions for Class One:

1. The enterprise is newly established.
2. At least 50 per cent of the total equity capital must be held by Japanese investors already in that line of business and at least one-third of the capital must be held by one such Japanese investor.
3. The Japanese representation on the Board of Directors of the company must be at least proportionate to the Japanese share of equity capital.
4. The decisions by the company are taken according to the provisions of the Japanese Commercial Code, and do not require the approval of any specific member of the Board of Directors or the unanimous consent of all shareholders.
5. The Japanese investors do not make contributions to equity capital in kind, other than factories, shops or warehouses.
6. The enterprise does not receive any transfer of business from an existing company and does not combine with an existing company immediately after its establishment.
7. The investment "does not have an exceptionally detrimental effect on Japanese interests".* (Does this rule conform with "automatic" approval?)

For investments in Class Two industries the conditions are 1, 5, 6 and 7 of the preceding list. The condition that the Japanese nationals must hold at least 50% of the capital, or any capital for that matter, has been dropped. Consequently Class Two has come to be called 100% liberalisation, whereas Class One is called 50% liberalisation.

Direct investment that does not meet the above conditions, or is in industries outside Classes One and Two is also automatically authorised provided that:

1. The total foreign equity holdings in the company do not exceed:

    (a) 15 per cent in the case of restricted industries such as waterworks,

---

* O.E.C.D., *Liberalisation*, p. 52.

railways, other transport, electric and gas utilities, fisheries, maritime transport, road transport, mining, radio, television, harbour operation, trustee business and banking;

(b) 20 per cent of the total equity capital in the case of non-restricted industries; and

2. No single foreign investor holds more than 7 per cent of the total equity.

Even when automatic or non-automatic approval for foreign investment is given, there is need for further permits for non-cash financing of foreigner's investment. Sometimes the foreign investor supplies a piece of equipment which is not readily available in Japan as his share of equity capital. In such cases a serious problem of valuation of the equipment arises, as otherwise some of the rules about foreign investment could be bent. Such valuations are made by assessors appointed by a Court of Justice, and can take a long time. Similarly, an important part of equity foreign investment is provision of technical assistance, or intellectual capital. The Japanese authorities carefully examine all such imports and their valuation. However, as long as the contract is not more than for one year and the annual fee is not more than US$30,000, all such forms of intellectual capital including the right to use a trade mark are approved "automatically".

REPATRIATION OF PROFITS AND OF CAPITAL

Profits of the subsidiaries and joint ventures may be transferred home under automatic approval after verification by an authorised foreign exchange bank. Transfer of profits made by wholly-owned *branches* requires permission from the Bank of Japan, which is automatic after detailed verification.

Repatriation of capital is free in all cases, that is it does not require any permission, but it does require verification.

GENERAL PROBLEMS FOR FOREIGN INVESTORS

Although the Code of Liberalisation of Capital Movements of the O.E.C.D. frees among other things the purchase of real estate and buildings by non-residents, Japan has obtained a waiver in this matter by lodging a reservation prior to joining the O.E.C.D. As a result foreign businesses require permits which are reported to be difficult to obtain. Similarly, a foreign investment project in Japan may require foreign personnel for whom entry permits are difficult to obtain according to foreign businesses though the Japanese authorities deny this.

"PORTFOLIO" INVESTMENT

Foreigners Investing in Japan. The main features of Japanese Stock Exchanges have been described in Chapter 6. Foreign interest in Japanese shares became evident in the early 1960s when Japan proved its economic potential and Japanese share prices were booming; when the share prices collapsed the foreign interest waned. However, with the recovery of the Tokyo share price index in 1968 and 1969 and a fresh boom in 1970, foreign portfolio investment reached record levels. The foreign share of purchases on the Japanese stock exchanges is still relatively very small. In the stock exchange boom years 1962 and 1963 foreign purchases represented mere fractions of 1 per cent of the total.*

Under the Japanese laws, Cabinet Orders, Ministerial Ordinances and Notifications, there are limits imposed on foreigners' purchases of Japanese securities. As from 1 July 1967, foreigners as a group may not hold more than 20 per cent of the equity of any Japanese enterprise, and in the "restricted industries" the limit is only 15 per cent. Any single foreigner may not own more than 7 per cent of the equity capital of an enterprise without specific permission. All foreign purchases require permission. Selling Japanese shares is free of control.

Because of the difficulty foreigners have in understanding the Japanese share market and therefore their difficulty in dealing directly on the Japanese exchanges, "Depository Receipts" and "Investment Trusts" have developed which hold title to Japanese securities and are located in France, Hong Kong, Switzerland, the U.K. and the U.S.A.

A depository receipt can be obtained in two ways: if a Japanese company makes an issue abroad, the subscribers obtain a depository receipt from the Western bank and its counterpart shares are deposited with a Japanese bank (for ease of collection of interest or dividends).

Alternatively, a non-Japanese who owns Japanese shares can deposit them with a Western bank which will pass them on to a Japanese bank and issue depository receipts to the owner. These depository receipts are then traded freely outside Japan in the over-the-counter markets, where the transactions escape all the taxes and charges applicable on Japanese Stock Exchanges.

Japanese Taxation of Portfolio Income. In general, non-resident portfolio investors, as in many other countries, pay a withholding tax which is 20 per cent on dividends and interest. Residents of countries which have concluded Avoidance of Double Taxation Agreements with Japan (see Chapter 3) are charged a somewhat lower rate of withholding tax.

Japanese Resident's Portfolio Purchases Abroad. Until February 1970 only the following Japanese institutions or persons could buy or hold foreign securities: "authorised foreign exchange banks" in respect to their working balances; insurance companies that have to maintain a deposit abroad; and immigrants and returning nationals, who may retain foreign shares bought before coming to Japan.

---

* O.E.C.D., *Liberalisation*, p. 90.

At the beginning of February 1970 the Japanese Government decided to permit some other portfolio investment abroad, subject to restrictions. Firstly, there is an (initial) maximum quota of U.S.$100 million that can be used for portfolio investment abroad. Secondly, individuals still are not allowed to make any portfolio investment abroad, a right reserved for investment trusts. The motive for this liberalisation lies in an "embarrassment of riches". Japan's external monetary reserves are rising fast and amounted to U.S.$3,630 million at the end of February 1970 with very strong prospects of reaching about $5,000 million at the end of the fiscal year 1970. (Some Japanese economists expect these reserves to reach about U.S.$12,000 million by 1975.) Such accumulation of reserves is embarrassing for Japan because the various deficit countries pressure her for an upward revaluation of her currency, as well as for a general economic liberalisation. Some relaxation of controls on investment abroad will tend to lessen the accumulation of reserves. It will also show that Japan is undertaking liberalisation.

STEPS IN THE PROCESS OF LIBERALISATION OF CAPITAL IMPORTS IN JAPAN

The first "liberalisation" of foreign investment in Japan took place on 1 July 1967. Its substance was not great. On 1 March 1969 the "Second Capital Liberalisation" took effect. On that occasion 135 industries were added to Class One, that is 50% liberalisation, and twenty industries were added to Class Two, or 100% liberalisation. In addition nine industries put into Class One in 1967 were upgraded to 100 per cent liberalisation in 1969. The Japanese claim that at that stage one-third of Japan's industries were liberalised. It should be noted that this is not a third by value of output, but one-third of the number of *items* in the Japanese industry classification, and that the Japanese chose to classify as separate industries producers of "fish finders", steel tubes, instant coffee, pickles, monosodium glutamate, vinegar, noodles, corn-flakes, tea and oatmeal. This method of industry classification gave Japan 600 separate "industries" and since after the Second Liberalisation over 200 industries were included in either 50% or 100% liberalisation, they can, in a way, claim liberalisation of one-third of the industries. However, the rest of the world thought that the liberalisation was a sham, in that it included industries where the Japanese were strongly established, or actual world leaders (fish finders, tyres, musical instruments, soy sauce), and industries like theatre, amusement centres, or independent specialised retailers (restricted to liberalised products only and restricted in size) where a foreigner would not have a chance.

As a result there were complaints about this Second Capital Liberalisation from the U.S.A., the U.K. and the Netherlands. The Business and Industry Advisory Committee of the O.E.C.D. formally expressed its disappointment and disapproval. In response the big Japanese business under the leadership of *Keidanren* (Federation of Economic Organisations) called for quicker and fuller liberalisation. Big business, interested in investing in the rest of the world and strong at home, has an obvious motive in calling for liberalisation to obtain favourable treatment abroad. The Japan Foreign Investment Council also called for quicker liberalisation. As a result in 1969 the Japanese Government started drawing up a list of industries to be included in the third liberalisation scheduled for the end of 1970. The fourth liberalisation is scheduled for March 1972. It may include automobiles, electronics, petrochemicals, and some other industries, but it is very likely that a number of industries will be left out altogether; among them will almost certainly be aircraft manufacturing, nuclear power industries, weapons industries and similar other industries.

CHAPTER EIGHT

Agriculture

The general condition of agriculture and its efficiency in any country depend primarily on the land tenure system. Land tenure is usually determined and altered through a political rather than economic process, partly because the mobility of land ownership or possession is usually very low. Usually the particular type of land tenure is determined by law or by a rigid and powerful convention. Land tenure directly or indirectly determines the size of the typical farm, the profitability of farming activities, the investment level, the variety of crops, and even agricultural technology.

The Former Land Tenure System

Japan has had two land reforms since the Meiji Restoration. One was at the time of the Restoration when the feudal land rights were abolished against government compensation in the form of bonds. At that time the *de facto* owners of the land became owners *de jure*, that is obtained the right to lease or to sell land. Their feudal dues were replaced by a land tax which amounted to 3 per cent of the government assessment of the value of land. However the *de facto* tenants of the Tokugawa period did not obtain any increased rights to their land. Indeed, when the Civil Code was later passed, tenants generally lost their former security of tenure.

The landlords, having obtained a legal right to terminate any tenancy and assisted by growing pressure of population on scarce land (at the time almost the only means of obtaining a livelihood) were able to charge exorbitant rents. The average rent came to be more than half of the annual crop and under those conditions it did not pay the larger landowners to cultivate their land themselves, or with hired labour. Better returns could be obtained by leasing the land to an eager tenant who did not have to be supervised. As a result large farms never developed in Japan and tenancy became more common than it had been.

It increased from 30 per cent of farmed land at the time of the Restoration to 45·5 per cent in 1914.*

After the Meiji Restoration the government did try to establish large farms in the new areas opened up in Hokkaido and in the reclaimed lands in the rest of Japan, but the large farms did not survive. The staple crop—rice—and its method of growing, coupled with the lack of suitable machinery at the time made large scale farming difficult. The high rents obtainable from numerous landless peasants were more attractive. Only now that a variety of agricultural machines have been developed have *technological* conditions for large scale farming been developed. In addition, high wages now exist, providing the *economic* condition for large scale mechanical farming. But social and legal obstacles to farm amalgamation persist.

The rarity of a large farm in Japan is revealed by the fact that when the Second Land Reform† came about (1947-1950), which abolished leased holdings roughly above one hectare, and owner-cultivated holdings roughly over three ha, the land compulsorily purchased from the landowners *leasing* the land amounted to over two million ha, but from landowners *cultivating* the land only 26,000 ha was taken.‡ (1 ha = 2·47 acres).

Economists now know that land tenancy, especially without security of tenure, is highly unfavourable for agricultural productivity. The insecure tenant has no incentive to improve the land by applying manure or fertilisers, or by any capital works which would give long-term yields. The landlord is liable to become an absentee landlord and lose contact with the farm and farming technology, so that he is unaware of the possibilities of improving the land. In addition, he is not as well placed to carry out land improvements (which have until quite recently been highly labour intensive) as the cultivator with permanent tenure. The well-motivated cultivator with security of tenure can devote his slack periods to improvement of the land, while it would be impracticable for the landlord to mobilise that spare time of the insecure tenant.

It could be concluded that the First Land Reform was not very favourable for agricultural productivity, in that it increased the area of tenanted land, and reduced the security of tenure for the tenants. However, it is almost certain that Japanese agriculture was already set up on an upward path of experimentation and improvement by peasants under the Tokugawa Shogunate. Obviously, the Japanese peasants of that period

---

* Takekazu Ogura, "Recent Agrarian Problems in Japan", *The Developing Economies*, Vol. IV, No. 2, June 1966.
† It should be noted that the term the Second Land Reform refers to land reform actually carried out according to the legislation of 1946. Some writers may refer by that name to another earlier Law passed by the Diet in 1945, which was, however, rejected by the Occupation Authorities as inadequate.
‡ Ogura.

were unusual as they experimented with various seeds of rice and cross-fertilised different kinds of seeds, and stealthily "imported" different rice seeds from other *hans* against legal prohibitions. One of the factors encouraging this very modern approach may have been the fact that under the Tokugawa feudal system the cultivator of land had an obligation to deliver a *fixed* annual payment in rice to the feudal lord. This meant that the individual peasant farmer had a very strong incentive to improve the land yield as all of the increase was his. The other factors for this extraordinarily progressive bent of the Japanese peasants may be difficult to discover. It is plausible that these progressive attitudes were carried over, even accentuated, in the post-Restoration age, although *some* of the features of the First Land Reform were not favourable to farm improvement. At any rate, as was pointed out in Chapter 1, Japanese agriculture in the last 100 years provided the base for general economic development.

The Second Land Reform

From the Meiji Restoration until the end of the last War, the *active* agricultural population of Japan was more or less constant at over 14 million. After the end of World War II about 9 million people consisting of repatriates from former Japanese colonies, demobilised soldiers and city workers who lost their jobs in the destroyed industries, moved into the villages. As a result the active agricultural population rose to an all-time record of 16·6 million, and could be given a livelihood in the villages only with extreme difficulty. Even before the War the countryside had some connections with left-wing parties and after the War there was ferment in the villages, promising grave political troubles.

In this situation land reform was one of the measures for democratisation included by the Occupation Authorities, along with the dissolution of the *zaibatsu*, anti-monopoly legislation and a new labour code. The land reform was to assist the absorption of numerous landless people in the countryside and to assist the development of agriculture. If the country was to regain economic self-support, especially under the circumstances where heavy industry was to be banned, and when food was desperately short, development of agriculture was particularly important. It was also expected that the land reform would prevent the development of political unrest such as there was in China.

It is doubtful whether an independent Japanese government, even a democratic one, would or could have accomplished as thorough-going a reform as was in fact carried out. Instructed by the Supreme Command of the Allied Powers to prepare a plan for land reform, the Japanese Government at first proposed something quite mild. It was the firm insistence of the occupation authorities that pushed the radical reform

through the Diet in 1946. This Second Land Reform virtually wiped
out land tenancy by making the vast majority of tenants the owners
of the land they had leased. The land reform was enacted by the
Revised Farm Land Adjustment Law, and the Owner-Farmer Establishment Law of 1946. The three main features of the land reform were
compulsory purchase by the government of some lands and resale to
peasants; establishment of limits on the future acquisition of land by
farmers; and fixing extremely low rents on the remaining tenanted land,
and giving the tenants a virtually absolute security of tenure.

There were three conditions for expropriation. Leased land owned by
absentee landlords (the landlords who had not lived in the village where
the land was situated in a specified period before the bill was introduced),
was to be compulsorily purchased, irrespective of the size of the holding.
When the owner of leased land lived in the village where the land was
located, a maximum limit was fixed by the Law and crop land above
this limit was to be expropriated. The maximum was highest for Hokkaido (4 ha), the next highest for Aomori Prefecture (1·5 ha), and
the lowest was for Hiroshima Prefecture (0·5 ha). The national average
maximum limit, however, was not to exceed 1 ha. In the case of the
land cultivated by the owner himself, the Law again fixed limits for each
prefecture. The highest maximum limit was for Hokkaido at 12 ha,
the next for Aomori Prefecture at 4·5 ha, and the lowest at 1·6 ha for
Hiroshima Prefecture. The prefectural governor had the power to
establish different regional limits within his prefecture provided that
the average maximum limit for the prefecture was not exceeded. For the
whole of Japan (except Hokkaido) the prefectural limits average was
not to exceed 3 ha. The limit for pasture land used by the owner was
set at 5 ha.

In practice, however, it was mainly the tenanted land that became subject
to expropriation, because large farms (even by the Japanese land reform
definition) were extremely scarce. The government did not confiscate
the land, but purchased it at a price worked out on the basis of the
price of rice and production costs in 1945 when the land reform plan
was being drafted, although the actual land reform was carried out
in the period 1947-1950. In 1945 the price of rice (the most important
determinant in the compensation formula) was 150 yen per 150 kg,
but owing to very rapid inflation in the following four years it rose
forty-one times to be over 6,200 yen in 1950. As a result the compensation became purely nominal and the land was in effect confiscated.
Professor Ouchi estimated that by 1950 the government price for average
paddy land would purchase only 5 per cent of the land's annual yield.*
Having taken over the land the government then resold it to the tenants

* Tsutomu Ouchi, "The Japanese Land Reform: Its Efficacy and Limitations", *The
Developing Economies*, Vol. IV, No. 2, June 1966.

at the same price but on easy terms with credit for long periods of time. Thus the tenants received the land virtually free of charge. This feature of land reform was very important from several points of view, even more important than the large area of the land involved.

Compulsory redistribution of land involved about one-third of the total farming land of Japan, though it is difficult to find the exact fraction because the official estimate of the total farming land in 1945 is highly suspect. In 1941 the total farming land amounted to about six million ha. The official figure for 1945 is only 5·1 million ha.

This last figure must be a gross understatement—the estimate was made after the Occupation Authorities had decreed compulsory food deliveries to the government at fixed prices and farmers had understated the area of cultivated land to reduce their quota for compulsory deliveries. In fact, in view of the large influx of a hungry population into the villages in the first few post-war years, it is probable that the total area of farming land grew above the normal level of over 6 million ha. The official figure for 1946 is 5·2 million ha, for 1947, 5·0 million ha and for 1949 (no estimate available for 1948) 4·9 million ha,† although the country population grew greatly during those years.

Thus it has to be assumed that when the land reform started the total farming land of Japan was about 6 million ha. In the course of the whole land reform the government compulsorily purchased: 1,968,000 ha of cultivated land; 394,000 ha of pasture land; and 1,272,000 ha of uncultivated land.‡ This adds up to 3,654,000 ha taken over by the government. The government did not sell all that land to the tenant farmers, but kept some and sold some for housing purposes. 1,938,000 ha of cultivated land and only 789,000 ha of pasture and uncultivated land (which adds up to 2,727,000 ha) were sold to tenant farmers by the government in 1950. The government spent 2,944 million yen in cash and 9,062 million yen in securities on the acquisition of the land. It received a total contract sum of 8,905 million yen* from the new owners, but virtually all of this was long-term credit.

The land reform directly reduced the tenancy rate to 10 per cent by 1950 from 46 per cent in 1945. Indirectly, there have been additional falls in the tenancy rate because the land reform legislation strengthened the tenant's position *towards* the landlord. This in fact gave the landlord an incentive to convert an existing tenancy into a sale and to avoid all new leasing of land. Land reform gave the tenant virtually absolute security of tenure and reduced the rent drastically. It also converted

† H. Arizawa and H. Inaba, editors, *Shiryo sengo ni-ju nen shi* (*Historical Material for Post-war Twenty Years*), Vol. 2 Keizai (Economics), 1966, Nihon Hyoron-sha Publishing Co., Tokyo, p. 128.
‡ Arizawa and Inaba, p. 126.
* Arizawa and Inaba, p. 126.

payment of rent from rice into money. In spite of two subsequent upward adjustments, the fixed rent is now almost completely nominal; since the landowner has to pay the Real Estate Tax which often exceeds the rent, holding onto the land can be a liability for the owner. As a result of these changes and the proceeding inflation, actual or potential leasing of land has often been converted into sales. Professor Ouchi† estimated that the tenancy rate by area of farming land fell to under 5 per cent by 1966. Thus the land tenancy system with all its social, and above all economic, evils was abolished.

From a moral point of view land reform had the weakness that it picked on the owners of farming land by in effect drastically taxing this particular group of asset holders, while exempting from levies other asset holders, such as owners of forest lands, valuable city land, and commercial and industrial capital. 1·8 million landowners lost on an average 1·1 ha each of cultivated land. The number of farmers who *bought* the land under the scheme was about 4·3 million, over 70 per cent of farm households in Japan.‡ These numbers explain in part the political attractions of the step.

In some cases the landowners were completely ruined, but probably most were merely severely impoverished. As a class they had better education than the general public, so that they were able to obtain positions in various agricultural institutions and governments, especially local government. Some of them had also other means of support, such as forest land (generally exempted from the land reform) or the land that they farmed themselves. The landowners did sue the government for "infringement of their constitutional rights" but their action was rejected by the Supreme Court. After Japan obtained independence the former landowners started a political movement with the objective of inducing the government to grant them compensation for their losses. Finally, in 1965, the government decided to give them a *partial* compensation which was officially called "reward for co-operation in the land reform". The motive for granting this compensation was, of course, purely political. The government believed that the landowners who lost their land still had a good deal of political influence in the villages apart from their own votes.

In general, since the land reform the government's economic policies have always tried to please the farmers. The land reform and the subsequent policies have turned the formerly politically restless countryside into solid and conservative Liberal Democratic Party supporters. These facts and the extraordinary growth of the whole economy have assured that any left-wing party, even the Socialist Party, has virtually

† Ouchi.
‡ *Farming Japan*, November 1967, Overseas Technical Co-operation Agency, Nihon Norin Kikaku Kyokai, Tokyo.

no chance of coming to power in the near future, unless there is a major international political or economic upheaval.

The economic effects of the land reform were even greater, and for the needs of the country they were all desirable. The vast numbers of people who flocked into the villages after the War ended were assisted in finding employment. Domestic food output was increased and thereby the pressure on the balance of payments was reduced. The virtual abolition of the tenancy system gave the cultivators greater incentive to improve the land and agricultural facilities. And the substantial redistribution of incomes in the villages reduced social class stratification, but above all it provided the cultivating farmer with the *means* to improve farming. The thrifty Japanese cultivators applied most of the income increase to farm investment: the purchase of improved varieties of seed; greater use of fertilisers, pesticides and mechanisation; new and wide use of vinyl plastics to protect early planted rice seedlings, which allows double cropping of land or rice growing in cold areas with a short growing season; and the widespread use of these plastics in hothouses for growing vegetables.

The Need for the Third Land Reform

The final result of these factors has been a great increase in agricultural output in spite of the rapidly declining labour force in agriculture since 1953. Paradoxically, however, almost every aspect of this great economic success of the land reform has now, in the quite different economic circumstances of the country, turned into a disability. In the early post-war period when alternative employment was not available, land reform was highly desirable as it aimed at and insisted on owner-farming, and attempted to give employment on land to as many people as possible. Now, with an extreme shortage of labour in the whole economy and much higher returns to labour in manufacturing, the excessive absorption of labour in agriculture has become uneconomic. It is reasonable to believe that if the tenants had not become landowners they would now be leaving the land more rapidly. The rigid maximum limits on the agricultural land holdings justifiable in the desperate immediate post-war years perpetuate the minute uneconomic farms. In spite of the remarkable Japanese industriousness and ingenuity, how could they have their farming on an economic basis when their average farm is still about 2·47 acres and the legal maximum limit varies between one half and four and a half ha?

The spectacular growth of productivity in manufacturing has created a wide disparity between incomes in agriculture and manufacturing. This disparity is not due to any neglect on the part of the Japanese farmers. In any other country the 3-4% increases of productivity which have been reached by the Japanese farmers would have been hailed as a great success. In Japan where increases in productivity in manufacturing often exceeded 15 per cent p.a., the trend represents a serious drag on the whole economy, especially as a general shortage of labour has developed. Even the substantial increases in farm productivity, inadequate in the sense that they have not matched the growth in manufacturing, yet so welcome in aiding the economy in the difficult fifties and much of the sixties, have become a burden towards the end of the last decade. Suddenly Japan has found itself with a vast surplus of rice, which promises to grow very rapidly to unmanageable proportions and which is already a heavy burden.

It is clear that the Japanese agriculture is in need of fundamental changes.

What the Japanese economy needs now is a faster outflow of labour from agriculture to other sectors, and an amalgamation of the tiny farms into much larger farms which would be economically viable in open competition with farmers in other countries, without the present massive and involuntary assistance by the Japanese taxpayer and the consumer. Even in the present legal, social and institutional set-up, a substantial outflow of labour force into manufacturing is taking place, but it is not fast enough and paradoxically does not lead to any significant decrease in the number of farms or increase in the average size of the farms. The best, most enterprising elements quit farming and leave the family farms to women and old folk. In other words the institution of part-time farm households and even part-time farmers is about to become the typical farming unit. This development would undermine the growth of productivity in agriculture and make it an even bigger burden for the nation. Briefly, only twenty years after the Second Land Reform, Japan is now in a great need of a Third Land Reform, larger and more thorough-going than the previous two. The Japanese Government is aware of the need and is not short of plans, but the political difficulties of this change are enormous.

The government has taken several steps to improve the structure of farming, apart from training farmers, extension work and financial assistance. In 1961 an amended Basic Agricultural Law was passed to relax the legal restrictions on the maximum area of land worked by a farming unit, to make possible an increase in the size of the average farm. The 1961 Law has two main features permitting family farms to exceed the existing maximum area limits, provided that the operations of farming could be "carried out effectively mainly with the family labour"; and relaxing the restrictions on the land size held by limited liability farming companies and co-operatives.

The limited liability farming enterprises (companies by registration but co-operatives in fact), as well as farm co-operatives proper did exist before the amended 1961 Agricultural Law. Then the attitude of the government to them was just permissive and otherwise neutral, provided that they complied with the principle of owner-cultivation. The new Law decided to encourage the farming co-operatives. The co-operatives are allowed to acquire more land than that contributed by the members provided that the area leased from non-members of the co-operative is less than half of the area of the land held by the co-operative, and that the quantity of hired labour is less than a half of the labour used by the co-operative.

The practical effects of these amendments to the 1961 Agricultural Law have been negligible. It is one thing to permit some acts and another to induce them. The size of the average family farm has not increased significantly. The effect on farming co-operatives has not been economically significant. It is true that there were only 589 farming co-operatives before 1960, that there were 3,178 in 1961, and that after the amendment of the Law they rose to 5,018 by 1965.* But these totals include two categories: total co-operatives and partial co-operatives. A total co-operative is one where all the productive activities of the members are run collectively. A partial co-operative is one where only some activities of the individual farms in the co-operative are run collectively. The important fact then is that four years after the amended Law was passed, in 1965, there were only 380 total co-operatives in the whole of Japan, and the 4,638 others were partial co-operatives. Further, very few of the total co-operatives bought or leased additional land, so that the objective of moving towards a larger, more economical size of farming unit has not been achieved so far.

It would appear therefore that the small area of the land *owned* by the typical Japanese farmer does not owe anything to the legal restrictions of maximum area of farms. This does not mean, however, that the consequences of the land reform do not have an indirect effect on the average size of the farms. The land reform which converted over four million tenants into landowners must have tied them more closely to the land, making them now more reluctant to leave the farms and thus reducing the labour mobility and farm mobility.

As for the area of land *cultivated* (though not owned) by the average farm, this is undoubtedly influenced by the present state of legislation on the side of supply of land for leasing. It should be noted here that the 1961 Agricultural Land Law reduced the restrictive provisions only on the *demand-for-land* side. In the first instance this Law still prohibits leasing of the land obtained under the land reform. Since about one-third of farming land falls under that category this limitation may be quite strong. Secondly, farming land rents are fixed at absurdly low levels,

* Ogura.

so that unless the farmers decide to go for black market leasing, and there is some of this, a legal leasing of land is not a business proposition. Moreover, farmers would not lease the land now because the tenancy laws are such that the landlord would not recover his land if he wanted it back, except through the tenant's kindness or fear of social pressures, if any, in the village. Further, should a landowner lease some of his land and later be compelled to move his residence out of the village, he would become an "absentee landlord" and his land would be compulsorily expropriated by the government at a nominal price.

In any case, increasing the size of the farms through greater resort to the tenancy system is not a satisfactory structural reform of agriculture.

As for the co-operative method of increasing the area of the typical Japanese farm to an economic size (strongly favoured by the Socialist Party of Japan), events have shown that the total co-operative is almost completely unattractive to the Japanese farmers, though partial co-operatives and village co-operatives are extremely popular.

In any case, even if the total co-operatives were somehow encouraged (by bribing the farmers?) this might not be enough. To do any good, that is to lead to a structural reform of farming (consolidation of plots, drainage, change of crops, establishment of new processing plants, etc.), it would be necessary to give the co-operatives the nature of a permanent and irreversible arrangement among farmers, and this would prove a very powerful deterrent to establishing such co-operatives.

This problem of Japanese agriculture being unable (in the present set-up) to evolve farms of sufficient size to make them economic, is the most intractable of all the Japanese economic problems. Certainly, all the other agricultural problems (to be discussed later) would be easily solved if this one were. The phenomenon of roughly the same number of farms, of roughly the same average size ($2 \cdot 47$ acres) continuing to persist despite a substantial outflow of labour requires detailed examination.

The decrease in the labour force in agriculture in the late fifties and in the sixties has three main causes. One is the state of high employment in the economy. The importance of this factor is shown by the fact that the outflow of labour from agriculture was small in the recession of 1958 and large in the boom of 1961. Similarly, but conversely, the inflow of labour into agriculture from the rest of the economy varied with the general level of activity. That is the inflow into agriculture has been higher in the recession of 1962-1964 than in the boom of 1961.*
Secondly, the very high productivity increases in manufacturing enlarge the income disparity. The higher the income disparity, the higher the pull of manufacturing and service industries.

* Masayoshi Namiki, *The Farm Population of Japan 1872-1965*, Agricultural Policy Research Committee, p. 58.

The third cause is the vast mechanisation of Japanese agriculture since the late 1950s. This mechanisation was largely due to the development of cheap, Japanese made, petrol-driven small agricultural machines, such as small garden tractors, power-operated but hand-pushed cultivators, power-operated sprayers, dryers, and so on. These machines saved labour and their availability allowed the typical farm household to spare one or more family workers to take an outside job. Towards the end of the sixties came an automatic power driven and operated rice-planting machine whose mechanical arm grabs and plants three rice plants at a time. At this stage, however, the causal relationship may have been reversed. Earlier, the cheap machines released some labour and allowed some members of the farm households to take outside jobs. By the end of the sixties farm labour became so short and expensive that a very complicated and expensive machine became desirable.

The outflow of labour from agriculture has been going on at various rates for the last 100 years. In the past daughters and second and subsequent sons (those who would not inherit the farm) left the farm for the city, either for permanent jobs or for casual jobs called *dekasegi*. Recently, however, the head of the farm household or the successor son have often resorted to *dekasegi*. In the past farmers took *dekasegi* in the off-season when there was little work on the farm, particularly in cold areas such as Tohoku, Hokuriku and Sanin, where a second winter crop could not be grown. Recently, however, even farmers from the double-crop areas engage in *dekasegi*, giving up the second crop. Apart from the inducement of high outside wages for taking casual outside jobs, their popularity is increasing because of the arrangements for social security insurance. The casual worker who has worked four months and twenty days will have paid the equivalent of four days' wages as unemployment insurance, for which he will later receive unemployment benefit of 60 per cent of his wage for ninety days.*

Given the fact that many farm family members leave the farm household jobs for good, why does the number of farm households not decline? Why are the small farms not bought up by the wealthier farmers even within the legal maximum area limit? It is noteworthy that transfers of land for non-agricultural purposes are livelier.

Transfers of land for increasing the size of farms are hindered by the three major factors. The first is inflation of land prices to levels at which a genuine and rational farmer may consider it uneconomic to buy the land *for farming*. This inflation of land values has been caused by excessively high capitalisation of land yields under farming by the less progressive farmers who put a low valuation on family labour used; rapid general inflation which makes land an excellent store of value;

* Namiki, p. 63.

and the fact that some agricultural land has or will come to be used for industrial or residential purposes, where its value will go up to very high levels. The heavy government price support for farm products makes a speculative behaviour in this area even more attractive.

In addition, housing in cities is extremely scarce and very expensive. Many families with most members commuting to work in cities decide to hold on to the family house in the village and this makes the sale of the land about the house either impracticable or less attractive to the owner. In any case the buyer would put only a low value on the farm house if he intended to integrate the purchase with his own land. But the farmer selling his farm and the house would have to pay an exorbitant price in the city. Further, the farmer would have to pay a heavy capital gains tax (on gains due to the sale of land). So he holds on to the farm.

The final reason for holding on to small farms is the inadequacy of old age pensions. Many of the part-time farm households hold on to the land to retire on. The Japanese are usually retired very early with a very small (if any) income, and on their own land they would be able to grow at least a minimum of food for themselves.

The Growth of Incidence of Part-time Farm Households

Like any other country Japan has had some "part-time farm households" in the past, as far back as statistics are available. However, in the last two decades there have been large quantitative and some qualitative changes in the incidence of this phenomenon. In the present Japanese statistics a part-time farm household is defined as one where one or more members are employed outside agriculture. The part-time farm households are classified into two categories. In Type I agricultural income is more important than outside income. Type II is where outside income is more important than agricultural income.

Table 8.1. *Changes in the Percentage of Various Categories of Farm Households.*

	1938	1950	1955	1960	1965	1967
Full-time Farm Households	45	50	35	34·3	21·5	21·2
Part-time Type I	31	28·4	37·6	33·7	36·8	31·0
Part-time Type II	24	21·6	27·4	32·0	41·8	47·7

Sources: Figures for 1938 from Namiki.
Figures for 1950–65 from *Nogyo Sensasu* (*Agricultural Census*), Ministry of Agriculture, Forestry and Fisheries.
Figures for 1967 from *Abstract of Statistics on Agriculture, Japan 1968*, Ministry of Agriculture, Forestry and Fisheries.

As Table 8.1 shows Japanese agriculture has been undergoing striking changes. If one assumes that the consistent trend of the sixties has continued until 1970 then in this year *agricultural* income has become a sort of casual occupation for more than half of the farm households. Further, only about one in every five farm households devotes itself entirely to farming. It would be interesting to know how many old couples are in that one-fifth still full-time in farming! This part-time farming must, of course, have serious effects on the future productivity in agriculture. If farming land is not taken out of the hands of half-interested people, the productivity growth in Japanese farming will lag even more behind manufacturing than it does at present. The Ministry of Agriculture, Forestry and Fisheries carried out a survey of productivity of various types of farmers. It revealed striking facts:

1. The shift to part-time farming increases the income of the household. This suggests that labour is pulled out of agriculture by other industries, not squeezed out of agriculture.

2. The average net *farming* productivity per 10 ares (1 are = 100 square metres) and especially per 10 labour hours is higher for Type I part-time farm households than that of full-time farm households. This fact appears to be somewhat against our hypothesis that a shift towards part-time farming leads to lesser efficiency of farming, but one fact and one surmise must be considered. Firstly, Table 8.1 shows that the Type I part-time farm households are steadily declining, and in recent years in particular many of them have been sliding into Type II where productivity undoubtedly falls. Secondly, our surmise is that among the full-time farm households (one-fifth of all farm households), there are many old couples whose sons and daughters have left—the farm household is full-time only because the old folks could not obtain any outside job. Naturally, such a farm household would be inefficient in farming and would tend to drag down the average productivity of the class.

3. The average net productivity in farming of Type II part-time farm households is much lower than that of the other two types of farm households. This effect appears with respect to the productivity per are of land and per work hour.*

The trend toward the rise of the proportion of Type II part-time farm households has been particularly strong in recent years (see Table 8.1) so that by now probably more than a half of all Japanese farm households are of Type II part-time. This means that Japanese agriculture has a built-in factor of deterioration. Agriculture simply is not getting any reasonable share of dedicated, enterprising, young and fit workers. As a result the farm is left to the care of the elderly parents or young wife, so that the average age of farmers is going up and the agricultural labour force becomes increasingly female. The actual position of part-time farming is even worse than the statistics show, because many

* *Noka Keizai Chosa*, Norinsho, quoted by Namiki, p. 66.

farmers taking casual jobs outside agriculture are not caught in the net of the compilers of statistics.

These part-time farming trends have various undesirable effects. With the loss of interest in farming and the growth of a tendency to hold land for other reasons, technological improvement and capital investment in farming are unlikely. With the great fall in the average number of family members engaged in farming, the second or winter crop is not sown, planting and harvesting is not done at the right time and generally the farm is neglected. The position is particularly acute here because of two factors. Replacing lost family labour by hired labour is restricted by the Agricultural Land Law. Replacing labour by machinery has been taking place but is inadequate (witness the fact that second cropping is often abandoned) partly because some types of machinery cannot be used on farms where the average farm is 2·47 acres, and where this small farm consists on an average of five separate non-contiguous plots.

Aware of these problems, the government set up the Committee for the Promotion of Structural Policies in Agriculture. In July 1967 the government revealed a general outline of the policies intended for the future. The objective is to increase substantially the average size of the farms. In principle this restructuring of farming, the greatest change in agriculture since the Meiji Restoration, is to be carried out by assisting farmers with larger farms to acquire more land; encouraging the organisation of co-operative farms by giving them financial assistance; and by creating a farmers' retirement pension system so that the older people would be more ready to leave the farms and sell the land.

The scheme envisages the classification of farmers into two or three categories according to size. According to the terms set for buying out the small farms, the policy might create resentment among the small farmers and they might turn from voting for the Liberal Democratic Party to voting for *Komeito*, Democratic Socialist, Socialist and even the Communist parties. This would be quite serious for the present Liberal Democratic government which relies heavily on the village vote. At present farming still has 5·6 million farm households with about nine million voters. Although any government-assisted redistribution of land would favour the large farmers to whom land would be redistributed, they would be much less numerous than the people who would lose their farms, that is the numerous very small farmers.

With the Japanese electoral system, which is not proportional, the votes of the (substantial) minority of farmers who would be pleased would be completely cancelled out by the votes of those who would be displeased so that possibly all rural electoral seats could be lost. Whether such a structural land reform would attract any present opposition votes in the urban electoral districts to the Liberal Democratic Party is uncertain. Such reform would require substantial taxpayer funds at the outset, and its benefits would come only in the longer run in the form of increased efficiency in farming and possibly reduction of food prices and farm subsidies. Even if some present opposition party urban voters could see the longer-run effects and even if they were thereby persuaded to vote for the Liberal Democratic Party, they could be felt only in the marginal seats, and would be swamped elsewhere. In addition, the nine million rural voters are much stronger than their numbers would suggest because the electoral boundaries were fixed over twenty years ago when the rural population was much higher and the urban population much lower than it is today, and the electoral boundaries have not yet been adjusted for the large population movements. Thus the present rural votes are in effect weighted two to three times as heavily as the votes of the urban voters. The present Liberal Democratic Party government which realises the need for structural reform also knows that it would be penalised at the polls if it did its duty. The matter is made more difficult for the government because the Socialist Party is opposed to creation of still larger farms out of the present "large" ones. The Socialist Party favours the co-operative solution.

There is a good deal of discussion among Japanese economists about the need for increasing the "mobility of land". Some believe that the problem of increasing the size of Japanese farms to make them economically viable without the crutches of subsidies and protection from imports could be achieved by increasing the ease with which land can be shifted from one user to another. For this purpose they recommend an amendment to the 1961 Agricultural Land Law, which would abolish legal rent ceilings; liberalise regulations on land leasing, which means restoring some of the powers of the landlord against the tenant; increase the maximum limit on the area of the land that a tenant can acquire; and would establish a public institution which would make use of such greater "land mobility" to assist setting up larger holdings.

A satisfactory restructuring of farming requires a complete and unreserved merging of small farms under individual ownership or under an irreversible co-operative ownership. Present *government-controlled* market mechanism is not producing either of the solutions, and the government will have to take sides on those issues. The government has two roads open to it in this matter. Since it is doubtful that individual farmers could be induced to join irreversible total co-operatives by any reasonable incentives, the government may have to fall back upon assisting private farm mergers, that is large farmers buying out small ones. This, however, requires government subsidisation which will *appear* to be subsidisation of large and rich farmers, although in the long run it would certainly be in the national interest and possibly even in the interest of the small farmers. This need for subsidisation of farm mergers arises from land prices inflated above the rational capitalisation of farm yield. The price demanded by the small landowner is very much higher than the price a rational *farmer* could pay. Thus the government may have to step in and pay the difference. This would establish a dual price system for land with a seller's price and a buyer's price. In addition, the government would have to establish and operate a system for the selection of those farmers who would be financially assisted in accumulating large farms. This would undoubtedly be difficult. The taxpayer cost of this policy would also be high, though in the longer run this policy would repay the cost when the direct and indirect assistance to viable farming was removed. One complication of such policy would be a certain, large increase in the land prices when it became known that the government was to finance a vast transfer of land.

If the dual-price method of converting small uneconomic farms into large economic ones were found to be politically unworkable, there is the alternative of the Third Land Reform. The government could compulsorily buy out small farms at a price reflecting the properly capitalised value of their income yields, and then resell them at the same price but on an easy instalment payment system to picked farmers. Under this solution it would be necessary to pick and compel the potential seller, and to find a suitable and interested buyer. There would be a variety of criteria for choosing the farmers to be compulsorily bought out. Economic efficiency would favour buying out all small farms, initially those, say, below 0·5 ha, or farmers manifestly inefficient, or those where the head of the family has had a permanent outside job at a certain date preceding the reform. Equity would favour repurchasing all of the land "sold" to the tenants under the last Land Reform. The farmers thus expropriated would still gain because they have used the land for twenty years, paid practically nothing for it, and now—to save them from hardship—they would be paid the capitalised value of the income yield of the land under farming.

It is doubtful whether the government will choose either of the policies. Probably, it will continue to temporise, making vague and general policy statements about a structural change and will hope that the burden of supporting an ailing agriculture will not become unbearable during its tenure of office.

Productivity: Japanese Farms are Highly Efficient but not Economic

Japanese farmers are heavily supported by the rest of the economy in several ways. Even so the average *farming* income per worker is much below the average worker's income in the cities. In the Japanese fiscal year 1967, agriculture contributed 2,800 billion yen to the net national income of 34,700 billion yen (8 per cent)*, but the labour force employed in agriculture represented 18·7 per cent of the total working labour force. The average rural *household* income in 1967 was 1,030,000 yen *per household* (U.S.$2,814). Of this figure *agricultural* income was slightly less than a half—the rest was income earned by the members of the farm household outside agriculture. Thus the remarkable fact is that the average Japanese farmer earns 510,000 yen p.a. (U.S.$1,416) from his average holding of 1 ha (2·47 acres) of land! This income has been rising very fast by the world standards of agricultural growth rates.

The increases in agricultural productivity have been so great that despite a much decreased agricultural labour force the output of almost all foodstuffs has been rising rapidly. The 1967 output was smaller than the 1950 output only in the relatively unimportant agricultural products, namely oats, maize, millet, buckwheat, rapeseed and bamboo shoots. All the other foodstuffs and feedstuffs registered large increases of output between 1950-1967. The largest increase was in forage crops (sixteen times) and pork (output in 1967 was twenty times higher than in 1926 and ten times higher than in 1935). The output of other products increased between 1950-1967: chickens ten times, sugar-beet ten times, sugar cane eight times, fruit seven times, milk cows seven times, vegetables as a rule several times, eggs three times in three years (between 1965-1968).

Rice production which occupies more than a half of Japan's cultivated land also has recorded substantial increases. The average annual yield of paddy (unhusked) rice was 833 kg per acre in the period 1874-1883. For the period 1904-1913 it was 1,027 kg, for 1951-1960 it was 1,420 kg, and in 1968, 1,817 kg per acre.† The increases in the output of rice, though not so spectacular as those of other products, have been large enough to produce an extraordinary surplus of rice in Japan that has become a heavy burden.

Table 8.2. *Average Annual Rice Yields, quintals per ha 1963-67.*

Australia	65·1	Greece	46·3
Spain	61·9	Ceylon	19·3
Morocco	51·9	Burma	15·3
Japan	51·8	India	15·3
Italy	48·9	Pakistan	15·3
United Arab Republic	46·4	Cambodia	11·4

Source: F.A.O., *The State of Food and Agriculture 1968*, Rome, 1968, p. 93.

* *Japan Economic Yearbook*, 1969, p. 93.
† E.P.A., *Keizai Yoran*, 1969, p. 147.
   Note: An English language Japanese publication: *Farming Japan*, November 1967, Overseas Technical Cooperation Agency, Nihon Norin Kikaku Kyokai, makes an error in these statistics by confusing ten ares with one acre.

In milk yields per cow Japan has the third place in the world after Bermuda and Israel, but before Denmark and Netherlands. These figures, however, are only *suggestive* of efficiency. They do not exactly represent efficiency because of differences in climatic and soil conditions. In any case a very high output per acre or per animal without consideration of cost is not necessarily a good thing economically. A very high price for a particular product protected by restriction of imports will certainly push up the yields per cow, or per acre, but whether this is economically desirable is another matter.

Table 8.3. Annual Milk Yields, kg per cow, Japan.

1948–1952	1952–1956	1962	1963	1964	1965	1966
2,920	2,738	4,379	4,341	4,345	4,284	4,300

Source: F.A.O., *Production Yearbook Vol. 21, 1967*, Rome, 1968, p. 383.

The general growth of agricultural productivity in Japan in the post-war period came from a substantial effort of farmers and a good deal of assistance from the government. The factors promoting agricultural output have been widespread farming education, increased level of investment, increased use of vinyl plastics for protecting young plants from frost, increased use of chemical fertilisers, protective chemicals, insecticides and fungicides, and widespread use of cheap farm machinery. In a sense the very high levels of protection from imports and expensive domestic price support policy have been most responsible for the large increases in productivity per acre, per cow and so on, because they provided the motivation for the extraordinarily intensive type of farming that Japan now has. High productivity increases, generally a virtue, have become a vice in this case by making Japanese agriculture technologically extremely efficient (if one ignores the problem of the size of the typical farm), and yet uneconomic.

Table 8.4. Use of Commercial Fertilisers
(In terms of N, P_2O_2, and K_2O) kg per ha of arable land in 1966/67)

Japan	350	Latin America	17
Western Europe	134	Near East (excluding Israel)	16
North America	61	Far East (excluding Japan and	
Oceania	41	Mainland China)	10
Eastern Europe and U.S.S.R.	39	Africa (excluding S. Africa)	2

Source: *The State of Food and Agriculture 1968*, p. 44.

Japan uses almost 100 times as much artificial fertiliser as India, and part of the reason for this is that the Japanese rice prices are much higher and fertiliser prices much lower than in India, so that the

Table 8.5. Mechanisation of Japanese Agriculture.

Year	Power-operated cultivators and tractors		Power sprayers	Power dusters	Ventilating and drying machines	Trucks and powered tricycles
	Pushed by hand	Power driven				
1964	2,183,000		524,000	180,000	724,000	358,000
1965	2,509,000		600,000	236,000	n.a.	418,000
1966	2,725,000	38,000	717,000	409,000	1,073,000	562,000
1967	3,021,000	57,900	905,000	724,000	1,367,000	884,000

Source: Bureau of Statistics, Office of Prime Minister, *Japan Statistical Yearbook 1968*.

Japanese farmer can buy *four* times as much fertiliser for the same quantity of paddy.*

Since the number of farm households in 1967 was 5·4 million, Table 8.5 shows that for every two Japanese farms there was then one hand pushed power operated cultivator or tractor, and roughly speaking for every five farms about one power sprayer, one power duster, one drying machine, and one truck or powered tricycle. Since a substantial proportion of these machines is co-operatively owned this means that the use of this machinery is accessible to virtually every farmer. Since the average Japanese farm is about 1 ha large these figures suggest an extremely high degree of power use per ha.

From the preceding discussion it follows clearly that Japan's agriculture today is almost completely un-Asian in most respects. It has the highest use of mechanical power per ha of cultivated land in the world. It has the highest rate of use of chemical fertilisers and of insecticides per ha in the world, and it has one of the highest yields per acre in the world. Yields per worker, while very high indeed by Asian standards, are low by Western standards. In education of farmers and technical farming education, Japan's agriculture is also un-Asian, and even surpasses some European countries. After leaving school Japanese farmers attend farming refresher courses every year and obtain assistance from government experimental stations and numerous extension officers. In addition, as Hemmi states: "Almost all the peasants in Japan read at least one monthly and one weekly agricultural magazine."†

In spite of these records, however, Japanese agriculture—a model for any Asian country—is a sick industry in the Japanese economy. Technologically it is remarkably efficient, yet it is uneconomic in its present

* *The State of Food and Agriculture 1968*, p. 110.
† Hemmi, p. 35.

Chart 8.1.

MECHANICAL POWER USED PER HECTARE IN
RELATION TO YIELDS OF MAJOR FOOD CROPS[1]

Per Hectare (Semi-logarithmic scale).

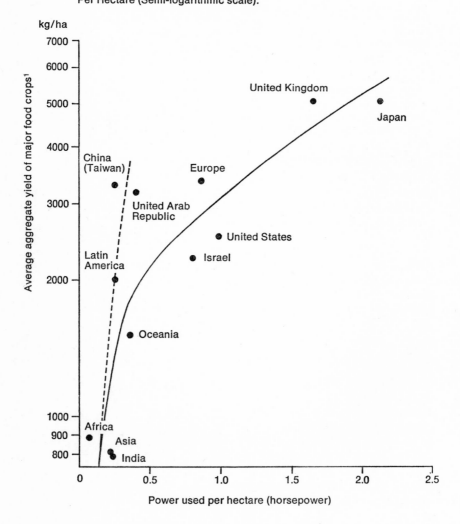

Power used per hectare (horsepower)

Note: 1 Cereals, pulses, oilseeds, sugar (raw), potatoes cassava,
            onions, tomatoes.
Sources: 1. *The World Food Problem*, a report of the President's
            Scientific Advisory Committee : Report of the Panel
            on thc World Food Supply, Washington D.C., 1967.
          2. Quoted by : *The State of Food and Agriculture 1968*, p. 93.

Table 8.6. *Index Numbers of Farm Productivity in Various Countries.*

Country	Index of farm output per unit of land	Index of farm output per labourer
Japan	100	100
Denmark	27·8	455
France	21·8	437
West Germany	31·7	302
U.K.	12·5	564
Italy	30·9	261

Source: E.P.A., *Economic Survey of Japan 1966/67*, Japan Times Ltd., Tokyo, p. 58.

size, structure, and income yield for present day Japan. A good deal about the nature of the Japanese economy is revealed by Table 8.6.

In the early post-war period Japan was often unable to produce and export enough manufactured goods to import enough foodstuffs. The economy did not have the capacity to expand the export sector any faster. Thus Japan gave the highest protection from imports to its agricultural products, and assisted agriculture in various other ways. This has given a great stimulus to the output of agricultural products per unit of land and Japan reached record levels of output per unit of land, but this policy did little to increase output per man employed in agriculture. This output per man *has* been rising but the rate has not been fast enough to keep pace with manufacturing. Admittedly the high level of protection, domestic food price supports, and reduction of the cultivators' rent burden did make higher investment in agriculture possible and thereby contributed to increases of productivity per farmer. But to put Japan's agriculture on a self-supporting basis like that of manufacturing, the size of the farming sector must be reduced, and the composition of its output must be changed. Basically, Japan's agriculture will ultimately shift substantially to providing those foodstuffs that are best consumed fresh, and most of the other foodstuffs will be imported. Under the present policy, Japan is over 100 per cent self-sufficient in vegetables and over 100 per cent self-sufficient in oranges and recently even in rice. But the cost of the present agricultural arrangements is very high to the taxpayers and to the consumers. The price of rice in Japan is three times the world price level and *in addition* it is substantially subsidised by the taxpayer. The price of wheat in Japan in 1965 was by far the highest in the world, 13·9 U.S. cents per kg, whereas the corresponding price was 3·9 U.S. cents in Argentina, 5·1 U.S. cents in Canada and 6·3 U.S. cents in Australia.* Barley was 13·6 cents per kg, whereas the U.S. price was 4·6 cents. Beef prices in Japan have been about five to seven time higher than in Australia.

* *Production Yearbook Vol. 21, 1967*, F.A.O., p. 520.

The taxpayers' costs must be added to the above consumer costs of agriculture in the present pattern.

The Rice Surplus Problem

Table 8.7 shows those taxpayer's costs that are "uneconomic", that is unnecessary in a rational system (but as such naturally it does not include costs such as governmental agricultural research and extension services).

Table 8.7. Foodstuffs Control — Receipts and Expenditure.

Fiscal year April to March	Receipts million yen	Expenditure million yen	Deficit million yen
1959	555,900	573,300	17,400
1960	579,900	612,200	32,300
1961	626,700	629,100	2,400
1962	672,900	726,700	53,800
1963	764,500	771,300	6,800
1964	791,100	929,100	138,000
1965	908,900	1,069,900	161,000
1966	964,000	1,225,500	261,000
1967	1,030,600	1,554,200	523,000
1968	1,094,400	1,642,100	547,000

Source: *Monthly Statistics of Japan,* September 1969.

The deficits were incurred mainly through the purchases of rice, although some other products such as wheat are also supported (but domestic wheat is not important in the total support costs). Each year the government fixes the price of rice at which the government (The Food Agency) will buy all domestic rice offered to it. This price was increased every year until 1968 on the principle of gradually reaching "Income Parity" between farmers and urban workers. In 1968 the government decided to stop the increases of producer prices because the fiscal burden of this proved to be excessive (see Table 8.10), given the fact that the government felt unable to increase the consumer prices of rice (because of fear of aggravating inflation). The total fiscal cost of the present rice policy of the government consists of two elements. One is the difference between the price at which the Food Agency buys rice and at which it sells the rice. The other element of cost is due to accumulation of vast stocks of rice. The costs here are for storage, rapid deterioration (the quality of much of the present rice stocks has already deteriorated greatly and some of it is unfit for Japanese consumption), the interest charge on moneys sunk into holding stocks, and the probability that the stocks will never be sold. To sell the surplus rice in the world markets would be difficult from the point of view of domestic politics because the government would not obtain one-third of the price it paid. The government is therefore temporising while admonishing(!) farmers to produce less rice and to switch to production of (the less profitable) vegetables. In the meantime to reduce the problem of storage costs, deterioration, and the interest on the capital sunk in the stored rice, the Japanese Food Agency in 1969 made a *loan* of 330,000 tons of rice (old stocks) to South Korea, and another one of 100,000 tons to Pakistan. The loan to Pakistan is for ten years after which period repayments in rice will be made over the following ten years in equal annual instalments— 10,000 tons annually on account of the principal and 2,000 tons annually as interest. These "loans" should be treated as gifts, because it is doubtful whether South Korea and Pakistan will have the will and the capacity to repay the "loan" in ten years' time, and if they did it is certain that Japan will not have the capacity to accept the repayment, unless the consumption and production trends in Japan are reversed.

The present rice surpluses are caused by a decline in consumption *per caput* to the extent that the total consumption declines in spite of the growth of population. The second reason for surpluses is the increase in output of rice due to greatly increased output per ha, and some increases of acreage under rice in recent years, due to rice planting in newly irrigated lands.

The government should not and could not do much about the decline in consumption of rice. As income *per caput* increases, consumption of rice is naturally substantially replaced by other foods such as vegetables and protein foods. In addition, rice is being increasingly replaced by wheat eaten in the form of noodles and bread. Thus the adjustment in the supply-demand position in Japan must come on the side of supply. Since it is impractical and undesirable to reduce output per acre, the acreage under cultivation must be reduced. But in spite of the exhortations by the government to farmers to switch to other crops, farmers find that with the assured sale of rice at a fixed and high price, in many cases

Table 8.8.   Consumption of Rice.

	Average 1934–38	1955	1965	1966	1967
Total consumption including use for seed, sake, etc. (thousand metric tons)	11,364	11,275	12,993	12,503	12,483
Consumption of table rice (kg/*per caput*)	135·0	110·7	111·7	105·8	103·3

Source: *Nihon Kokusei Zue*, Kokuseisha, Tokyo, 1969, p. 217.

Table 8.9.   Rice Production.

Year	Area planted 1,000 ha	Output 1,000 metric tons	Output kg per ha
1900	2,805	6,220	2,220
1940	3,152	9,131	2,900
1950	3,011	9,651	3,210
1960	3,308	12,858	3,890
1961	3,301	12,414	3,760
1962	3,285	13,009	3,960
1963	3,272	12,812	3,920
1964	3,260	12,584	3,860
1965	3,255	12,409	3,810
1966	3,254	12,745	3,920
1967	3,263	14,453	4,430
1968	3,280	14,449	4,410

Source: *Nippon: A Charted Survey of Japan 1969*, p. 139.

rice pays best. This has been the case in spite of substantial increases in the price of vegetables.

A comparison of Tables 8.8 and 8.9 shows very roughly the balance of supply of and demand for rice in Japan. Domestic supply of rice was inadequate until 1966 when a further fall in consumption and a somewhat smaller rise in output produced a surplus. In 1967 there was a further fall in consumption, though a slight one, but this time domestic output of rice showed a dramatic rise. This development was repeated in 1968 and in 1969. Thus it cannot be viewed as an accidental effect due to some climatic factors. Large surpluses of rice are now a structural feature of the Japanese economy. These surpluses are accentuated by the fact that (despite the existence of a system of government import controls on rice) Japan has continued to import rice when she has already had surpluses! There are two reasons for this. Firstly, Japan has some essentially barter type bilateral agreements with some Asian countries such as Communist China, and if she stopped importing Chinese rice, Japanese exports of manufactured goods would fall through too. Secondly, imported rice, which is much cheaper than the domestic rice, is used for manufacturing purposes for products like glucose, biscuits and so on. The domestic industries using this cheap imported rice would be severely hit if their main raw material were to double in price, and they may be a strong pressure group. The government could, of course, cut the price of the domestic rice to be used for manufacturing purposes, but this would produce complications as others would ask for the reduced price, and in any case the reduced-price sales would show large deficits. As a result imports of rice help to swell domestic rice surpluses held by the government.

Table 8.10. Balance of Acquisition and Disposal of Rice by the Government
(thousand metric tons)

"Crop Year"	Stocks at the beginning of "crop year"			Purchases during "crop year"			Grand total at the disposal of Government during the year	Grand total disposed of during the year
	Domestic origin	Imported origin	Total stocks	Domestic	Imported	Total purchases		
1960	3,051	288	3,339	5,534	206	5,760	9,079	5,249
1961	3,596	234	3,830	5,365	140	5,505	9,335	5,715
1962	3,442	178	3,620	6,455	173	6,628	10,248	6,480
1963	3,621	147	3,768	5,466	177	5,643	9,411	6,498
1964	2,819	94	2,913	5,941	410	6,351	9,264	6,725
1965	2,454	85	2,539	6,614	883	7,497	10,036	6,912
1966	2,968	156	3,124	6,369	887	7,256	10,380	6,997
1967	3,099	284	3,383	9,239	457	9,696	13,079	7,233
1968	n.a.	n.a.	5,846	n.a.	n.a.	n.a.	n.a.	n.a.

Source: E.P.A., *Keizai Yoran*, 1969, pp. 148-9.
Note: "Crop year" starts in November of year 1 and ends in October year 2, but it carries the name of
    year 2.

Basically the rice surplus problem arises from the fact that rice is too profitable for the Japanese farmer in comparison with other farm products. The government could solve the rice problem by cutting the producer rice price. This would alienate the rural population, because it would lead to falls of income. Theoretically the government could compensate this loss by increasing the support prices for other foodstuffs, for example vegetables (it could not very well increase the prices of protein foods of animal origin because they already are extraordinarily high). Quite apart from the difficulty of finding the right level of such compensatory price support and the dangers of surpluses developing there, this arrangement would not aid the losing rice grower if he does not grow many vegetables. The rice problem is a typical result when a government starts trading with the objective of holding the price at a particular level. The political pressures exerted by producers, to which the government is very susceptible, are sure to produce that problem.

Controlled Marketing of Foodstuffs

The government controls rice, wheat and barley marketing under the Food Control Law of 1942. Originally the intention of the Law was to assure "fair distribution" of staple foods, but now it is operated in favour of farmers to assure them of high incomes comparable to wages in cities. Rice is purchased by the government on the basis of "advance sales application system" (*Jizen uriwatashi moshikomi sei*). Most other important agricultural products are also subject to controlled marketing. Livestock (meat and dairy) products are controlled by the "Law Governing Price Stabilisation of Livestock Products" (*Chikusanbutsu no Kakaku Antei nado ni kansuru Horitsu*). The Livestock Industry

Promotion Corporation, a government agency, has the function of controlling marketing. The Ministry of Agriculture fixes the maximum and the minimum price limits for dairy products each year, which creates a system of guaranteed prices. However, milk for manufacturing purposes is sold at a lower price, "the standard dealing price". The difference between the guaranteed price and the standard dealing price is covered by a government subsidy to farmers called "deficiency payment". The Livestock Industry Promotion Corporation buys up all the livestock products, including beef, pork and eggs, that fall below the set price and stores them for release at a future date. The Corporation has also the sole right of importing livestock products. Because domestic demand for the foodstuffs other than rice is rising, they have never created the same problems as rice. In any case if an unmanageable surplus threatened, the Corporation would just shut off imports which in this case would be feasible and adequate. In the case of egg production, the market managed to clear the supplies, but at prices that were considered too low, and in 1966 the government set up production guidance programs and a National Egg Prices Stabilisation Fund (*Zenkoku Keiran-Kakaku Antei Kikin*) which makes "deficiency payments" to farmers.

Vegetables production and marketing are also subject to government guidance and control under the Vegetables Production and Marketing Stabilisation Law (*Yasai Seisan Shukka Antei Ho*). The government fixes "specific (producer) basic prices" on cabbages and onions and when market prices fall below that level, farmers are partially compensated. In addition, the government designated some areas as vegetable producing areas and gives the farmers full information on the supply-demand situation.

Sugar-bearing raw materials, such as sugar beet, sugar cane, sweet potatoes, and white potatoes (the last two are used in the production of glucose and starch for textiles) are controlled in price, and if necessary the government purchases all domestic sugar at a minimum price. Imports of sugar cannot be shut off because they were liberalised in 1963.

Silk is still an important export product, and the industry is controlled under the Cocoon and Raw Silk Price Stabilisation Law of 1951. Through its agency, the Japan Raw Silk Export Custody Company, the government buys all raw silk at a fixed floor price and sells it at a fixed ceiling price. The government has established a Special Account for financing those operations. Production of silk cocoons is subsidised through the government owned Japan Cocoon Corporation.

The "Food Combinats"

In order to reduce the handling of various semi-finished food products, and the associated costs, the Economic Planning Agency and the Ministry of Agriculture *in co-operation with private manufacturers* have sponsored and are promoting groupings of allied food processing industries in one locality under the name of "food combinats". A food combinat is a kind of vertical-horizontal integration of various industries linked by output-input relationships, where all the linked plants are deliberately located on contiguous sites to facilitate the flow of materials from one plant to another. A typical combinat consists of firms at three levels of production. Level I consists of warehouses and silos for various domestic and imported raw foodstuffs such as grains and nuts. Level II consists of flour mills, rice mills, vegetable oil extraction plants, peanut processing plants, feedstuff factories and sugar refineries. Level III consists of final processors, such as bakery, confectionery, noodle, starch, rice jelly, dairy products and frozen food factories. The Japanese expect substantial savings from such arrangements. The following "food combinats" have already started operating or are planned: Chiba Combinat (Chiba Prefecture); Funabashi Combinat (Chiba Prefecture); Sano Combinat (Osaka Prefecture); Kobe Combinat (Hyogo Prefecture); and Fukuoka Combinat (Fukuoka Prefecture).

Report of the National Agricultural Council on Recent Agricultural Situation and Needed Policy Changes

In September of 1969 a report of the above Council made an assessment of the condition of agriculture and recommended the following policy changes.*
1. The expected annual consumption of rice is 12·4 million tons, whereas recent average annual output of paddy (unhusked) rice is 13·7 million tons. By the end of 1969 the Government held about 5·6 million tons of rice that was stored over one year (and at that age deterioration begins). Relief must come from a reduction of output. In the 1969 "crop year" the government hoped to divert 10,000 ha from rice (about one-third of one per cent of the total rice acreage) but in fact the diversion amounted to only a half of that. The Council saw three possible solutions: effective measures for diversion of paddy land to other uses; reduction of price support for domestic rice; or production quotas.
The National Federation of Farmers' Co-operatives expressed willingness to reduce paddy acreage by 300,000 ha to 350,000 ha in the 1970 "crop year" if the Government paid a compensation of 400,000 yen (U.S.$1,111) per ha of diverted land. On 31 January 1970 the Government decided that 240,000 ha of paddy land will be diverted out of which 130,000 ha will go to other crops and 100,000 ha will go to

* This section is based on information that has been supplied by courtesy of Professor Kenzo Hemmi, a member of the Council.

non-farming use. The Government will pay a compensation of 350,000 yen (almost U.S.$1,000) per ha. Moreover, the Government, farmers' organisations and business circles are considering how to switch 118,000 ha of paddy land (which produces 500,000 tons of unhusked rice annually) out of farming altogether.

2. The Council recommended that generally Japan should not reduce the ratio of her food self-sufficiency below 80 per cent, but that the output of cereals should be reduced, and the output of animal products, fodder, feedstuffs, fruits and vegetables should be increased, with regard however to the costs of doing so.

3. About 70 per cent of Japan's agricultural production is directly or indirectly supported by the government. The support is discriminatory and it produces a shortage of vegetables and meat on one hand, and a surplus of rice on the other. The Council recommended that price support policies should be re-examined, taking into consideration their structural effects and the needs of the country as well as movements in world prices of farm products.

4. The Council recommended modernisation of processing and marketing of farm products.

5. Recognising that international trade expansion is indispensable for economic development, the Council recommended further import liberalisation in foodstuffs. It recommended a shift from the reliance on import quotas to import levies and deficiency payments. The Council recognised that it is desirable to increase imports of farm products from South East Asia and "other developing countries especially".

6. The Council recommended assistance to outflow of farm population to non-farming pursuits through a special retirement pension program, encouraging commuting to cities, encouraging establishment of factories in rural areas and expansion of employment exchange services.

7. Looking towards 1977, the Council envisages that to maintain some sort of parity with non-agricultural incomes, the average agricultural household income in that year should be 2 million yen (U.S.$5,555). In order to make that possible the typical rice farm should be four to five ha, and a dairy farm should have twenty milking cows at least. Further, it would be necessary to introduce even more mechanisation, to extend co-operative farming in suitable circumstances, and finally to improve the land market. For these last two, it would be necessary to amend the present Agricultural Land Law and the Co-operative Law.

8. The Council recommended improvement of attractiveness of living conditions in rural areas as well as introduction of non-farming activities (such as electronics industries), both as instruments of siphoning off labour from farming and as a relief to cities' congestion.

CHAPTER NINE

General and Concluding Remarks

The growth of the Japanese economy in the last 100 years should demonstrate that national economic development, poverty or wealth are not dependent on the natural resources at the disposal of the nation, but are mainly a cultural phenomenon. The word "cultural" is used here in its widest sense, including not only learning and the arts, but also social institutions, value judgements, beliefs, mores and attitudes to life. Some nations develop, in a long series of historical accidents and rather rarely as a conscious choice, a favourable "culture" pattern for economic growth, while other nations develop an unfavourable one. Natural resources sometimes may help development and sometimes are obviously irrelevant. What seems most important is the nation's determination to increase its output of goods and services. This determination can be gauged by the priorities assigned to increasing production among other social objectives. Ever since the Meiji Restoration Japan has assigned the highest priority to economic development. Not many developing countries pursue the objective of economic growth with the same devotion and single-mindedness. This determination is the secret of Japan's success. It should be stressed that this determination to succeed economically has not arisen with the motive of achieving consumption habits of the "barbarians ", a motive which would have produced scorn in the Meiji leaders. In fact in the Tokugawa and Meiji periods and for some time afterwards the Japanese felt themselves *superior* because they did not consume the modern type of goods. Even now the under-developed countries are often really quite complacent about their consumption standards (though it would be unfashionable not to voice the desire for consumption growth). The Meiji leaders wanted economic growth for the sake of military power. The motive for modernisation of the economy was not greater consumption, but the defence of the country from the onslaught of European imperialism in the nineteenth century. This case illustrates the need for some profound shock to the fundamentally complacent under-developed societies to start rapid modernisation.

While the fear of becoming a European colony provided the motivation for modernisation, the immediate instrument of modernisation chosen was education: formal education, and on the job training. Manufacturing was fostered by the Japanese governments mainly because it was needed to provide weapons. By coincidence, rapid development of manufacturing was also indicated on purely economic grounds by Japan's natural endowment.

Unlike many under-developed countries of today, Japanese agriculture has been very progressive within the institutional limits since the second half of the Tokugawa Shogunate. Agriculture provided the basic minimum of food for the growing population, that is a work force more or less constant until the end of World War II and declining afterwards, kept increasing the food supply. Agriculture provided the labour force for the growing industries, as well as the lion's share of its savings. In addition, in the seventy years or so prior to World War II, agriculture (silk in particular) provided the bulk of foreign exchange earnings needed for the purchase of modern technology. While Australia and New Zealand moved to prosperity on the sheep's back, Japan's modernisation was spun by silk worms until World War II. After that war, however, fundamental changes occurred both in the motives for and the path of development. The armaments industries disappeared, though they are now back on a smaller scale. Suddenly Japan became a consumption-oriented society, where modern Western-type gadgets (though not yet Western diet) have become the desired objective and a status symbol. Briefly, Japan has become a consumer's society with assembly line mass production methods being applied to manufacture of any conceivable product, even pianos which have been considered unsuitable for mass production techniques.

During the 1950s and 1960s Japan undertook the development of heavy industries (*jū-kōgyō-ka*) and became one of the world's top producers of steel, and the largest shipbuilder in the world, building standardised ships under mass production techniques while the other countries continued to build costly "made-to-order" ships. Further, in 1963 when the well-known economist, C. P. Kindleberger, cast some doubt about Japan's future capacity to export motor vehicles,[†] she was exporting over 14 billion yen worth of passenger cars, a figure that has been almost doubled each year to reach 90 billion yen in 1967.[*] Electronic products, a wide variety of complex manufactured products, capital goods and often complete industrial plants came to be the bulk of Japan's exports gaining the role formerly played by textiles. In fiscal 1968 heavy industry and

[†] C. P. Kindleberger, *International Economics*, 3rd edition, R. D. Irwin, Homewood, Ill., 1963, p. 127.
[*] Bureau of Statistics, Office of Prime Minister, *Japan Statistical Yearbook 1968*, 1969, p. 299.

chemical industry exports were worth over 9 billion U.S. dollars out of a total of 13·7 billion dollars of exports.

It is possible that taking a view of a little more than one generation, losing the last war was a blessing in disguise for the Japanese. If Japan had won the war new enemies would no doubt have appeared in the eyes of her marshals and admirals. In addition, marshals and admirals of all nations, like peasants, are obsessed with the idea of acquiring more land. While for a single peasant acquiring more land is always desirable, for a nation acquiring more land is as a rule a heavy burden on the economy both in acquisition and holding it. The marshals and admirals, if victorious, would have pushed the Japanese nation to further sacrifices for "defence". As it happened after the defeat Japan has turned her attention away from military adventures to solid economic achievement, which is now bringing better life for consumers than they have ever had, or could hope to have in the course of any alternative development. The conquest of the whole of Asia could not possibly have given Japan the present standard of living, and even less the standard of living that Japan will have in the coming ten years, when she should be among a handful of the richest countries in the world *per caput* of population.

Although Japan's low defence expenditures (0·8 per cent of G.N.P. in the fiscal year 1967) have aided the growth rate in that so much more has gone to investment without the hardship and social unrest that consumption cuts would have brought about, this should not be taken as the cause of the rapid growth. If Japan had armed forces at the level of some other countries, her defence expenditures in peace time could have been higher by only a few per cent of the G.N.P. In many countries where the investment rate is very low, not much above 10 per cent of G.N.P., this level could be very important. In Japan, however, where capital formation now exceeds 30 per cent of the G.N.P., this low level of defence expenditures is not decisive, though it helps.

Although land area limitations are not now a significant restrictive factor for economic growth of any *single* country, a high rate of population growth can be inhibiting as it reduces, other things being equal, the availability of capital *per caput* and even the availability of education. Further, at present a rapid growth of population in most countries, certainly in Japan, reduces the quality of life by creating congestion in cities, on the roads, in holiday resorts and generally by reducing access to the limited number of natural or man-made objects of beauty. Pollution of our total environment is a rapidly increasing function of population growth and density. It is noteworthy that Japan has controlled her population growth rate over the last 100 years to keep it at about one-third of the rate of the present under-developed countries. Even so, life in many parts of Japan becomes uncomfortable or unbeautiful

Table 9.1.   Population Changes in Various Countries in 1967.

Country	Birth rate per 1,000 pop.	Death rate per 1,000 pop.	Natural increase per 1,000 pop.
Taiwan	28·5	5·5	23·0
Japan	19·3	6·7	12·6
Netherlands	18·9	7·9	11·0
Italy	18·1	9·7	8·4
U.S.A.	17·9	9·4	8·5
U.S.S.R.	17·5	7·6	9·9
U.K.	17·5	11·2	6·3
West Germany	17·3	11·2	6·1
France	16·9	10·9	6·0

Source: *Nippon: A Charted Survey of Japan*, 1969, p. 42.

because of the direct or indirect effects of high population density. From this point of view, the present increases in Japan's population are excessive.

As Table 9.1 shows, at present Japan has a birth rate quite comparable to that of any advanced country, low compared with the under-developed countries. But partly because of the improvements in health and welfare and partly because of the age structure of the population, the death rate in Japan is very low. The net result is that among the advanced countries Japan has now a very high rate of net increase of population. In view of the environmental evils of high density of population it might be desirable for Japan to control the birth rate even more than she has been doing while the death rates are so low.

Table 9.1 exaggerates (though only a little) the demographic trends in Japan. The birth rate for 1967 (quoted in the above international comparison) has had a slight abnormality in the case of Japan, as can be seen from Table 9.2. The slight abnormality in 1967 was caused by what might be called the spill-over effects of a larger abnormality in 1966. 1966 is considered by some superstitious people in Japan to be very unlucky for any girl born in it.* It is believed that girls born

* The Japanese have two ways of naming a year. One resembles the Western way in so far that each year is numbered consecutively from the first year of the reign of the current emperor, thus for example 1970 is referred to *in all official statistics* as *Showa* 45. (Note: to convert a Showa year to the Western denomination it is necessary to add 25 to the Showa year number.) In addition the Japanese have an old way of naming years inherited from the Chinese. In that system years are grouped into ten categories. The ten categories of years are called by the names of "basic elements": Ki-no-e ("Senior" Wood Year), Ki-no-to ("Junior" Wood Year), Hi-no-e ("Senior" Fire Year), Hi-no-to ("Junior" Fire Year), Tsuchi-no-e ("Senior" Earth Year), Tsuchi-no-to ("Junior" Earth Year), Ka-no-e ("Senior" Metal Year), Ka-no-to ("Junior" Metal Year), Mizu-no-e ("Senior" Water Year), Mizu-no-to ("Junior" Water Year). Each particular year is named after 12 animals in the following sequence: rat, cow, tiger, rabbit, dragon, snake, horse, sheep, monkey, hen, dog, and wild pig. The

Table 9.2.   Japanese Demographic Trends.

Year	Birth rate per 1,000 pop.	Death rate per 1,000 pop.	Natural increase per 1,000 pop.
1926	34·6	19·1	15·5
1930	32·4	18·2	14·2
1935	31·6	16·8	14·9
1940	29·4	16·5	12·9
1947	34·3	14·6	19·7
1950	28·1	10·9	17·2
1955	19·4	7·8	11·6
1957	17·2	8·3	8·9
1958	18·0	7·4	10·5
1959	17·5	7·4	10·1
1960	17·2	7·6	9·6
1961	16·9	7·4	9·5
1962	17·0	7·5	9·5
1963	17·3	7·0	10·3
1964	17·7	6·9	10·7
1965	18·6	7·1	11·4
1966	13·7	6·8	7·0
1967	19·4	6·8	12·7
1968	18·6	6·8	11·8

Source: E.P.A., *Keizai Yoran*, 1970, p. 42.

in that year will bring bad luck to their husbands and may kill him. As a result the superstitious people took great care not to have a child born in that year in case it turned out to be a girl. This reduces the actual birth rate in that year. It may also have some effect on the births in the preceding year and the following year to the extent that couples decided to try to advance the arrival of the baby, or to postpone it. The majority of the non-superstitious people have a good practical reason to have the birth of a girl in an unlucky year registered (illegally) as born outside that year, either the preceding or the following one, whichever is the nearer, because a correct registration could make a girl unable to marry. This reduces the official figure of births in that year and "increases" the number of births in both the preceding year and the following year.

As can be seen from Table 9.2, the abnormal year 1966 has had some effects on the birth rates both in the preceding year and in the following

full name of a particular year consists of the "element" name and "animal" name which follow their own sequence independently of the other. As time passes different combinations of those two names appear. It is traditionally believed by a section of the population that girls born in Tiger Year will be stubborn and will make the family unhappy, and the Fire and Horse Year combination is particularly unlucky (girls born in that year will be likely to bring bad luck to the husband and are likely to kill him). Year 1966 was such a "Special Horse Year".

one, as we would have expected. The effect, however, on 1968 birth rate would be negligible, if any. Thus if we take the 1968 birth rate as more or less normal for some time to come, it transpires that the Japanese annual natural increase in the population is about 12 per 1,000, and as such is comparable to the Dutch increase, but is certainly much higher than that of the other developed countries. And the Dutch demographical developments may not be optimal.

It should be noted here that, unlike in Japan, the Dutch government actively assists emigration, the Dutch are much more willing to migrate than the Japanese and the legal immigration restrictions against the Dutch are much smaller than those against the Japanese in most of the countries receiving immigrants. As a result the annual Dutch emigration is much larger than the Japanese one even in absolute terms, not to mention in relative terms. In recent years annual emigration from Japan varied between only 4,000-6,000, more than half of whom went to the U.S.A. (mostly marriage and adoption cases), although at the end of 1968 the majority of 1,210,000 Japanese living abroad were in Brazil.*

It is significant, however, that the Japanese Government, businessmen and many Japanese economists have *very recently* formed the opinion that Japan's population growth is now too low. The practical expressions of this are shown in two new policies. The Japanese Government, which used to assist emigration by giving free passages to emigrants, cancelled the policy in 1969 and closed down the Emigration Bureau. In 1970 a new system of child allowances was introduced partly to raise the birth rate. One of the motives in this case was probably economic, though there could have been other motives too. In general the economist's attitude to population growth is not as simple as the popular belief holds. All depends on the other circumstances of the economy, such as the availability of capital (or other resources) *per caput* of the growing population. Japan now experiences two phenomena unique in the history of mankind. Firstly, her G.N.P. grows at an extraordinarily high rate, and secondly an extraordinarily high proportion of that G.N.P. (about 40 per cent) is being saved. As a result in an almost unbelievable reversal of circumstances population growth suddenly ceased to be an economic problem for Japan. Japan can now provide every additional baby with enough (man-made) resources to enable it to make a living. However, from a statement that Japan *could* accommodate a higher population growth, there is a long and uncertain path to a statement that it would be in her interest to encourage a higher population growth. Admittedly, a higher population growth does supply a certain dynamism to an economy *provided that the availability of capital* is assured (as it indeed now is in Japan). But exactly how does this population growth

---

* *Nippon: A Charted Survey of Japan*, 1969, pp. 36 and 41.

affect economic growth? It has a dual effect. Higher population growth creates a larger market and therefore gives more scope to the industrialists. However, this factor may be of some significance only for a country that experiences some special difficulties in expanding external markets, and Japan certainly is not in that position. On the other hand, higher population growth increases the supply of labour, which is always welcomed by industrialists, and would be especially welcome now in Japan which is at present short of labour and is strongly set against importing any foreign labour. Since the Japanese Government now can be called a businessman's government, these facts would tend to explain the government's attitude. But the businessmen and those economists that favour higher population growth rate have not proved their argument. Clearly, the essence of modern civilisation and technology is to replace labour by capital. Only if the Japanese businessmen lost their confidence in their ability to invent and to introduce new capital equipment and technology that are even more labour saving than in the past would their concern about population growth rate be justified.

It is possible, of course, to view the problem from a few quite different angles. One of them is concerned with the age structure of population, more precisely with the proportion of the working age population in the total population *in a particular period*.

Table 9.3 shows that from the point of view of current ability to produce goods and services the age structure of Japan's population has been steadily improving in the last decade. *Somewhere between 1970-1975 it will start to deteriorate, and that deterioration will be particularly*

Table 9.3. The Age Structure of Japan's Population in Various Years, Actual and Projected.

Year 1 October	Total	Numbers in thousands			Percentages of total		
		Aged 0–14 years	Aged 15–59 years	Aged 60 years and over	Aged 0–14 years	Aged 15–59 years	Aged 60 years and over
1960	93,884	28,012	57,582	8,290	29·8	61·3	8·8
1961	94,732	28,098	58,204	8,530	29·6	61·4	9·0
1962	95,614	27,216	59,624	8,775	28·5	62·4	9·2
1963	96,542	26,325	61,170	9,047	27·2	63·4	9·4
1964	97,475	25,428	62,764	9,282	26·1	64·4	9·5
1965	98,403	24,767	64,098	9,538	25·2	65·1	9·7
1970	103,327	23,810	68,424	11,092	23·0	66·2	10·7
1975	108,635	24,620	71,039	12,976	22·7	65·4	11·9
1995	120,225	21,545	76,210	22,470	17·9	63·4	18·7
2015	119,015	20,226	67,118	31,671	17·0	56·4	26·6

Source: E.P.A., *Keizai Yoran*, p. 39. Estimates made by the Institute of Population, Department of Welfare, Government of Japan.

marked at the end of this century. This deterioration will be caused by a doubling of the number of old people between 1970 and the end of the century. It will also be accompanied by a decline of both the absolute number and the proportion of the young people from some date around 1975.

It is very easy to misconstrue the meaning of such trends and data. Whether one considers them favourable or unfavourable *on balance* depends on many "value judgements": generally speaking the relative valuation of various aspects of the population changes as well as the valuation of their timing. Firstly, the economic growth rate in Japan is so high that the narrow economic effects of the changes in the age structure of population would be easily swamped by other factors. Secondly, an increasing proportion of the old people in a society is, other things being equal, an excellent index of the degree of advancement of civilisation. So is the decline of the proportion of the young people. A look at Table 9.4 (in particular the Indian figures and the figures for any advanced country) bears this out.

Thirdly, if a country wished to and actually did "improve" its age structure in some future period (fifteen years after Year One), by this very fact it would be deciding to worsen its age structure in the period of the first fifteen years! Thus on balance, why should the present generation undertake this special burden to make things so much easier for the generation living between Year Twenty and Year Sixty-five? It should further be noted here that such "improvement" in the age structure of a population would be short-lived, that is to say, would automatically turn itself into a deterioration (other things being equal) when Year Sixty was reached. Thus any conscious, deliberate intervention now by government in the age structure of population could make sense only if the government could be sure that the nation was going to face some particular challenge in the period between Year Fifteen (rather Year Twenty) and Year Sixty. In other words the government would have to feel that the nation was relatively speaking facing no problems between Year One and Year Twenty, and no problems between Year Sixty and, say, Year Eighty! If a case for the existence of such a situation cannot be established there is no case at all for a government trying to affect the age structure of the population, but there still *is* a case for the governments of almost all nations controlling their population growth rate in general. Indeed the day is not too distant when nations will negotiate on the basis—we shall not increase our population provided that you will not increase yours—as nations now bargain about tariffs. But in any case, even from a narrow nationalistic point of view it is doubtful whether any interests of a nation (especially as large as Japan) would be fostered by the growth of numbers, and it is certain that some interests (the quality of life) would be adversely affected.

Table 9.4. The Age Structure of Population in Selected Countries.
Percentages of various age groups in total population in 1965.

Country	0–14	15–64	65 and over
Japan	24·3	68·9	6·8
West Germany	22·6	65·5	11·9
U.K.	23·0	64·7	12·3
France	24·6	62·9	12·5
U.S.A.	30·1	60·4	9·5
India	41·0	55·9	3·1

Source: U.N., *Demographic Yearbook 1967*, Copyright, United Nations 1967. Reproduced by permission.

Table 9.4 demonstrates that at present Japan is fortunate in having a very high proportion of population in the productive age group. The United Kingdom and France, on the other hand, have a large proportion of old people, while India has an extraordinarily high proportion of children.

While an underlying assumption in some of the preceding discussion has been that Japan has a population level higher than "optimal", in other words, that Japan is in *some sense* an over-populated country, or a short-of-space country, it has to be admitted that many of the environmental evils of high density of population in the cities and around them are not so much due to the overall density as to the pull that large cities exert on industries. All the same high overall density of population *contributes* to excessive local densities at points where density matters, such as various public amenities.

The preceding statement is borne out by the fact that, for example, Australia also has a very high concentration of her population in large cities—in 1968 over 60 per cent of total population lived in capital cities.* Yet the environmental evils of capital cities' population concentrations in Australia are not nearly so great there as they are in Japan. For example, Nagoya, with a population of 2 million in 1965, and Yokkaichi, population 219,000 are *incomparably* more polluted than (the larger) Sydney, population 2·6 million in 1968, or Melbourne, population 2·3 million. Nor is this higher pollution in the Japanese cities due to any higher level of industrialisation in Japan as a whole. In fact in Australia workers employed in manufacturing represent a higher proportion of the total labour force than in Japan! In 1967 in Japan 25·9 per cent of the total of employees worked in manufacturing, while in Australia in that year the percentage was 36·9.†

* The Australian News and Information Bureau, Department of the Interior, *Australia in Facts and Figures No. 101*, Canberra, p. 38.
† (a) The Japanese figure from: *Nihon Kokusei Zue*, p. 97.
  (b) The Australian figure from: *Quarterly Summary of Australian Statistics*, December 1968, p. 14.

The preceding passage should therefore prove that a high overall (national) density of population *is* a serious aggravating factor.

The localised heavy concentrations of population are essentially induced by economic, social and cultural attractions of living, working and up to a point even playing in large cities. The problem is universal all over the world, but in Japan it is more acute than in any other country. The problem arises from the fact that private costs and benefits are quite often unequal to social costs and benefits. A family or an enterprise moves to a large city because of better access to various facilities. The move may be advantageous for the individual unit, but the sum of these shifts to cities creates enormous social costs. In most countries the solution lies in planned creation of medium sized cities, or satellite cities. In Japan, a mountainous country where flat land is extremely scarce, this solution is not so easy and may not be very attractive, not yet anyway. In any case in some prefectures the density is already so high that rural areas hardly differ from urban areas.

The paradoxical feature of Japan's population movements is that in the period 1960-1967 the prefectures which already have a relatively low population density, such as Iwate, Fukushima, Tottori, Tokushima, Oita, Akita, Niigata, Toyama and Yamagata have experienced declines of population. On the other hand, the prefectures that already have a very high density of population, such as Tokyo, Osaka, Kanagawa, and Aichi have experienced the largest additional influx of population. The cause of this demographic reshuffle lies in the movement of agricultural population to manufacturing industries. It is also called urbanisation. The cause is in a sense uncontrollable and should not be controlled. The effects of this demographic shift, however, should be mitigated. Until recently Japan was concentrating so hard on income creation that she did not invest much in environmental improvement, or even protection from worse things which are coming. In the Social and Economic Plan 1967-1971 a beginning was made in this field of improvement of the environment but much needs to be done yet. Japan has now the means to recover gradually what was destroyed in her environment by the modern industry and the density of population. But it will take a long time before cities like Yokkaichi or Nagoya will have reasonably clean air.

At the roots of Japan's recent and future economic growth lies the very high standard of education of the mass of the people. The Japanese are now quantitatively the second-best educated people in the world (after the U.S.A.) and if one allows for quality of education, they could be the best educated. This will assure Japan's economic growth and prosperity. Doubts are occasionally cast on the future economic prospects of Japan by references to the alleged Japanese high dependence on foreign trade. Those people who make such references do not define their term "dependence on trade". Presumably they mean the ratio of imports to G.N.P. If so, the arguments are quite wrong. In terms of the percentage represented by imports in the G.N.P. in various countries, Japan is now one of the less dependent countries of the world.

Table 9.5.   Imports as Percentage of G.N.P.

Netherlands	37%
Belgium	35%
Sweden	20%
Canada	17%
U.K.	16%
Italy	14%
West Germany	14%
Australia	14%
France	11%
Japan	10%

It could perhaps be argued that much of the Japanese imports are essential raw materials and that therefore a cut in imports might have higher repercussions—owing to a sort of multiplier effect—than a similar cut of final consumption goods would have. The answer would be that capital goods and producers' goods, which loom large in the imports of other countries, would also have such multiplier effects. In Australia, for example, imports of *consumer* goods are less than 20 per cent of total imports. In any case, short of a general depression or a world war, there is no danger of Japan being unable to obtain the raw materials she needs, although the Japanese are extremely sensitive about the security of supplies. If a world depression came, then no country would have high growth rates, though judging by her record during the Great Depression of the 1930s, her high structural flexibility and capacity for wage and profits restraint, Japan would do better than most. If a world war came, no country's economic growth would matter.

Index

Agencies, government-affiliated, 103-4
Agricultural
  Improvement Fund System, 91
  Modernisation Fund System, 91
Agriculture
  Changes needed in, 250
  Competition between food and silk,
    39
  Co-operatives, 154
  Deterioration factor, 225
  Experimentation in Tokugawa period,
    16, 17, 19, 244
  Government aid, 90
  Labour
    excessive absorption of, 249
    nature of outflow, 253
  Labour force, 9
    decline of, 252, 253, 255
  Machinery, ownership of, 261
  Output
    estimates 1878-1917, 7-8
    factors promoting increased, 260
    underestimation by Meiji govern-
      ment, 8
  Productivity
    effect of first land reform on, 244
    effect of part-time farming, 250,
      255
    increases in, 258
  Progress in, 191
  Protection
    from imports, 6, 263
    costs to consumer, 263
  Recommendations of Committee for
    Promotion of Structural Policies
    in, 256
  Reform hindered by political factors,
    256

  Report of National Agricultural
    Council on situation and needed
    policy changes, 269
  Shift to production of foodstuffs that
    are consumed fresh, 263
  Support of, 257
  Un-asian attitude toward, 261
Agriculture, Forestry and Fisheries
  Finance Corporation, 92, 154
Anti-Monopoly Act 1947, 79
  Breach of, 224
  Mergers, 82
  Obstacle to reconstruction, 79
  Relaxation of, 79-80

Balanced budget principle, 107-8
Banks
  Administrative guidance to, 149
  Assets, 141
  Borrowings, 139
    from Bank of Japan, 140
  Central Bank for Commercial and
    Industrial Co-operatives, 89-90
  Central Co-operative Bank for Agri-
    culture and Forestry, 91
  City, 135
    holdings of foreign exchange, 141
    shortage of funds, 136-7
  Class A Foreign Exchange, 146-7
  Class B Foreign Exchange, 146-7
  Commercial, 135, 137
  Commercial system, 133
  Credit card service, 138
  Deposits, 137-9
  For Commercial and Industrial Co-
    operatives, 153
  Foreign Exchange business, 146-7
  Liberalisation of activities, 150